Hi Greg.

Sherry and I thank you for
your interest in our book.
We learned a lot writing
it and hopefully it will also
help you in your interest in
the breed.

Sincerely

Bobbie Brooks
6-18-04

THE ALASKAN
MALAMUTE

I am watching. . .

    The white road for

    My brothers and sisters,

I am waiting. . .

    For you to bring them

    Back from the frozen lands

Watching. . .

              —S. Wallis

THE ALASKAN MALAMUTE

Yesterday and Today

BARBARA A. BROOKS

SHERRY E. WALLIS

Alpine
Blue Ribbon Books
Loveland, Colorado

Permission to quote from copyrighted material was given by:
Hoflin Publishing, Ltd, for portions of *Seppala, Alaskan Dog Driver*, the *Malamute Quarterly*, and *Alaskan Malamute Annual*.
Wendy Volhard for her *Puppy Personality Profile*
The Escanaba Daily Press for photo of Paul Voelker and accompanying article
Carole Owens for "Epilepsy: A Roundup of Facts and Ideas"

Library of Congress Cataloging in Publication
Brooks, Barbara A., 1937-
The Alaskan Malamute: Yesterday and Today/ Barbara A. Brooks, Sherry E. Wallis.
p.   tm. Includes bibliographical references and index.
ISBN 0-931866-96-0
1. Alaskan Malamute   I. Wallis, Sherry E., 1947-   .   II. Title
SF429.A67B76   1998   98-9655
636.73--dc.21   CIP

The pronouns "he" or "she" have been used in the generic sense to refer to dogs or people of either sex. No bias toward a particular sex is intended.

Many manufacturers secure trademark rights for their products. When Alpine Publications is aware of a trademark claim, we print the product name as trademarked or in initial capital letters.

Alpine Publications accepts no responsibility for veterinary medical information, suggested treatments or vaccinations mentioned herein. The reader is advised to check with their local, licensed veterinarian before giving medical attention.

This and other Alpine books are available to breeders and clubs at special quantity discounts. Write to Customer Service, Alpine Publications, P O. Box 7027, Loveland, CO 80537.

A portion of the proceeds from this book will be used to establish the *Malamute Fund,* administered by the authors and used solely for the welfare of Alaskan Malamutes.

Credits:
Cover and text design and layout: B. J. McKinney
Copyediting: B. J. McKinney and Nancy Wilson; Proofreading: Sharon Anderson
Front Cover Photos: Center portrait: Am. Mex. Intl. Ch. Atanik's Life's Short—Play Hard, WTD, WPD, WWPD, ROM. Breeder/Owner, Kimberly Meredith. Photo by the owner. • Sled team: Bill Matott's ten-dog team. • Agility: Purdy's Psyche Passion, photographed by Mormont de Henau.
Back Cover: Painting by Dorothy Redding.
Text photos not credited are by an unknown photographer or assumed to be the property of the owner.

1 2 3 4 5 6 7 8 9 0

Printed in the United States of America.

CONTENTS

PART I. TODAY:
LIFE WITH AN ALASKAN MALAMUTE

Part II. YESTERDAY:
THE MALAMUTE THROUGH HISTORY

Dedicated to

Mrs. Delta Wilson Smith

and to

"Bowser," Ch. Windrift's Nakoah, ROM,

Barbara's beloved companion.

FOREWORD

In 1976 I had the privilege of meeting Barbara Brooks. I was a novice, at that time, to the Alaskan Malamute Breed. Barbara took it upon herself to take my wife Joyce and me to some dog shows. While attending these shows, I could see the excitement and thrill a quality Malamute brought to Bobbi's face. The excitement became contagious! She was the first breeder from New England to produce an All-Breed Best in Show winner, her beloved Ch. Windrift's Nakoah.

Barbara's feelings for this magnificent breed have not changed. When she saw the need for a comprehensive book about the breed—from its earliest beginnings to it's progress through the decades—that same enthusiasm gave her the will to write it. This eye-opening treatise will not only be of interest to breeders, but will be a source of information for historians and education for dog show judges. She covers the breed from the heroic duties Malamutes performed in Antartica and in World War II to the 21st century issues of health and Malamute rescue.

The authors' purpose in writing this book is not confined to the show dog fancier. They accurately describe the working Malamute with its unique ability to survive and work in extreme weather conditions, its legendary endurance, and its great strength that enables it to pull loads many times its body weight. The mentality and personality of the breed are also thoroughly covered.

This book will entertain and educate those who have yet to become full-fledged "Malanuts." It covers more aspects of the breed in greater detail than any other publication before it. I am honored to write the Foreword on this authoritative work about our breed. I believe that all who read it will want to recommend "The Alaskan Malamute Yesterday and Today" to other fanciers.

Bill Matott
Sendaishi Kennels, Manchester, NH
Breeder, exhibitor, weight pull and race dog driver.
1996

ACKNOWLEDGMENTS

Our starting push came from Delta Wilson Smith who sent us a wealth of material collected over her lifetime in the breed. We hope we've done it justice.

We'd like to thank the many Alaskan Malamute owners, including all those outside the United States, who sent information about and pictures of their wonderful dogs. All our contributors deserve special thanks above and beyond just their name above their articles. Our goal at the outset was to make this a book for all Malamute people. Thanks to your participation, we think we've succeeded.

When Dorothy and Bob Page offered us access to the Archives of the Siberian Husky Club of America, we gratefully accepted. In addition to supplying us with pictures, they generously shared their own memories of Short Seeley as did Wendy Wilhauck and Natalie Hogdens. Carol Williams went above and beyond, giving us all sorts of information as well as opening her scrapbooks for us, as did Tracy Young in sharing her pictures from Beulah Robels. Bob Zoller generously recounted his experiences and reminiscences about the "old days," and Gail Skoglund did a terrific job of assembling material on Arthur Walden.

Keith Hurrell gave us the benefit of his much greater experience in working Malamutes, and Sue Fuller and Sue Renkert contributed information about working dogs. We owe a special thanks to Shilon Bedford for looking up all those dates, to Ilene Stewart for getting the National Specialty list together, Susan Richardson for the ROM statistics, and Billie Stewart for the obedience history.

Updates on health issues came from Linda Dowdy and Dr. Joceyln Jacobs-Knoll and other concerned individuals. We'd also like to thank Lori Schmidt and Scott Barry for giving us so much information on wolves and wolf hybrids.

Thanks also to the staffs of the Houston Public Library; the American Kennel Club Library and *Gazette*; Marge Heath at the University of Alaska Polar Archives; and Doug Pfeiffer of Graphic Arts N.W. Editions, Hoëbeke, Paris, France.

Especially, we would like to express our gratitude for the help of our families. Steve Brooks gave Mom her computer and became her support network. Meredith and Jennifer Wallis took care of the dogs when Mom was away. Our husbands, Richard Brooks and Robert Wallis, have kept up with their own jobs as well as the dogs, fish, cats, birds (for the Brooks's), and kids (for the Wallis's), all the while offering tireless support and encouragement.

ABOUT THE AUTHORS

Barbara's love of Malamutes began when she bought one as a pet in 1965. Her Windrift dogs are well known and compiled a remarkable record for a small kennel, finishing nineteen Windrift champions, several of which were also ROM producers. Her first litter produced Ch. Windrift's Leah of Aurora, who was three times BOS at the National Specialty, and Ch. Aurora's Micah of Windrift who was WD at the National. Leah and Ch. Aurora's Noatak of Windrift produced Barbara's best-known dog, a multiple Best in Show and Best in Specialty winner, Ch. Windrift's Nakoah, or "Bowser".

A native New Englander, Barbara was active in the New England Sled Dog Club, two New Hampshire area kennel clubs, and the AMCA. Short Seeley was a personal friend and a frequent guest in the Brooks' home. In 1979 the Brooks family moved to Texas, where Barbara became a member of the Kennel Club of Texarkana. She has served as secretary, president, and show chairperson, and taught a puppy socialization class. They have recently returned to her native New Hampshire.

Judging since 1983, Barbara is now approved for the Working group, Australian Shepherds, and Pomeranians. Besides judging in the U.S., she has officiated in Europe and Mexico. Although virtually retired from showing and breeding, she has continued her interest in Malamutes by putting on seminars around the U.S. and in Europe. Her articles on the breed have appeared in many Malamute publications in the U.S. and abroad.

Barbara was instrumental in forming the Quadrangle Cluster with the Kennel Club of Texarkana and the Hot Springs National Park Kennel Club. It was first held in 1991 and has seen an increasing entry each year.

Sherry Wallis began showing, training, and breeding German Shepherd Dogs in 1970. Her interest in Malamutes began with a co-ownership with one of her obedience students. Unfortunately, her husband Robert preferred Shepherds. Eventually, they compromised on Akitas, which they still breed and show. She has bred over twenty Akita champions, including a Register of Merit, and finished championships on German Shepherd Dogs, Malamutes, a Ridgeback, and a Papillon. She has also completed obedience titles on numerous dogs. Sherry worked as a professional trainer, conducting training classes for the Houston YMCA and several training clubs.

Also a judge, Sherry is currently approved for German Shepherds Dogs, Alaskan Malamutes, Akitas, Samoyeds, and Siberian Huskies. She is a member of the Ft. Bend Kennel Club and Houston Kennel Club, as well as the German Shepherd Dog Club of America. She served on several committees (Rescue, Judge's Education, and Web Page) for the Akita Club of America and as president of the Lone Star Akita Club of Houston.

Sherry has written extensively about Akitas as columnist for both *Akita Dog* newsletter and *Akita World* magazine. Her articles on other breeds and dog-related activites have appeared in numerous other publications.

A native Texan, Sherry has lived in Houston all of her adult life. She has two children. In addition to dog activites, she and her brother, Stephen, design and maintain web pages.

INTRODUCTION

We've known each other for more years than either of us wants to admit. When we first met, we lived a thousand miles apart; later, a scant three-hundred. Now with Barbara's move back to her native New Hampshire, we've come full circle. We have followed similar paths in the realm of dogs, first breeding, training, and showing; then, judging. In addition, we have studied multiple breed books as part of the process of obtaining approval for new breeds. As we read them, we discussed their virtues and vices. These talks naturally led to sharing ideas about what we would include in an "ideal" breed book. We never dreamed that those ideas would become a reality, but here they are!

To document the breed's history, we've been able to locate many pictures of Malamutes working on Alaskan teams long before anyone had heard of them in the lower forty-eight states. We're very excited about the photographs; not only the archival ones, but also those we received from Malamute people.

Their response to our requests was so overwhelming that we unfortunately are able to use only a fraction of the photos we received. Truly, the single most difficult task associated with this book has been choosing which photographs to send to the publisher. Even then, only some will find their way into the book. We would like to have used them all, but with publishing costs as high as they are, had we done so, no one would be able to afford to buy the book.

Several artists shared their work with us, and people with specialized knowledge about the breed generously provided material. Their contributions have added greatly to the depth and detail of *The Alaskan Malamute Yesterday and Today*.

Its focus is specifically on Alaskan Malamutes, and while some material may apply equally well to other breeds, much is breed specific. Where we have provided general material, such as that on buying a puppy, we have done so because we feel most sources are not specific or thorough enough. On the other hand, so many books and videos are available on subjects like breeding and whelping puppies, that we have little to add. Libraries and bookstores are full of books about specific subjects or about dogs in general. We urge you to explore these as additional resources and have provided a bibliography to get you started.

The Alaskan Malamute as a breed developed from disparate and sometimes conflicting sources. We have tried to recognize the variety of contributions, whether from people or from dogs, in a balanced and objective manner. It is also a breed of disparate types, all of which have their admirers and detractors. Regardless of your preferences, within these pages you will find quality examples of all of these lines.

To meet our goal, we also had to cover the many different activities in which Alaskan Malamutes are engaged. The amazing versatility of this breed and its owners is reflected in material depicting Malamutes doing all sorts of things ranging from the traditional sledding and showing to work in search-and-rescue and movies.

When we began this project, our collective experience with Malamutes covered over four decades, and we thought we knew a lot about the breed and about dogs in general. We've been astonished at how much more we've learned about both. We are honored and delighted that our discoveries are with you now.

Barbara A. Brooks
Sherry E. Wallis

Part I

Today

Life with
an Alaskan Malamute

Malamutes—man's best friend! Courtesy Sel and Joanne Levy. Be sure the adult dog is what you want before you succumb to the puppy. Photo by Sel Levy.

ALASKAN MALAMUTE – RIGHT DOG FOR YOU?

The Alaskan Malamute is certainly one of the finest of the few breeds we Americans claim as our own. Honed by centuries of work as a sled dog, he has earned a unique place in American history. He has worked the gold fields hauling freight and packing gear; he has pulled sleds across Antarctica, and rescued downed flyers in Greenland's icy expanses during World War II. Despite a constitution tough enough to survive the rigors of work at both poles, this breed's gentle, affectionate nature has enabled him to make the transition from worker to companion with ease.

From his Alaskan home, the Malamute has found his way across the globe and into the hearts of people from Australia to Sweden, from Indiana to Italy. The same adaptability which served the Alaskan natives who developed the breed so well fits the Malamute neatly into today's lifestyles.

He competes in long-distance races, in weight pulls, dog shows, agility, or obedience trials. He is part of a recreational sled team or pitches in at the family camp-out by packing his share. In regions where snow seldom covers the ground, he can be hitched to a rubber-tired cart. Regardless of whether he pulls a sled, performs search and rescue services, or sits at the window, the Alaskan Malamute is always ready to answer the human need for companionship.

Perhaps you have a Malamute providing these benefits for you already, or perhaps you are trying to make a decision concerning the breed. Either way, to understand and appreciate the Malamute, you should have an accurate idea of what an adult looks like and how it will tend to behave.

If everyone could and would be satisfied with one breed, only one type of dog would exist. Obviously, this is not the case; what one person adores, another may find unappealing. Those who like Malamutes are impressed by the dog's imposing stature, lush coat, and clean markings. Others may be intimidated by their size, appalled at the amount of hair they shed, or find their markings and colors boringly similar. Even fanciers of the breed may find their dwelling space inadequate for such a large, energetic dog.

You can easily lose track of practical considerations when you see a Malamute puppy. Be forewarned, they are almost irresistibly cute and cuddly. However, that adorable bundle of fur quickly disappears, giving way to a gawky, curious, energetic youngster, a stage that is followed by an even larger, furrier adult. Be sure that the adult dog is exactly what you want before you succumb to the puppy, because the adult dog is what you will eventually have.

MALAMUTE TEMPERAMENT

Not only should you be sure that the appearance of the adult Malamute is what you want, but you should be sure the personality of the breed suits you as well. As the standard describes temperament, "The Alaskan Malamute is an affectionate, friendly dog, not a 'one man' dog. He is a loyal, devoted companion, playful on invitation, but generally impressive by his dignity after maturity." Broadly speaking, this description fits most Malamutes; however, it leaves much unsaid.

Malamutes are often described as "laid-back," meaning that they accept many situations with aplomb and are seldom nervous or anxious. Adaptable and amiable, they easily make themselves at home wherever and however they find themselves.

Although they are rarely idle barkers, Malamutes are quite talkative and have a wide range of vocalizations to express their feelings. A Malamute may continue doing something that he does not really want to do at your command, but rest assured he will tell you just what he thinks of it all the while!

Typically, Malamutes are willing, even enthusiastic, about meeting new people. Many Malamute owners say that their dogs have never met a stranger. Some dogs do become more reserved as they age, but "impressive dignity" may be a long time coming.

Their lack of suspicion is among the traits that make the Malamute such a pleasant companion in public places such as campgrounds and trails. They are unlikely to make a nuisance out of themselves by guarding the grounds, barking or growling at every passer-by.

On such outings, they are more than willing to contribute their share of work. Give a Malamute a challenge, and he will meet it with unswerving determination. Tough, rugged, and hardy, they are quite capable of coping with rigorous trails and harsh conditions and are even more willing to snuggle up and keep you warm at night.

Alaskan Malamutes genuinely like people and enjoy being around them. At the same time, their independent nature keeps them from being pests. If you are not paying attention to him, a Malamute is usually able to amuse himself. In the process, his antics may entertain you as well. A few laughs are all the encouragement a Malamute needs to clown around. The healthy, cared-for Malamute brings zest and enthusiasm to everything he does. His sheer joy in life is one of the most endearing and appealing qualities of his nature.

FINDING YOUR MALAMUTE

Once you have decided that the Alaskan Malamute is the breed for you, the next step is finding the particular Alaskan Malamute that is the dog for you. Where you look for a dog and what dog you select should be governed by several criteria: your family's needs and individual personalities, your reasons for wanting a dog, their availability, and your budget.

Companionship is the most common reason for getting a dog. However, the versatile Alaskan Malamute loves backpacking and weight-pulling, sledding, skijoring, and carting. He shines in the show ring and can be quite competent in obedience. The tasks to which you put him are limited only by your time, willingness, and abilities.

Just as some people seem to be adept at anything to which they put their hand, so too, some dogs seem able to perform well in many arenas. Am/Can Ch. Black Ice's Aleutian Dream, WLDX, WTDX, WWPD, and Am/Can Ch. Avalanche at Snow Castle, Am/Can CD, WLD, WTD, WWPDX, WPD, for example, are both champions in two countries and holders of working certifications as lead, team, and/or pack dogs.

Currently the most titled Alaskan Malamute is BIS/BISS/ Am/Can/Mex/Ber/Int/World/CACIB/CACM/CAC/FCI/ FCM Ch. Chinome's Arctic Invader, Am/Mex CD/PC, TT, CGC, IWPA, WPD, WTD, WLD, WWPD, IWA-PAX, WTDX, WLDX, WWPDX. He has multiple championships internationally, obedience titles in two countries, a temperament certification, a canine good citizen's certifi-

Ch. Brok'n Ice's Transantarctica, winning Best of Breed. Breeder/owner, Kevin Redding.

cate, and working certifications in weight-pull, packing, and lead and team dog work in both American and International events. More than that, he is an outstanding example of the multi-faceted Alaskan Malamute. His achievements would be hard to duplicate, but they demonstrate that a sound Malamute with working temperament is a very versatile dog indeed. A bitch, Ch. Onak's Twitterpated Fool UD, WPD, WPDX, WTD, WLD, WWPD, WWPDX, TT, HT, NA, has proved that girls can do it all, too.

Most people and most dogs are better at some things than others. A realistic assessment of what you want in a dog will determine what you look for in parents and puppies and where you go to find them.

A FRIEND FOR LIFE

When you look for a new car, you take into consideration not only the needs of the primary driver but also those of everyone else who will ride in it. You want something that is attractive and functional and affordable. You look for a manufacturer whose product is durable and trustworthy, a company that will cooperate with you and stand behind its product should a problem develop, and that will be around for the duration of your ownership.

When you consider that the dog you choose will probably be around for a longer period of time, does it make any sense to shop less carefully for your dog than for your car? After all, your dog is your friend for life and offers far more than any machine.

Temperament, both yours and your prospective dog's, is your first consideration. As with the car, the needs of all "users" must be considered; the dog's innate personality should mesh with yours and your family's. If you are very assertive, an alpha-type dog—brash, bold, and strong-

Your Malamute will do just about anything you do! This Mal and his friend are enjoying a swim.

willed—may suit you, but if others in your family are timid, the dog will make them miserable. When push comes to shove, the dog may be out of a home. Compromising on a milder, more moderate dog will make everyone happier, including the dog.

If you are fortunate enough to find a breeder who uses the Puppy Aptitude Test, review the results and make use of them. You can use the dominance evaluations for your own impromptu checks of puppies that you are considering. Dominant and independent puppies are generally not good choices for homes with small children or infants.

After seven weeks, experience will begin shaping the puppy's behavior, so a good environment will strengthen a dog's weaknesses while a poor one may make them worse. The mother, or dam, is an important influence, not only because the puppies inherit components of their temperament from her, but more importantly, because they learn very quickly from her example. Observe her away from her puppies and decide whether you want a dog that acts like her for yourself.

Having puppies is no excuse for poor behavior on the dam's part. With newborn puppies, even the mildest mother may be fiercely protective, but by the time the puppies are old enough for viewing, her comportment away from them is probably an accurate reflection of her everyday temperament.

Females are commonly bred to outside dogs. Although the sire may not be on site, you may be able to see him if he is in the area. He, too, should be a dog with which you would like to live, since he contributes half the puppies' genes.

You can probably get information about an off-site sire as well. Start by calling the owner and asking about the dog. Owners may tell you what they think you want to hear, but what they say tells you a lot about what traits they value. You might be surprised at the number of people who prize aggressive behavior in any dog, no matter how inappropriate to the breed. If you ask how the dog responds to strangers and are told that he likes almost everyone he meets, he is probably a typical Malamute. Discount any dogs portrayed as suspicious, unfriendly, or aggressive, regardless of their other accomplishments.

THE EXTRAS

If you want to participate in special activities with your dog, you will require more than an Alaskan Malamute with good temperament, although you should never settle for less. Your requirements will also depend on the depth of your participation. For instance, a dog that runs on the occasional recreational team is quite different from one competing in long-distance freighting. Not all Malamutes can obtain advanced obedience titles, nor does every one belong in the show ring. Only a few of those shown achieve championships.

Realistically assess what you want to do before you look for your dog, and let that assessment determine where you look for him. If you have already gotten a dog, be realistic about his potential and let his abilities and talents shape what you do with him. Trying to make the proverbial square peg fit will be stressful and unproductive for both of you. Make the best of what you have and learn all that you can from your experience.

PUPPY VS. OLDER DOG

Consider whether your needs might be met better by an older dog. They are often for sale by the owner or available for adoption from various humane or rescue groups.

Although buying an older dog may be the ideal choice for a particular person's lifestyle and intentions, many people are afraid of being stuck with someone else's problem.

Puppies are adorable and entertaining—but are they right for you? Photo © Mormont De Henau, Belgium.

The second-hand dog is regarded with often-unwarranted suspicion. An older dog's temperament, appearance, health, and abilities are easier to assess than those of a puppy.

CAVEAT EMPTOR

Caveat emptor, Latin for "let the buyer beware," should be taken to heart. Dog-related purchases comprise a huge share of the multi-billion dollar pet industry in the United States; yet the production and sale of the market's initial product, the dog itself, are governed only by the rules of applicable registries such as the AKC, state consumer protection laws, and voluntary guidelines such as the AMCA Code of Ethics. Knowing what to look for is your responsibility.

FINDING THE RIGHT BREEDER

Breeders who maintain high standards may ask you a lot of questions. They will give you a written contract, which may be quite detailed. Don't be put off by either of these circumstances. Your answers to her questions will help the breeder determine whether the breed is right for you, and if so, which puppy will best suit your personality and needs. Remember that although you will be responsible for your puppy's upbringing, the breeder is responsible for its existence and its effect on the breed. Good breeders take this responsibility seriously.

You should expect a written sales contract or bill of sale that gives the name and address of the seller as well as the registration information on the dog. It should also clearly state any warranties and the specific remedies under it that are available to you as well as any agreements for future action by any party and what will happen if the agreements are not carried out. Verbal agreements not specified in the contract may not be binding under state law and are difficult to prove even if they are considered so.

A detailed agreement may seem daunting at first. You may even be suspicious about why anyone would have so many provisions about what should be a simple transaction. However, when any agreement is activated by circumstance, problems always arise when the assumptions of one party do not match the assumptions of the other. Reading through an agreement and giving it some thought may be more trouble than just writing a check and leaving, but consideration in advance is never as much trouble as wrangling at a later date.

The first indication of a breeder's concern is how they care for their dogs and puppies. While young puppies make neatness difficult, cleanliness is essential. When you see her, the dam will probably be out of coat and thin; most females look pitiful after weaning a litter. Still, she should be bright-eyed and healthy. The house and kennel may not look like a *Home and Garden* showcase, but the dogs' housing should be clean, secure, and comfortable with plenty of room for exercise. Both dogs and puppies should have plenty of contact with people and other dogs of good temperament.

Ask whether the breeder has any dog club affiliations. Being a member of the AMCA or a local Malamute club does not make one breeder's dogs better than another's. It does say something positive, though, about their commitment to the breed and their desire to learn more about it. They may also be signers of the AMCA Code of Ethics which details the minimum standards under which the national club feels dogs should be raised and sold.

If you cannot visit breeders, ask for video tapes of the dogs and the puppies and for a copy of their contract. Check references with people from area dog clubs.

CERTIFICATIONS

You should not be reluctant to inquire about health concerns regarding a dog you are considering. In addition to its having current vaccinations and being parasite free, its parents should be screened for genetic health problems found in the breed. Anyone who breeds Malamutes should readily show you certifications that the parents' thyroids, eyes, and hips are normal and that they are certified clear of producing dwarfs. If you are buying an older dog that has such certifications, the seller should provide them at the time of purchase.

The seller should be informed about these issues. Shy away from people who tell you that they don't do genetic screens because they've never had any problems. No responsible breeder fails to evaluate their stock before cementing their dogs' genes into another generation. Mark anyone who doesn't do genetic health screens off your list of prospective breeders.

PET SHOPS

Pet shops and other types of commercial marketers should not be on your list either for a variety of reasons. In many instances, the employees know little to nothing about dogs, much less specific breeds. In fact, after reading this book, you will probably know more about Malamutes than most of them.

Since neither of the parents are present, you can make no determinations about their temperament or appearance. So that they reach the market when they are "cutest," these breeders ship their puppies at a very early age. As a result, the puppies often lack proper social skills in dealing with both other dogs and humans. Because they are forced to eliminate in the wire cages in which they are kept, many pet-shop puppies are very hard to housebreak.

Sometimes, good dogs can be purchased from these outlets, but you are more likely to find one from a conscientious hobby breeder.

WHEN YOU WANT SOMETHING MORE

When you also have more in mind for your dog than companionship, the field from which you select your dog will become even narrower. Check references on kennels from which you contemplate purchasing a dog and give serious thought to what you want in a dog. For instance, if you want a dog primarily for sledding, look at kennels with working dogs; for showing, kennels with champions; for obedience, kennels with titleholders.

The puppies most likely to be successful in your endeavors are ones from breeders who both participate in the field successfully and have some experience in breeding. Here, especially, you need to check the "track record" of the breeder—not just how many pointed or champion dogs he has, but how many he has bred and sold to other people. Your concern is the merit of what

*Ch. Sabaka's the Heat Is On winning the points at the Lowell Kennel Club show. Breeder/Owners, Mike and Jackie Consentino.
Ashbey photo.*

When faced with a choice like this, how do you decide? That's why it is important to make up your mind about why you want a puppy and what you want it to do before you go shopping. This adorable group was bred by J. M. Brown of Scotland.

Selecting a dog for show becomes easier as the dog becomes older. Movement is easier to evaluate; most of the adult teeth are in and the bite should be fairly stable. You don't have to guess about size and substance. Kaila's the Witch Is Back. Breeder/owners, Chris and Eileen Gabriel.

A promising show puppy should be trained to stack, alert to bait, and move smoothly on lead at an early age. Practicing at matches before your puppy is six months old will get him used to showing. Ch. Windrift's Rruff N Tuff got his start here going Best of Winners from the puppy class at six months of age. Breeder/owner, Barbara Brooks.

Visiting National and Regional Specialty (all Malamute) shows is an excellent way to find a puppy. A wise buyer stays to watch the Stud Dog and Brood Bitch classes. Here you will see a dog or bitch with two of their puppy or adult offspring. You'll have an opportunity to see some of the Malamutes that are Register of Merit producers, as well as younger sires just starting their careers as a stud dog. Puppies from the latter may be more of a gamble, but the price will be more reasonable. Look for Malamutes that are proven winners with a type you like and a prepotent ability to reproduce their own good qualities. If you watch enough shows, the bloodlines and stud dogs you most admire will become evident. Photo by Joan Smith.

Ch. Alcan Private Label, Best of Breed at the 1989 National Specialty, with his famous daughter Ch. Echo Simply Snazzy. Breeder, owner, Dian McComb. Photo by Ross. Note the resemblance of daughter to father.

Ch. Chena's Penny From Heaven is the dam of three Specialty winning daughters. Breeders, owners, Sel and Joanne Levy. Ashbey photo.

At left, the beautiful Akela's Song of Ordan, owned by E. Terryjn, Belgium. Photo © Mormont De Henau. Above, a lovely red daughter of his, Quertakela of Keema's Wolfpack, age nine weeks. Again, note the resemblance in overall type. When picking a puppy for show or breeding, look at the grandparents as well as the parents. Choose a line you like and pick a puppy with strong familial type.

Malamutes make great camping companions! Courtesy Chris Eisenga.

you can buy not the show record of what the breeder keeps. Never make the mistake of equating advertising with excellence.

Show quality animals are usually more expensive and may have contractual restrictions. Asking for a show-quality puppy which you do not plan to show because you think "pet" puppies are somehow inferior is a mistake. As long as success is measured by achievement, show breeders will place their best puppies where they are confident that the dog will be shown. For a breeder to sell you a show-quality puppy he knows will not be shown is really quite illogical.

Legitimate show-quality puppies or adults are seldom available to just anyone. You will have to convince the breeder that you are offering not only a good home but a good show home. You may have to agree in the contract to some show obligations. In turn, the seller should offer you some minimum obligations, including eventual certification of hips and eyes and an acceptable CHD rating, presuming that most show animals will be bred.

PURCHASING YOUR DOG

When you decide to purchase a dog, the seller should provide you with registration information, a pedigree, and a written contract—these three items are essential. Other supplemental information is nice, but not essential.

REGISTRATION

The AKC's Registration Department provides free information about their services which you can obtain by writing, or phoning, or through the AKC web site. Beginning with the initial breeding, registration of a dog has several steps. The papers you obtain from the seller will depend on the seller's progress in this process. Ideally, the breeder will give you the puppy's blue slip or his individual registration. Sometimes, papers are in transit for a number of legitimate reasons, from obtaining signatures from out-of-town co-owners to having them returned for mistakes or omissions. However, the owner should provide you with adequate documentation to this effect.

Blue Slips—Registration begins with an Application for Litter Papers which must be completed by both the sire's owner and the dam's owner. It must be mailed to the AKC before the puppies are six months old. After processing, the AKC returns to the breeder an individual Application for Registration for each puppy in the litter. Since these are blue, they are referred to as "blue slips." Occasionally, they are referred to as "puppy papers" or "litter papers."

Both you and the breeder complete the blue slip and send it with the appropriate fee to the AKC which then returns a white Certificate of Registration to you. This is the individual registration or the dog's "papers."

Once the dog is registered, ownership can be transferred. The AKC will record the change and issue new papers reflecting to the new owner; everything else on the registration remains the same. The dog's individual registration stays with him for life; however, blue slips are only valid for a year from issuance. If you fail to apply for an individual registration within that time period, you will not be able to register your dog unless you can demonstrate extenuating circumstances.

Supplemental Transfers—When you receive any registration papers, whether blue slips or individual registrations, make sure that each person listed there has signed the form. If the seller is not named on the papers, he should have a supplemental transfer slip from AKC which documents the transfer of the puppy to someone other than the recorded owner. You should avoid buying a dog from anyone without the proper papers.

Anyone who transports animals across state lines for sale is subject to the USDA regulations on dog brokers, must be registered with them, and must meet certain minimal standards. A broker who does not have a supplemental transfer form is violating the AKC rules but is leaving no paper trail. Trouble with the federal government is more serious than trouble with the AKC.

Individual Registration—Two types of individual registration are available, unlimited and limited. The registration certificate of an unlimited registration has a blue border. Dogs so registered can be shown in any AKC events for which they are eligible. If they are bred, their progeny are eligible for registration.

The limited registration has an orange border. It restricts the dog from exhibition at dog shows and excludes any progeny from AKC registration. Because the breeder may convert the limited to an unlimited registration at any time, the limited registration affords him the opportunity of evaluating stock at a more appropriate age and reserving final decisions on breeding until then.

Dog shows are a forum for breeding, so dogs with limited registrations are not eligible for competition (although this may change in the future). However, they can compete in other AKC-sponsored events such as obedience, agility, and performance events like weight pulls and backpacking.

Even an unregistered purebred can compete in many events. If you obtained your Mal from a rescue or shelter, you may be able to obtain an Indefinite Listing Privilege (ILP) by consulting the AKC Registration Department.

PEDIGREES

A pedigree is nothing more than a family tree, and all dogs have one. However, the family tree of a registered dog is traceable back to the initial registrations. While in some breeds this covers a considerable span, Alaskan Malamutes have a relatively short registration history with some pedigrees going comparatively quickly to "Unknown." The American Kennel Club guards the integrity of its registrations carefully, and its certified pedigrees are the most accurate pedigree source. You can order one when you register your puppy by checking the box on the blue slip and sending the fee or by sending a copy of your registration papers along with the fee to AKC.

However, the pedigree your puppy's breeder gives you should be sufficient and may provide more information. If the breeder does not supply one, confuses the registration papers for the pedigree, or just does not know what you are talking about, go on to the next breeder on your list.

A REPUTABLE SELLER WILL PROVIDE:

1. Registration paper (litter or individual).

2. A three or four generation pedigree.

3. A sales contract or bill of sale.

4. Health records, including immunizations given, a record of any illnesses or veternary visits, and written records of any tests for hereditary problems that have been performed.

5. Any warranties the seller makes will be clearly stated in writing and signed by the seller.

6. A supply of the food the puppy is currently eating.

7. The breeder's name, address and phone number.

8. The name, address and phone number of any veterinarian(s) that have previously seen the pup.

9. Brief care and feeding instructions, plus a list of booster immunizations needed and the date.

A comfortable, clean place to call home is important for your Malamute. Akela's Song of Origami, owned by Col. Robert Gill, enjoys her place on the doorstep of the kennel. Photo by Gill.

CARING FOR YOUR MALAMUTE

Although many generations have passed, the Arctic's ruthless natural selection of their forebearers still provides the Alaskan Malamute with a remarkable constitution. Individual dogs, for the most part, are hardy and healthy. Provided that you keep his vaccinations and preventive medications current and he has no genetic disorder, your dog will probably see his veterinarian only for checkups and boosters.

Breeders and researchers have been working for decades to eliminate both genetic and acquired diseases in dogs. Their efforts, coupled with advances in preventive medicine, help ensure a healthier, longer life for your dog. Ultimately, however, his welfare is dependent on your knowledge.

YOUR HEALTH CARE PARTNER

Your partner in your pet's healthcare is your veterinarian, and you should choose one before you get a dog. In fact, many sellers require a check-up immediately after purchase.

The ideal veterinarian is someone who is familiar with your breed and who keeps up with advances in the field. His location is also important because the time it takes to get to his office might make a difference in a life-or-death situation. Find out about available emergency care before you need it and choose a veterinarian that provides some sort of twenty-four-hour coverage.

Veterinary medicine has a number of practice areas. Veterinarians in rural areas usually have a varied one that concentrates on large animals. If you need something beyond routine work, you may need a veterinarian who treats dogs or even a specialist. Specialists are certified in fields such as radiology, pathology, dermatology, internal medicine, dentistry, surgery, and oncology, to name a few. Because of their more limited practices, specialists are usually located in larger cities or at veterinary colleges and may see only referrals from other veterinarians. However, most will make an exception for someone with little access to good resources.

Many times, you will have to use your own judgement about your dog's health. To ensure that your judgement is good, you must educate yourself about health problems and their symptoms, available preventive care, and good husbandry practices.

Your consultations with your veterinarian will be much easier, and your veterinarian will be able to make a better diagnosis if your dog is not afraid and stressed by his visit. To help with this, make sure your dog is comfortable in the car and meeting strangers. Schedule a few visits to your veterinarian's office, take some treats, and ask the staff to give them to him.

When your dog is ill, keep track of his symptoms, jotting down their frequency and the circumstances that caused them. In the office, your dog should be on leash. Letting him socialize with other dogs can spread contagious disease. If you think your dog has one, such as parvovirus or distemper, alert the staff in case they want you to come in another entrance.

FEEDING AND SUPPLEMENTATION

A feeding program that meets his nutritional needs will get your Malamute off to a good start. Optimum development requires proper nutrition. Your dog's metabolic needs will depend upon his age and activity level; the growing puppy is very different from the mature dog, and the geriatric dog is yet another case.

FEEDING PUPPIES

Malamute puppies grow quickly and need a diet which promotes reasonable growth—high quality proteins with increased calcium and the vitamins and minerals necessary for their proper utilization. Calorie intake must be high enough for growth, but Malamute puppies should be kept thin enough to see a waistline. Too much weight, especially in a puppy as large as a Malamute, puts undue strain on an immature structure and may induce muscular and skeletal problems.

FEEDING THE MATURE DOG

At maturity, calories and protein levels should be scaled back unless the dog is working or under particular stress. For instance, lactating females need much more food than a non-breeding pet. Likewise, a working sled dog requires more fat and protein than a dog being shown one weekend every month.

FEEDING THE OLDER DOG

The appetite of a geriatric dogs (over seven) may be decreased due to a reduced sense of smell and taste. Digestive or absorption problems also may make weight maintenance difficult. Keeping weight off may be a problem for older dogs with decreased activity and a slower metabolism. Older kidneys, liver, heart, joints, and muscles still need high-quality proteins, but less of it, along with fewer calories and salt.

DOG FOODS

Exactly what you feed your dog will be determined by several factors: availability, cost, and your dog's response to the food. To tempt your pet's palate, a dizzying array of products are sold for a variety of prices at outlets ranging from the grocery store to private dealers.

The best food for Malamutes is dried or baked kibble which comes in several textures, from tiny pellets to large chunks. Dry food has the highest calorie content, is the most nutritionally complete, and helps remove tartar build up on teeth while also exercising gums. A few spoons of canned food or leftovers added to dry food may improve its appeal but should never be the sole food source.

Dogs are carnivores, but they also will graze on choice greenery and eat the stomach contents of herbivorous kills. They are so well assimilated into human culture that they can survive on a human diet, although they will not thrive on one.

Their nutritional requirements are different from humans. They have difficulty digesting many complex carbohydrates, make their own vitamin C, and do not suffer from the cholesterol woes of humans. In fact, dogs need saturated fats in their diet.

Quality commercial dog foods are so well formulated today that they need little, if any, supplementation. To determine the quality of the ingredients used, read the labels. Premium foods use meat, not meat by-product or soy, as a primary source of protein. These foods are more readily absorbed, so less food provides more nutrition. In-creased absorption also means less waste, so clean-up is easier.

Supplementing a complete food can cause problems. Many vitamins are toxic at higher doses, and others must be present in special ratios to be utilized. If you feel you must supplement, use a balanced multivitamin.

You may need to adjust food seasonally. In freezing weather, dogs need more calories, best supplied by fat, to maintain weight, especially if they are working. However, continuing such a rich diet into the summer may aggravate any tendency to skin problems.

EATING PROBLEMS

Nutritional needs vary between breeds. Malamutes are what horse people call "easy keepers" or "thrifty." Most have hearty appetites and can survive on very little—a legacy from their predecessors.

Malamute eating problems are invariably "man-made." Spoiled dogs may refuse plain food, holding out for goodies. You can correct this quickly by putting down food for only fifteen to twenty minutes twice a day, then removing it. When he is hungry enough, the dog will eat.

Some people advocate self-feeding. In theory, the self-fed dog will ultimately regulate his intake, thus maintaining an optimum weight. Since most Malamutes live to eat, their interpretation of "optimum" might differ from yours or your veterinarian's. As a by-product of their heritage, Malamutes make the most of their food and gain weight very easily. Self-feeding works best with only one dog since Malamutes are great competition eaters. Watch food left in self feeders as it is subject to spoilage from moisture and attracts insects.

Malamutes may also recycle. Coprophagia, or stool eating, is not uncommon and is no cause for alarm. Sometimes this reflects a need for more calcium, as does eating oyster shell or stone. If supplementation does not curtail this behavior, use one of the food additives that make stools less attractive to your dog. If this fails, clean up more frequently.

WATER

Your dog has a constant need for fresh, clean water. You can leave out a bucket or bowl, use an attachment on your hose or water faucet that provides water on demand, or install a self-filling dish. Even though Antarctic puppies had to survive by eating snow to meet their water needs, your house pet may not be able to deal with a

TO VACCINATE OR NOT TO VACCINATE

Jean Dodds, DVM, is one of the foremost veterinary researchers in canine immunology and has written about immune-mediated diseases in publications for both veterinarians and dog breeders. Asked about immunizations against Lyme disease, Corona-virus, and Bordatella, she replied that vaccines for these are "all somewhat questionable." She points out that in some cases the vaccine for Lyme Disease sets up an antibody-antigen complex causing the same arthritis-like symptoms as the disease it is supposed to prevent.

"The balance between the level of infection minimal enough to build antibodies without making the dog ill and a level sufficient to stimulate maximum antibody production is a fine one indeed. The effect of vaccines on healthy, normal dogs is usually minimal, but in animals with even minor immunologic problems, the effects can be serious." She advocates a more conservative approach to vaccination, weighing the risk factors of the disease and the likelihood of its contraction against the hazards of immunizations.[1]

block of ice in his water bowl, so in freezing weather, remember to provide fresh water.

IMMUNIZATIONS

Immunization is a very important step in protecting your dog's health. Vaccinations are available for many canine diseases.

As new vaccines are developed, manufacturer's tend to combine them into mixtures given with one injection. This is called a multi- or poly-valent vaccine. Recently, some veterinarians have questioned the wisdom of assaulting the immature immune system with so much at one time.

Another controversy surrounds the use of a modified live virus instead of a killed virus in vaccines. As Dr. Jean Dodds points out, "Killed vaccines do not replicate in the vaccinated animal, do not carry the risk of residual virulence, and do not shed attenuated viruses into the environment. Furthermore, killed vaccines do not bear the risk of contamination with adventitial viruses present in the tissue culture cells used to grow modified-live virus vaccines."[2] If they are slightly less effective, boosters can be given more frequently.

IMMUNIZABLE DISEASES

Immunizations are available for the following diseases which can occur in the dog. A few, such as rabies, are zoonotic (can be passed from species to species).

Rabies is a fatal viral disease which is passed on to other species through the saliva of infected animals. The virus is usually transmitted through a bite and attacks the brain and central nervous system.

Distemper, a viral disease, wiped out whole kennels before the vaccine was developed. It was first tested at Chinook Kennels on the dogs leaving for the second Antarctic expedition. All dogs should be vaccinated at regular intervals throughout their lives.

Hepatitis is caused by canine adenovirus type 1, while type 2 results in a respiratory infection. Type 1 can cause liver and kidney damage severe enough to cause death. Type 2 is a factor in kennel cough.

Leptospirosis is a bacterial infection that can cause permanent kidney damage. It can also be transmitted to other species, including humans.

Parainfluenza is a virus which causes "kennel cough," an annoying respiratory infection. Puppies, sick, or old dogs can require extensive treatment.

Parvovirus invades the intestinal tract causing severe, dehydrating diarrhea which can result in death, especially in puppies or old dogs. Puppies with parvo may also have cardiac complications. It is highly contagious.

Coronavirus is another highly contagious intestinal infection. In young puppies especially, the dehydration from vomiting and diarrhea can be fatal.

Bordatella is a bacterial infection which may occur alone, resulting in kennel cough. It may also be present with distemper, adenovirus type-2, parainfluenza, or other respiratory problems.

Lyme Disease is a bacterial infection transmitted by ticks, resulting in arthritis-like symptoms. Its highest incidence is in New England.

You can discuss these issues with your veterinarian. If he uses multi-valent, modified-live virus vaccines, perhaps he will alter his schedule if he knows that you are concerned and that you will return for boosters.

PARASITES

FLEAS

The most common external parasite is the flea, an insect of remarkable athletic ability and equally remarkable survival skills. In warmer climates, these pesky insects can make everyone, dog and human alike, miserable. A Malamute with fleas can render himself hairless in an amazingly short time.

The key to flea control is in not only getting rid of the ones you have but preventing adult development, thereby interrupting the cycle of infestation. Everyone associates dogs and fleas, but in actuality, the flea spends much of its life off the dog in the grass, bedding, carpet, cracks in the concrete, etc., jumping on the dog for dinner or transportation. These areas, therefore, also must be treated at the same time as the dog is treated.

Hundreds of products are available for flea control ranging from organic materials to chemical pesticides. They can repel or kill adult fleas or inhibit the growth cycle. Some have a residual effect and may pose health hazards to both you and your dog.

To exterminate fleas, you can tackle the project yourself, hire a commercial exterminator, or both. If you live in an area where fleas are a problem, you must start your control program early in the year and continue measures throughout the warm weather to be completely effective.

Regardless of the methods you use, follow directions diligently and be careful not to overdo. If you bathe your dog in flea soap, dip him in a pesticide, put on a flea collar, and then apply pesticides to his living area, you may not have to worry about fleas because you may no longer have a dog!

Fleas can contribute to many skin problems. Scratches can become infected, and dogs can contract tapeworms from fleas, both of which require medical treatment. Worse, some dogs develop an allergy to the flea saliva injected with each bite, causing further coat and skin problems. Although flea control requires effort at regular intervals, the alternatives are more expensive, more unpleasant, and pose a danger to your dog's health.

TICKS

Ticks carry several diseases which can affect mammals, including Rocky Mountain or Spotted Tick Fever, Canine Ehrlichiosis, and Lyme Disease, all of which pose serious health problems for affected animals. Ticks can be found in wooded areas, land used for grazing livestock, in high grass, and in coastal areas.

During the warmer months in tick-prone areas, be sure to check both yourself and your dog for these pests. Pulling one off will leave the head embedded in the skin which can cause irritation and infection. Instead, put alcohol (rubbing or drinking) or nail polish remover on it to intoxicate or kill it. When it releases its grip, the tick can be removed safely and either burned or dropped into pesticide or alcohol.

Tick collars will repel ticks, but flea sprays may not, even though they will kill a tick on the dog. If you have a problem with ticks in your house or kennel, you should consult a commercial exterminator about control. Fortunately, they are seasonal.

FLIES

Flies love ear tips and will torment some dogs and ignore others. A petroleum jelly coating may provide adequate protection; insect repellents work fairly well but need reapplication frequently.

During fly season, you may need to schedule an extra yard clean-up, since feces attracts flies. Unlike fleas and ticks, however, flies are wide-ranging, and your yard might not be the source of the problem.

If you use a jar-type fly trap, be sure to hang it safely away from the dogs. Full of flies, the jar can be poisonous, and, if the dogs get into it, you will be in for some heavy bathing duties!

INTERNAL PARASITES

Your pet's vigor can be also be sapped by internal parasites. The intestinal tract of the dog can house many types including hookworms, roundworms, tapeworms, giardia, whipworms, and coccidia. Except for tapeworms, all of these can be detected by microscopic examination of stool samples. Tapeworms shed segments which look like rice grains and are easily visible in the stool and occasionally around the anus.

Since they attach themselves directly to the intestinal lining and feed on the dog's blood supply, hookworms are the most dangerous, especially to puppies and young dogs. Their presence is often signaled by signs of anemia,

New outdoor runs at Windrift had to be filled in to make ground level before cement could be poured. Runs are portable. Cement is the easiet surface to keep clean and free of parasites. Brooks photo.

pale gums and pale inner eyelids. Intermittent diarrhea, bloody stools, lack of appetite or increased appetite with no weight gain, poor coat, and running eyes are all signs of infestation.

Your veterinarian may not detect whipworm or giardia with only one stool sample. Whipworms are commonly asymptomatic, except for a constantly shedding coat that is dry and brittle; the hair may even break off. When symptoms do appear, they are often dramatic and include bloody diarrhea and a loss of appetite.

Giardia should be taken very seriously. Unchecked, it can cause seizures and eventual death.

Parasite Prevention—Because many internal parasites are transmitted through fecal material and/or water, cleanliness is very important to your dog's health. A classic cycle of infestation begins when the dog walks through infested fecal material and then puts his foot in his water or food dish or licks his pads, thereby infecting himself. Backpacking Malamutes may also get giardia from contaminated streams. If you are not supposed to drink the water, don't let your dog drink it either.

Insect vectors carry some parasites. These include fleas which carry tapeworms, flies which carry coccidia, and mosquitoes which carry heartworm. The latter poses a significant danger to infected dogs.

HEARTWORM

Heartworm larvae injected into the bloodstream by a biting mosquito eventually mature into worms that lodge in the heart. As they grow and multiply, the heart has increasingly less room for blood. Eventually, the dog dies. Because the process is slow, changes to the dog's vigor are gradual enough to escape early notice.

Treatment is hard on the dog and may not be possible if he is in poor health. Even after the heartworms are gone, the dog may have resulting lung and heart damage. The best way to deal with heartworms is to prevent them.

Fortunately, several products are available from veterinarians to prevent not only heartworms but other internal parasites such as hookworms and roundworms. Daily or monthly dosages are given orally.

YOUR DOG'S MEDICINE CHEST

Your medicine cabinet is probably full of things to deal with minor medical needs, and many of these products can be used for dogs. A few added items will complete your pet's medicine chest.

Since you cannot ask your dog to hold a thermometer under his tongue, you will need a rectal thermometer and some petroleum jelly to ease its insertion. Normal temperature for a dog is between 100° to 103° Fahrenheit or 38° to 39° Centigrade, depending on the ambient temperature and his activity level. A transient rise in body temperature may occur in a heavily coated Malamute that plays or works hard in warm weather, but the dog's temperature will return to normal with rest. Fever, however, is a prolonged, elevated temperature and should be taken seriously enough to consult your veterinarian.

Additional items to have on hand include:
- sterile gauze and self-adhesive bandages
- antiseptic soap
- adhesive tape
- tweezers
- alcohol
- scissors
- plastic bags for stool samples
- large (10 cc) syringe for liquid medicine.

Always keep the phone number of your veterinarian and/or emergency clinic close to the phone.

Over-the-counter medicines to have on hand for your dog include:
- antibiotic and cortisone ointments and creams
- anti-diarrheals such as Kao-Con, and/or Pepto-Bismol (Imodium, while effective in humans, can cause intestinal problems for dogs)
- antihistamine such as Benadryl
- Ascriptin, which embeds aspirin in an antacid matrix should be used judiciously instead of plain aspirin, and should be given with food. (Dogs should not be given Ibuprofen or Tylenol.)

MEDICAL PROBLEMS

BITES

Insects and Spiders—Insect stings can cause problems for some dogs, although others seem quite impervious to them. If the dog worries at a spot or chews it, give him a weight-appropriate dose of Benadryl, which should reduce the reaction, but may make him drowsy and thirsty. If the symptoms do not abate after a couple of hours, consult your veterinarian.

Venomous spider bites are another matter and warrant a visit to the veterinarian. The area around the bite may immediately begin forming pus, and further problems can develop.

Snakes—Snake bites also need medical intervention as soon as possible, although dogs seem less sensitive to snake venom than humans. Keep the dog calm and put cool compresses on the bite if possible until you can get to the veterinarian. You can give him Benadryl to help with any allergic response.

DOG FIGHT INJURIES

Dog fights can produce several types of injuries depending on the severity of the fight, including broken limbs and bitten-off ears which clearly call for medical help. Other injuries, such as punctures, will necessitate immediate attention from you. The hair around the bite should be clipped back, and the wound washed with antiseptic soap and covered with antibiotic ointment or cream. If punctures and shallow cuts are the only injuries, call your veterinarian to find out if he wants the dog on antibiotics.

Slashing teeth can cause tears that require stitches. If the cut is bleeding, apply a clean compress and exert direct pressure on the wound to try to stop it. Do not remove the bandage to see if the bleeding has slowed or stopped; you will pull off the clotted blood and start the bleeding again. As soon as the bleeding has stopped, bandage the compress on snugly and transport the dog to the veterinarian.

CAR ACCIDENTS

While some dogs are quite careful of cars, others seem unable to comprehend either their size or speed. No one can provide for every whim of fate, and the best-supervised dogs can have run-ins with automobiles.

If this happens to your dog, do not panic. The mobile dog's first instinct is to run away, so try to calm him and keep him with you. Get him in your car, restrain him with some sort of tie, or find someone to help you. Call your veterinarian and tell him what has happened.

If the dog is so agitated that he is snapping, protect yourself with a blanket, coat, towel, or large piece of cloth. He may calm down when he realizes you are helping him.

An immobile dog can be put on a board or car seat. If you are alone, try to stop any serious bleeding before you leave. Put compresses on the wound and apply direct pressure, bandaging the compress on without removing it. If you have help, let them drive while you help the dog. He will be happier with you than with a stranger.

DIARRHEA

So many diseases have diarrhea as a symptom; its occurrence can signal anything from a dire problem needing immediate medical attention to an overly excited dog. Common causes are changes in food or a reaction to medication, especially antibiotics. You should be concerned if your dog has several soft, watery stools more frequently than normal.

Give him an antidiarrheal agent such as Kaopectate (not Imodium unless instructed to do so by your veterinarian). Diarrhea causes dehydration, so make sure that your dog has access to water, but remove all his food and let his stomach rest for a day. Then, begin feeding him foods that are easy on the stomach, such as rice or oatmeal cooked in broth and not drained. You can mix in other binders such as cheese, eggs, cottage cheese, and/or yogurt, which has the added advantage of replacing food-digesting bacteria that may have been stripped from your dog's intestinal tract. Feed him several small meals of this type, and if his stools improve, gradually add his regular food over a couple of days until he is back to normal.

Stools that have fresh blood or are black and tarry are cause for alarm, as is persistent diarrhea. Consult your veterinarian immediately. Keep other dogs away from an affected dog and the areas in which he has defecated to prevent the spread of any disease.

FROSTBITE

Frostbite most often affects the tips of the ears, the tail, the toes, and sometimes the scrotum. It is usually the result of prolonged exposure to subzero temperatures. However, dogs moved from warmer climates to cooler ones are most susceptible. Prevention should be obvious, but when it fails, recognizing the symptoms quickly is important for successful treatment.

Initially, the affected areas feel cool and may be pale. As the tissue thaws, it may become reddened and painful. Mild cases may escape notice until hair over the damaged area turns white later.

A dog with mild frostbite will recover quickly. A severely frostbitten area should be rapidly thawed by gentle applications of warm water; the tissue will irritate very easily if not handled with extreme care. Protective ointments such as petroleum jelly will keep it from drying. If severe, however, amputations and surgical debridement may be necessary if the area does not heal after a reasonable time period.[3]

HEAT STROKE

Like all the "Northern" breeds, the Alaskan Malamute is particularly susceptible to hyperthermia, or heat stroke. This tendency is not restricted to warmer climates, but heat stroke does occur more frequently in areas with high humidity and heat.

Recognizing the clinical signs accompanying hyperthermia is very important because treatment should begin as soon as possible. At first, the dog might have raspy breathing with increased production of thick, ropy saliva. Mucous membranes usually turn very dark red, and the whites of the eyes tend to become bloodshot. This stage may be followed by very heavy respiration which becomes labored. Most dogs will then lie down and will eventually become comatose as the condition worsens. Many will manifest their shock with bloody vomitus or diarrhea.

Treatment should begin immediately before transport to a veterinarian. Spray the dog with cold water and literally pack him in ice if possible, giving special attention to the groin, armpit and pads. Contact your veterinary clinic before transport so that the staff and doctor can be ready to administer emergency care. On the way to the veterinarian, turn the car air conditioner on high or open the windows to maximize cooling.[4]

The danger of heat stroke is always present when dogs are left inside a car, even if the outside temperature is moderate. The sun coming through the windows warms the small interior, making the car a hothouse. Every year thousands of dogs die in cars while waiting for their owners to finish shopping. Leave your Malamute at home when the weather warms up.

POISON

Dogs and children are especially at risk for poisoning. Fortunately, children grow out of the compulsion to taste everything, but dogs never do. They may lick poisonous material off their feet or inhale toxic substances into their lungs.

Be alert to dangers and keep materials out of reach and tightly sealed. If you find spilled, open, or chewed containers; material on the dog's feet, coat, or mouth; an abnormal odor to the dog's breath or body; burns or

Puppies are fond of nibbling on house and garden plants, some of which are poisonous. Nine-week-old puppy from Belgium.

POISONOUS PLANTS

Following is a list of poisonous plants. Many are irritants to the skin, throat, stomach or intestine. Others produce lameness, cardiac irregularities, convulsions, or hallucinations.

Aconite or monkshood, Almond, Alocasia, Amaryllis, Angel's trumpet, Apricot, Autumn erocus (Colchicum),

Balsam pear, Baneberry, Belladonna or deadly nightshade, Bloodberry or baby-pepper, Bird-of-paradise bush, Black locust, Blackberry, Bittersweet woody nightshade, Buckthorn, Bull nettle, Burdock,

Cacti, Caladium, Calla lily, Candlenut, Cardinal flower or Indian tobacco, Carolina nightshade, Castor bean, Chalice vine, Cherry, Christmas candle, Chinaberry, Chokecherry, Clemantis, Clusia, Common boxwood, Coral plant, Coriaria,

Daffodil, Daphne or spurge laurel, Dumbcane (Diefenbachia),

Elephant ear, English holly, English ivy, Euonymus,

Flag iris, Foxglove, Foxtail,

Garden sorrel, Glory lily, Goatshead, Golden chain (Laburnum), Ground cherry,

Henbane, Honey locus, Honeysuckle, Horse chestnut or Buckeye, Hydrangea,

Jack-in-the-pulpit or Indian turnip, Japanese plum, Jerusalem cherry, Jessamine, Jimson weed or Thorn apple,

Kentucky coffee tree,

Larkspur, Lily of the valley, Lords-and-ladies,

Malanga, Marijuana, Matrimony vine, Mescal bean, Mock orange, Moonseed, Morning glory,

Needlegrass, Nettle, Nettle spurge, Nutmeg, Nux vomica,
Oleander, Oregon root,

Peach, Periwinkle, Peyote or mescal, Philodendron, Poinsettia, Poison hemlock, Pokeweed, Pongam, Potato, Privet (ligustrum),

Raintree or monkey pod, Rhubarb, Rosary pea or precatory bean,

Sandbox tree or monkey pistol, Sandbur, Skunk cabbage, Soapberry, Stinging Nettle,

Tobacco, Tripleawn,

Virginia creeper,

Water hemlock, Western monkshood, Wild barley, Wild brome, Wild cherry, Wisteria,

Yam bean, Yellow allamanda, Yews (all).[5]

painful areas on the skin or mouth, you should think about the possibility of poison.

Ingested poisons may cause cramping and pain, vomiting and/or diarrhea. Drooling and generalized weakness and slowed respirations should set off alarm bells. Inhaled poisons are signaled by coughing, sneezing, shortness of breath or blue mucous membranes. Severe cases may have very labored breathing, or respiration may stop altogether. Materials that can be absorbed through the skin will cause localized redness and pain, even peeling, and the mouth and nose may be severely irritated.

Many ornamental plants are poisonous to varying degrees. Ethylene glycol antifreeze has a particularly enticing smell and taste and is lethal for the dogs that drink it. A dog that drinks from the toilet may be poisoned by a flushable bowl-cleaner, and those grazing on lawns or clippings may also be ingesting pesticides, chemical fertilizers, fungicides, and/or herbicides.

Immediate medical attention is essential for any symptoms and evidence of poisoning. If you can identify the substance or plant, take it and any labels with specific antidotes listed with you to the veterinarian. When transport time is a problem or if the dog is advanced in his symptoms, take appropriate first aid and/or antidote instructions into your own hands if possible.

REPRODUCTIVE SYSTEM DISEASE

As dogs age, they are subject to various diseases associated with the reproductive system. Veterinarians used to recommend waiting until after puberty to neuter or spay dogs; however, increasingly, they are advocating sterilization before sexual maturity. If your motivation for acquiring a dog is companionship, the health benefits of spaying and neutering far outweigh the expense and inconvenience of surgery. The most immediate advantage is sure birth control. A by-product of being a "natural" dog, Malamutes have a very strong sexual drive. Malamute females want to find a mate, and the males are real Lotharios. Keeping one in your yard when a neighborhood female is in season can be unbelievably difficult.

Neutered dogs will not develop testicular cancer or infections, and spayed females will likewise never have uterine or cervical cancer. Early neutering virtually prevents a variety of prostate problems as well as tumors around the anus, and mammary tumors and cancer, which are quite common in intact females. Females no longer have hormone-induced sheds, and neither sex displays as much intersex aggression. Some behavioral problems associated with sexual activity, such as mounting and marking, and some dominance behaviors are decreased or eliminated.

Pyometra is an inflammation of the uterus to which intact Malamute females seem prone in their later years. It can result in death if left untreated, which is why spaying a producing female after her last litter is good idea.

SEIZURES/EPILEPSY

Seizures result from the uncontrolled electrical discharge of neurons in the brain. Epilepsy is a term referring to recurrent seizure activity where no active underlying cause exists, although it may be secondary to a previous problem. While determining the type may be difficult, it can help in diagnosis. There are three types: generalized, partial, and partial with secondary generalization.

Generalized Seizures—Generalized seizures are caused by "[t]otal, or bilateral involvement of the brain . . . . They may be mild and cause no loss of consciousness, or they may be severe, causing total loss of consciousness."[6] Metabolic problems, poisonings, nutritional deficiencies, or inherited epilepsy are the most likely causes.

Typically, at the beginning of a generalized seizure cycle, the dog becomes restless and anxious. He may look off into space or ask for attention. This behavior is followed by loss of consciousness with dilated pupils. Accompanying motor action may involve chewing motions with salivation, stiff legs, paddling or running motions that alternate with rigidity of the legs and a stiffly arched back. The dog may urinate and/or defecate during the seizure. Although they seem to last forever, most seizures are over within a few minutes. The dog may pop up as if nothing has happened, or he may be disoriented for a short time.[7]

Partial Seizures—In a partial seizure, the electrical discharge is localized in a specific area of the brain. They are usually the result of brain damage caused by disease, tumor, or trauma.

"Partial seizures include many forms of behavior you may have seen, and perhaps never equated as being seizures . . . unilateral muscle twitching of the face or limbs; bizarre and aggressive behavior, chewing, lip smacking and excessive swallowing; running; confusion; 'fly biting;' 'star gazing;' hallucinations; episodic tail chasing; self-mutilation; and some chronic episodic vomiting and diarrhea."[8]

Partial Seizures with Secondary Generalizations—Partial seizures with secondary generalizations are difficult to identify because the activity typical of the partial seizure may be quite brief and unobserved by the owner. Since these seizures are most commonly associated with a non-inherited lesion, differentiating them from a generalized seizure is important in determining cause. One important tip-off is the presence of asymmetric motor activity.[9]

What Should You Do? Although full-blown seizures are difficult to watch without doing anything, nothing is exactly what you should do. When your dog has recovered, you should call your veterinarian, and if your dog has more than one seizure, you should have a thorough examination.

The most important thing you can do for your dog is to observe and record the circumstances surrounding his seizure. Tell your veterinarian: What the seizure looked like throughout. How long do they last and how often do they occur? Are signs of partial seizure present? Has your dog been ill or had a fever. Has he been exposed to toxins (include plants, new carpet, dips, sprays, etc) or been in a pound, shelter, or kennel recently? When and with what was he vaccinated? Do any littermates or relatives have seizure problems? What and how often is he fed?[10]

Causes—The most common, non-inherited causes of seizure activity are infectious, inflammatory brain disease such as distemper or other encephalitis-causing viruses. The next-most common are traumas to the head in which

seizure is an after effect; these are followed in frequency by metabolic problems, the most common of which are hypoglycemia, poisoning, and tumors.[11]

Oftentimes, symptoms other than seizures can help identify the problem. A dog with a tumor may also have weakness or paralysis of a limb. Blood tests can reveal the presence of infections or low-blood sugar.[12]

Unfortunately, the underlying causes of epilepsy are not always possible to determine despite careful observation by both owners and veterinarians or extensive work-ups. When no reason can be found, the diagnosis is termed "idiopathic epilepsy."

Treatment—Seizures can usually be controlled by anticonvulsant drugs, the most common of which is phenobarbital. Also used with dogs are Primidone (Mylepsin or Mysoline) and diphenylhydantoin (Dilantin), although primidone may cause liver problems and diphenylhydantoin may be ineffective in dogs.[13] A new therapy involves the use of potassium bromide alone or in conjunction with phenobarbital.

Other suggestions to help with seizure control are: a low-protein balanced diet, daily rather than monthly heartworm medication without a vermifuge, avoidance of any organo-phosphates for parasite control and of any drugs known to lower seizure thresholds. These include digitoxin, dipyrone, chloramphenicol, amphetamines, acepromazine or other phenothiazine tranquilizers, phenyl-butazone, and griseofulvin.[14]

Sendaishi dogs wait patiently to get on the road. Courtesy of William Matott.

SOFT PADS

Before you take your Malamute backpacking among the rocks, road-working on concrete, or pulling a cart on asphalt, consider his feet. Even dogs on snow get booties for protection.

You can help toughen your dog's feet while he is still used to a soft surface by applying Tincture of Benzoin to his pads. This is available at pharmacies and is sold under a variety of names by pet suppliers. It does not sting or hurt, but it does stain, so let it dry before allowing your dog in the house.

TOAD POISONING

Malamutes love to hunt, and in semitropical climates, sooner or later, they will run into a toad. You'll know immediately because your dog will be frothing at the mouth and drooling from the toxins in the toad's saliva.

To treat your dog, wash his face, mouth, and eyes with a lot of cool water. More powerful toad toxins can cause seizures, rapid heartbeat and breathing, and even death, so if you suspect that your dog is having further problems, get him prompt medical attention.

EXERCISE

An important adjunct to good health is proper and sufficient exercise. If you jog or walk regularly, your dog will realize the same benefits from it that you do. Recognize, however, that he also needs to become accustomed to it; you cannot expect your potato to hop off the couch and trot five miles.

Their heritage as Arctic sled dogs gives Alaskan Malamutes a very thrifty metabolism resulting in quick and easy weight gain. Fortunately, they also form muscle tissue with the same facility. Even self-exercising dogs with a naturally high activity level benefit from additional regular exercise.

An exercise program should gradually increase in distance and duration. The dog should be worked at a medium to slow trot, preferably on a soft surface. If you do not jog, you can lead your dog beside a bike, golf cart or from the tailgate of a car, (be careful to keep him away from exhaust fumes).

Puppies and young dogs need regular exercise, but save heavy-duty roadwork until bone growth is finished. If your dog is overweight, reduce his food and walk him until his ribs can be felt but do not show. Then begin road-working him to build muscle; otherwise, he may become too bulky.

HOUSING

Many problems can be avoided by housing your dog properly. Dog-proofing should be as important as child-proofing if your dog will be living with you in the house. Dogs are generally happier, relate better to people, and live longer if they are treated as family members and receive individual attention.

Even a housedog needs both regular exercise and some room to run around unsupervised. This can be provided by a fenced yard or a fenced-off dog run.

NO DOG SHOULD EVER BE ALLOWED TO RUN LOOSE. If you think confining a dog to a house or yard or walking him on leash is cruel or too restrictive, then you should not own one. The days when dogs could roam the neighborhood are long gone if, in fact, such a time ever existed.

FENCING

Fencing is important for keeping your Malamute safe. Chain-link is very serviceable as long as the wire is strong

SAFE IN SPITE OF HIMSELF

Always remember that a Malamute who wants to escape can probably do so. Chained dogs become especially strong in the forequarter from pulling, and metal rusts and wears out. A dog can hang himself if he is chained close enough to a fence or other obstacle that he can try to jump.

When sex enters the picture, a dog's brain seems to leak out his ears. Normally, crate-trained dogs will stay in a crate even though they would prefer being out. One Malamute owner paid a high price for complacency when she left her dog and a female in season crated next to each other. Her dual-titled champion-companion-dog strangled when he got his head through the top of the crate but couldn't get out and couldn't get back in.

Another safety tip comes from a well-known breeder who had a terrible fire in her kennel building. She said the only dogs that survived were the ones in plastic crates, because they escaped when the crates melted from the heat. The dogs in metal crates were trapped and died.

A little vigilance and attention to changing circumstances can keep your dog safe. This might mean boarding your dog during risky periods, or making other housing arrangements.

Inside a modern kennel building. Note raised beds for dogs. Sliding dog doors allow access to outside runs, but can be closed when necessary. Brooks photo.

enough to resist chewing. It is used for both permanent fencing and for portable runs. Periodically, be sure to check the tension wire at the bottom of a permanent installation and the fastenings that hold the wire to the frame on portable pens to see that they have not rusted or been pushed loose.

Board or privacy fencing has the advantage of blocking both your dog's view and your neighbor's view, although wood rots and can be chewed. All fencing, but especially wood, will be stronger if the uprights are put on the side of the fence opposite the dog's yard.

If you have more than two dogs, you may have to resort to a kennel set-up. Schemes for these are as simple as a stake-out chain and dog house or as elaborate as a kennel building with indoor/outdoor runs. Construction techniques and requirements differ widely depending upon area climate.

Because they are so amiable, Malamutes are easily stolen from unsecured yards, so put a lock on your gates. The commonly used U-shaped gate latch should be secured with a bolt snap to keep your dog from nosing it open.

Interior runs like these can be built by anyone handy with a hammer and saw. The wide double doors provide good ventilation. An air conditioner is mounted on the back wall. Brooks photo.

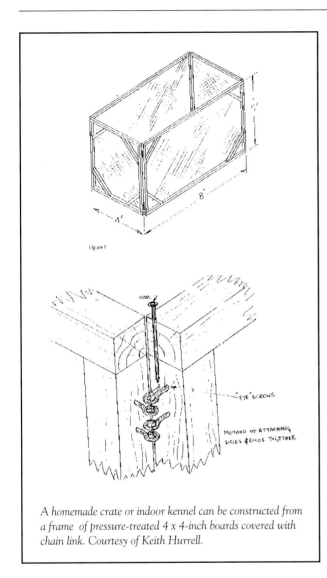

A homemade crate or indoor kennel can be constructed from a frame of pressure-treated 4 x 4-inch boards covered with chain link. Courtesy of Keith Hurrell.

Invisible fencing may be the only solution to fencing needs if you live on rocky terrain or in subdivisions that restrict fencing. A buried wire forms the fencing and sends a signal to a special collar receiver. Whenever the dog gets too close to the wire, the collar emits a warning tone. If he fails to heed it, as he gets closer, the collar gives him a mild shock.

This type of fencing presents a few problems. Malamutes can be more determined than pain-sensitive and may cross the wire despite the shock. Unfortunately, they are rarely so motivated to return that they will cross the wire to get back into the yard. Instead, the dog will require an escort—you—to come home. Even if the fence does keep your dog in, it will not keep marauding animals out. You may have trouble with other people's loose dogs

and cats. Therefore, the invisible fence is best used with some other kind of barrier.

Dogs that climb or jump are always a problem. Runs can be covered with wire topping, and sometimes a tall enough fence will surpass their abilities. For the Olympic contenders, however, you should consider a fence charger. These are powered by house current or batteries and can be found at Sears, Montgomery Ward, feed, or hardware stores.

SHELTER

Your dog should never be left outside without shelter or shade. If he is allowed access to your house or garage, a number of "dog" doors are available commercially which let him come and go as he pleases. For strictly outside or kenneled dogs, shade can be provided by shade-cloth coverings, trellises, or solid covers. He should also have a pallet and/or dog house.

Your dog's exercise area should be cleaned daily. Stools can be buried, put in the trash (check to see if this is permitted by your local government), or washed into a kennel septic system or sanitary sewer for just that purpose. If the dog is on a brick, concrete, or gravel surface, these materials should be periodically washed with bleach and allowed to dry thoroughly before the dog is returned. These measures will help control not only odor, but internal and external parasites.

CRATES

Dogs are denning animals. Unlike most humans, they feel safe and secure in small, closed-in spaces. In the home, the den can be simulated by a dog cage or "crate." They can be made from wire, plastic, wood, or metal and may be disassembled, sometimes easily, sometimes not, or they can be conveniently folded into a suitcase shape for easy storage. Crates are available directly from manufacturers who advertise in catalogs and dog magazines or from pet supply and some discount stores.

A crate will provide your dog with a place he can call his own and will satisfy his need for privacy. In a busy household, it may be the only place a young dog can get the sleep he needs. If your dog is ill or if you have a house full of undoggy people, a crate is a place to secure your dog, where he can rest or just be alone. It is an invaluable aide in housebreaking, and homes with more than one dog can avoid food-related spats by feeding each dog in his own crate.

A crate used for travel or shipping should be just large enough for the dog to stand up and turn around—any larger and he may be knocked about unduly. A crate used only at home where the dog is confined for longer periods should be larger to allow the dog more room to stretch out. A "large" size accommodates all but the biggest Malamutes which may need an "extra-large."

Once a dog is accustomed to a crate, it is the safest, most peaceful, and comfortable place to be. It provides a "home away from home" for dog shows, car and airplane travel. Many hotels will only allow dogs that are crated when unsupervised.

Crates are not intended for punishment purposes; rather, they are a place for the pup to take an undisturbed nap, eat without anxiety, or keep out of trouble when the family is out of the house.

COLLARS AND IDENTIFICATION

No dog should wear a choke collar when he is unsupervised. If the collar catches on something, the dog may strangle himself struggling to get free. Instead, use a loose buckle collar on him and attach his current rabies and identification tags.

People who would ordinarily not pick up a wandering dog will often help a dog that is wearing tags. In many areas, animal control officers will try to contact owners, but dogs without identification are euthanized after the required holding-period. Along with tags, you should consider some kind of permanent identification such as a tattoo or an implanted microchip.

ENDNOTES:

1.   Jean Dodds, DVM, Personal communication (April, 1994).

2.   W. Jean Dodds, DVM. "Vaccine Safety and Efficacy: Killed Virus Versus Modified-Live Vaccine." *Kuvasz Quarterly* (Spring, 1992), 11.

3.   Randall S. Murray, DVM, Personal communication (March, 1994).

4.   Murray.

5.   Robert W. Kirk, DVM, *First Aid for Pets*, (New York: E. P. Dutton, 1975), 46-49.

6.   Carol Fry Owen, "Epilepsy: A Round-Up of Facts and Ideas," *The Bagpiper*, Scottish Terrier Club of America, 1993, #4, reprinted in *The Pomeranian Review* (August/September, 1995), 11.

7.   Owen, 10.

8.   Owen, 11.

9.   Owen, 11.

10.   Owen, 10.

11.   Owen, 12.

12.   Malcolm B. Willis, Ph.D., *Genetics of the Dog.* (New York: Howell Book House, 1989), 181.

13.   Owen, 13, 16.

14.   Owen, 17.

Leonhard Seppala's sled dog kennel in Alaska is typical of those in the Gold Rush days. Photo courtesy of Alaska and Polar Regions Dept., University of Alaska. From the Loman Family collection.

3

TRAINING PRINCIPLES

Canine education begins with an owner who wants to form a close partnership with his dog—one that establishes the foundation for all joint activities: companionship, dog shows, obedience trials, agility events, backpacking, sledding, racing, skijoring, or weight pulling. Training is essential if you are to enjoy a pleasant relationship with your dog. At the least, your dog should come when called, walk beside you on leash, sit, down, and stay.

In addition to being housebroken, your Malamute should be trustworthy in the house. He should not chew or jump on furniture, nor drag clothes out of hampers, nor wrap the house in toilet paper. His greetings should be restrained; no one should need to fear damage to their clothing or their person when entering your home. Outside, a walk should not disintegrate into a contest of wills, and your neighbors must not fear for the well-being of their pets.

WHEN TO TRAIN

Some of your Malamute's education must be done at home. More formal training may be done at a training class. Class training has many advantages, including more socialization with other people and dogs, more distractions, and the opportunity to work in a different location. You will have additional information sources and a class full of "yardsticks" by which to measure your progress.

Dogs are not so different from humans. In both, the foundations of adult behavior are laid during childhood, where rapid and effectual learning occurs that will shape the rest of the individual's life. Since most training classes are geared toward dogs of six months or older (even kindergarten puppy classes usually require puppies to be four months old), educating your young puppy will be up to you and your family. A puppy learns a lot during this time period, and he will either learn from you what you want him to do, or his education will be left up to happenstance.

At two to three months of age, a puppy is virtually a blank slate, guided mostly by instinct. You need only to work with those natural tendencies and his own

personality. This is a wonderful time when your efforts will not be hindered by prior experiences nor will you have to contend with a lot of adolescent defiance or adult attitude. Puppies are eager to learn and eager to please. Training them can be one of the most enjoyable experiences you ever have with a dog, and it will certainly make your subsequent life with him more pleasant.

WORKING WITH A PUPPY

Working with a puppy will require some special consideration on your part. Concentration is a learned skill, and

A puppy is virtually a blank slate for you to mold. This pretty pup is owned by F. Seidl, Czech Republic.

29

young dogs have little experience with it. Training sessions should be extremely brief, but frequent; several five-minute sessions during the day are far more effective than one fifteen minute lesson. Sessions should be followed by a few minutes of play to reinforce training as a pleasant experience.

Never lose your temper, especially with a puppy. He will undoubtedly not associate your anger with his transgression. Confused dogs approach training with either fear or belligerence—neither of which fosters learning. Instead of getting angry with him, rethink what you are doing; try looking at what happened from the dog's perspective and see if the problem lies with your methodology. If that does not suggest a solution, consult some of the excellent books on training that are available and/or an experienced trainer.

Never start a training session when you are in a bad mood. Malamutes are incredibly responsive to their owners, and if you are frustrated or annoyed, your dog will sense this and not perform his best. If you have a positive, upbeat attitude towards training, your dog will, too.

BACKGROUND TRAINING CONCEPTS

Whether you work with a puppy or an adult, alone or in a class, familiarity with canine reasoning skills and an understanding of pack behavior and communication will improve your ability to "think like a dog." Keeping a few basic concepts about the dog's learning ability in mind can help you become a skilled trainer, regardless of what tasks you and your dog tackle.

CONSISTENCY IS THE KEY

Consistency is extremely important when training. Always use the same command in the same tone of voice. Always make sure that performance of a task is not left up to the discretion of the dog. For instance, while you may not mind your dog jumping on you when you are wearing grubbies, you surely do not want him messing up your good clothes (nor should any guest have to submit to such behavior regardless of attire). The dog is not capable of distinguishing between suitable and unsuitable clothes, so, he must learn that jumping up on people is unacceptable in *all* circumstances.

The same thing applies to a puppy's tendency to mouth or bite for attention. As a rule of thumb, you should never allow or encourage a puppy to do anything that would be undesirable if done by an adult dog.

Keep this in mind when choosing toys. If the dog could confuse a toy with something you would not want chewed, find a different toy. How would a dog know the difference between your favorite shoes and a pair you have discarded? How can he recognize that a stained towel is different from the towels hanging in the bathroom?

Always provide plenty of toys that the puppy understands belong to him, then never allow him to play with anything else. Rawhide chews, Nyla-bones, hard rubber balls (be sure they are too large to get stuck in his throat), tug-toys, and toys made out of stretchy latex are excellent choices. Keep a supply of these about the house and yard so that when you observe your puppy with something you do not want chewed, you can correct him immediately and offer him a permissible alternative.

TIMING IS EVERYTHING

The timing of corrections and praise is every bit as important as offering them in the first place, because the dog's ability to correlate cause and effect is very limited. To be associated with an action, a correction optimally should occur within twenty seconds, although in an older, more experienced dog, the span might be as long as a minute.

One of the most common misapplications of correction occurs during housebreaking. The owner discovers that the dog has had an "accident." Dragging the dog over to his offense, she administers some sort of correction—yelling, shaking, hitting. When the behavior continues, the owner often feels that the dog is acting out of spite or defiance. Owners invariably interpret the dog's expression as one of guilt. "I'd swear he knows he's done something wrong," the owner maintains, "because every time I come home he looks guilty and tries to avoid me!"

However, the canine interpretation of the events is quite different from that of his human master. What the dog does know is that whenever the master comes home, walks around the house and has a certain expression on his face, tone of voice, and body position, trouble is coming. His subsequent demeanor expresses anxiety and fear rather than guilt.

In order to feel guilt, the dog would have to have the intellectual sophistication to understand the concepts of right and wrong. He would have to believe that his action was wrong, know that it is an occasion for disapproval, and know that punishment will follow. He would have to know that the punishment is directly related to his action, regardless of the time span between them. Operating at this level requires higher reasoning skills which the dog simply does not possess.

That we can so easily assign our own emotions and faculties to the dog is a complement to his ability to integrate with humans. In training, however, we must always guard against doing that. Otherwise, we end up training the dog in ways wholly unintended.

Mis-timed praise can result in the same type of problem, and one of the most commonly seen examples arises when the owner attempts to reassure a fearful dog. As an example, the dog encounters something that elicits a fear response which the owner does not want to encourage or reward. The owner often tries to alleviate the dog's fear by gently stroking him and murmuring softly, "That's all right. It's okay." Of course, the dog's behavior is not okay, and the dog does not understand those words. What he does understand is that when confronted with a certain stimulus, the emotions he experienced and the response he demonstrated to them met with the approval of his master. So the next time he encounters that stimulus, his reaction pattern is established. Rather than reassuring the dog that his fears are misplaced, the owner actually is encouraging the fearful response by rewarding it.

DOGS DO NOT SPEAK ENGLISH

"Learned first, learned best" is an adage which dog owners may experience firsthand when a particular training technique has backfired. For instance, if you thought you were teaching the Sit-Stay but instead taught the dog to jump up and stand, you may despair of getting the dog to unlearn what he learned so well the first time.

Take heart. Fortunately, dogs do not speak English or any other human language. The words "sit" and "stay" alone have no more meaning to a dog than "chair" and "table." If your dog has learned something other than what you want when you say "sit" and "stay," change the words to something else. Use "place" and "wait," for example, and begin anew with more care to teach the correct behavioral association.

DOGS ARE ROTTEN GAMBLERS

If you tried to unlock a door and succeeded in opening it once by lifting it slightly, the next few times it stuck, you might try that again. However, after ten or so times, if the once-successful technique failed, you would probably quit trying it. When the odds are no longer favorable, you abandon that technique and move on to another.

On the other hand, if a dog gets out of the yard once because the gate was left unlocked, he will check that gate *every time he goes outside.* Even if it is locked for the next thousand attempts, he will continue to check, just in case.

Dogs cannot calculate odds, which makes them really rotten gamblers. One success is unlikely to be canceled out by thousands of failures. You can never depend on a dog giving up a behavior that achieved the desired result previously just because his last few attempts have failed.

When you begin off-leash heeling in obedience training, your Malamute must be thoroughly under your control. This is at least as important as his knowing how to heel to begin with. Make sure he never has the opportunity to

Canine education begins by forming a close partnership with the dog that will become the foundation for all other activities. If you want to enjoy your Malamute, a walk should not turn into a pulling contest, and the dog should know how to sit, stay, and lie down. Good training makes it easy to handle a group like these four Mals on the beach in Europe with owner Luc Verbustel.

succeed at leaving your side. It is much easier than trying to convince him not to leave once he has learned it is possible.

Similarly, if he had a spectacular romp around the neighborhood after finding a hole in the fence, a Malamute will forever check that fence for weakness. It is much better for you to routinely check your housing for escape potential. What your dog does not know will not hurt either of you.

Put some thought into your training so that the dog does not succeed at anything you want to avoid, especially if his action will put him beyond your direct control, making correction virtually impossible.

FROM CRIB TO COLLEGE

Contributed by Vicky Jones

In general Malamutes are a patient, loving breed, devoted to their family and equally adored by their owners. Conscientious breeders strive to produce excellent temperaments that will assure buyers a companion that they can enjoy for a lifetime. The Malamute, however, is a "primitive" breed with all of its natural instincts intact, including the tendency to lead or be led. This fact alone is probably responsible for the greatest majority of Malamutes that find themselves in shelters or rescue situations.

DOMINANCE

The Malamute was bred to survive the most difficult of environments, which included extreme cold, hard work, and starvation. He relied on his own wits and skills for generations and was extremely survival-oriented. Therefore, when the Malamute's owner fails to direct or control his behavior, the result is that the Malamute acts on his own primitive instincts—whether they are good or bad.

Having taught obedience classes for twenty-five years, I have seen Malamutes that represent every stage of temperament problems, ranging from the youngster who is testing the waters to see what he can get away with to the fully-mature adult who has obtained complete control of the household and will accept no instruction from any human without bared teeth and a growl.

Dominance behavior can be observed in pups as early as two to three weeks of age, when they are first learning to walk. They begin toothlessly grabbing each other by the muzzles, posturing over the backs of their littermates, and growling. They are hilarious to watch, but, make no mistake, they are hard at work, defining their future position in the pack. As they age, they will incorporate raised hackles, stiff legs, and erect ears to further indicate their intentions.

The dam will usually watch carefully and allow the pups to work out their own pack order, but she will interfere when she feels that a puppy is getting out of line. She will always single out the most dominant pup by grabbing its neck and pinning it to the ground until it stops yelping and struggling. Mom also teaches all the pups how hard they are allowed to bite before being disciplined; this bite inhibition is eventually passed on to humans. Clearly, allowing puppies to interact with their dam until they are at least seven to eight weeks of age is very important.

DISCIPLINE

In both the human and canine world, those who misbehave are disciplined. The keys to making discipline effective are *method* and *timing*. Methods vary and many are quite successful. Timing is absolutely essential.

Verbal discipline is the most common method used with young puppies and, if an extremely good foundation is set, it may be the only form of correction the dog ever requires. Of course, this does not mean discussing his transgressions over a cup of coffee. Instead, the tone of voice should be harsh and loud, and the handler should use only one-syllable words, such as "No," "Stop," "Hey," "Ah." The deep, harsh voice reminds the pup of his mother's growl which he undoubtedly heard when he bit too hard, pulled on her tail, or aggravated her somehow.

All puppies use their mouths to play or in some way establish contact with their human companions. *You must teach puppies that teeth are never allowed on flesh, especially if you have children in the household.*

When a puppy nibbles on you, make a yelping, crying sound, telling him he has hurt you. Whether it actually hurts is irrelevant. If the puppy has been properly taught, this will cause him to release. Consistently doing this will quickly discourage biting behavior altogether. Failure to respond to this correction indicates either a poorly taught puppy (blame it on mom) or one with a problem temperament. In either case, you will have to use more severe dominance corrections.

When dogs are angry at each other, they use growls and snaps to indicate their displeasure, followed, if necessary, by a grab to the throat and a pin to the ground until the lesser animal gives up. This type of correction is excellent when verbal corrections are ineffective, and it should be used on *any behavior that you would consider unacceptable in an adult dog.* Stopping the problem when the puppy is young means you won't need to conquer it when he is an adult.

Puppies begin to establish dominance at an early age. Obviously both of these puppies want to be number one! Photo courtesy of Del Biagio, Italy.

Dominance posturing—strong eye contact, showing teeth, and strong, upright stance— versus the lower posturing and sideways glance of the submissive individual.

The dog on the left has now gained complete dominance over the other dog, which is submitting without resistance. Note how the dominant dog has grabbed the neck scruff and is shaking it. Above two photos courtesy of Bob Mouthaan, Belgium.

As a Malamute puppy moves into adolescence, he can challenge authority in minor or major ways. These challenges can be a growl or a stiffening over his food bowl, refusal to obey verbal commands when his attention is elsewhere, or raising his lips and arguing over being forced to do something he doesn't want to do.

While a rolled-up newspaper secured with tape is an effective tool (I have used it for years in class to curb aggressive dogs), few of us walk around with one stashed in our purse or pocket. Likewise, when a person strikes a puppy (or adult dog, for that matter), the puppy may view it as a snap from another dog and often will snap back at the offending hand. If the owner resorts to another smack, the fight can escalate into a real battle from which no one emerges the winner.

Specifically how would natural corrections be applied? A good example is one of the most common problems of aggression, protection of the food bowl. Like many other problems, this does not emerge overnight, although to the owners it might seem so if they failed to recognize early warning signs.

FOOD DOMINANCE

Food dominance problems usually begin with the puppy stiffening over his bowl and emitting a low growl when humans approach. If this behavior is not stopped at this point, it can become a household nightmare. I have actually known of cases where the owner could not enter the kitchen as long as the dog was eating!

With a young puppy, occasionally stroke him and talk soothingly while he is eating. This keeps him from being frightened that his food will be taken away when humans are near.

If and when he decides to "protect" his food by crouching over the bowl and growling, the first step is a verbal correction—a quick, sharp "NO." If this proves ineffective, stage two involves grabbing the puppy by the back of the neck, lifting his front feet off the ground while giving him a shake and a strong verbal correction. This is borrowed from his mother's "growl" and "neck grab" technique.

The youngster or adult dog will require a more serious correction using a collar, since a heavy dog is nearly impossible to lift by the back of the neck. Stage three of correction involves grabbing the dog by the neck, shoving him to the ground on his back, and pinning him there until *all* fighting reactions cease. Verbal corrections, ("No," "Stop") are still given in conjunction with the physical discipline.

This may take several minutes, but the owner absolutely

must be the victor. Once the dog becomes completely submissive, the owner should allow him to get up and finish his meal without interference. Many dogs will try to beg forgiveness at this point, but ignoring their offers and giving no praise for a short time is the best course. After all, the dog made a mistake, and he should be forced to remember and learn from it.

Even with a breed as proud, assertive and self-confident as a Malamute, improper discipline can cause a dog to become neurotic and fearful. Praise should always be sincere, and corrections should always be quick, meaningful, and above all, *consistent*. Disciplining harshly for an action one day and ignoring the same action the next day will make the dog confused and resentful. Overdoing discipline can also be extremely counterproductive.

Puppies will be puppies, and if losing a pair of shoes or some shrubs to an active puppy is beyond tolerance, then perhaps a dog does not fit your lifestyle. Harsh corrections should be reserved for cases of unacceptable temperament

The dog's positioning depicts the pack order in this household. The white puppy is last in line and waiting patiently. Courtesy of Chris Eisenga, Belgium.

Enjoy your puppy while she's still cuddly. In a very short time she will be much too large to carry. Akela's Song of Origami at three-and-one-half-months of age. Owners: Col. Robert and Melvi Gill.

such as growling or snapping at humans or other animals. The dog must learn to look to his master to guide his behavior, and he should not be allowed to make his own decisions regarding aggression. The Malamute will never hate his owner for giving him a fair correction, instilling respect without fear.

TRAINING CLASSES

Contributed by Keith Hurrell and Vicky Jones

If you have never trained a dog before, you will benefit from class instruction. Although the usual age to start training is six months, some locales offer puppy training classes earlier, and for a Malamute, sixteen weeks is a good age to start. Classes are usually held once a week and involve a commitment to practice the lessons during the rest of the week on your own.

Most communities have at least one dog obedience school run by the local kennel club, veterinary clinic, private trainers, or pet supply store. Look for an instructor

HOUSEBREAKING

The most successful housebreaking techniques take advantage of the dog's natural instinct to keep his living quarters clean. The trick is keeping this area small enough, from the dog's perspective, to encourage him not to eliminate. Even a small bathroom may seem large to a puppy. An appropriately sized crate or pen is the best choice for housebreaking confinement. It should be just large enough for the dog to stand up, turn around, and lie down comfortably.

When you cannot supervise the dog, you should put him in his crate. He may have a few mistakes, but he will quickly learn that he is stuck with them and will have to wait to be let out. When you return, immediately put him outside and praise him when he goes. Be sure to let him finish all his business before you let him back into the house.

Let your pup out just before bedtime and first thing in the morning. Very young puppies may need an outing in between, but by three months they should be able to make it all night. Keep a regular schedule for trips outside during the day. Other times to be watchful are after napping, eating or drinking, or during playtime. An excited puppy may suddenly stop his activity and begin sniffing about—a sure sign that he is looking for the "right" spot. Put him outside immediately and remember to praise him when he is good. If problems continue, either you are not supervising him adequately or your confinement area is too large.

As the dog grows in size and experience, he will need to go out less often and will begin "asking" to go out by whining, barking, or scratching at the door. He may come and stare at you, showing excitement as you walk toward the door. When he is reliably asking to go out and has no nighttime slip-ups, you can allow him to sleep loose in a room.

A dog that is allowed free run of the house will always choose the room farthest from his living quarters in which to eliminate. Candidates for this include formal rooms reserved for special occasions (the one with the white carpet and good furniture) or guest bedrooms—anyplace your family does not routinely use. Even after your dog is reliable in the house, you may want to put a baby-gate across these doors to mark them as off-limits.

who is knowledgeable about large and/or Northern breeds, and if you have choices, visit each a few times and watch. No two instructors use the same training technique, so see how they each work with the handlers and dogs, then compare. Even better, visit on graduation night to evaluate the progress of the dogs. This can be the deciding factor for which class you choose.

There are basically two methods of dog training, force or reward, although some trainers use a combination of the two. In many classes today, the reward method is in vogue. It teaches verbal discipline, praise, and food reward as the primary road to success. Owners in these classes whose Malamutes do not respond to these methods are often afraid of physical correction, having been led to believe it is abusive. The problems multiply, and the owner is soon faced with the dilemma of either isolating his dog for life or having his unmanageable animal euthanized or placed in a shelter.

Avoid classes that do not allow physical discipline or those that rely strictly on food as a training mechanism. On the other hand, you should not attend classes in which the instructor insists on muzzles for dogs with temperament problems or uses hanging techniques for failure to perform exercises (hanging or choking a dog is reserved only for the most severe aggressive behavior, such as attempting to bite). The best teacher for both dog and owner is the one who is highly experienced and who presents a sensible combination of praise and discipline.

You may run into a trainer who arbitrarily refuses to take Malamutes. They may even have a list of breeds they do not accept along with a list of problems of each breed which render it unsuitable for their class.

If you are refused admission to a class because of your dog's breed, breathe a sigh of relief at the trainer's honesty and find another class rather than feeling rejected or doubting your dog's abilities. A person who has spent his entire career training Golden Retrievers and Shetland Sheepdogs may well have difficulty working with breeds outside the herding and retrieving groups. Their refusal of your dog is merely an expression of their own limitations or preferences.

Malamutes in general have sharp senses, fast reflexes, and great intelligence; however, this does not make them easy dogs to train, especially for those more familiar with gun dogs or herders. Malamutes have a low tolerance for boredom; they were not bred to do the same activity over and over. They are more resistant to repetition than sporting or herding dogs. Your challenge is to teach an exercise while ensuring enough variety to keep it interesting. Your class director should be able to show you ways to do this.

While you can force a Malamute to repeat the same exercise endlessly, it will take the spirit out of him. Nothing is more miserable than a spiritless Malamute, so remember that variety is the spice of life.

Iceborn's Amazing Grace and Iceborn's Against All Odds, bred by Marilyn Rice.

4

THE EDUCATED MALAMUTE

Regardless of what activity you intend to do with your Malamute, whether it is sledding or just sitting together on the patio, he should be a well-mannered dog. That requires basic obedience training, which can open the door to many other activities you can enjoy with your dog. Recognition of your Malamutes' achievements can be obtained in a number of different ways.

The Malamute, like all working breeds, likes to have something to *do,* and you will find him a good candidate for a variety of activities. While it used to be said that a dog you expected to pull a sled should not be obedience trained, today a single Mal often performs a multitude of tasks requiring differing skills and abilities. This breed is both versatile and intelligent; truly a companion you can live with and enjoy in many ways.

CANINE GOOD CITIZEN TEST

In September, 1989, the AKC launched the Canine Good Citizen Program (CGC) in response to a flood of proposed anti-dog legislation across the United States. The level of training required is no more than would be expected from any well-behaved, socially-acceptable dog, and many Malamutes have been certified as Canine Good Citizens, including the youngest dog to receive the title, Ch. Poker Flat's Yukon Law CGC, TD.

CGC Tests can be held by organizations of all varieties and are open to all dogs, whether registered, unregistered, purebred or mixed. AKC registered dogs which earn the award can use the letters CGC after their name, although it is not an official AKC award like an obedience title. In several instances dogs with CGC titles have been granted special privileges in areas that place restrictions on dog ownership or prohibit the presence of other dogs. Like a school diploma, the CGC says that your dog is mannerly and that you are a responsible owner.

To demonstrate his confidence and self-control, the dog must be willing to be groomed or examined, accept strange people, and tolerate other dogs. He must be able to walk on a loose leash even in crowds and reliably perform the most basic obedience commands such as sit, down, and stay.

OBEDIENCE TRIALS

Obedience trials have much in common with dog shows. Instead of judging against a standard of appearance, the obedience judge uses a standard of performance. There are set requirements for fulfilling each level.

The dog and handler perform a set of exercises together, each of which is allotted a certain number of points which add up to a perfect score of 200. To qualify, a dog must earn at least 170 points *and* over 50 percent of the available points for each exercise. To earn a title, the dog must obtain three qualifying scores, referred to as "legs," under three different judges. While the mechanism for earning the titles is the same for all three obedience titles, the level of difficulty increases from one title to the next.

The titles available are: Companion Dog (CD), Companion Dog Excellent (CDX), and Utility Dog (UD). The initials are used after the dog's name once he has achieved the award. He must complete a CD before a CDX, and a CDX before a UD. He may continue to compete for additional awards, including an Obedience Trial Championship (OTCh.—which appears before his name) and Utility Dog Excellent (UDX, used after his name). The method for achieving these two titles differs from that of the others.

AWARDS

Competitors in each obedience trial class are placed first through fourth based on qualifying scores. At the end of the class judging, the judge passes out the placement ribbons and trophies. In addition, each dog and handler with a qualifying score receives a green qualifying ribbon.

The obedience trial equivalent of a Best-in-Show is High-in-Trial, the winner of which must come from the regular classes and have the highest qualifying score. Many clubs also offer an award for High-Combined, which is for the dog with the highest combined qualifying scores from competition in Open B and Utility.

Shows with more than one obedience judge are usually arranged so that the A and B classes of each level are split between them. Anyone who already has a leg under the person judging one class then might be able to earn a qualifying leg towards his title by entering under the other judge.

COMPANION DOG (CD)

The first obedience level is the Companion Dog or CD title. It is the only one in which the dog is on-leash for part of the work. It begins with a Heel on Lead and a Figure 8, after which, the lead is removed and the dog completes a Heel off Lead; Stand for Examination; Recall; a Sit-Stay for one minute, and Down-Stay for three minutes. During both stays, the handlers stand on the opposite side of the ring from their dogs.

Two classes are available for entry, both with different eligibility requirements. Novice A entries are restricted to people who have never completed a CD title on a dog. Everyone who competes in Novice A is on equal footing as a beginner. The Novice B class is unrestricted; competitors can run the gamut from novices to professional trainers.

Ch. Storm Kloud's Marketa of Awanuna CDX, WLP, WTD, Can. CD, WLP, WTD, CGC, wins a High in Trial and impressive trophies for owners Rick and Bev Pfeiffer.

COMPANION DOG EXCELLENT (CDX)

The Companion Dog Excellent exercises build on the dog's previous training. They consist of a Heel with a Figure-8; a Drop on Recall, where the dog does a down

A blast from the past (l. to r.): Ch. Poker Flat's Midnight Cowboy CD, WWPD; Ch. Poker Flat's Reluctant Dragon CD; Poker Flat's Jacks or Better; Ch. Poker Flat's The Soft Parade CD; Poker Flat's Queen Jane HPPROX, CD; Ch. Poker Flat's I'm No Angel CD; and double Register of Merit holder, Ch. Malesa's Mischief Maker CD, ROM, OB-ROM. Photo courtesy of Robin Haggard and Jim Kuehl.

as he returns to the handler; a Retrieve on the Flat and Retrieve over the High Jump (in both of which the dog fetches a dumbbell); and a Broad Jump. The Long Sit and Long Down require the dogs to sit for three minutes, and down for five minutes with the handlers out of the dogs' sight. Since all open work is off lead, the dogs must be able to work reliably and independently, and they should have some athletic ability. For large dogs such as Malamutes, good hips and shoulders are a necessity.

CDX classes are also divided into Open A and Open B, both of which require the dog to have completed a CD title. At the Open level, class eligibility pertains to the dog rather than the handler. Open A dogs may not have completed a CDX, while Open B is unrestricted. Dogs with a Utility title may compete in Open B as well.

UTILITY DOG (UD)

The exercises for Utility also build on and go beyond the tasks the dog has already mastered. All work is off-leash, and the handler gives almost all commands by hand signals. First is the Signal Exercise during which the dog does a heeling pattern that ends with the handler leaving the dog on a Sit Stay. He then signals the dog from across the ring to Down, return to a Sit, Come, drop into a Down halfway back, and then complete the return. The dog Stands for Examination and then performs two Scent Discriminations where he selects both leather and metal articles which the handler has touched. The dog also is Directed to Retrieve one of three identical gloves and Directed to Jump a bar jump and a solid jump in an order specified by the judge.

Ch. Tamarock's Yukon Sugruk Aklak CDX, UDT. Owner, Sue Renkert.

Am. Can. SKC Ch. Vykon's Oklahoma of Kenworth CDX, Can. CD, WPD, CGC. Owners, George and Judy Jackson.

Apkut's Klondike of Natsha CDX, WPD. Owner, George and Judy Jackson.

Historical Notes – Malamutes in Obedience Competition

By Billie Stewart. Adapted from publication in THE AMCA Newsletter.

Jackie, CD, was the first Malamute to be awarded an obedience title, on October 5, 1944. The dog's owner was Roland Lombard. Jackie was unregistered, and his sire and dam were unknown. A full six years passed before another Malamute, Ch. Yukon Timber Grey, CD, was awarded his title on October 22, 1950. He, too, was unregistered. His owner was Mr. Scott and his breeder was Beulah Robel of Ro-Ala-Ken Kennels.

In 1952, two registered Malamutes that were also champions earned CDs. The first was Ch. Husky Pak Black Hawk, owned by E. Truchon and bred by Robert Zoller. In his honor, the Alaskan Malamute Club of America annually gives the AMCA Black Hawk Memorial Award (first presented in 1973) to the Malamute with the highest average qualifying scores in Novice whose owner is an AMCA member. The second CD was Ch. Yukon Gray Avalanche, CD. Mr. Scott was listed as the owner and breeder. Since he was sired by Ch. Yukon Timber Grey, CD, they became the first father and son to earn obedience titles.

Ch. Cliquot of Husky-Pak, whose head study graces the AMCA logo, earned his CD in 1955 and went on to a CDX in 1957. Cliquot was owned by the Aningers and bred by Robert Zoller. Cliquot's daughter, Ch. Husky-Pak's Flaming Flirt, was the first female Malamute to achieve a CD and a CDX. Flirt was owned by Merry Stockburger and bred by Zoller/Sykes. The Flaming Flirt Memorial Award, established in 1973, is given annually by the AMCA to the opposite sex qualifier for the Black Hawk Award.

Another AMCA award is given annually to the dog with the highest average of qualifying scores for advanced titles. The Oonanik Memorial Award commemorates Ch. Coldfoot Oonanik, UD, who had obedience and breed titles from several countries. Owned by P. Anctil and bred by Coldfoot Kennels, Oonanik's UD title was the first for a Malamute and was awarded on December 4, 1966.

Between 1940 and 1960, Malamutes earned nineteen obedience titles. As the breed increased in popularity, more Malamutes entered the obedience rings and by February 1988, thirty-three years after Cliquot received his CDX, the fifty-seventh title was awarded to Annie Velletri's female, Nicklesworth of Kaila, Am/Can CD, WPD, CDX. AMCA awards in obedience are offered to both American and Canadian members. In 1988, the Oonanik Memorial Award was presented to a Canadian dog, Ch. Malhaven Chasing Rainbows, CDX, bred and owned by Karen Ibbitson.

Other awards offered for obedience achievement by AMCA to its members are the Award of Merit and Obedience ROM. The former is awarded to a Malamute who wins an advanced title (CDX, UD, TDX, OTCH). The OB-ROM title is given to dams with at least four obedience-titled offspring and sires of at least six offspring with obedience titles. By1990, fourteen sires and seventeen dams had achieved the OB-ROM.

In November, 1991, Northeast Tahkela Amorok CD, TD, owned by Sharon Robinson, became the first Mal to receive a Tracking Dog title. Two other females owned by Roslyn Stendahl, Black Ice's Sparkplug TDX, and Black Ice's Spell Breaker, TD, have completed tracking titles.

Ch. Yukon Timber Grey, CD, born in 1949, was the second Malamute to earn a CD degree.

Utility classes are divided into A and B. Like the Open divisions, A classes are only for dogs with a CDX but no UD; whereas B is for any dog with a CDX or higher title.

UTILITY DOG EXCELLENT

A recently instituted award is the Utility Dog Excellent (UDX). To earn this, a dog must obtain qualifying scores in both Open B and Utility B at the same show for ten shows. The scores must be won as a set.

OBEDIENCE TRIAL CHAMPION

At the utility level, dogs also compete for championship points, which are awarded for first or second places in either Utility and Open B. Like the points in a dog show, these are based on the number of competitors in the class. An Obedience Trial Champion (OTCH) must earn a total of 100 points to complete this title. He must win at least three first places, one of which must be in Utility B with at least three dogs in competition, another in Open B with six dogs in competition, and a third first place from either. These must be under three different judges.

TRACKING TESTS

Tracking is not only a wonderful sport for you and your Malamute; it is also very useful. Every dog with a nose has the ability to track, and the skill is often put to use in search and rescue work or simply asking the dog to find a lost set of keys. Unfortunately, tracking tests are difficult and expensive to stage and can only accommodate a handful of entrants at any one time, but tracking is becoming more popular, so the number of trials is increasing.

TRACKING DOG (TD)

Receipt of a Tracking Dog Award is designated by the letters TD after the dog's name; a Tracking Dog Excellent, by TDX. The names of Utility Dogs with Tracking Awards are followed by UDT (Utility Dog Tracker) or UDTX (Utility Dog Tracker Excellent).

In order to participate in a TD test, your Malamute must first be certified as ready by a tracking judge. This certification lasts a specified time, during which the dog must either pass a tracking test or be recertified.

The area for the track has certain terrain requirements, and a separate track must be laid for each participant. The dog works on a harness, rather than a collar, to which a 30- to 50-foot lead is attached. The dog must work without guidance from the handler (who is himself not informed of the track's path). The track is between

Ravenhill's Ghizhavay CD, TDX, wins an award for owner Cathi Carr-Lundfelt. Hansen photo.

440 and 500 yards, and the scent is between one-half to two hours old. It is laid by a stranger wearing leather-soled shoes and follows a course marked the previous day with flags. As he lays the track, the tracklayer picks up all but the two beginning flags.

As the dog runs the track, he must clearly be following the scent, although how he works will depend on the terrain and the prevailing winds. At the end of the track, he must find a leather object left by the tracklayer. A dog either passes or fails; he receives no score and no second chances.

TRACKING DOG EXCELLENT (TDX)

Dogs which have completed the TD can complete a more advanced test which builds on the skills required for the TD. Even more difficult to stage, TDX tests are a separate event from TD tests.

The TDX track is longer and older, with more turns over more difficult terrain. It also has cross-tracks laid by people other than the tracklayer which the dog must *not* follow. The TDX is a challenge that Malamutes should be more than able to meet. Their keen noses, athleticism, and love of the outdoors stand them in good stead here.

VARIABLE SURFACE TRACKING

The newest tracking degree available is the VST. The Variable Surface Tracking test requires that the dog follow the scent of a person across a variety of ground surfaces, including grass and pavement, on a single track. This test more closely parallels work done by search and rescue dogs. Successful completion of one licensed tracking test certifies the dog to have the initials VST used after his name.

Ravenhill's Kawiara Chukayugtug TD, owned by Cathi Carr-Lundfelt, was the first Malamute to earn the Tracking Dog title in Alaska. Hansen photo.

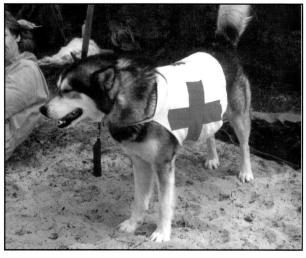

Many tracking dogs go on to do search and rescue work. Above: Williwaw's Ladyhawk being raised in a sling harness as part of practice for search work. Photo by Mike Abel.

Center right: Ghizha digs to indicate where a person is buried. Owned by Sue Renkert.

Below right: Yortok, owned by Marijke Baas of Holland, displays the rescue dog blanket, indicating he is qualified and ready to work.

AGILITY

Beginning in Great Britain, the sport of agility has exploded in popularity across the world. It capitalizes on the dog's athletic ability rather than formal training, although, like many other activities, it does require basic obedience skills.

Founded in 1986, the United States Dog Agility Association (USDAA) was the first organization to sponsor agility events. In 1994, AKC began sponsoring Agility Trials.

Like obedience trials, agility trials have several levels of graduated competition. The dog must earn three legs under three different judges in order to obtain a title, although in agility a qualifier must earn 85 of a possible 100 points with no non-qualifying deductions.

Agility is an international event!
Top: Shuyak walking the bar in agility
with owner-trainer Helly Vogt of Switzerland.

Right: Purdey's Psyche Passion
going over an agility bar jump.
Mormont De Henau photo.

Below: Purdey's Psyche Passion going
through the tire jump. He is owned and photographed
by Mormont De Henau of Belgium.

Titles and classes are similar to those of obedience, beginning with the Novice Agility (NA), then Open Agility (OA), and finally Agility Excellent (AX). A Master Agility Excellent (MX) is available to dogs who go on after finishing the AX title to qualify in ten additional AX classes.

Obstacles include an A-frame which the dog scales, poles through which he weaves, a table, a pause box (where he does a Stay), see-saw, raised walk, cross-over, crawl, open and closed tunnels, and assorted jumps and hurdles. Jump height depends on the height of the dog. Most Malamutes will have vertical jumps 24 inches high and horizontal ones of 48 inches.

As the dog runs off-lead through an obstacle course, he is timed and scored on a fault system similar to that used in horse-show jumping. Not only is agility fun for the dogs and handlers, it is a very exciting spectator sport.

Besides the AKC, several other organizations have agility competitions. Most of them are open to all dogs, while AKC events are open only to registered or ILP dogs.

THERAPY DOG

Material contributed by Sandra Shallbetter

Dog owners are familiar with the enjoyment and comfort that a dog can bring, but there is also a medical aspect to this human/animal bond. The therapeutic effects of interacting with an animal, such as reduced blood pressure, reduction in tension and stress, and diversion from pain, have been documented and are becoming more widely recognized by the medical community. Children especially benefit from the diversion and comfort provided by animal contact. In addition, playing with the dog can temporarily mask pain and provide motivation for the child to exercise. Parents are often grateful for the distraction.

An increasing number of healthcare facilities are now actively seeking properly screened and trained handler and dog teams to participate in these programs, generally referred to as Animal-Assisted Activities (AAA) or Animal-Assisted Therapy (AAT). These organizations facilitate an informal interaction between the handler/dog team and patients, with no specific objective other than providing comfort, diversion and improving the quality of life for the patients. A visit requires little or no documentation, and no measurable results are expected.

Animal Assisted Therapy, on the other hand, is a formal involvement in the treatment program of a patient which must be prescribed by the attending physician or therapist. They formulate a treatment plan involving the handler/dog team with specific goals and objectives. The progress of the therapy is documented and closely monitored.

The Malamute's gentle, affectionate nature makes him a good candidate for therapy work. In addition to his friendliness, size, and striking appearance, the wide variety of activities in which Malamutes engage are a marvelous conversation starter, initiating interaction with the patient.

Not every dog, regardless of breed, is suitable for service as a therapy or visitation dog. Each animal must be extensively screened and evaluated to determine if they have the temperament, controllability, and the predictability required to handle the stress of interacting in a confined setting with strangers who may have various physiological and/or emotional problems. Properly screened and trained, Malamutes have the necessary intelligence and intuitive qualities to adapt to the unusual environment of a healthcare facility.

Screening criteria may vary depending upon the type of facility and the extent of contact in which the dog will be engaged. Typically, in addition to basic obedience skills and a Canine Good Citizens award, the dog must pass a stringent temperament/aptitude test which exposes the dog and handler to various situations which may arise during a visitation.

These include the unexpected, rapid approach of persons using walkers, crutches, and wheelchairs; walking down a narrow hallway with persons seated on both sides who reach out to touch the dog; a tray of metal pans falling to the floor near the animal, and other similar stressing scenarios. In each case, the dog must react non-aggressively and non-fearfully and must remain under the handler's control. A number of Malamutes have qualified on these stringent tests and are active in both AAA and AAT programs.

Another important requirement for the therapy dog is a thorough health screening, repeated at regular intervals. The extent and frequency of the examination depends on the type of facility to be visited and the concerns regarding infection control.

Throughout the therapy dog's life, the owner needs to provide a great deal of petting, hugging, and cuddling. Dogs need to know that they can always trust and depend on their handlers to take care of them. Playing lots of games with your Malamute will also give him a valuable rapport with you. You should, however, avoid games

Certified therapy dog Williwaw's Ladyhawk O Shalla TT, CGC, WTD, WOD and owner Allen Shallbetter visit Allison Korvas.

where he "play bites" or paws anyone. Play should always be controlled. A seemingly harmless behavior practiced during play can get out of control in a stressful situation; even a scratch inflicted on a patient can have serious repercussions.

Though the rigors of the testing, health checks, training, and the visitation or therapy sessions may seem rather taxing, the reward is seeing the comfort, relief from boredom or pain (even if just for a little while), and, in the case of the AAT, actual improvement in the persons condition.

Spending time with a dog is therapeutic to owners, too. Here Arctic Legend Andra Noeri enjoys a surfboard ride with his friend. Photo by Chris Eisenga.

Canada's first certified therapy dog, Wintertrail's Cinnamon Snowbear WTDX, CGC, with owner Dave Hardie. Photo by A. Smith.

Right: Ch. Tikiluk's Nikola of Windrift winning High in Trial for owner/handler Beverly Turner. Smith photo.

Below: A dual ROM, Wayeh Needa Mist, TT, bred and owned by Billie and Horace Stewart.

REGISTER OF MERIT OBEDIENCE MALAMUTES

An Obedience Register of Merit is awarded by the Alaskan Malamute Club of America to males that have sired six or more offspring that have earned a Companion Dog or higher award in obedience, or dams that have produced four or more offspring that have earned a CD or higher. That so many of these also are Register of Merit producers of champions testifies to the continuing working ability and versatility of the breed. The following list is through 1996.

Sires
Ch. Aristeed's Frost Shadow, CD
Adventureror de Korok
Ch. Cold Foot Oonanik, UDT
Ch. Glacier's Storm Kloud, CD
Ch Inuit's Sweet Lucifer, ROM
Ch. Maluk of Northern Star, CDX
Ch. Sarge's Candy Man of Big Paw
Ch. Shuyak Caro of Cold Foot, CD
Ch. Snopaw's Snoqualmie, CD
Ch. Storm Kloud's Emcee of Awanuna, CDX

Dams
Actiondale's Kara, CDX, TD
Ch. Aesir's Geri of Hill Frost, CD
Ch. Beowulf Thosca of Snow Foot, CDX
Beowulf Thadja-Kimit, CD
Ch. Beowulf's Lynaska Dolly, CD
Ch. Dorry's Sitka of North Wind
Ch. Malesa's Mischief Maker, CDX
Natasha of the Red Moon
Ch. Polarpaw's Akela Akamai
Ch. Skagway's Get Up 'N Boogie, CD
Snookum's Paria of Amorak, CD
Ch. Sno Foot Mushy
Ch. Storm Kloud's Forever Yours, CD
Ch. Storm Kloud's Hhumble Shaman
Ch. Storm Kloud's Vvanilla Pudding
Ch. Timberlane's Misty Rainbow, CDX
Ch. Win-Kre's Akamai Fury
Wayeh Needa Mist

Left: Ch. Onak N Tanunak's Tough Choice, CD, WTD, WPD, WPDX. Bergman photo.

Below: Certified therapy dog Inuit's Driftwood, bred and owned by Sheila Balch.

Above: BIS Ch. Breakfast in America Del Lago Degli Orsi practices the recall. Breeder, Gloria Urbani. Owner, the Trevisans of Italy.

Shukeenyuk powerfully clears the bar jump in Open competition. Keith Hurrell, owner.

Carol Williams enjoying a sledding expedition with her pure Kotzebue team.

5

THE WORKING MALAMUTE

The Alaskan Malamute is no longer essential to man's survival in the Arctic. Although the snowmobile and other motorized vehicles have replaced him, the dog's need to work has not diminished.

Malamutes thrive when they work. As long as their health and welfare needs are met, dogs that work live longer and are healthier than dogs that do not work. Whether you just enjoy your dog at home or go for some of the various awards, we urge you to find some type of activity in which you and your dog can participate.

THE AMCA WORKING DOG PROGRAM

In order to encourage registered Mal owners to work their dogs, the Alaskan Malamute Club of America initiated a Working Dog (WD) Program in 1977. Dogs can be certified in four fields: sledding, backpacking, weight pulling, and skijoring. Sledding awards are: WTD (Working Team Dog) or WLD (Working Lead Dog). WPD (Working Pack Dog) is available in backpacking, and WWPD (Working Weight Pull Dog), in weight pull and a Working Skijor Dog (WSD).

The program was expanded in 1985 to include an additional level for each certification. Upon completion of the more stringent requirements, an "excellent" is added to the original title, designated by the initial "X."

Each field has a number of specific requirements which must be met. These are set out in the Rules which are available from the AMCA. Unlike most breed club working programs, the AMCA's Working Dog Program allows the dog to meet the certification requirements by participation in non-AMCA sponsored events and in non-competitive events such as backpacking and sledding trips. An applicant need only provide the required forms, signed by the official or an impartial witness.

This chapter was prepared with the assistance of Keith Hurrell, Sue Fuller, and Vicky Stiller MacLean, Past Chairwoman for the AMCA Working Dog Certification Committee.

The program is open to both members and non-members of AMCA, and the Working Dog Class, a non-regular class for certified dogs, is offered at many regional specialty shows as well as the AMCA National Specialty. The response to the program has been excellent. Hundreds of dogs have obtained certifications in the working programs.

The WD level requires a minimal amount of training and conditioning and is not beyond the reach of any sound Malamute. The WDX, on the other hand, signifies a considerable achievement. Without a good attitude and physical ability, a dog will not be able to complete these requirements.

PACKING

Backpacking is an activity in which you and your dog can participate no matter where you live. Malamutes packed mining equipment all over Canada and Alaska and supplies for soldiers through European mountains during both World Wars. Yours can certainly help with the family camping trip. If you are a serious hiker and camper, a pack dog can expand your horizons considerably. Not only can he lighten your load by carrying up to one-third of his weight in food and equipment, he can keep you warm on a cold night. He will also provide companionship and protection on the trail and in the campsite.

TRAINING

If you and your dog are beginners, build your abilities gradually, trying a few easy trips at first. Before taking a backpacking trip, the dog should have some basic obedience training and be in good condition, and he must be reliable off-leash. Chasing wildlife can cause irreparable damage to the dog pack and its contents. A rambunctious dog that collides with the backpacker's legs or bumps him with his pack can also be a problem on the trail.

His feet should be strong and tough from plenty of exercise and conditioning hikes, and if the trips are into

49

Backpacking is one activity almost any dog owner can enjoy. Not only can your Malamute carry part of the load—he is both good company and protection. Allan Shallbetter and Shalla's Nuka Kinau CGC, WPDX, WLD take a break.

WORKING DOG SHOWCASE

The Working Dog Showcase, developed by Cindy Adams, premiered as a National Specialty event in 1988 and has become a regular feature since then. To be eligible for entry, a dog must have either two AMCA working dog titles or one working dog title and one leg toward an Excellent title.

In competition, dogs are evaluated on a point scale by three judges. Although the scale from the standard was used initially, this was changed to emphasize features that are most important in working dogs. Points are awarded for: general appearance, body, movement, conditioning, feet, temperament, front, and rear. The top four dogs with on the highest combined score are recognized. The Showcase is a unique opportunity to see and recognize dogs with both excellent conformation and working ability.

WINNERS

Date	Dog	Owner
1988	Am/Can Ch. Icelandic's Omen of Black Ice	Schraad
1989	No competition	
1990	Ch. Poker Flat's Deputy Dan	Haggard/Kuehl
1991	Am/Can Ch. Oopik's Lil' Bit A Canuck	Muir
1992	Ch. Nor-Sky's Bear Creek Kazan	Johnson
1993	Ch. Black Ice's High Speed Chase	Bedford
1994	Am/Can Ch. Icelandic's Omen of Black Ice	Schraad
1995	Ch. Sendaishi's Diamond Jim	Matott
1996	Int. Am. Ch. Onak N Tanunak's Touch Choice	Corr
1997	Winterchill's Sable Mischief	Murray

the back country, you should expose the dog to crossing streams over log bridges and scrambling over unusual obstacles.

When the going is rough, the dog should be able to handle each situation with confidence, which can only develop through previous training or exposure to such hazards. Agility work transfers well to backpacking, giving the dogs experience and confidence in tackling unusual conditions, thereby preparing them for the rigors of the backcountry.

EQUIPMENT

Many backpacking and mountaineering stores carry dog packs, and several mail order outfitters supply dog packs, doggie booties, and hard-to-find backpacking equipment. A creative person with access to a sturdy sewing machine can make much of the equipment and special material. Many excellent books on backpacking techniques and the equipment you will need are available.

Your dog will need his own backpack. It should be suitable to your needs and be fitted to his body. The pack should ride over the withers and back; this position is controlled by means of the front, or sternum, strap. If the pack is to be used by different dogs, the front strap should be adjustable. The neck strap should be attached to both the front strap and the front center of the pack assembly, and it should be reinforced to accept a harness ring for attaching the leash. The harness ring must be strongly attached to serve as a restraint or hoisting point.[1] The dog may have to be helped up an extremely steep incline or helped back onto its feet after sinking into deep snow. The harness ring can also be used if the dog has to pull a tired child or adult. Some packs have a single belly strap, but two straps are better, one close to the pack front and the other close to the rear. All buckles on both straps should

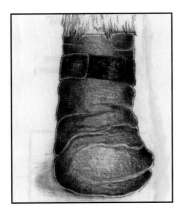

Dog bootie. Photo courtesy Black Ice Kennel.

be the quick-release type for fast pack removal when the dog has to wade or swim in deep water.

On some dog packs, the harness and pack can be separated. If the pack is attached to the harness by Velcro, you must be careful to keep the Velcro clean of undercoat hair or the pack will not stay on.

Sometimes mountain trails are made of decomposed granite or sharp rocks that are hard on feet. To prevent damage that might mean canceling your trip, you should carry at least one set of booties for each dog. You should also take along a dog dish for food and water and a spring scale to make sure both sides of the dog's pack are evenly balanced.

An old gunny sack can serve as your dog's sleeping bag, providing protection from sharp rocks and insulation from the cold ground. It can also serve to cushion the dog's back from sharp objects in the pack.

A stakeout chain or cable to restrain the dog is another necessity once camp is established. Some campgrounds only permit dogs if they are kept on leash, since other campers in the area may not appreciate a loose dog in camp.

Apply flea dip or spray before the dog leaves home. In some areas, ground squirrels and their fleas are known to carry bubonic plague and other diseases.[2]

PLANNING

Planning a trip is very important for your enjoyment and safety. Remember neither of you will have fun if you or your dog is overloaded. Review all of the available literature and any topographical maps of the terrain under consideration; check the weather and make sure dogs are allowed on the trails and in the campsites. Each area is different.

Many recreation or wilderness areas require the use of a water filtering kit or recommend boiling drinking water to kill giardia or other contaminants in the streams and lakes. Mountain areas may have rivers to wade, very steep or rocky trails to climb, or possibly even ice fields at higher elevations. You can encounter hazards of many sorts, including wildlife, such as snakes or bears. Failure to take

the necessary precautions can easily place both of you at risk.

Always inform someone when and where you are going and when you expect to return. With adequate preparation, a backpacking trip into the wilderness with a Malamute can be a wonderful adventure.

WORKING PACK DOG REQUIREMENTS

For certification as a Working Pack Dog (WPD)[3], a Malamute must carry a daily initial weight equal to a minimum of thirty percent of his body weight. Consumption of food and water will lighten the load, but it cannot be otherwise reduced. At least two pack trips on natural terrain must be completed.

Two options are available:

1. The dog must pack a minimum total of 30 miles, and each trip must be at least 10 miles per day. One overnight camp out of at least 10 miles round-trip must be included.

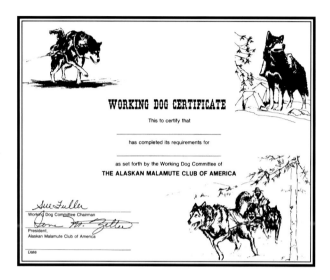

MALAMUTES THAT HAVE EARNED THE TITLE OF WORKING PACK DOG EXCELLENT

Date	Dog	Owner		Date	Dog	Owner
1988	Wakon's Kaleb	Hediger			Texmahl Oo-La-La of Oonanik	Texmo
1989	Passion of Snow River	Matosky			Fjelstad's Sweet William	Ezell
	Nanook	Matosky			Texmahl Kobuk of Wolflodge	Ezell
	Alyeska's Konoshka Snow Belle	LaBelle			Ch. Greenbriers's Born Tu B Wylde	McCracken
	Ch. Hyrum's Alaskan Bandit	LaBelle		1994	Ch. Chinome's Arctic Invader	Walden
	Maska's Torque in Motion	Rolfson			Onak's Nabo Tis Hels Apoppin	Ivey
	Kazan's Kasstoff in Maska Pak	Rolfson			Tatanka's Petawin Kel at Nabo	Ivey
1991	Grizzly's Alyeska Siatnak	Karamatic			Nabo N Tanunak Roy Pizazz	Guadagna
	Ch. Onak's Taku Tufentumble	Karamatic			Nabo's Tell Me Lies	Guadagna
	Onak's Fool of Razzmatas	Karamatic/Corr			Nabo Tyler's Tamana	Guadagna
	Ch. Snookum's Tamon of Onak, CD,	Corr			Onak Tannunak's Tough Choice	Corr/Richardson
	Ch. Onak's Tomfoolery	Corr			Onak's Northern Juneau	Covarrubia
	Ch. Onak's Tuffenuf For Us	Corr			Vanderal's Mukluk the Bear	Morelli
	Ch. Storm Kloud's Ddriving Reign	Texmo		1995	Onak's Totem of Tongass	Griffiths
	Texmo Chippewa of Oonanik	Texmo			Onak's Tumalo's Teeka	Griffiths
	Kiska Tinau Taniska	Caudill			Tatanka's Tokha of Toneeka	Griffiths
	Shalla's Nuka Kinau	Shallbetter			Toneeka's Times Could B Tuffr	Griffiths
	Onak's Speck of Cinnamon	Karamatic			Toneeka's Red Ruby	Kreuger
	Onak's Twitterpated Fool	Corr			Tanunak's Arctic Dasher	Silva
1992	Euga Luga Babouska	Caudill		1996	Onak's Yukon Chief	Sams/Corr
	Kachiri	Caudill			Onak's Tuff as Nails	Corr
	Sweet Chopaka Tesseract	Olsen			Onak's Tougherenhell	Corr
1993	Vanderval's Kayak the Bear, CD	Morelli			Onak's Too Tough To Handle	Corr
	Vanderval's Tundra Eagle	Morelli			Onak's Taylor Made	Sams/Corr
	Vanderval's Ghost Nugget	Morelli			Onak's Catch Me If You Can	Eberline/Corr
	Temahl the Storm's Reign Beau	Texmo			Onak's Timber of Tamon	Wannamaker/Corr
	Kalluk Koosa Ki of Tanana	Bertling			Onak's Shadow of Tough	Vitale/Corr
	Yakone's Masked Mischa	McAdams				
	Flying Eagle's Montana Skye	McAdams				

2. The dog must pack at least 40 miles, each day's trip being at least 10 miles, but no overnight camp-out is required.

For both the WPD and WPDX, if you are hiking on slopes, an elevation gain may be substituted for mileage in the following manner: 1,000 feet of elevation is equivalent to 1 mile of flat terrain. Elevation gain is figured as the difference between the highest and lowest points of the trip.

For the Working Pack Dog Excellent (WPDX), the dog's weight and the weight of his pack must be verified by an impartial witness or trip official prior to the start of each trip. Overall, he must pack for over 120 miles in one to three trips, each of which must be at least 40 miles. Packers must average 10 miles per day under normal conditions such as maintained trails and normal weather. Any day trips from a base camp will be counted only if the weight requirement is met.

More challenging for both dog and person, trails must be backcountry (remote areas inaccessible and unsuited to vehicular traffic) where support is not generally available. These distance requirements make camping overnight necessary, and these overnight camps must be back-country, not at trailheads, roadside campgrounds, and the like. Suitable locations for pack trips include national forests, state parks, hiking trails and undeveloped natural terrain, depending on local regulations.

Dogs owned by Gilbert Dubied, Switzerland, shown at a camp in the snow.

Frangilak, owned by M. T. Pottier of France, wears a soft-sided nylon pack.

Many Malamutes with pack dog titles are also show dogs. Above left: Ch. Istari's Tinuki of Artic Wind, WTD, WPDX, ROM, bred and owned by John and Helen Schultz.
Above right: Ch. Tikiluk's Shoshoni Stone Fox, WPD, bred and owned by Beverly Turner.

Lynne Hurrell and Wicked cross a log over a deep chasm. This is a time for real caution.

A freighting or weight pulling harness. All sled dog drawings in this chapter by Linda Duke.

WEIGHT PULLS

An owner with only one dog can also participate in weight pulling, a sledding activity. Again, basic obedience is advisable before starting a mature dog on weight-pull training. A young dog's bones are still developing. *Never work a young Malamute with a heavy load.*

It will amaze you, however, to learn just how much weight a Malamute is capable of pulling. Many owners get involved in this sport just for fun, while others are serious about setting records.

Weight pull contests were a natural outgrowth of the type of work Malamutes did everyday. By 1934, Fairbanks, Alaska, was hosting the North American Championship Weight Pull Competition, and pulls were popular adjuncts to sled dog races. Today, many specialty clubs hold weight pulls in conjunction with their shows or with all-breed shows. Some are open only to Malamutes.

In 1970, Taaralaste "Naki" Neiu of Roger Burggraf's Taaralaste Kennels in Alaska set a record in the North American Championship pull. She pulled 2,350 pounds over 60 feet. She had to break loose a sled that had steel runners to do this. Today, the distance from start to finish varies depending on the rules under which the pull is held. Most pulls use a 16 foot distance from start to finish, although in Alaska some contests require a 25-foot pull.

The pulling surface determines whether a sled or a wheeled cart is used to hold pre-weighed objects placed in the bed. The dogs take turns at pulling. The handler may drive the dog from behind if the dog is familiar with sledding or call him from across the finish line. Overcoming inertia, getting the sled or cart moving, is the hardest part of the weight pull; once it is moving, the work is much easier.

Once all the dogs have pulled, the weight is increased by approximately 100 pounds and the dogs continue taking turns until the handlers "pass" or a winner is determined. Winning can be based on either the overall weight pulled or on the most weight pulled in proportion to body weight. Weight pulls are one of the few areas where larger dogs have an advantage; they can pull more weight overall and are often stronger. While the Malamute's abilities as a freight-hauler suit him to weight pull, he was not bred for it, nor was the weight pull ever meant to be anything more than a sport.

EQUIPMENT

You can purchase a weight-pull or freighting harness through mail-order catalogs, or you can make them at home. Be sure your measurements are accurate; measure the dog's body, not his fur.

You will also need a tug line to fasten the harness to whatever he is pulling. This should be a long, strong rope or chain with a swivel snap at each end.

The freight harness (sometimes called a single-tree harness) appropriate for weight pull has a spreader bar a few inches from the rear which helps distribute the weight evenly to both sides of the dog's body, while at the same time holding the harness away from his legs. When you put the harness on the dog, pull it tight behind him to make sure that it will fit properly when he is working. The spreader should neither hit his rear nor be too far back, and around the neck, the harness should be neither too tight nor too high. All the straps should lie flat; snug, yet not tight. It should be well padded, especially across the chest.

TRAINING

Serious training should wait until the dog is at least eighteen months old. He should be fitted with a well-made freighting harness. If you want, you can also begin teaching sledding commands at this time. Regardless, never make training hard work or boring; the most important part of any training is making it fun.

Once your dog accepts the harness, start training by attaching a light object to it, such as a truck tire or a wooden box on runners into which rocks or dirt can be placed. Wheeled vehicles are less suitable because they do not provide a constant drag. Begin with light loads and work up, always finishing with a load that the dog can move comfortably. Initially, he should pull the empty drag to earn his food three days a week over a smooth course, either

Mountain Home's Yukon WLDX, WWPD shows excellent weight-pull form. Owned by Roy and Sue Fuller.

Fire pulling 2,300 pounds at the 1992 North American Championship pull at Fairbanks. Owned by Gordon and Barb Heppner. Photo by Carlson.

Ch. Istari's Hobbit Forming WTD, WWPDX, owned by John and Helen Schultz, shows how it is done.

WORKING WEIGHT PULL DOG EXCELLENT

Date	Dog	Owner
1988	Ch. White Water Bitteroot Shuyak	Adams
	Sasha Serenade	Adams
	Ch. Nanook of the Northern Lights	Johnson
	Ch. Bitteroot Shuyak Kachemac	Adams
1089	Ch. Winkre's Bootes O'Starwind, CD	Johnson
	Maska's Sure-Foot Sheba	Rolfson
1990	Am/Can Ch. Wakon's Glacier Ice Bear	Sternberg
1991	Wolflodge Knickinick, CD	Malcolm
	Black Ice's Amiable Force	Stenger
1992	Bitteroot's Snopaw Rogue	Adams
	Awanuna's Winter Flake, CD	Pfeiffer
	Ch. Nor-Sky's Bear Creek Kazan	Johnson
1993	Kiskatinau Taniska	Caudill
	Grey Mist's Whirling Wind	Stenger
	Euga Luga Babouska	Caudill
	Conan Chief of the Tundra, CD	Talalay
	Ch. Tikiluk's Wraith of Damien	Turner/Ritter
	Ch. Storm Kloud's Oomiak	Russell
	Kazan's Kasstoff in Maska Pak	Rolfson
	Maska's Torque in Motion	Rolfson
	Whisper Pine Northland Sitka	Bedford
	Black Ice's Persuasive Force	Bedford
	Can Ch. Black Ice's Shear Force	Bedford
	Maska's Amarok of Storm Kloud	Rolfson
	Ch. Istari's Smokey Buccaneer	Marsicek
1994	Storm Kloud's Jason's Magic	Bell
	Am/Can Ch. Avalanche at Snow Castle, CD	
		Schultz
	Ch. Istari's Tinuki of Arctic Wind	Schultz
	Ch. Istari's Hobbit Forming	Schultz
	Wotan's Steel Whirlwind	Biss
	Am/Can Ch. Storm Kloud's Keep the Win	
		Russell
	Ch. Foxfire's Szatahni Tosah	Lieske
	Ch. Chinome's Arctic Invader	Walden
	Kachiri	Caudill
	Buccaneer's Murphys Law	Marsicek
	Sno-King's Kodiak Teddi Bear	Kirchner
	Foxfire' Lil Boni Tazs	Lieske
	Storm Kloud's Wwright Won Baby	Russell
	Sarge	Beauchamp
1995	Rose of Sharon's Meeshka	Holmes
	Tikiluk's Windstorm	Cox
	Sno-trek's Kingsdale Granite	Olson
	Kingsdales Ready For Kombat	Olson
1996	Storm Kloud's Kkilling Time	Cocking
	Thunderstorms Innocent Ayla	Cox
	Chevelier Breezy	Malcolm
	Rosss of Sharon's Pyka	Corr
	Sorcha's Aonair Barron	Wallis
1997	Polarstorm's Buccaneer Blend	Marsecik
	Storm Kloud's Corner The Market	Russell
	Onaks Yukon Chief	Sams

level or on a gentle upgrade, if possible. Measure off 20 feet or more; the training course should always be longer than the official competition course to discourage quitting.

Leave the dog on a stay or have someone restrain him while two large scoops of food are put in a dish which is placed at the 20-foot mark. Let the dog see his dish and call him. When he pulls to it, give him a small bit of food. Repeat five times; the last time give him the remaining food.

After the dog accepts the drag, add a few rocks or an extra tire, but increase the weight gradually. Your dog's confidence that he can indeed pull the load behind him is an important part of his ability to actually do it. You build that confidence by letting him always be successful. If he

Am/Can Ch. Avalanche at Snow Castle Am/Can CD, WLD, WTD, WWPDX, WPD, owned by John and Helen Schultz.

Yukon Pride's Nanook Horizon WWPD is pulling 2850 pounds. Owner, Gordon Heppner. Photo by Ken Blade.

has to strain, or if he dislikes or fears the exercise, your work will be for naught.

After a month or more, your dog is ready to start building more muscle. Start each set of pulls with a light pull and increase the weight each time, until the fourth pull makes him really exert himself. As before, keep the weight within

Weighing in before a pull.

his ability to pull. For the fifth pull, reduce the weight back to that of the third. By this point, the dog knows the exercise, and it can be varied to suit each individual dog. When you start, put down an empty dish, and when the dog completes the pull, hand him a treat from your pocket. Once he is familiar with this, eliminate the dish. Eventually the dog will only receive praise with an occasional treat since you cannot bait a dog in competition.

If your dog wins a weight pull competition, let that be the last pull he makes, unless you are confident that he can pull more weight and want to provide a demonstration or if you need a few more pounds for a certification requirement. However, in tough competition, the weight he is required to pull may just be too heavy. So that he does not lose his confidence, grab his harness and help him pull it the complete distance. He must believe that he can always complete his pulls and *ALWAYS* give lots of praise when he finishes.

WEIGHT PULL DOG REQUIREMENTS

For certification as a WWPD or a WWPDX, the International Sled Dog Racing Association (ISDRA), AMCA, or International Weight Pull Association (IWPA) rules must govern the event. Required distances for the pull depend on the pulling surface.

For a WWPD, the dog must qualify in four separate events. On a natural surface, the weight pulled must equal or exceed eight times the dog's weight. On artificial surfaces such as concrete, carpet, etc., the weight pulled must equal or exceed 12 times the dog's weight.

For a WWPDX, the dog must qualify in five separate events. He must pull 14 times his body weight on snow with a sled or 16 times his weight on any other natural surface with a wheeled cart. On a man-made surface such as concrete or carpet, divisions by weight determine how much he must pull to qualify. At 60-80 lbs. he must pull 23 times his weight; 81-100 lbs., 21 times his weight; and over 100 lbs., 19 times his weight. In addition, to obtain a WWPDX the dog must place in the top third of his class in each event. If three-fourths of the competing dogs pull the required weight, the pull is disallowed.

SLEDDING

The Alaskan Malamute's desire for harness work and his joy in its performance runs bone-deep. It is so intrinsic to his character that a dog without it is really not a true Malamute at all.[4]

Many people do not realize how suited Malamutes are to recreational work since they are often overshadowed in races by their swifter cousins. Unfortunately, sledding can seem so specialized and daunting, that even in areas with plentiful snow, many people never try it. It requires more equipment than other activities, more training, more conditioning, and if it is a small team, more assistance from the driver. On the other hand, it does afford your dog the chance to do what he was bred for, and sledding keeps both of you in excellent condition.

EQUIPMENT

To work, you will need harnesses, slip collars, a gang line, and neck lines for each dog as well as a training cart and, eventually, a sled. On the racing harness, the tug line attaches on the back above the tail, while on the freighting harness, it falls just below the rump, altering the dog's center of gravity. It can be used with or without the spreader.

Regardless of which harness is used, the attachment sections should be kept as light as possible. A heavy harness ring and metal snap may whip around, painfully slapping the dog's rear. All the necessary equipment can be purchased from a mail-order dog outfitter or made by a resourceful person.

Racing competitions also require that the driver carry a dog bag in which an injured or exhausted team dog can be

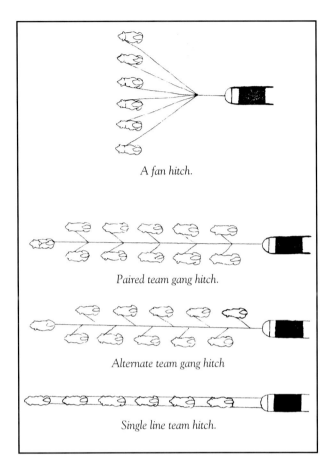

A fan hitch.

Paired team gang hitch.

Alternate team gang hitch

Single line team hitch.

carried to a drop off point. A large gunny sack with a draw string around the neck is usually acceptable.

A snow hook or tie-line used to restrain the sled and team while they are being hitched to the sled is essential, A spare tug line and harness should also be carried.

HITCHES

Dogs can be hitched to a sled in various arrangements depending on the terrain, type and amount of snow, and custom of the area. In the vast treeless expanses of Greenland and the Arctic, teams are usually fan-hitched, whereas on the trails of Alaska and the Yukon, dogs were almost always in a gang or tandem hitch.

The fan hitch has several advantages. Here, the leader is in the center with the strongest dogs on either side and the weakest on the outside. This hitch lessens the chance that part of the team might pull the rest into danger, into a crevasse or through a break in the ice, for instance, and the work load is distributed more evenly than in the gang hitch.

Some of the fan's disadvantages are pluses for the gang hitch. Here, a single line runs from the sled to the lead dog. Team dogs are hooked either side-by-side or on alternate sides of the center tug line. In this style of harnessing, the front dogs break trail, which can be very tiring. If it is too difficult, the driver might have to join in the efforts. Dogs can be rotated to interior positions for a respite, while on the fan hitch, each dog breaks his own trail.

Today, most mushers use a gang hitch. One or two lead dogs are followed by the point dogs. Following them may be any number of swing dog pairs—the first swing, then second swing, and so on. The pair closest to the sled are called wheel dogs and are usually the strongest, since they take the brunt of the sled's weight. Sledding may be done with any number of dogs, though for racing, three dogs are the minimum for a team.

TRAINING

A dog needs to have basic obedience but not formal leash training. A dog trained to heel may be confused by being required to move out in front of the trainer and to keep a tight line. He should certainly have learned the Down Stay and to come at some signal—a whistle or verbal command. These two commands can be life-savers in an emergency.

To run a dog team, a lead dog must be trained to obey trail commands for starting, turning, going straight ahead, passing other teams, and stopping. A novice musher will soon learn the value of a good lead dog; the first dog, after he is trained, will train the next dog by example.

There are numerous commands for starting off—some drivers give a shrill whistle, others yell, "Hike," "Let's Go," or whatever works. However, the commands for turning are standard, "Gee" for right, " Haw" for left and "Whoa" for stop. Other auxiliary commands may be developed for "Straight ahead" when the dog tries to make an unwanted turn.

The first requirement is a well-fitting harness, a four-foot tug line or leash, an agile trainer, and a trail with lots of possible left and right turns. Once at the training area, fasten the tug line to the harness-pulling ring and command the dog to move out, pulling you. At the first turn, yell the necessary command and pull the line in that direction. Pointing the direction frequently helps the dog to understand what is required. Give lots of praise when he does the right thing.

A team of National Park Malamutes hauls freight in Mt. McKinley National Park, Alaska. Courtesy of Sue Renkert.

Yukon sledding harness. Drawing by Linda Duke.

An X-back racing harness. Drawing by Linda Duke.

Mals bred and owned by Bruce and Charlotte Tuck move in unison.

Toboggan fully loaded for a camping trip. Courtesy Black Ice.

Dave Herdman Cathman, Scotland, running a wheel rig.

Truck used by Sendaishi kennel to travel to races.

All Alaskan Malamute team owned by Robert and Nancy Russell, Storm Kloud Kennels, and driven by Jamie Nelson in the 1994 Iditarod. Photo by Robert Russell.

Below: Roger Burggraf's team of Malamutes hauling freight up the East Fork of the Toklat River in Alaska in the 1970s.

Malamutes That Have Earned Sledding Excellent Titles

WORKING LEAD DOG EXCELLENT

Date	Dog	Owner
1989	Mountain Home's Yukon	Fuller
	Snowshoe	Fuller
1990	Am/Can Ch. Black Ice's	
	Aleutian Dream	Bedford
1991	Canjor's Kaijuh Tu	Collins
	Storm Kloud's Here I Am	Nelson/Russell
1992	Kiskatinau Taniska	Caudill
	Ch. Black Ice's High Speed Chase	Bedford
	Oopik's Country Bumpkin, Can CDX	Muir
	Can. Ch. Oopik's Ebony Reflection	Muir
	Kinarctic Kaila's Arctic Wind	Hardie
	Tangeluq's Maximum Overdrive	Larkin
	Euga Luga Babouska	Caudill
	Ch. Chinome's Arctic Invader	Walden
1995	Storm Kloud's KKruzin Along	Richards
	Storm Kloud's Hhailstone	Nelson/Russell
1996	Taro D'Emisca	Circe
	Inuk D'Emisca	Circe
	Emisca Bianca D'Ericlam	Circe

WORKING TEAM DOG EXCELLENT

Date	Dog	Owner
1987	Aldar's Tongas	Stiller
	Kaheltna's Hoot Owl	Stiller
	Aldar's Glacier Tubby	Stiller
	Trolldom's Chug Along	Stiller
	Trolldom's Mouse	Stiller
	Trolldom's Ophir	Stiller
1988	Valden's Kodiak of Kanjor	Collins
	Trolldom's Sparky	Collins
	Kohoutec's Canjor Mia	Collins
	Canjor's Uno Kissima	Collins
	Canjor's Kaiyuh Tu	Collins
	Aluk's Aklaya of Canjor	Collins
	Trolldom's Dawson	Collins
	Aluk's Panik of Canjor	Collins
1989	Mountain Home's Twisp Twist	Fuller
	Mountain Home's Libby	Fuller
	Mountain Home's Raven Ridge	Fuller
	Mountain Home's Band on the Run	Fuller
	Mountain Home's Saskatoon	Fuller
	Mountain Home's Loganberry	Fuller
	Northernstar's Jasper	Fuller
	Northern Light's Kodiak	Fuller
	Can Ch. Black Ice's Shear Force	Bedford
	Black Ice's Aleutian Tugboat	Bedford
	Am/Can Ch. Black Ice's	
	Aleutian Dream	Bedford
1990	Battan's Arctic Williwaw	Fuller
	Black Ice's Frozen Ingot	Bedford
	Am/Can Ch. Black Ice's Winter	
	Obsession	Bedford
1991	Snowshoe	Fuller
	Mountain Home's Yukon	Fuller

Date	Dog	Owner
	Thunderpaw of Mountain Home	Fuller
	Mountain Home's Blackberry	Fuller
	Mountain Home's Rocky Ridge	Fuller
	Mountain Home's Drift Buster	Fuller
	Mountain Home's Serenade	Fuller
	Mountain Home's Frosty Morn	Fuller
	Mountain Home's Pine Fores	Fuller
	Mountain Home's Comet Cora	Fuller
	Trolldom's Elsa	Stiller
	Malaworth's Trolldoms Texas	MacLean
	Trolldom's Aldar Orbit	MacLean
	Canjor's Cariboo	Collins
	Canjor's Coyote	Collins
	Canjor's Zephyr	Collins
	Can Ch. Oopik's Ebony Reflection	Muir
	Oopik's Country Bumpkin, Can CD	Muir
	Marlayne's Black Gem of Oopik	Muir
	Can Ch Icelandic's Snomischief	
	of Oopik	Muir
	Am/Can Ch. Oopik's Lil' Bit A Canuck	Muir
	Black Ice's Amiable Force	Stenger
	Storm Kloud's Hhailstone	Nelson/Russell
	Storm Kloud's Hhanniba	Nelson/Russell
1992	Grey Mist's Morning Dew	Stenger
	Black Ice's Lightening Strikes	Stenger
	Grey Mist's Gifted Force	Stenger
	Grey Mist's Whirling Wind	Stenger
	Prairie Wind Gift to Grey Mis	Stenger
	Grey Mist's Shear Delight	Stenger
	Grey Mist's Shear Zone	Stenger
	Grey Mist's Midnight Storm	Stenger
	Euga Luga Babouska	Caudill
	Black Ice's Thundering Thor	Bedford
	Can Ch. Oopik's Snow Enticer	Muir
	Can Ch. Oopik's Mystic Keyrea,	
	Am/Can CD	Muir
	Can Ch. Oopik's Canadian Cruiser,	
	Am/Can CD	Muir
	Lady Katherine De Chabek	Hardie
	Wintertrail's Cinnamon Snowbear	Hardie
	Tangeluq's Tuxedo Junction	Larkin
	Tangeluq's Gypsy Queen	Larkin
1993	Kiskatinau Taniska, CD	Caudill
	Shape Shift's Ice Crystal	Caudill
	Shape Shift's Aurora	Caudill
	Shape Shift's Colde Duck	Caudill
	Shape Shift's Tu Isis Colde	Caudill
	Ch. Storm Kloud's Eez Remarkable	Russell
	Ch. Storm Kloud's Hhuckleberry	Nelson/Russell
	Storm Kloud's Hhear the Drum	Nelson/Russell
1994	Tigara's Winds of War	Walden
	Ch. Chinome's Arctic Invade	Walden
1995	Barnstormer By Storm Kloud	Russell
	Storm Kloud's Ggrandslam	Russell
	Windhaven's Missy Magoo	Screpanski
	Storm Kloud's KKruzin' Along	Richards
	Storm Kloud's Ilcess	Russell

Date	Dog	Owner	Date	Dog	Owner
	Storm Kloud's Tabetha	Russell	1996	Oopik's Lil Panda Bear	Murray
	Storm Kloud's MMy Last One	Russell		Oopik's Whirlwind Romance	Murray
	Storm Kloud's At It Again	Russell		Niki 2nd	Murray
	Storm Kloud's Wwon in Great Taste	Russell		Sendaishi's Polar Trax	Matott
	Storm Kloud's YYes Just Say Yes	Russell		Sendaishi's Eskimo Eddy	Matott
1996	Taro D'Emisca	Circe		Sendaishi's Chuck the Duck	Matott
	Emisca Maverick Pride and Joy	Circe		Sendaishi's Lester D Molester	Matott
	Emisca Blizzard D'Ericlam	Circe		Sendaishi's Shaktoolik Joe	Matott
	Inuk D'Emisca	Circe		Sendaishi's Diamond Jim	Matott
	Emisca Bianca D'Ericlam	Circe		Sendaishi's Pleasure is Mine	Matott
	Panuck D'Emisca	Circe		Timlo's Just Plain Jake	Tuck
	Emisca Uayack D'Ericlam	Circe		Sno-Trek's Kingsdale Granite	Olson
	Timlo's Dark Side of the Force	Tuck		Kingsdale's Ready for Kombat	Olson
	Timlo's Mystic Warrior	Tuck		Kingsdale's Desert Storm	Olson
	Timlo's Winter Witch	Tuck		Kingsdale's Oprah's On	Olson
	Timlo's Rambling Rose	Tuck		Kingsdale's Big Bad Buck	Olson
	Mighty Illamar	Murray		Kingsdales Kobalt Kali	Olson

Left: Northernstar Jasper, WTDX, bred and owned by Roy and Sue Fuller.

Above: Mountain Home's Yukon, WLDX, WWPD, was the first to earn a Working Lead Dog Excellent title. Bred and owned by Roy and Sue Fuller.

Left: Snowshoe WLDX, WWPD, the first bitch to earn a Working Lead Dog Excellent title. Breeder/owners Roy and Sue Fuller.

At first, make all your turns in the same direction until the dog understands, then do all turns in the opposite direction. When he understands both, mix left and right turns and straight-aheads. It is surprising how fast a good dog will catch on.

If sled-command training is started at an early age, around four months or so, two dogs may be trained at the same time. If they prove too strong and active or encourage each other to make the whole outing a big game, go back to just one, or they will run your legs off.

If the dogs are eighteen months or older, a light three-wheeled training cart is nice to have. You can work the dog or dogs while riding on the easy sections and running on the upgrades.

Once the first dog is working satisfactorily, you can add a second dog, preferably behind the first. The more experienced dog can keep the newcomer from taking off in the wrong direction and creating confusion. As the second-dog hears your commands and realizes what to do, the two dogs will work efficiently and may eventually be run as a brace or double lead.

As each new dog becomes trained, you can add the next dog to the team or run with the first one or two, or whatever method of training appears to work the best.

Tom Knoll skijoring at a race in Aspen, Colorado.

However, be careful when placing a young dog into an experienced team. If they run too fast or for too long, the newcomer can easily become discouraged.

A local sled-dog club that holds workouts and races throughout the year can be of considerable help for novice sled dog or weight pull trainers. At these workouts, veteran trainers and racers take time to talk and teach newcomers. You may also be able to examine, buy, or borrow equipment. In addition, some clubs also have weekend dog sledding seminars or equipment-making parties that can be very beneficial.

WORKING TEAM AND LEAD DOG REQUIREMENTS

The Sledding Program encompasses work on both sleds and wheeled carts. The AMCA certifies Working Team Dog and Working Lead Dog. An Excellent rating can be obtained with further work.

All events are held under International Sled Dog Racing Association (ISDRA) rules. A dog does not have to run on the same team all the time, nor does the team have to be all Malamutes. The dog must qualify pulling a cart or sled in some combination of race or excursion, or both. Classes may be sprint or freight. A lead dog must satisfy the same requirements running single lead on at least a three-dog team. The Excellent rating requires more miles in harness.

SKIJORING

Skijoring has been popular in Scandinavia and Europe for a long time. It offers a simpler, less expensive alternative to sledding but requires a very proficient skier. Most skijorers use only one dog, but it may be done with more depending on the ability of the skier and the training of the dogs. A well-trained team leader is a must.

The skijorer may also pull a small sled or toboggan or carry a backpack for longer trips. He can hold a towbar or use a hip belt to free his hands for poling.

Slightly more stable than using just the skis, is a pulka which is a streamlined frame of 44 pounds (20 kg.) to which the dog is harnessed. Pulk racing is extremely popular in Europe, especially in Scandinavia.

A regular racing harness with about an eight-foot tug line works well. The low-draft design of freighting or weight-pull harnesses makes them unsuitable for skijoring because the skier's hands are higher than the dog's back, which pulls the tug line of a freighting harness out of its proper working position.

Multiple champion Bareebinyackzan, Dutch CD, WTD, racing in the Scandinavian or Pulk class in Germany. Owned by Marijke Baas, Holland.

Skijoring in Belgium. Photo courtesy Mormont De Henau.

In a three-dog skijoring team, the distance between the lead and points should be about 6 feet. Just as in waterskiing, the takeoff is crucial. The first forward lunge tends to pull you off-balance, so you will have to be prepared by taking up any slack in the line and leaning back a little.

Once launched, you are in for a very exciting ride. For one thing, you have no brake to slow the dogs down as you do on a sled. This is just one of the reasons why you should be an accomplished skier with well-trained dogs.

Sharp turns can be dangerous, especially if your dogs decide to take off after a rabbit or a deer. You may side-slip on the icy surface and get wrapped around a tree. In some instances, you may have to let go of the tug line and ski to a stop. When stopping or slowing down, be careful not to run into the dogs with your skis.

For skijoring, dogs should be at least eighteen months of age, in good health and physical condition, and should be thoroughly reliable in following sled-dog commands. Most dogs will follow a trail that is well travelled, but it is necessary to have your dogs' full confidence and trust when you want them to travel unmarked or virgin territory.

Skijoring is a wonderful way to spend time with your dog, but you must be extremely careful and responsible. Try not to let go of your dogs. Even though they may get along with each other, they may fight with other dogs or run off and get their tug line tangled around a tree.

During the big Carnivals in Alaska, skijoring with dogs is a regular feature. It is gaining popularity in Canada and the United States and is a great way to break puppies to harness. The Alaskan Malamute Club of America will certify Skijoring dogs; to pursue this, contact the AMCA for the names of the Working Dog Committee members.

ENDNOTES:

1.   Keith Hurrell, "Keith's Klinik. A Snow Tail, " Alaskan Malamute Quarterly, 12:2 (Winter, 1993-4), 19. The standard's recommendations are important for all the work the dog performs. Some consideration must be given to the size of the dog, even in backpacking.

In an account of a backcountry packing trip, Mr. Hurrell observes, "The next problem was getting the dogs across. This was a good example of why a pack dog should not be too heavy to lift. Lynne brought one dog to the edge and I lowered him to the water. . . . I picked him up and helped him onto the far bank." In Arctic works, dogs often have to be pulled out of crevasses and out of the water.

2.   Carried by rodent's fleas, bubonic plague has steadily moved east across the United States since its introduction into the San Francisco area at the turn of the century.

3.   All Working Dog requirements are taken from the AMCA rules effective October, 1992.

4.   Although you may not be able to work your own dogs in harness, you can maximize your chances of retaining a desire to work in your breeding program by utilizing dogs with working certification as breeding partners.

Number One Working Dog and Number Two All-Breeds in the United States for 1997, Am. Can. Ch. Nanuke's Take No Prisoners, "Tyler," is the top winning Malamute in breed history. He has won of over 45 Best in Shows. Tyler also won the 1997 National Specialty, 16 Best in Specialty Shows, Best of Breed and Group One at Westminster Kennel Club in l998, and Best of Breed and Group Two, Westminster Kennel Club show in l997. Bred by Sandra and Rosemarie D'Andrea, and co-owned by Kathy Leuer, Dr. William Newman and Sandra D'Andrea. Booth photo.

6

THE ALASKAN
MALAMUTE STANDARD

A general definition of the word standard, according to Webster's, is: "Something that is established by authority, custom, or general consent as a model or example to be followed." Applied specifically to dogs, it is the accepted description of a breed. For those breeds recognized by the American Kennel Club, it is formulated by a breed club designated as the national or "parent" club.

The writers of the standard attempt to portray verbally the characteristics unique to the breed, to emphasize the features which enhance its intended functions, and to specify those that are undesirable or totally unacceptable. Breeders use the standard to shape their choices as to what dogs to breed, which partners to use with them, and which of their offspring should be bred in the next generation. Likewise, when they are asked to evaluate the dogs presented to them, dog show judges measure each dog against their interpretation of the standard and rank the dogs accordingly.

Writing a standard and making changes to it can be every bit as stressful and arduous as serving on a jury in a complicated, controversial trial. Once the national club's standard committee has thrashed out a draft, it must be ratified by the general membership. Although breed standards can be and are changed, such changes are never undertaken lightly.

A standard is basically a blueprint. Just as homes built from the same blueprints can differ in appearance, individual dogs can conform very well to the same standard and still be far from identical. The latitude of these differences is determined by the specifics of the standard, and those specifics are essential to preserving the character and function of the breed.

One person's vision and emphasis will always differ from another's, depending on the experience and background of the evaluator. Such variation is integral to the evaluative process and helps maintain balance in the breed.

THE FIRST STANDARD

The Alaskan Malamute Club of America adopted its first Standard on April 17, 1935, and much of its language survives today. For size, it recommended a range: "Height—Of male dog averaging from 22 to 25 inches. Of bitch averaging from 20 to 23 inches. Weight—Of male dog averaging from 65 to 85 pounds. Of bitch averaging from 50 to 70 pounds."

INTERIM STANDARDS

Although the first revision to the Standard, approved on April 12, 1960, changed the format and wording somewhat, its most substantive differences were in the areas of size and color. Instead of the weight and height ranges specified previously, the new Standard recommended only the upper height and weight from its predecessor. Further, it added a cautionary note that soundness be considered before size.

Color provided another area of controversy. The original Malamutes were seals, wolf-grays, and silvers, but the acceptance of new lines into registration after World War II brought in dogs with a wider range of colors. Recognition of the solid white Malamute was made as a concession to these new dogs. In addition, language describing undesirable marking patterns was inserted with the description of coat color, and the scale of points was deleted.

On August 10, 1982, the Standard was amended to include blue eyes as a disqualification. The words "dogs and bitches" were changed to "males and females," and the scale of points was included again.

CURRENT STANDARD

In the 1990s, the AKC requested that breed clubs reformat their standards. To further facilitate the study of and reference to breed standards, the AKC designated Spira's book *Canine Terminology* as its official lexicon.

While the essential description of the Malamute is unchanged, the latest version of the Standard is in a different order and has some rewording. The most significant additions are: acknowledgment of the red (liver) color; description of proportions of depth and length; a discussion of proper side gait; and deletion of the scale of points once again. Trimming is restricted to neatening the feet.

RELEVANCE OF THE STANDARD

Every version of the Alaskan Malamute Standard describes the optimum dog for freight work in the coldest climates. While the original Standard was based on observations of dogs whose ability was proven in both the Arctic and Antarctic, few Malamutes today do sled work and even fewer live in the harsh conditions of their ancestors.

While these circumstances do not make the standard any less relevant, they do make it easier to lose sight of how important some aspects of the Standard are to maintaining the breed's working ability. Fortunately, even in modern times, graphic examples of the Standard's relevance arise. Two important examples regarding size and coat are in Will Steger's account of his TransAntarctic Expedition, *Crossing Antarctica.*

Steger's experience reinforces the validity of the ideal freighting size contained in all versions of the standard. The standard committees have stood firm on this, despite continuous pressure to raise both height and weight.

Steger's crew was acutely aware of every calorie the dogs needed for work. In assessing their performance, Steger says:

> The true stars of the expedition have been Geoff's dogs. Their spirit is constantly high, they pull at a continuously strong pace, and because they are smaller they eat less. . . He has proved to me that a sixty-to-seventy-pound dog is the best for these conditions. By comparison, my dogs average between ninety and one hundred pounds.[1]

Likewise, his experience with Sawyer points out the importance of a correct coat. While dogs with woolly or long coats can and do work in Arctic conditions, such coats can be life-threatening for a dog in prolonged sub-Arctic temperatures. Steger says:

> . . . Sawyer collapsed from exhaustion. . . . One of Sawyer's problems is his long hair; he looks like a musk ox and ice collects on his inner layer of fur costing him insulation, thus warmth and strength. Eskimos always kill long-haired puppies for this reason, but we had taken Sawyer to Greenland and he had worked out well. Here it is another story. The poor dog is carrying more than forty pounds of ice and snow in his fur. . . . Sawyer will have to be sent out the next time we are visited by a plane.[2]

Ch. Kachina's Cujo ROM, *a multiple specialty winner and three-time BIS winner, owned by Paul and Ruth Levesque. Graham photo by Sabrina.*

To maintain a dog which can work in the harshest of climates, the coat described in the Standard is essential. Long-coated dogs can work well in many capacities including sledding, backpacking, obedience, and agility. However, because of the genetics involved using them for breeding may well result in many generations of improper coats.

The Malamute Standard by its very nature as a blueprint is brief, with little or no explanation about its specifications. However, they are neither arbitrary or frivolous. Its specifications are designed to create an ideal freighting dog for polar climates.

To make it easier for the newcomers to understand, we are presenting the AKC Standard with accompanying comments and explanations. Much of the material for this commentary was provided by Sheila Balch, a distinguished judge and long-time Malamute breeder. Best known for her two-time National Specialty winner, Ch. Inuit's Sweet Lucifer, Balch's stock forms the foundation for many Malamute kennels in the U.S. and abroad.

Ch. Glen Haven's Arctic Knight BIS, BISS, Pedigree Award winner and number one Malamute in 1995. Owned by Terry and Gloria Toussaint.

Multiple Best in Show and Best in Specialty Show winner Am. Can. Ch. Sno Ridge Blue Ice Lady O War, ROM. Breeder/owner Eileen Kinnas. Olson photo.

Am. Can. Ch. Iditarod's Inupiat Warrior, a BIS winner bred by Jackie Lund and owned by John Dewing.

AKC STANDARD FOR THE ALASKAN MALAMUTE
(Approved May 31, 1994)

GENERAL APPEARANCE

The Alaskan Malamute, one of the oldest Arctic sled dogs, is a powerful and substantially built dog with a deep chest and strong, well-muscled body. The Malamute stands well over the pads, and this stance gives the appearance of much activity and a proud carriage, with head erect and eyes showing interest and curiosity. The head is broad. Ears are triangular and erect when alerted. The muzzle is bulky, diminishing only slightly in width from backskull to nose. The muzzle is not pointed or long, yet not stubby. The coat is thick with a coarse guard coat of sufficient length to protect a woolly undercoat. Malamutes are of various colors. Face markings are a distinguishing feature. These consist of a cap over the head, the face either all white or marked with a bar and/or mask. The tail is well furred, carried over the back, and has the appearance of a waving plume.

The Malamute must be a heavy boned dog with sound legs, good feet, deep chest and powerful shoulders, and have all of the other physical attributes necessary for the efficient performance of his job. The gait must be steady, balanced, tireless and totally efficient. He is not intended as a racing sled dog designed to compete in speed trials. The Malamute is structured for strength and endurance, and any characteristic of the individual specimen, including temperament, which interferes with the accomplishment of this purpose, is to be considered the most serious of faults.

COMMENTS

The Alaskan Malamute was created by nature rather than man. In his native environment, natural selection assured only the strongest, most vigorous animals survived to reproduce, and today he retains much of that hardy strength.

The Malamute served as the utility dog of the Inuit and he should still demonstrate a well-built, beautifully conditioned athleticism. His work required both strength and endurance, and he should strike a balance between them. He should never be overdone with thick bunchy muscles like a weight-lifter. His legs and feet must be perfectly formed, his front and rear assemblies well-balanced. Head shape, markings, and ear-set are important elements of breed type.

In writing the standard, the parent club wanted to emphasize differences between the freighting and racing dogs. Unfortunately, traits described as a comparison are sometimes construed as absolutes. In describing the Malamute as a "heavy" freighting dog, for instance, the intent is to contrast the Mal with dogs such as his cousin, the Siberian Husky.[3] While Huskies were used in freighting, they are suited better to lighter loads and greater speeds. Siberians can and do compete in races; the typical Malamute is not intended to be a racing dog.

Ch. Kaila's Paw Print is an excellent representative of Malamute type—well balanced, good pigment, substantial bone, and beautiful eyes and ears. Breeder/Owners, Chris and Eileen Gabriel. Ashbey photo.

COMMENTS

In almost sixty years of existence the AMCA has not budged on the desirable freighting sizes and weights, despite considerable pressure to change the standard to fit the trends of the time. From the days of the Gold Rush to the latest Antarctic expedition, the 25-inch, 85-pound dog has proven his superior efficiency for pulling steadily over long distances with minimal food.

The thick coat over the withers must be factored into any estimation of size; however, the Malamute should never be evaluated solely on that basis. Because the profuse coat can be misleading, evaluating proportion may require a hands-on approach.

The Malamute is never short-legged or stumpy nor is he tall or coltish. He is not square but should not be overly long, since such length weakens the back and interferes with his function. He should never be overweight or out of condition.

SIZE, PROPORTION, SUBSTANCE—

There is a natural range of size in the breed. The desirable freighting sizes are:
  Males, 25 inches at the shoulders, 85 pounds;
  Females, 23 inches at the shoulders, 75 pounds.
However, size consideration should not outweigh that of type, proportion, movement, and other functional attributes. When dogs are judged equal in type, proportion, movement, the dog nearest the desirable freighting size is to be preferred. The depth of chest is approximately one-half the height of the dog at the shoulders, the deepest point being just behind the forelegs. The length of the body from point of shoulder to the rear point of pelvis is longer than the height of the body from ground to top of the withers. The body carries no excess weight, and bone is in proportion to size.

Ch. Sendaishi's Diamond Jim WTDX, a multiple group and specialty winner. Breeder/Owners, Bill and Joyce Matott. Tatham photo.

The Malamute should be slightly longer than he is tall. Leg from elbow to floor should be half the height of the dog. Measure height from point of withers to floor; length from point of shoulder to ischium. Drawing by Linda Duke.

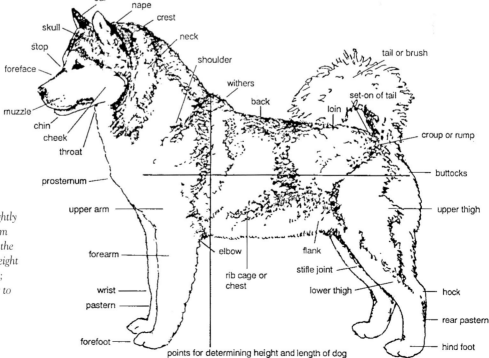

HEAD—

The *head* is broad and deep, not coarse or clumsy, but in proportion to the size of the dog. The expression is soft and indicates an affectionate disposition.

The *eyes* are obliquely placed in the skull. Eyes are brown, almond shaped and of medium size. Dark eyes are preferred. *Blue eyes are a disqualifying fault.*

The *ears* are of medium size, but small in proportion to the head. The ears are triangular in shape and slightly rounded at the tips. They are set wide apart on the outside back edges of the skull on line with the upper corner of the eye, giving ears the appearance, when erect, of standing off from the skull. Erect ears point slightly forward, but when the dog is at work, the ears are sometimes folded against the skull. High set ears are a fault.

The *skull* is broad and moderately rounded between the ears, gradually narrowing and flattening on top as it approaches the eyes, rounding off to cheeks that are moderately flat. There is a slight furrow between the eyes. The topline of the skull and the topline of the muzzle show a slight break downward from a straight line as they join.

Ch. Kaila's Son of A Witch exhibits a nice profile, correct stop, dark pigment, tight flews, and eyes that are correctly placed with the corner right at the bottom of the ear. Breeder/Owners, Chris and Eileen Gabriel.

*Right: A head with too much stop.
Drawing by Linda Duke.*

COMMENTS

The Malamute's head immediately distinguishes him from other Northern breeds. His expression is soft, never harsh or unfriendly, and comes from his lovely brown eyes, their almond shape and oblique placement. While the eyes can be varying shades of brown, the preferred color is dark brown. Yellow eyes detract from the softness of expression and black eyes are too hard. Not only are round, protruding eyes unattractive, they are more likely to be damaged by Arctic weather.

While the standard uses the word "medium" to describe the size of both the ears and eyes, this term is relative to those found in Northern dogs, since the extremities of all Arctic species are small to protect against heat loss and frostbite. The Malamute's ears should be smaller in proportion to his head than those of the Siberian Husky, for instance, but both are considerably smaller than a German Shepherd's. The ideal Malamute ear is no longer than 3-4 inches in length from the tip to the outer attachment. The thick ear leather should not fall or wobble as the dog stands or gaits. Ear set is important to the Malamute's appearance. They are widely set with the lower, outside edge in line with the outside corner of the eye. They should never be set atop the skull nor will they be parallel to each other. A dog may fold his ears back when working or to show

amiability, especially so in females and puppies.

The head is shaped like a broad wedge and is never coarse, overdone, fine or snipey. Fashioned as one piece, like the wolf's, the head has little break from skull to muzzle. Thus, the stop is relatively slight. Too abrupt or sharp a stop results in incorrect eye placement and shape. Likewise, too little stop makes the eyes too close together. The muzzle is bulky and tapers only slightly; too much makes it snipey. It should be the same length as the skull.

Some dogs lose pigment on the inner lip with age; however, the outer lips, nose, and eye-rims are black (liver in reds), never pink. A center stripe of lighter pigment on the nose is a "snow nose" and is acceptable but is not at all the same thing as an unpigmented nose.

The lips should be close-fitting, since this is also a weather adaptation, as is the slight dewlap and the padded appearance of the head. That the Inuit removed the dog's teeth to keep them from chewing has nothing to do with today's dog. The tendency toward missing teeth is inherited, and full dentition and a scissors bite should be encouraged. There should be 6 upper and 6 lower incisors; 2 upper and 2 lower canines; 4 upper and 4 lower premolars on each side; 2 upper molars and 3 lower molars on each side, for a total of 20 teeth in the upper jaw and 22 in the lower jaw.

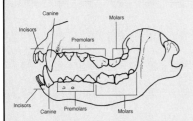

Drawing by Nancy Robinson.

The *muzzle* is large and bulky in proportion to the size of the skull, diminishing slightly in width and depth from junction with the skull to the nose. In all coat colors, except reds, the *nose, lip, and eye rim pigmentation* is black. Brown is permitted in red dogs. The lighter streaked "snow nose" is acceptable. The lips are close fitting.

The upper and lower jaws are broad with large *teeth*. The incisors meet with a scissors' grip. Overshot or undershot is a fault.

Left: The correct eye and ear set. Drawing by Eugene Terryn.

Below: A beautiful head study of a bitch, Ch. Uyak Indian Inez, ROM, bred by Dr. Harold Schwatzapfel and owned by Terry Sewell. Photo by Krook.

NECK, TOPLINE, BODY—

The neck is strong and moderately arched. The chest is well developed. The body is compactly built but not short coupled. The back is straight and gently sloping to the hips. The loins are hard and well muscled. A long loin that may weaken the back is a fault. The tail is moderately set and follows the line of the spine at the base. The tail is carried over the back when not working. It is not a snap tail or curled tight against the back, nor is it short furred like a fox brush. The Malamute tail is well furred and has the appearance of a waving plume.

Ch. Sendaishi's Kandu Can-Do, ROM. Breeder/Owners, Bill and Joyce Matott.

Ch. Midnight Sun's Winter Love, ROM. Breeder/owner, Tracy Young. Yuhl photo.

COMMENTS

A dog with a good shoulder will have enough length of neck to present a pleasing arch when viewed from the side. A neck that appears too short results from a too straight front which reduces the dog's efficiency, as does a shallow chest. Well-developed lungs are essential to satisfy the oxygen demands of an endurance animal.

On the other hand, the chest should not be so broad that it displaces the elbows or weakens the front. From the side, the forechest should be visible, although care should be taken to assure that it is chest and not coat. Without a properly defined forechest, the front assembly cannot be correct.

As with all Arctic denizens, the Malamute has a compact body. While the back should be fairly short, the loin must be long enough to permit easy tireless movement and flexibility but not so long that it is weak.

The ideal tail will curl nicely over the back and touch the topline with a waving tip. A perfect tail may drop when the dog is hot, tired, bored, or unhappy and should be taken as an expression of mood rather than a poor tail so long as the correct carriage is assumed when the dog gaits. When working, dogs often have a trailing tail, where it is carried out behind them just below the level of the topline.

Many show dogs have been trained to carry their heads up or do so as the result of poor shoulders. Working dogs will lower their heads as they trot and should never be penalized for this head carriage.

The Malamute topline slopes gently. This is never a steep, downward exaggeration. When gaiting, the topline should be firm and stable without a side-to-side roll. Poor toplines indicate weakness and must be penalized.

COMMENTS

Proper shoulders ensure adequate reach during movement. The shoulder blade (scapula) and upper arm (humerus) should be of equal length, although many of today's dogs suffer from a short upper arm. A proper front, when present, should be rewarded.

The forelegs appear as straight, parallel columns from the front and must not turn out at the pasterns. Of the Northern dogs, Malamutes have the heaviest bone; however, this description should be taken in the context of comparison with other Northern Dogs and not all dogs generally. Excessive bone makes a dog ponderous and clumsy; a Malamute should never resemble the giant breeds such as the St. Bernard or Newfoundland, who have truly heavy bone. Creative grooming may make bone appear larger, so the foreleg must actually be felt to check size.

Although they have a slight slope for flexibility, pasterns bent any more will weaken the stride. Since they serve as shock absorbers for the forequarter, in a dog the size of a Malamute, weak pasterns will eventually break down. Completely upright pasterns usually accompany a straight shoulder.

An old adage says, "Sled dogs are built from the ground up," meaning that good feet are essential for performance. The foot is always deep and compact with highly-muscled toes. To some extent, all dogs pick up some snow in their feet which melts from their body heat and then refreezes forming ice balls that can injure the foot. No space should be visible between the toes, as splayed feet foster this problem. Snowshoes are preferable to high heels for walking in snow. Just as the size of a snowshoe distributes weight over a larger area, reduces pressure and helps a person stay atop the snow, larger feet better suit the Malamute's function than tiny cat-feet.

FOREQUARTERS—

The shoulders are moderately sloping; forelegs heavily boned and muscled, straight to the pasterns when viewed from the front. Pasterns are short and strong and slightly sloping when viewed from the side. The feet are of the snowshoe type, tight and deep, with well-cushioned pads, giving a firm, compact appearance. The feet are large, toes tight fitting and well arched. There is a protective growth of hair between the toes. The pads are thick and tough; toenails, short and strong.

Below, left: correct snowshoe foot. Below right: incorrect feet, the one of the left is splayed, the one on the right is a short, round cat-foot.

Bottom: correct and incorrect fronts. Drawings by Tracy Pounds.

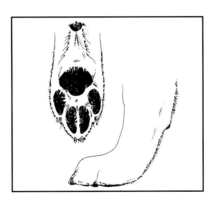 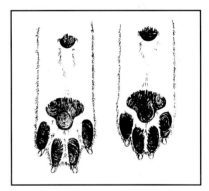

Good front   Toeing in   Toeing out

HINDQUARTERS—

The rear legs are broad and heavily muscled through the thighs; stifles moderately bent; hock joints are moderately bent and well let down. When viewed from the rear, the legs stand and move true in line with the movement of the front legs, not too close or too wide. Dewclaws on the rear legs are undesirable and should be removed shortly after puppies are whelped.

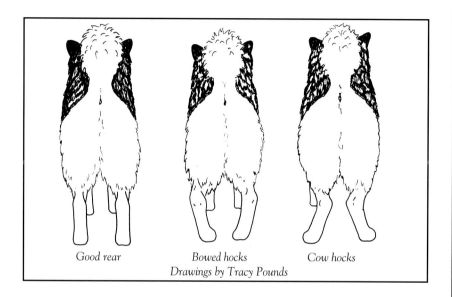

Good rear   Bowed hocks   Cow hocks
Drawings by Tracy Pounds

COAT—

The Malamute has a thick, coarse guard coat, never long and soft. The undercoat is dense, from one to two inches in depth, oily and woolly. The coarse guard coat varies in length as does the undercoat. The coat is relatively short to medium along the sides of the body, with the length of the coat increasing around the shoulders and neck, down the back, over the rump, and in the breeching and plume. Malamutes usually have a shorter and less dense coat during the summer months. The Malamute is shown naturally. Trimming is not acceptable except to provide a clean cut appearance of feet.

COMMENTS

The muscling called for elsewhere is echoed in the hind legs. The croup has a gentle slope and is neither steep nor flat. Like the shoulder and upper arm, the upper and lower thighs should be equal in length and should meet at the same angle so that the dog moves with balance. A well let-down hock aids the powerful drive needed in the rear. From the rear, the legs are parallel and perpendicular to the ground when standing. Cowhocks and toeing out are faults.

The texture, composition, and quality of the coat are critical for the Malamute's survival. The outer coat is comparatively harsh with a soft, wooly undercoat. Too harsh a guard coat will result in coat that stands-off, opening the undercoat to weather, while a too-soft guard coat regardless of length, allows penetration by ice, snow, and water. A soft coat that is too long (woolly) is doubly undesirable, and a dog with no undercoat unless the result of seasonal shed, is unthinkable.

Along the sides, the coat is about 1-1/2 inches long, but on the back, rump and tail, this increases to 3 to 4 inches, although females usually have less coat than males. Any attempt to artificially texturize a too-soft coat or to disguise a too-long coat by trimming is unacceptable. Trimming is allowed only to neaten the feet.

A long-coated adult. Woolie coats often lack the correct, harsh texture.

This cute long-coated puppy will make a wonderful pet.

COMMENTS

The standard has been changed with each revision to include some marking and color variations members consider novel and attractive. The latest revision adds red and sable, but still does not address blues.

Regardless of color, the markings of the Malamute contribute to his distinctive appearance. They are typically and ideally symmetrical. Asymmetrical white markings that extend unevenly into the margins of the color and/or white splashes in the color should be penalized.

Since the Malamute is a dog who works for a living, soundness of gait is critical; he is a superbly athletic endurance dog. Movement is effortless with no wasted motion up or down or side to side. His powerful rear drive thrusts him forward and is matched by a complementary reach. If the Malamute's front and rear assemblies meet the criteria set down in the standard, he will never crab, overreach, or interfere.

From the front, the legs reach forward straight and true with no lateral movement at the pasterns, no wobbly elbows, and no paddling feet. From the rear, the strong propelling drive is apparent. The rear pads should be just visible as the dog's leg moves backwards. Pads that face the sky before coming forward for the next step are a sign of excessive follow-through. While this movement might seem quite dazzling, it is inefficient and wastes energy. Whether fore or aft, movement is neither close nor wide, converging instead towards the center as speed increases. Any deviation from soundness and effortless gait must be seriously faulted.

A Malamute moving around the show ring may display an extended trot. While this is eye-catching, it is hardly typical of a working sled dog. Balance and power are more important than exaggerated speed and suspension.

COLOR—

The usual colors range from light gray through intermediate shadings to black, sable, and shadings of sable to red. Color combinations are acceptable in undercoat, points, and trimmings. The only solid color allowable is all white. White is always the predominant color on underbody, parts of legs, feet, and part of face markings. A white blaze on the forehead and/or collar or a spot on the nape is attractive and acceptable. The Malamute is mantled, and broken colors extending over the body or uneven splashing are undesirable.

GAIT—

The gait of the Malamute is steady, balanced, and powerful. He is agile for his size and build. When viewed from the side, the hindquarters exhibit strong rear drive that is transmitted through a well-muscled loin to the forequarters. The forequarters receive the drive from the rear with a smooth reaching stride. When viewed from the front or from the rear, the legs move true in line, not too close or too wide. At a fast trot, the feet will converge toward the centerline of the body. A stilted gait, or any gait that is not completely efficient and tireless, is to be penalized.

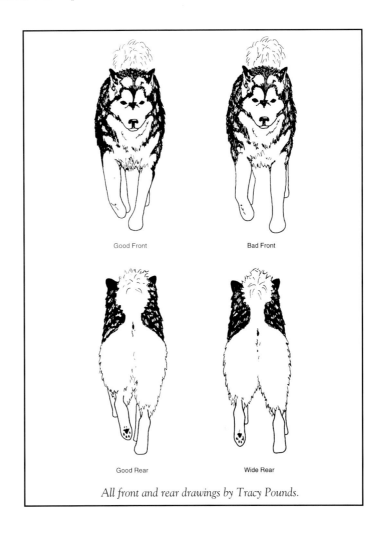

Good Front   Bad Front

Good Rear   Wide Rear

All front and rear drawings by Tracy Pounds.

Above: Ch. Mushateer's Lewis Moon, ROM, displays the balance of movement so essential to endurance in harness. Owner, Chris Fallas Cameron.

Right: Ch. J. Allen Yukon Hug a Wolf shows great economy of motion, which also contributes to endurance. The legs form a straight column of support from upper arm to foot. Owner, Billie Stewart. Cynde Johnson photo.

Below: The slightly sloping topline of Ch. Toalan's Flying Colours adds to the powerful thrust of this Malamute's rear. The photo shows excellent balance and coordination, making this a picture of perfect side gait. Breeder/owner, Ron Pohl, Canada.

COMMENTS

Although the Malamute some-times demonstrates dominance over other dogs by aggressive behavior, he should always be friendly and gentle with people. Any sign of aggression towards people is unacceptable. A Mal is not a guard dog that warns of a stranger's approach by growling or snarling. Dogs with such behav-ior do not exhibit correct, typical temperament, and certainly should not be permitted in the show ring.

The Malamute in its correct form is a marvel of efficiency. While he is well-muscled and more-heavily developed than his other Northern cousins, he is never an overblown cartoon nor is he is a slow, clumsy, plodder.

Soundness of limb and move-ment are vital to the Malamute's function. When interpreting the standard, as much emphasis must be given to the attributes of soundness as to those describing substantial build. Throughout the standard in varying forms, the three words used most often to describe the Alaskan Malamute are strong, powerful, and sound.

TEMPERAMENT—

The Alaskan Malamute is an affectionate, friendly dog, not a "one man" dog. He is a loyal, devoted companion, playful in invitation, but generally impressive by his dignity after maturity.

SUMMARY

IMPORTANT: In judging Malamutes, their function as a sledge dog for heavy freighting in the Arctic must be given consideration above all else. The degree to which a dog is penalized should depend upon the extent to which the dog deviates from the description of the ideal Malamute and the extent to which the particular fault would actually affect the working ability of the dog. The legs of the Malamute must indicate unusual strength and tremendous pro-pelling power. Any indication of unsoundness in legs and feet, front or rear, standing or moving, is to be considered a serious fault. Faults under this provi-sion would be splay-footedness, cowhocks, bad pasterns, straight shoulders,

Ch. Frostfield New Expectations, owned by Wendy Willhauck. Ashbey photo.

lack of angulation, stilted gait (or any gait that isn't balanced, strong and steady), ranginess, shallowness, ponderousness, lightness of bone, and poor over-all proportion.

Disqualification:

Blue Eyes

FOREIGN STANDARDS

Since the Alaskan Malamute originated in the United States, most countries simply translate our Standard directly, as does the international show organization, the Federation Cynoloiges Internationale (FCI). Differences usually center around the issue of size.

In response to pressure from members, France and the United Kingdom increased the range for height and weight. In the UK, The Kennel Club Standard has a range for males of from 25 to 28 inches; and the females, 23 to 26 inches, as does the Australian Standard. However, at least one club there, the Alaskan Malamute Club of Victoria, has adopted the American Standard.[4]

Am. Can. Ch. Williwaw's Sunbear of Targhee, ROM, winner of thirteen BIS and nine BISS awards. He has a full mask as well as a necklace. Notice the excellent set to his well-furred ears and his very dark pigment. He is the sire of Am. Can Ch. Williwaw's Seahawk O Targhee, ROM. Breeder/owners, Al and Mary Jane Holabach.

MALAMUTE COLORS

Describing color is always difficult, especially when terminology is not consistent from breed to breed.[5] In one breed, one basic color with a variety of shadings might have a separate name for each shade, while in another, all such shades might be lumped into one category. For instance, a dog described as "brown" in one breed might be fawn, champagne, silver-beige, cream, biscuit, toast, mahogany or red in another. Also, several factors contribute to the overall appearance of the dog's color.

FACTORS CONTRIBUTING TO COAT COLOR

Guard Hair—Coat color description begins with the guard hair. Alaskan Malamutes have three basic colors of guard hair: black—each hair is black from the tip to the base; agouti[6]—the individual hairs are black at the tip and barred in several bands of brownish or blackish shading to the base; white—hair is white from tip to base, although the shade of white can vary from ice-white to cream or biscuit.

Other colors present in this breed are blue and the color called red in Malamutes (also Siberian Huskies and Doberman Pinschers) but liver in others (Spaniels, Dalmatians, Poodles). Reds are seen much more frequently than blues.

Undercoat—Because it is oily and of softer texture, the undercoat color appears different from the guard coat just as silk and wool of the same color look different. Its color may be similar to or different from the guard hair.

Markings—The colored guard hair and undercoat cover the back and sides, forming a "mantle," which is always bordered by white markings (points). These are found in varying amounts on the legs, feet, underbody, and face and may vary from a bright white to an ivory.

The only solid color allowed is white. Irregular white markings typical of the marking pattern known as pinto[7] may appear in the breed. Since these are not typical, perpetuation of such mismarks is strongly discouraged by the standard. Malamutes should have symmetrical markings.

Trimmings—Accompanying the markings, undercoat, and guard hair colors may be what are called "trimmings." Found in various shades of brown, these are usually around the margins of the color and frequently extend into the markings.

COLOR DESCRIPTION

The terms used to describe coat color are actually the sum of these individual factors. The perception of overall color provided by the undercoat, trimmings, and guard hair determines how the dog's color is described.

Because the AKC registration application requires a color description, the AMCA attempted to clarify color descriptions in 1993. It wants to properly describe every color present in the breed and have it accurately depicted on the dog's individual registration certificate.[8] (See Table 1.)

AGOUTI COLOR

When a fabric is woven from different-colored threads for the warp and woof, the human eye perceives an overall color different from either of the component ones. In an agouti dog, the color bands have a similar effect, so that the perceived color of the dog depends on several factors. Among them are the extent of the black at the tip, the colors of the other bands and how they are distributed, and the color and presence of the undercoat.

All Malamutes except for the black and the solid white are agouti in color, although such variation in appearance results that these dogs are referred to as silver, wolf-gray, and seal. The wolf-sable is an agouti dog with the addition of brown trimmings.

Silver is the lightest of the agouti shades. Wolf-gray falls in the middle, while seal is the darkest. In the seal, black extends well down each hair shaft. Seals often show a dorsal stripe when they are puppies, and the hair on the back retains much more extension of black down the shaft than the hair on the sides and front even in the adult.

Some breeders distinguish further between seals depending upon the color or the bands on the guard hairs and the color of the undercoat when it is present. Some appear so dark as to be almost black while others are almost brown. So many gradations appear in this color that it defies one or two word descriptors, and the fullness of the dog's coat and undercoat will make his color vary from season to season.

BLACK AND SEAL

Black Malamutes have guard hairs black from bottom to top. The undercoat is usually a very dark charcoal color; whereas, seals have a lighter undercoat which can vary from dark cream to white. Dark seals and blacks may be quite similar in summer coat, but are easily distinguishable in the winter. Since banded hairs are stiffer than solid

TABLE I. Coat Color

Color	Description
	BODY COLOR
Black	Black guard hair with black or dark gray undercoat.
Alaskan Seal	Black or black-tipped guard hairs with white or cream undercoat. Dog appears black at a distance, but is not a true black because of the light undercoat.
Wolf Sable	Black or gray guard hairs with a reddish undercoat and red trimmings. Both black and red factors evident.
Wolf Gray	Gray guard hairs with light gray, cream, or white undercoat. Dog definitely appears gray even though there may be some black hairs on the topline. No red factor evident.
Silver	Light gray guard hairs with white undercoat.
Red	A definite shade of red. Either light or dark, with liver lips and nose and light eye color. No black factor evident.
Blue	An off-black or bluish-charcoal color. Eye color may be affected. No black factor evident.
White	Both guard hairs and undercoat are white. Often evidence of a mask in cream color. Only solid color allowed.

TRIMMINGS

Shades of gold, cream, buff, brown, or reddish hues often found on legs, ears, tail, and face between white areas of the underbody and the dark color above.

FACE MARKINGS

Cap	A cap of color covers the top of the head and the ears, usually coming to a point in the center of the forehead.
Goggles	Dark areas under the eyes, extending sideways to the cap.
Bar	A dark area extending from the center point of the cap down the nose.
Eye Shadow	Dark markings under the eyes which do not extend out to the cap.
Star	A small white spot in the center of the forehead.
Blaze	A white mark extending from the center point of the cap back up the forehead. Width and length can vary.
Closed Face	A cap covering the head with no other markings on the face.
Full Mask	Combination of cap, goggles, and bar.
Mask	Combination of cap and goggles.

CHEST MARKINGS

Necklace	Curving band of dark color across the chest.
Eagle	Two bands of dark color protruding partially across the chest forming a pattern resembling the eagle emblem.

NECK MARKINGS

Collar	White band of color encircling the neck.
Withers Spot	White mark varying in size but centered at the withers or at the base of the neck.

A Rainbow of Malamute Colors

This lovely watercolor of Ch. Windrift's Nakoah, a multiple BIS and BISS winner owned by Richard and Barbara Brooks, was painted by Linda Duke.

Right: The open face of Am. Can. Ch. Storm Kloud's Corner The Market, WTD, WWPDX contributes to his lovely, soft expression. Weight pull winner at the 1997 National. Breeder/owner, Nancy Russell.

Below: A silver and white female, Ch. Kaila's Second Sight, has a feminine appearance that says "Make no mistake, I'm a girl." Breeder/owners, Chris and Eileen Gabriel.

Top: Ch. Kee-Too's Kijik Kougarok is a black seal. Breeder/owner, Linton and Kay Moustakis.
Bottom: Ch. Chena's Ain't She Sweet is a brown Alaskan seal. Breeder/owners, Sel and Joanne Levy.

Ch. Chena's Magic Wand shows a full mask, goggles and bar. Note the small, well-furred, correct ears and stand-off, brown seal coat color. Owner/breeders, Sel and Joanne Levy.

Left, top to bottom:

Ch. Artic Luv's Bear Bright Blade owned by Bernadette Quercio is a striking red mahogany with a full mask. Color affects coat texture; his appears nicely harsh.

Wolf sables have reddish brown in their coats, but have black pigment. Ch. Alki Polar Panzer owned by Terry Sewell, like many dogs of his color, has cream markings rather than white. Head markings include a bar and eye shadow.

Ch. Tanunka's Dakota Chief, CGC, a brilliant red, is one of only two red Mals to win a Group First. (The other was Ch. Alcan's Jack O'Diamonds.) Breeders, Susan Richardson and Dian McComb; Owner, Susan Richardson.

Ch. Bar-B-R'S-TIC Frosty, CD, was the second white champion and the only dual-titled white in the U.S. Dogs of this quality should not be ignored because of their color. Breeder, Barbara Baxter; Owner, Susan Ruff.

Below: Can. Ch. Kipmik's Driving Force, a gray, is shown winning a Group 4. Breeder/Owner, Adele MacGillivray. Alex Smith photo.

Top left: The white haw and the pink splotches over the nose suggest that this dog might produce unevenly marked or mismarked offspring if bred to a mate with similar indicators. The best choice of mate would be a Mal with even markings, dark haws, and black pigment. Photo courtesy Mormont De Henau.

Top right: Tricolor occurs so rarely in the breed that it is not even mentioned in the Standard. Wolfpack Nikkienookabear. Owner, Mr. Fourie, South Africa.

Center left: Lack of sunlight caused the decreased pigment or "snow nose." Ch. Windrift's Cajun Queen O'Sabaka regains her normal dark pigment in summer. Owners, Mike and Jackie Consentino.

Center right: Blue is not mentioned in the Standard, but it does exist. The coat is dark to slate gray and the pigment charcoal gray. Photo courtesy Linda Birmantas.

Below: A true black and white often does not have the stand-off coat. Ch. Kiwalik's Vykon Indiana Jones, CD, ROM, sire of 20 champions. Owner Vicky Jones.

Markings Make Each Mal Unique

Am. Can. Ch. Poker Flat's Yukon Law, WTD, ROM, is a lovely wolf gray with an open face, cap and star, and a broken necklace. Note his nicely rounded ear tips, soft expression, and black pigment. This excellent representative of Malamute type was the 1996 National Specialty Best of Breed. Breeder/owner, Robin Haggard. Co-owners Kathy Stortzum and Brendan McKiernan, DVM. Photo by Pet Care Plus.

Above left: These are very controversial markings. The white around the neck is clearly a shawl rather than a collar since it extends behind the withers. The white extending up from the legs and belly to connect with the shawl makes the dog predominantly white. Whether these markings should be faulted, and to what degree, is not really clear from the Standard. Ch. Wahkeen's Chrome Plated Caddy, bred by Linda Allen. Cott photo.

Above right: Ch. Kiwalik's Snowbear of Kipnuk, ROM, is another top winning sable. He is open faced with a beautiful head, well-set ears, proper tail carriage, and a slightly sloping topline Breeder, Shelton Sewell; Owner, Ken Hyatt.

Right: The width of topskull, well-furred, correctly shaped and set ears, broad muzzle, and very dark pigment on this dog more than make up for his eyes, which are slightly round. He has a full mask with slightly lighter shading than his very dark coat markings. Ch. Chena's T'Dawkins of Kanutoak, bred by Sel and Joanne Levy. Photo by Sel Levy.

Face Markings: Left, Because this dog's face markings extend into his cap, they are technically considered goggles. Cold Valley's Quot Erat Kinuk. Owner, Mario Van Alebeek.

Center: This dog has faint eye shadow and a narrow blaze. Note the correct eyeset. Am. Can Ch. Kipoo's Icy Karhma. Owner, Carol Williams.

Below right: A distinct bar with a little eye shadow accompany a deep cap. The color necklace rests above eagle chest markings. Owner, Herman Nicole.

Am. Can. Ch. Oopik's I'm a Warrior TOO is a black and white with a full mask, full goggles, bar, and very dark eyes. Breeder, Lorna Muir; Owner, Lynda Birmantis. True black and white Mals are not as common as dark seals.

The contrast of white coat with very dark eyes and pigment contributes to the appeal of Poker Flat's Easy Living. Owner, Hiram Daitch. Most white dogs have biscuit or off-white shading, which should not be penalized.

Below: Am. Can Ch. Inuit's Sweet Lucifer, Am.Can.ROM, Am. Can. Ob-ROM, was the winner of thirteen specialties, including two Nationals, and a very influential sire. Breeder, Sheila Land; Owner, Sheila Balch.

black hairs, the coat of a black dog will tend to lie flat while an almost-black seal's coat will stand out.

BLUE AND LIVER (RED)

Blue is not addressed in the current color listing, but it also does occur. Unless they are compared in good lighting, distinguishing a blue dog from a black can be as hard as separating navy blue and black socks. However, a blue can be easily identified by inspecting the nose, lips, eyerims, and pads. Instead of the normal black, these will be dark bluish-charcoal rather than black. Likewise, a "red" will have liver pigment in these areas.

RED (BROWN)

A lot of confusion has been created in Malamutes because the term "red" has been used interchangeably to describe both liver and the brown color found in the wolf sable. Coat color formed from brown pigment has a different chemical composition from that formed by black pigment and is unaffected by either the blue or black genes. It is genetically and chemically different from liver pigment and can be anything from mahogany to buff.

Brown (red) is found in the trimmings of the wolf sable. It may be confined to a few areas or extend into the mantle. Distinguishing between the two colors called red is quite easy. Red (livers) will also have red (liver) noses, eye-rims, and pads, while those of the wolf sable will be black.

COLOR IN THE SHOW RING

Ideally, a judge should recognize that the standard offers great leeway regarding coat color. However, in the real world, a judge is more likely to ignore the standard's restrictions on the distribution and pattern of the white markings than to acknowledge a white dog of quality. Because they are the most common colors, grays and seals naturally fit most people's image of the Malamute, and judges are not immune to being comfortable with the familiar.

While some very fine representatives of the breed have been red and have had very successful show careers, even their most enthusiastic supporters will agree that showing reds can be an uphill struggle. Although a good white dog should be just as acceptable as a gray, their almost total absence from the ring speaks for itself.

Among show breeders, what are called "mismarks" are somewhat controversial. On the one hand, some breeders feel that a "good dog cannot be a bad color" and accept a wide range of markings, including half-collars and very asymmetrical face and leg markings. The strictest consider any asymmetrical markings and collars unacceptable even though the standard allows them.

Part of the problem arises from the standard's failure to set limits on the extent of white. For instance, if the collar extends back over the withers so that it is really a shawl, is that considered a mismark? If a white spot on the nape of the neck extends up between the ears and below the withers, is that a "spot" or a "splash?" The interpretation is left up to the individual.

Even the most vehement detractors of mismarks, however, would agree that these markings have no bearing whatsoever on the dog's value as a worker or pet. In fact, such a cosmetic defect may provide the pet buyer with an opportunity to purchase an otherwise outstanding puppy which might have remained with the breeder or been sold to a show home.

ENDNOTES

1.   Will Steger and Jon Bowermaster. *Crossing Antarctica.* (New York: Alfred A. Kopf, 1992), 235-6.

2.   Steger, 98-9.

3.   Any knowledgeable person should be able to tell whether an individual dog is a Malamute or a Siberian. If the differences are not apparent, the dog has very poor breed type. A Malamute that resembles a Siberian Husky is not a good Malamute and vice versa.

4.   Wilma Livingston, Traralgon, Victoria, Australia, personal communication.

5.   Having Spira's *Canine Terminology* as a common reference source makes this slightly less confusing.

6.   This color takes its name from a rodent species in which the individual hairs are banded with black and various other lighter shades.

7.   Many breeds have a pinto marking pattern which may also be called pied or piebald. Among them are the Siberian Husky, Akita, Greyhound, Pointer, many spaniels and hounds. This is distinct from an extreme white or extreme piebald (a dog predominately white with spots of color remaining about the head, ears, tail, and/or back. The Bull Terrier and Great Pyrenees are examples of this marking pattern.)

8.   Among the AKC color choices was "brown"—actually fawn like a boxer. Such a Malamute would represent a throwback to outside dogs like the Mackenzie River Husky, some of which were behind very early M'Loot dogs. Neither author has seen a brown Malamute.

Ch. Echo's Simply Snazzy is impeccably groomed with every hair separated. She is one of the top-winning bitches in the history of the breed. Owned by Dian McComb. Photo © Warren and Vicky Cook.

7

GROOMING YOUR MALAMUTE

Grooming for a show is more detailed than that required for upkeep, but all grooming is easier if the dog has a naturally correct coat with a thick undercoat and coarse, but not brittle, guard hairs of proper length. Proper nutrition, regular grooming, and freedom from parasites are essential if you want your Mal to have a good coat. Fancy grooming techniques can improve the look of a poor coat, but nothing compares to the beauty of a healthy, genetically correct one.

A basic grooming regimen will help to keep your dog healthy and happy. Just a few additions will get him ready for the show ring. The Alaskan Malamute is a natural breed, and he should not be altered or artificially changed in any way.

EQUIPMENT

Although you can get by with just a minimum of equipment if you are not showing your dog, investing in the right tools will make grooming a pleasure, and by purchasing a few additional items you can make your dog look his best for visitors, photo sessions, or special occasions.

Essential equipment includes at least one spray bottle, several brushes and combs, nail clippers, a tooth brush, shampoo, and perhaps a coat conditioner. A pair of good trimming shears will be helpful.

SPRAY BOTTLES

Large spray bottles that hold at least a quart, plus a few smaller bottles, are used to mist or wet the dog before brushing. They also help conserve supplies, especially shampoo, by directing a concentrated amount just where it is needed.

This section was prepared with the generous help of Peggy Hemus (Pegini), who took the closeup grooming series photos, Linda Allen and Al Holabach, who groomed for the photos, and Jerry, Linda, and Tacy Sommersett.

BRUSHES

At least two or three brushes are a must. The flat-backed brush with slightly bent metal tines known as a slicker works well for leg and tail hair, while a pin brush with straight metal or plastic tines set in a rubber backing is needed to get through the undercoat on the body. For baths, a large human nail brush will help scrub the shampoo into the coat. The Mason-Pearson brush is expensive, but its natural boar bristles are easy on the guard hairs, yet strong enough to penetrate the thick undercoat, making it an excellent choice for show grooming.

COMBS

You will need two metal combs: a 7-inch long greyhound or Resco comb with 1-inch teeth, and a 4-inch-long comb with 2-inch teeth to get through the undercoat to the skin. In addition, a teflon-coated rake will remove dead undercoat when regular combs quickly clog with fur.

NAIL CLIPPERS

Several tools are available for trimming toenails. Toenails clippers come in either the guillotine or scissor types; both are equally effective, but be sure to buy them for jumbo or extra large nails.

A Dremel or nail grinder is a small appliance that allows you to file the nail into a neater shape. Some dogs prefer the grinder over clippers; others object to the noise, although the battery-operated grinders are quieter.

SCISSORS

If you have to make do with only one pair of scissors, get curved ones with rounded tips. Otherwise, get a pair of flat shears eight to ten inches long as a second pair. Good quality shears are essential for show trimming, so purchase the best you can afford. Keep in mind that using scissors on wet hair will dull and rust them, so to help maintain their condition, be sure to clean them after each use and store them in a dry place. Scissors should be sharpened periodically by a professional.

Grooming supplies, left to right: trash bag, blow dryer, spray bottles, various brushes, scissors, tooth scaler, wet wipes, whitener, coat conditioner, chalk, waterless shampoo. Behind is a tack or grooming box. The lid holds assorted leashes. Supplies are sitting on a large grooming table.

TOOTHBRUSH AND SCALER

Many health problems in older dogs begin with poor dental care as youngsters. Teach your puppy to let you brush his teeth—you will save on veterinary expenses over the long run, your dog's breath will be fresher, and his teeth will be whiter. Special dog toothpastes are available to use with a toothbrush or with a washcloth over your finger.

Owners who are confident in handling their dog's mouth can purchase a tooth scaler at a pharmacy or dog supply shop. Ask an experienced handler or your veterinarian to show you how to use it properly to remove tartar from your dog's teeth. You must be careful not to cut the dog's gums when using a scaler.

DRYER

Another essential for showing is a forced-air livestock dryer (which really is not a dryer at all but a vacuum cleaner with the hose attached to the wrong end). If you're not showing, you may be able to utilize your household vacuum in exactly this way. Although air passes over the motor and is slightly warmed, the force of the air coming out of the nozzle actually blows the water out of the coat. It also blows out loose hair, debris, and any chalk you have around you, so be considerate and watch where you are aiming!

SHAMPOO

Use a shampoo that is especially formulated for dogs; their coat is different from human hair. For showing, you may want shampoos with optical brighteners for specific colors such as black, red, silver, or white.

Malamutes, especially those kept on concrete, may get stains around the elbows which are difficult to remove. Chemical bleaching results in porous hair that stains even more easily and may cause chemical burns to the dog's skin and/or hair breakage. Instead, try a combination of whitening shampoo and Clairol Metal-X™ shampoo, available at beauty supply stores. Never use Metal-X™ around the eyes, and be very careful not to get any in either the dog's or your own eyes.

SELF-RINSE SHAMPOO

Several brands of self-rinsing shampoo are available. It comes in very handy for emergency clean-ups or for general cleaning over several days of showing.

CONDITIONER

A conditioner should moisturize without softening, thus keeping the proper coat texture. To protect your dog's hair from sun damage, you can use a spray-on protein protectant with sunscreen. Black and red dogs are especially susceptible to sun-bleaching.

WHITENERS/GROOMING POWDER

Bathing a dog at a show is not always possible. On a dirt surface, in muddy weather, or over several days, the white areas of your dog's coat may need some help. Whiteners are available from vendors as powders or chalk blocks. Many products can be used, including cornstarch or baby powder, or a mixture of the two. If you try a new product, be sure you have seen it on another Malamute or test it well before the show. Surprises before you go in the ring are not good.

If you use chalk, you can also use Kolesterol hair dressing sold at beauty supply stores or a chalk helper available from show vendors or catalogs. All chalk must be brushed out before the dog enters the show ring.

GROOMING TABLE

A luxury for pet owners, a grooming table is essential for show exhibitors. Your back will thank you, and your improved access to the dog will help you to see things you might miss otherwise. You need one with a large surface and a height that suits your stature. Add a grooming arm that is tall enough to secure the dog while standing.

Until they learn to jump on and off, help by putting the dog's feet on the table . . .

. . . then lift or help him up. Linda Allen demonstrates.

Start teaching a puppy to stand on the grooming table while he is very young.

Secure his head to the grooming arm with the strap so he is reminded to stay on the table. Never leave a dog unattended. Pegini photos.

Clean, well-groomed dogs are a pleasure when you travel. (l. to r.) Royale's Solitaire, Tigara's Mountain Brier, and Tigara's Royale Sea Star wait for owner Barbara Alexander, Scotland.

WEEKLY HOME GROOMING

In the best of all possible worlds, you would clean your dog's teeth after every meal, just like your own. In reality, you probably will not manage this but you should brush them at least several times a week.

Malamutes should have strong nails for traction on the ice. Regular maintenance will keep nails at a proper length, although a Malamute with good feet that is kenneled on cement may keep his nails short without trimming. Trim off the tip of the nail. If you accidentally cut into the quick, styptic powder such as Kwik Stop™, available from pharmacies or dog show vendors, should quickly stop the bleeding. The styptic does sting, so be prepared for some discomfort on the dog's part. When properly trimmed, your dog's toenails should not quite touch the floor when he walks.

Many people are under the mistaken impression that a shedding coat can be kept if it is not brushed. Nothing is farther from the truth. In fact, new hair will not grow in until the old hair is out. Constantly removing the old coat stimulates new growth.

To help keep coat on a dog that is being campaigned, you should brush daily. This gives you a barometer as to when he will be totally out of coat while hastening the new coat's appearance. Dying coat is often brittle and easily broken, so as you brush, mist the coat with plain water or a mixture of water and a water-based conditioner, such as All Systems coat conditioner or Alpha Keri bath oil.

Two or three times a week, brush the coat vigorously back and forth, first against the lay of the hair and then with it, using a pin brush. A similar procedure will be used when preparing the dog for the show ring.

Keep the toenails clipped back to maintain a nice tight foot.

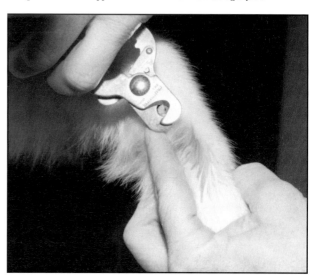

Don't forget to trim the front dewclaws, too.

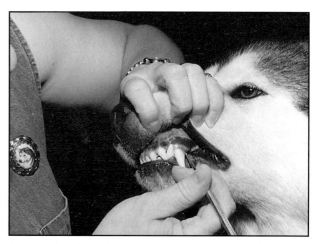

Use a tooth scaler to clean the teeth every two weeks. Pegini photos.

BATHING

Dogs that are brushed regularly will stay fairly clean. Still, when a dog is dirty, he needs a bath. Always comb your dog before you bathe him. When he is in a full-blown shed, the loose undercoat hair will need to be raked, brushed, and combed completely out before he is bathed. Shampoo collected in clumped hair may not rinse out, and the soapy clump will be sticky, attracting more hair, and eventually forming a mat. If your dog chews himself because the underlying skin is irritated, an oozing "hot spot" can result.

The logical place to bathe your dog is your bathtub, but a stock watering tub on a table works just as well. Or, as shown in the photos at right, in warm weather you can bathe your Malamute outside with a hose. Regardless of where you bathe the dog, the procedure is the same.

Thoroughly wet the dog with warm water. Spray shampoo on his coat and work it in with your hands, a wash cloth, or a small brush. Get the soap all the way to the skin and throughout the coat. You may have to rewet sections of coat as you shampoo.

Before a show, or if your dog is stained, wash all the white areas with whitening shampoo. (Using one on the colored coat will brighten it at first, but eventually the optical brighteners in it will cause fading.) Apply it to the white areas and let it sit while you shampoo the colored coat. Here you can use a regular shampoo, or one especially formulated for your dog's coat color.

Al Holabach's technique is the most efficient way to comb out a dog before bathing and also before a show. He separates the coat in layers and combs from the skin out before bathing the dog.

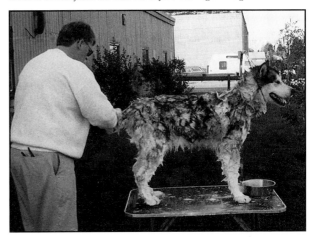

Al demonstrates how to bathe a dog in warm weather or if you don't have a tub. Place the dog on the grooming table. Wet him down with a hose and work in the shampoo.

Starting with a dog like this? Use a rake or comb to get the loose hair out. Follow with a good bath to loosen the rest.

Rinse thoroughly with the hose and allow him to shake.

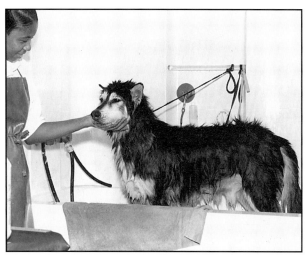

The first step in bathing is to thoroughly wet your dog. Here the dog is in a raised tub, with the lead fastened to a towel bar.

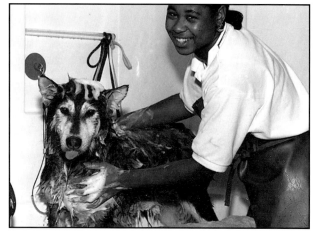

Work the soap into the coat so it penetrates the undercoat and reaches the skin. A brush is helpful on heavily-coated dogs. Keep the soap out of your dog's eyes. A drop of mineral oil in each eye will help protect against chemical burns.

Wash the entire dog, being careful in areas with delicate skin such as the scrotal and anal areas. Wash the face and under the chin, but never use the water full force on these areas or your dog will try to avoid this part of his bath.

CALLUSES

Large dogs often develop annoying red spots at pressure points where they lie or sit. Elbows and rear pasterns (the area from hock to foot) are the most commonly affected. First the area becomes red, then the hair wears off and a thick callus forms.

You can help prevent calluses by providing thick padding in the dog's crate or sleeping area. If red stains appear on the coat, start applying Vitamin E oil to the pressure spots on a daily basis. Prevention is better than trying to get rid of a callus after it forms.

A bare, crusty, callused area is quite unsightly. Treat a callus with Vitamin E oil as above. If ingrown hairs appear in the rubbed area, pluck them out so that normal outward hair growth can begin. It will take quite some time for a callus to be replaced by new hair growth.

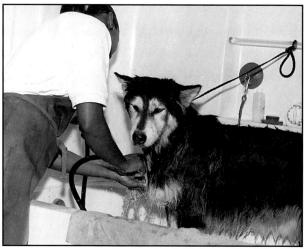

Be sure to rinse thoroughly. Soap left in the coat will irritate and make the coat gummy. Whitening or colored shampoo can be absorbed by the undercoat and leave a stain that is difficult to remove.

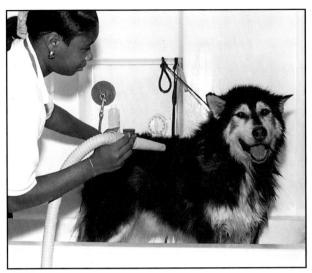

Drying the dog in the tub is quick and easy. Towel off excess water and begin blow-drying at the head and neck. To ensure your own safety, make certain that you are not wet or standing in water. If you are drying just before a show, you will probably want the dog on a grooming table for better access to his legs and feet.

Rinse thoroughly, using the brush again to help permeate the coat. Squeeze off the excess water with your hands, then let the dog down to shake, but keep him on leash or he will undo all your work in the nearest dirt pile.

DRYING

If you live in a damp, warm area, you *must* dry the dog after bathing or his undercoat will mildew. Constant dampness can cause skin irritation and coat loss. Using a blower to dry the dog also prevents the coat from matting or clumping.

For your own safety, move the table to a dry location, dry yourself off a bit, and put on dry shoes. Then plug in the dryer and systematically begin to blow your dog's coat dry, beginning at the neck and working downward.

When the dog is almost completely dry, brush him out as illustrated on the following pages.

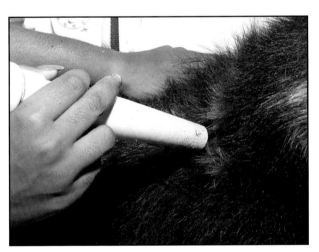

Left: Blow against the grain of the hair, paying particular attention to areas where the coat is thick. A forced-air dryer works better than your own hair dryer because heat makes the dog uncomfortable and will dry and damage the coat. If you must use a regular hair dryer, keep it on cool setting and move it around quickly to avoid burning the dog's skin. For safety reasons, never use a hand-held dryer around the tub.

Below left: Wet hair clumps together. As the dog dries the hair begins to fluff out. Before a show you should also brush the hair as it is dried. Brush all the way to the skin and into the undercoat.

Below right: Work down the back and sides. Dry the legs and feet last.

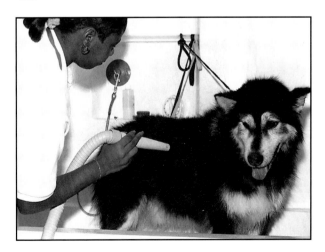

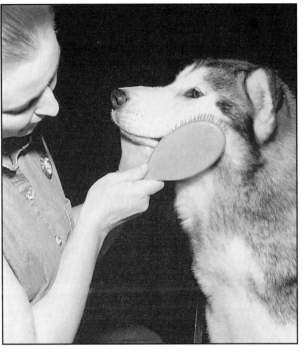

Begin brushing at the head and work back and down the dog, brushing against the lay of the hair. Linda Allen is using a pin brush.

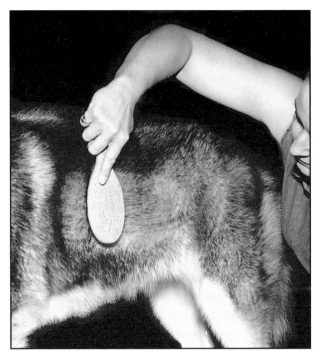

Brush the sides forward and up.

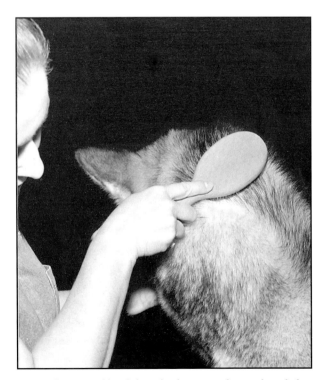

Section the coat and brush from the skin outward to get through the thick undercoat. This pulls the skin oils out onto the hair, hardening the coat.

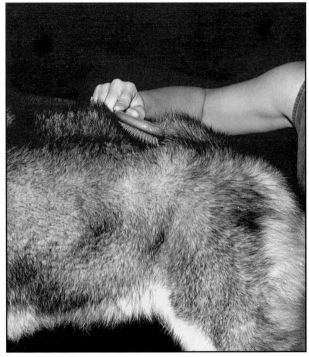

First, brush the hair on the top of the back up or forward. All photos on these two pages by Pegini.

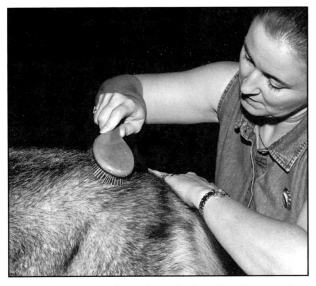

Above: Then smooth it down. If your dog has a lot of hair over the croup, or is a little high in the rear, you can brush or comb out some of the undercoat to improve the look of his topline. Lightly dampen the area and smooth it down with your hand.

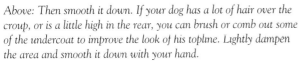

Above right: Get down to the skin, brushing outward on the breeches.

Below right: Then brush the hair back to finish up.

Below: End the session by brushing out the hair on the top and bottom sides of the tail until it stands outward in a plume.

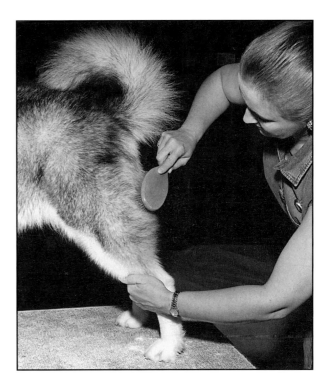

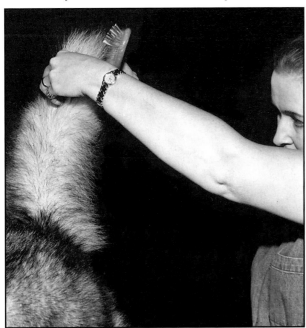

Grooming the Malamute

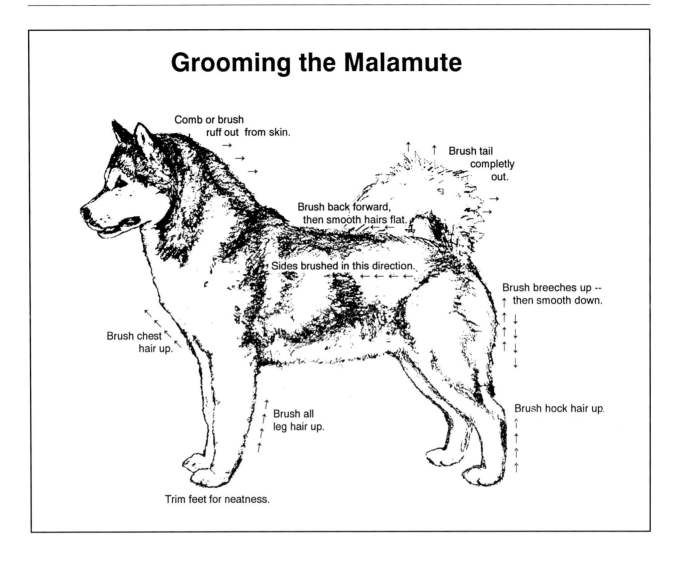

Comb or brush ruff out from skin.

Brush tail completly out.

Brush back forward, then smooth hairs flat.

Sides brushed in this direction.

Brush breeches up -- then smooth down.

Brush chest hair up.

Brush all leg hair up.

Brush hock hair up.

Trim feet for neatness.

SHOW GROOMING

Dogs going to a show should always be bathed the day before departure, unless the shows have bathing facilities on site. Under no circumstances should you ever bathe your dog at the hotel. Hotels that have to hire plumbers to clear hair-clogged drains after a dog show solve their problems by not renting to any people with dogs.

TRIMMING

After the dog is completely dry from his bath, his feet should be neatened. Sometimes dogs have such shaggy hair on the rear pastern that it obscures the outline of the leg. Even though the Standard only allows trimming of the feet, some people still neaten this. Trim only enough to show the straight outline of the leg, but not enough to detract from the appearance of heavy bone (See illustration).

Whiskers provide the dog with sensory information, and many people, both exhibitors and judges, prefer that they be left alone. Others like the cleaner, smoother look, and most dogs seem unaffected by their whiskerless condition. If you do trim whiskers, though, do a good job. Leaving the dog with half-inch prickles is the worst of both worlds. Battery-operated trimmers are easiest to use, but unless you are very careful, you can nick the skin, leaving very unattractive bare patches. If you shave whiskers, do it before the bath to get rid of those pesky hairs that the trimmer removes with the whiskers.

Dogs with hairy feet slide more when gaiting. You can improve traction by applying a rosin-like product (available from vendors) on your dog's pads. Be sure to apply it at ringside just before walking into the ring; otherwise, dust, loose hair, and chalk will stick to the dog's feet and make him more likely to slip.

TRIMMING

Linda Allen demonstrates trimming. Photos by Pegini.

Top left and center: Separate the toes and carefully trim away the hair. You can lift the front feet up. To trim the back feet, firmly grasp the foot and flex it so the pad faces upward.

Below left: Using a round-tipped scissors for safety, snip at the base of each whisker. Your dog will pull the whiskers back into his skin, so you will have to brush the whisker up and then catch it with the blade.

Below right: This dog's foot is now trimmed clean. If you want to neaten shaggy hair on the rear pastern, first brush the hair so it stands out. Then trim carefully, keeping a long, straight scissors perpendicular to the leg bone.

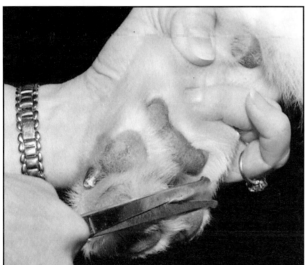

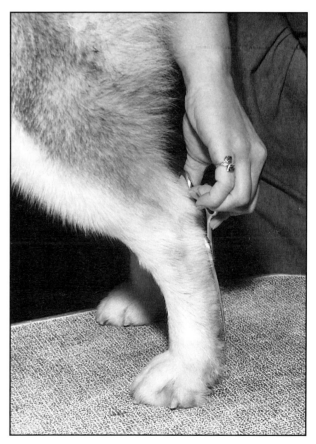

WHITENING

There are several methods to whiten your dog; use the one that works best for you and for the situation.

Method 1—The night before the show, or very early in the morning if you have adequate drying time, spray self-rinse shampoo or water on all of the white areas except the tail (it's too hard to get chalk out), wetting them thoroughly and working the moisture in evenly. Pack cornstarch, a mixture of cornstarch and baby powder, or a commercial grooming powder for medium-coarse hair into the *wet* coat. (If you've just finished bathing the dog, you can immediately pack his white areas and dry only his face and colored coat.) Work the powder down to the skin using your hands or a bristle brush (a cheap one, not your Mason Pearson). The final product should look like a flocked Christmas tree; if not, powder more. Put the dog in his crate until the powder dries. As it does, it will drop out of the coat. Be sure to clean out the crate before you put your groomed dog back inside.

Dogs cleaned this way have a special gleam to the white, and the hair looks and feels more natural. Be aware that if the air is really damp the mixture will not dry as well and will be very difficult to remove from the coat.

Method 2—To clean the entire dog when bathing facilities are not available, spray the entire coat thoroughly with self-rinse shampoo and rub it into the coat. Towel dry the dog and finish with the blow dryer. This will clean but not whiten the coat. Bathing is better, but this method is good in a pinch. After several uses the shampoo will leave a residue.

Method 3—Chalking will help whiten a dog, especially if his white is creamy. It also helps build up a sparse coat, giving the illusion of bone. While you do not have to use it, a chalk helper such as Kolestral or Chalk Mate helps hold the chalk in the coat while protecting the hair from its drying tendencies. You can use the same whitener mixture as in Method 1 or a large chalk block. Spray-on chalks do not work as well.

Regardless of which method you use, always practice at home to see how long it takes you to get the material out of the coat. The dog should not be ready too soon, yet you do not want to go racing up to the ring with clouds of chalk billowing out of your dog.

All signs of chalk and conditioners must be removed before your dog goes into the ring. If a judge goes over your dog and comes up with chalk on his hand, your dog will be excused from the ring, and all your effort will be wasted.

While chalking and when brushing out, your table should be covered with towels or newspapers so that the excess powder can be thrown away instead of flying everywhere. Using a soft bristle brush (again, not your Mason Pearson) or your slicker, begin brushing against the lay of the hair, loosening all the powder. When it all appears to be out, clean up your table. Then, use the blow-dryer to remove the residue that is still in the coat, checking the colored coat for wayward powder. When you are sure it is all out, tidy up the dog's toenails with a wet paper towel.

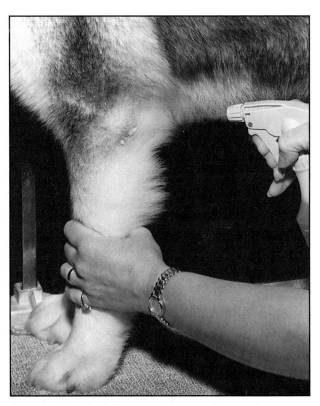

Spray the hair to be chalked with plain water. You can also use chalk helper. Rub it into the dog's legs, working upward against the grain of the hair. The elbow area needs special attention.

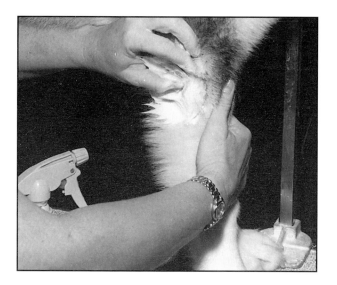

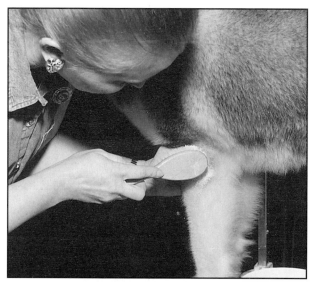

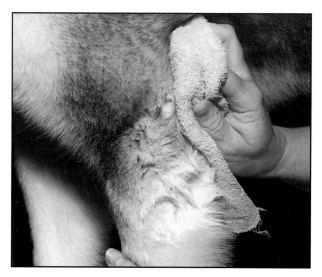

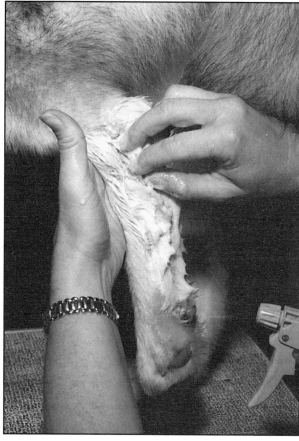

WHITENING

Left: Use either your hands, a soft brush dipped in powder, or a cloth to apply chalk to the moistened hair. Use an upward motion, working against the grain of the coat. Let the chalk dry thoroughly before brushing it out.

Above: Among the factors that determine how heavily to chalk is the amount of time you have for it to dry. On long circuits where bathing facilities are not available, using a self-rinsing shampoo instead of water will help keep the white areas looking clean. This dog's rear pastern has been thoroughly moistened and will be heavily packed.
All photos by Pegini.

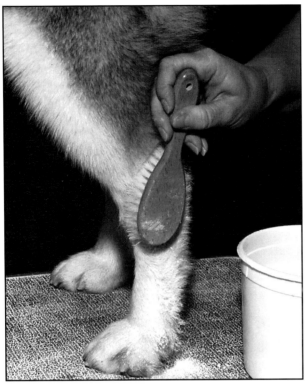

Legs coated with a helper like Chalk Mate or Kolestral, or lightly dampened, will hold much less chalk and take a lot less time to dry.

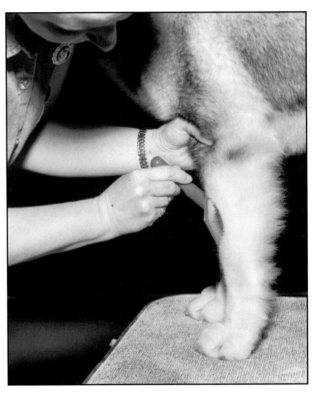

When the dog is thoroughly dry, a quick brushing will confirm that all the chalk is out of your dog's coat before you go into the ring.

COMBING OUT

A comb out just before you go into the ring adds the finishing touch to your grooming efforts. Beginning with the head and ears, working backwards and down the sides, comb the hair up. Lightly brush the hair down on the back and rump. Run your comb through the leg hairs and take it with you to the ring for touch-ups.

SPRAYS, MOUSSES, AND GELS

Dogs with poor coats or poor coat texture are often moussed, gelled, and sprayed in an attempt to improve their coat. Many of these products are drying agents which exacerbate dry coats and brittle hair.

By the time a person gets to be a judge, he has had enough experience to recognize the use of artificial substances on the coat as soon as he touches the dog. These are particularly obvious in damp or wet weather because they get gummy. A judge might turn a blind eye to some hair helpers, but not if his hands stick together after he goes over your dog!

You can pick up many hints and tricks by watching the pros in the grooming area before a show. Be sure to read the AKC booklet *Rules and Regulations for Dog Shows* first; everything you witness behind the scenes may not be in accordance with the rules.

Try everything at home first. Learn to trim on a dog you won't be showing for some time. Experiment with different products long before the date of your next show, and be sure to experiment with their use daily over a period of several days such as you would experience on a weekend or week-long show circuit. What works on one dog may be disastrous on a dog with a different coat type. If a particular product doesn't work well for you, ask a grooming supplier at one of the shows to recommend alternative products.

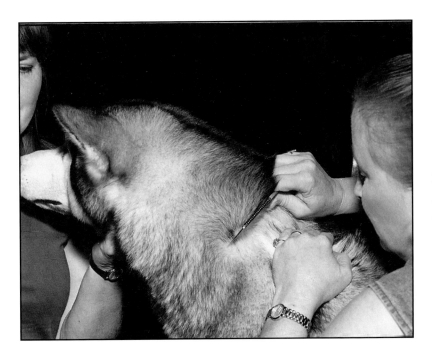

Section the hair and comb upwards. You must get down to the skin, through the undercoat. Don't just run your comb over the top of the hair. If you hit a snag, gently work through it so you don't pull out the undercoat. Pegini photos.

COPING WITH THE DOG HAIR PROBLEM

Cleaning up the shed coat is really a small price to pay for your dog's glorious coat the rest of the year. Here are some tips to make this stage easier.

First, sweep up all the hair that you can to protect your vacuum cleaner from clogs. You can minimize hair on your furniture by covering it with sheets while your Malamute is changing clothes. These can then be cleaned by shaking them outside and washing. A fabric softener sheet will take hair off clothes in the dryer. Be sure to clean your lint filter after every load.

If the situation becomes desperate, stay away from dark fabrics, especially wool and gabardine which seem to attract dog hair. Should you find hair on your tux, remove it with a velvet clothes brush. The sticky kind quickly become coated and have to be replaced; likewise, brushes get too clogged with hair to be effective.

There are many uses for dog hair. Some people save the hair and have it spun into yarn to make a sweater or blanket. You'll find advertisements for this service in the dog magazines or at show booths. If you're into bird watching, bag some of the hair in a net onion sack and hang it out for birds to use for building nests.

A well-groomed Malamute makes his owner proud to take him anywhere. Cold Valley's Quot Erat Kinuk, owned by Mario van Alebeek, at twenty-one months of age has just won a Best of Breed at a show in Holland. Wim van Vugt photo.

Am. Can. Ch. Taolan Arctic Cat ROM, a National specialty winner, Best in Show Winner, and multiple group winner, always owner-handled. Breeder, Ron Pohl. Owned by Richard and Virginia Grefe. John Ashbey photo.

8

SHOWING YOUR MALAMUTE

Dog shows are an event at which championship points are awarded and are second only to horse racing as a continuously held sporting event.[1] As they move into their second century, much about them has changed, but dog shows still provide a place to display the results of breeders' efforts and to obtain independent evaluations of their stock. They are also a forum where breeders can exchange ideas and information. They offer opportunities for participation at many levels and are the only sport we know of where amateur, professional, men, women, and children compete as equals.

THE AMERICAN KENNEL CLUB

In addition to its duties as a registry, the American Kennel Club sponsors dog shows in the United States although it does not hold any shows of its own as in other countries. Instead, shows are put on by clubs that are either members of the AKC or licensed by it for that purpose.[2]

SANCTIONED MATCHES

Matches sanctioned by the AKC are strictly regulated and may be either Plan B (or OB for obedience), which are same-day affairs and the most common, or Plan A (OA for obedience). The latter is similar to a regular show with pre-entries by mail before a certain date and a prepared catalog. Most clubs only hold an A-match as a preliminary to licensing.

Matches provide practice for the show-giving club, exhibitors, puppies, and potential judges. A club may only hold two shows a year but may have several matches.

DOG SHOWS

All-breed clubs usually hire a professional show superintendent licensed by the AKC to help with their shows. Superintendents do much of the paperwork associated with the show, including the premium list and judging program for which they maintain a mailing list, catalog, and armbands. They also supply, set up, and break down the show equipment. Most specialty and obedience clubs handle their own shows through a show secretary who handles the show paperwork, including mailouts.

From two months to six weeks before a show, the superintendent or secretary mails out the premium list, a pamphlet which contains information about and entries for the upcoming show. In it are: the name of the show-giving club, the type of exhibition (dog show, obedience trial, etc.), the dates, location, judges, and all premiums offered for wins. Additional information about the show site and any special rules or requirements are also contained in the premium list.

On the entry form is the name of the secretary or superintendent as well as the closing date and time after which no entries will be accepted. This is usually noon on the Wednesday two weeks before the show.

Any AKC entry form or a photocopy of one can be used to enter a show, as long as the name and date of the show are on the front and both sides of the form are included.[3] The entry form and payment for the entry must be received before the closing date and time printed in the premium list and on the entry form. Entries received too late are returned unopened.

After the closing date and before the show, you will receive an acknowledgment of your entry with a judging program. (If not, call to check on your entry.) The program has routes to the show and a list of hotels that accept dogs. It also has a schedule for each ring, showing the judge for that ring and the times for breed judging. A breed may be judged after the published time, but under no circumstances will it ever be judged before it.

DOG CLUBS AND THEIR EVENTS

Depending on their function, dog clubs fall into many categories. All-breed, group, specialty, and national breed clubs are the ones which hold dog shows. An obedience club can hold an obedience trial.

Under its auspices, an all-breed show may hold several AKC events—a dog show, obedience trial, tracking trial, or performance event, depending on the abilities and desires of the club. These are open to all of the recognized breeds eligible for the event.

The activities of a group club are restricted to dogs within that group, and at a group show, the highest award would be Best in Group. They can also hold obedience trials, and whatever performance events are appropriate for that group.

Specialty clubs have an interest in only one breed. Only the national breed club can be a member of AKC, but independent specialty clubs can be licensed to hold a variety of different events depending on the breed including dog shows, obedience trials, tracking trials, field trials, earth trials, herding tests and trials, hunting tests, lure coursing tests and trials, and Coonhound events.

The AMCA holds a national specialty show annually and allows unlicensed, affiliated local clubs to hold regional specialties in different areas of the country under their auspices. Independent specialty clubs hold their own license from AKC for shows and can have their own shows and obedience trials. They often offer weight-pull, although this is not an AKC-sanctioned event.

At this time, working certificates for sled dogs are awarded by the national breed club, the AMCA. If the AKC continues on its current path, tests for these abilities may be incorporated into their program, helping breeders to preserve breed purpose and type.

You can estimate when your breed might begin by allowing two minutes for every dog before you, but understand that some or all of those dogs might be absent, in which case your estimate will be wrong. No one calls or looks for you; you are responsible for having your dog ringside at the proper time. If you are too late, in almost all cases, you are out of luck.

ELIGIBILITY

Not all dogs can be shown. AKC has certain basic eligibility requirements. At matches, the dog must be registerable, but for shows, he must have a regular individual registration or papers must be in process.

Because dog shows are for breeding stock, certain physical standards must be met. "A dog which is blind, deaf, castrated, spayed, or which has been changed in appearance by artificial means except as specified by the standard . . . or a male which does not have two normal testicles normally located in the scrotum, may not compete at any show and will be disqualified."[4] At specialty shows only, neutered males and spayed females are allowed in Stud Dog and Brood Bitch classes and in Veterans. A lame dog or any dog with grooming materials in its coat or whose color or markings have been changed artificially will be excused without any award.

The judge must be able to examine the dog, including checking testicles on a male without fear for his safety. Dogs destined for the show ring should be used to handling. If your dog menaces or threatens anyone in the ring, the judge will excuse him; however, if he attacks anyone, he will be disqualified and cannot be shown again.

Ch. Kikikook's Get Down-N-Dirty, one of the top winning bitches in the South. Breeder, John McCarthy, Jr. Owner, Linda Summersett. Photo © Pegini.

DOG SHOW CLASSES

REGULAR CLASSES — **Classes are divided by sex. Dogs show first, then bitches.**
Regular classes must be offered at every licensed show; however, there are not always entries in all classes.

Puppy	For dogs over six months but under twelve months. May be divided by age: 6 to 9 months and 9 to 12 months.
Twelve to Eighteen Months	For dogs that are over 12 months but under 18 months. These "teenagers" may not be physically mature enough to compete with older adult dogs.
Novice	For dogs that have not previously won three firsts in any class other than Puppy or 12-18-Months, and have not acquired one or more points toward a championship.
American Bred	Open to any dog bred and whelped in the United States. Used as an in-between class for dogs too old for Puppy and not mature or experienced enough for Open class. Sometimes used by handlers who have several dogs to show.
Bred By Exhibitor	Dog must be owned wholly or in part by the person or spouse of the person who was the breeder or one of the breeders of record and handled by the same or a member of their immediate family.
Open	The most competitive class, open to any dog six months of age or over. It is primarily entered by dogs or bitches seriously competing for the championship points.
Winners	This is the only class you cannot enter before the show. The first place winners of the regular classes compete. Winners Dog is judged after the regular dog classes, and Winners Bitch after the regular bitch classes.
Best of Breed	The first intersex class in the competition. Open to champions of record, those finishing a championship after entries closed, the winners of any single-dog non-regular classes, as well as the Winners Dog and Winners Bitch.

NON-REGULAR CLASSES
Names and requirements for non-regular classes vary with the show and breed. Single-dog entry classes are held before Best of Breed judging since the winners are eligible to compete in that class. Non-regular classes with more than a one dog entry are held following Best of Breed. Common non-regular classes are:

Veterans	Dogs or bitches seven years or older, which may or may not be champions,
Working	Offered at Malamute specialties, this class is open only to dogs that have some kind of working certification. They may or may not be champions.
Stud Dog	A sire and at least two of his offspring (get), which must also be entered in the regular classes.
Brood Bitch	A dam with at least two of her offspring. which must also be entered in regular classes.
Brace	Two dogs of either sex owned by the same person(s) and exhibited by an owner.
Team	Four dogs exhibited together by one person.

JUNIOR SHOWMANSHIP
For youths between 10 and 18 years of age where awards are based on the handling ability of the youth instead of the quality of the dog. Junior division is for boys and girls at least 10 and under 14 years. Senior division is for boys and girls who are at least 14 and under 18 years old on the day of the show.

Novice	For youths who, at the time entries close, have not won three first place awards.
Open	For those who have won three or more first place Junior Showmanship awards at licensed shows with competition present.

Left: Liane Dubois winning Best Junior Handler at the 1993 National Specialty with Heritage Kotzebue Balthazeaar. Tatham photo. Center: Leanne Wolf takes Best of Winners with Gothic's Bright Morningstar, proving that junior handlers can do well in the regular classes, too. Photo by Petrulis. Right: Eleven-year-old Bryan Willhauck handling Frostfield High Flyer to a Best of Breed. Tatham photo.

Paula O'Neal winning Best Junior Handler with Ch. Mals-About's Rowdy of Snow Song, owned by Hank and Barbie Corwin.

Kristin Levesque winning Best Junior Handler with Ch. Greenbrier's Rais'n Kane at the '93 AMCA Regional hosted by the Yankee AMC. This show followed the National, so it was a very big win for her.

Part of the Brace class at the 1979 National. In the foreground are eleven-year-old Ch. Williwaw's Chena, C.D. (left) and her daughter Ch. Williwaw's Shemya, CD. Breeder/owner, Mary Jane Holabach.

Ch. Inuit's Moon Unit, ROM and Inuit's Hat Trick winning Best Brace in Show. Owner, Sheila Balch.

The winner of the 1981 National Specialty Stud Dog class, Ch. Lorien's Man O' War of Snoridge ROM, and his get. Thompkins photo.

Ch. Chena's Leading Lady takes Winners under Judge Lina Basquette for breeder/ owners Sel and Joanne Levy. JC Photo.

EQUIPMENT

The array of equipment for showing and grooming that some people bring to a show can be daunting to a new-comer. Over time you will accumulate material that is helpful to you, but to begin showing, all you really need is a dog with a collar and leash.

Malamutes are shown on choke collars, usually chain link. The collar should be just large enough to go over his head, with links that are strong enough to hold a lunging dog, yet not so bulky that handling the collar is awkward. It should be unobtrusive and have no dangling tags.

Your leash should be of good leather or soft nylon with a medium-sized bolt-snap. Likewise, the width should be enough to restrain the dog without danger of snapping, yet narrow enough to be folded inside your closed hand.

CRATES

If you have used a crate at home, you will find it quite an advantage when you begin showing. Your dog will re-gard the crate as "home" and feel secure in it. A large dog requires a crate of corresponding size. If this is a problem for your vehicle, investigate the various "suitcase" crates that fold for traveling.

FOOD AND WATER

Even for a short outing, you should always have a bowl and water. Overnight trips call for food, too. Malamutes may be sensitive to food and water changes, so bring them from home or buy distilled water. Your dog's response to change may be that traveler's anathema—diarrhea. In case the worst happens, you should take paper towels, a few old towels, and some wet-wipes for quick clean up.

Some dogs are picky about eating on the road. If you need to encourage your dog's appetite, add a tablespoon of canned food—but no more—to his dry variety.

ATTIRE

A good rule of thumb is to dress as nicely as the judges do, but remember they are not showing dogs. Men can never go wrong with a coat and tie. Women may wear pant suits, suits, dresses, or a blouse and split skirt or nice walking shorts. Running in your clothes should be easy and comfortable. They should be long enough and loose enough to protect your modesty when you bend over your dog.

Both men's and women's shoes should be comfortable, with non-skid soles. They should also provide cushioning and support for running. Men should empty everything that rattles and clinks from their pockets, and women need to watch their jewelry. Long necklaces can get tangled about the dog's head or in his collar, and bangle bracelets can be very distracting.

JUDGING PROCEDURE

Dogs are shown by individual breeds in whatever order fits the superintendent's time restrictions. Within the breeds, however, the order is unvarying. All regular dog classes are held before Winners Dog after which all regular bitch classes are held before Winners Bitch. The Winners Bitch class is followed by Best of Breed judging unless any non-regular single-entry classes such as Veteran are held. They will come between Winners Bitch and Best of Breed. Any multiple-entry, non-regular classes, such as Brace, Stud Dog, or Brood Bitch, are held after Best of Breed. Their order is up to the club, but it must be published and followed.

Judging proceeds within each sex by class, always beginning with the lowest class with entries and proceeding to Open. The number of dogs and bitches entered may differ, sometimes markedly.

First and second place dogs from each class should remain at ringside, but other dogs may be put up. When the judge makes the placements for the last class in that sex, each first-place winner enters the Winners class. No other dogs are eligible for this class. When the judge selects his Winner, that dog goes to the 1st place marker and receives his ribbon and any prizes and then leaves the ring. Only the Winners Dog and Winners Bitch receive championship points.

Then the dog which placed second to the Winner in the regular class comes in, and the judge selects the Reserve Winner. Like the runner-up to Miss America, if the Winners award is revoked for any reason, the Reserve Winner receives the points. Although disqualification of a win happens infrequently, it does happen, usually as a result of improper entry or having the wrong handler in the Bred-by-Exhibitor class.

The Best of Breed class is called to the ring after the judging of Reserve Winners in bitches or after non-regular class judging, if any are offered and entered. Into Best of

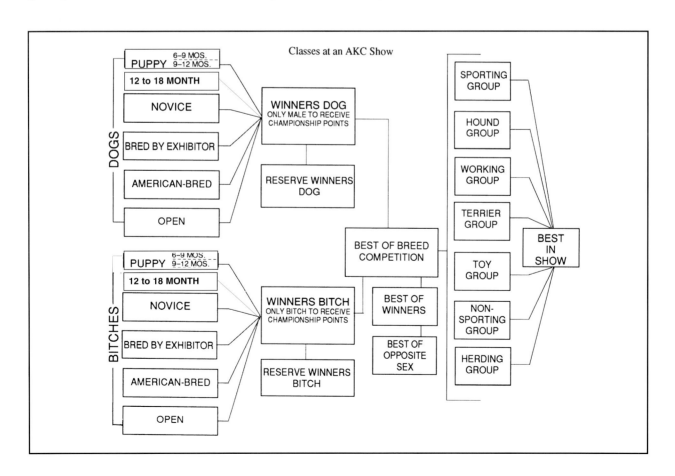

Breed go champions entered or moved up from the regular classes because they finished after entries closed, the Winners Dog and Winners Bitch, and winners of any non-regular, single-dog entry classes.

Regular awards are: Best of Breed, Best of Winners, and Best of Opposite Sex (to Best of Breed) or BOB, BOW, BOS, respectively. At specialties, additional prizes may be given for Best Puppy, Best Veteran, or Best Bred-by-Exhibitor. Eligible dogs will be called into the ring and judged after the Best of Breed judging, unless a previous award may have decided the outcome, in which case, the award is presented at the same time.

Every dog in the Best of Breed class is eligible for the Best of Breed (BOB) award, but only Winners Dog and Winners Bitch compete for Best of Winners (BOW). If one of the Winners is excused or does not return to the ring, or only one sex is represented in competition, no BOW is given. Best of Opposite Sex (BOS) competition is between the dogs of opposite sex to the BOB.

A Winner that is BOB is automatically BOW. The Winner of the opposite sex is still eligible for consideration as BOS, however. This is important because if extra non-regular trophies are offered and the BOB dog came from either a non-regular class like Veterans or from Winners, such an award may have been decided by the BOB award. For instance, a BOB from Veterans is automatically Best Veteran. Likewise, a BOB Puppy is automatically Best Puppy.

Other wins have the same sort of effect. If Winners Bitch is from the Puppy class, she has defeated the other bitch puppy by going Winners, so competition for Best Puppy would be between her and the dog puppies.

HOW A DOG BECOMES A CHAMPION

A dog becomes a champion by winning a total of fifteen points under at least three different judges. He must win two majors (shows worth three or more points) under two different judges.

Theoretically, you could finish your dog's championship in three five-point majors. In actuality, this rarely happens.

Results from the show are sent to the AKC from the show superintendent or secretary and posted to each dog's record by the AKC Show Events Department. This department keeps track of each dog's show career and when a championship is completed, sends a championship certificate to the owner.

CHAMPIONSHIP POINTS

Points for Winners Dog and Winners Bitch are independent of each other and are based solely upon the number of dogs in competition and the area in which the competition occurs. The point schedule is reassessed each year. The new one is published in the May AKC *Gazette* and becomes effective on June 1st.

In competition above the Winners level, both Winners may have the opportunity to win more points. The governing principle is that a dog always receives points equal to those that would have been awarded to any dog he defeats. However, such increases are not additive.

The first opportunity for additional points comes with the BOB or BOS award. A Winner awarded either BOB or BOS get the count of the total number of males or females in competition in the regular classes plus the number of same-sex dogs competing in the BOB class. If neither Winner goes BOB, the judge decides BOW. The BOW gets points equal to those of the defeated Winner if that dog's points for the show are greater. However, there is no penalty if that dog's points are less. The possibility for increased points can occur, too, when any defeated dogs are added to the class entry if BOS is one of the Winners. If BOS was defeated in the BOW competition, the BOW gets the benefit of the enhanced points as well.

This carries on to the Group and Best-in-Show competition. A dog that wins Group or Best in Show gets the same number of points as the highest available points of any dog or bitch he defeats. However, most of these winners are already champions, and in the United States, once a championship is completed, points are no longer relevant.

AT THE DOG SHOW

How far ahead of your judging time you arrive at the show depends largely upon whether your plan to groom on-site or at home. If you are rushed you may get flustered and nervous. Your dog will take his cues from you and become unsure and jittery, too, so allow plenty of time for unloading and set-up. There will be an assigned grooming area where dogs and handlers can park their belongings, set up a grooming table, and arrange supplies.

After picking up your armband at ringside and checking in with the ring steward, take a few minutes to watch your judge's procedure. Find out if the judge wants you to enter the ring in catalog order. If not, try to be first or among the first in the ring.

Many exhibitors feed their dogs very lightly before a show, but be sure the dog has adequate water. Give your dog some rest breaks during grooming. He can get very tired of standing. If he arrives at the ring with every hair in place but is utterly exhausted, you have defeated your purpose. Take him out for a "potty break," before going to the ring to wait your turn. Like human travelers, a dog can become stiff from the traveling, crating, and standing, so it's a good idea to move him briskly for a short time before your class. Most importantly, always try to make dog shows FUN for your Mal!

HANDLING YOUR OWN DOG

Alaskan Malamutes have a long tradition of having owner-handlers, many of whom have had top winning dogs. With practice and attention to detail, you can be there too. You have some significant advantages over a professional. For instance, you know your dog intimately. He has been trained for the ring, feels secure with you, and looks up to you for guidance. He will be much happier with you than with a handler, and that shows in the ring.

To show, both of you need to practice setting up and moving, and you need to learn what goes on at a show. Look into handling classes which are often available from area kennel clubs. Your dog will have to be familiar with having his teeth and testicles examined, so having other people help with this before he goes into the ring is useful. Matches will give you a chance to try out your new-found skills.

STACKING (POSING)

When evaluating your dog, a judge looks at him from several angles. He or she assesses physical soundness by watching movement and mental soundness from attitude and demeanor. In addition, the judge will appraise an elu-

This handler has trained his dog to "free stack" or stack himself on a loose lead—which many judges prefer. Note that he is using bait, carefully concealed, to get the dog's full attention.

Am. Can. Ch. Farouk De Chabek, ROM, is a multiple American and Canadian Specialty winner, including the National Specialties in both countries. Breeder/owners, Andre and Lise Lepine. Alex Smith photo.

sive quality known as "type." A dog with type exemplifies the breed; he has all those characteristics that readily identify him as an Alaskan Malamute.

The judge's impression of your dog's type comes from observing it standing, mostly in profile. To present the best picture possible, you must position your dog in a manner consistent with the Malamute standard. This is called "stacking," "setting-up," or "posing" your dog. The more proficient you and your dog become at this, the more likely you are to win.

When your Malamute sets up reliably, you may begin baiting him with food treats or a special toy to make him look particularly attentive and alert. You must learn to set your dog up by hand, and your dog must learn to accept this before you begin using bait.

Before you begin working on your dog, try some experiments in physical dynamics on yourself. Stand with your feet slightly apart, facing forward. Then, turn your head around to the right and try to look at something behind your left shoulder. You will take your weight off your right leg, or you may even move it. When your dog moves his head, he does the same thing. This is why controlling the head is the key to setting up your dog.

Now, get on your hands and knees. The most stable, comfortable position is with your hands directly under your shoulders and your knees under your buttocks. Move your arms forwards slightly and see how much pressure this puts on your wrists. Eventually, you will want to move your knees forward or your arms back under you. Stretch your lower legs out behind you. This places pressure on your back, and you will want to move either your arms or legs. The same things happen with a dog that is propped or set too far out in the back.

In setting up your Malamute, you will stand at his right shoulder, since he is always on your left. You will always work from front to back and within that framework, from side to side.

First you will secure the head. Using the leash itself or the leash-ring of the collar gives the dog at least three inches of play for neck movement. As you have seen by your own experiment, the body and then the legs tend to move with the head. Keeping his head somewhat immobile will keep him from shifting about.

Therefore, hold the dog by the collar. You can do this by gripping under the collar so that your knuckles point forward and your palm faces the dog's withers. You can

If you are working with a puppy, place him on a grooming table. Tacy Sommersett has just begun working with this puppy. His pose is typical of a beginning dog. After he relaxes it will be easier to set his rear legs out more. Patience is the key to training. Pegini photo.

When you stack your dog, hold the collar and gather up the leash in your hand. A dangling leash is very distracting. Photo by Wallis.

tighten the collar, then, by twisting your fist upward. A dangling leash is distracting, so gather it into your hand. The collar is your physical restraint, so do not let go.

The order in which you work should be: Inside front, outside front, outside rear, inside rear, check the front. Repeat this order to yourself until it is firmly fixed in your mind and practically second-nature; otherwise, nervousness will make you forget all the little steps when you are in the ring.

At first you will be slow and awkward in setting up your dog. You will be lucky just to get his front positioned. Take heart—you will improve with practice. When only minor corrections are necessary, you can begin working with bait.

Use a command, such as Stack, and continue to use it every time you set the dog up. Talk in a reassuring tone and use a word like Steady if he starts to move. Using your most "get excited" voice will only encourage him to jump around.

Work for short periods and do not expect perfection overnight. You should be firm, but not discouraging, patient and pleasant. At first, your dog will be unsure of himself and may seem downcast and confused. If you are lavish with your praise and make the rest of the work session pleasant, he will become more confident and secure as he learns what is expected of him.

Your movements should be purposeful, smooth, and fast, not quick and jerky. If you are too tentative you will make your Malamute anxious, and he will have time to fidget. Take time at the shows to watch other handlers, especially at the group level, and notice different techniques.

SETTING UP THE FRONT

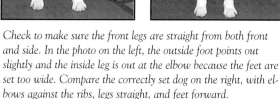

Check to make sure the front legs are straight from both front and side. In the photo on the left, the outside foot points out slightly and the inside leg is out at the elbow because the feet are set too wide. Compare the correctly set dog on the right, with elbows against the ribs, legs straight, and feet forward.

Top row, left to right:
Hold the collar with your left hand. Slide your right hand down the shoulder, grasping the right leg at the elbow. Lift slightly and straighten the leg as you set it down. Hold the elbow tight against the dog's ribs. The leg should be straight from elbow to pad, with the foot pointing forward.

When the inside leg is satisfactory, switch hands on the collar. Reach over the dog, sliding your hand down his shoulder to grasp the left elbow. Use the same technique to place the left leg in line with the right one.

A dog that is set up in an uncomfortable or off-balance position will usually move to correct it. Linda Allen handling. Photos by Wallis.

Do not grab the dog in the middle of the leg or by the paw. This does not straighten the entire leg, and it will also mark you as a beginner.

SETTING UP THE REAR

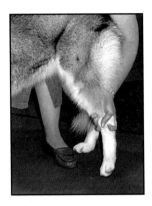   

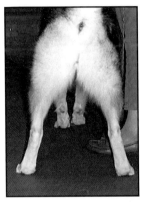 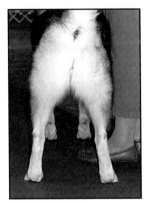

Top row, left to right:
Run your hand down the dog's back to the left rear hock. Gently but firmly grasp the hock joint and lift the leg slightly. Bend the hock a little to the outside as you place the rear foot. An alternate method is to reach under the dog's body and grasp the outside leg at the stifle.

Set the inside leg in the same fashion,.

Twist the hock joint out slightly before placing the foot on the floor.

The leg should be perpendicular to the ground from the hock to the foot, and straight from hip to foot when viewed from the rear.

This page and facing page: Linda Allen handling; Photos by Wallis.

Compare the photo on the left, where the rear is set too wide and the front to close, to the photo on the right, where the dog is set correctly. The rear legs should be just slightly outside the plane of the front legs.

At home, work in front of a large reflective surface, such as a mirror or patio door, so you can see what you are doing from the judge's vantage point. Your Malamute should look balanced in his stance. Think of him as a table; if he looks like he might fall, you are not positioning him well or else he is nervous. Very tense dogs will hunch their backs and stiffen their rears, but practice usually relaxes them.

Well-built dogs will naturally stand squarely, so you may only have to make minor adjustments. However, most dogs are not perfectly angulated nor are their limbs perfectly placed, so they are bound to fall short of perfection.

If a leg is planted too firmly to move, remember your experiment and shift the dog off balance. Linda has pulled the collar towards herself, forcing the dog to transfer weight to the inside leg while Linda moves the outside leg.

SETTING UP – SIDE VIEW AND TAIL

Top left: This dog's stance is referred to as "rocking horsed," "propped," or "bridged," because her front is too far forward. This makes her shoulder angulation appear too straight. This is one of the hardest things to gauge correctly. Practice in front of a mirror. Hint: if you can see the dog's toes when you look down, her legs are probably too far forward.

Top right: This dog is off balance because her rear is set too far back. The rear pastern is not straight, and she is pushing her weight forward causing her front to sink slightly. Her head carriage is forced slightly forward and down. This trades problems: the front appears better; the rear looks worse than in the previous photo.

Top center: Unless your dog's tail is naturally correct, place it by gently moving your hand from the base to the curve. Don't try to keep it up by pushing it into the dog's side. The result, as here, will be that the dog appears to have an incorrect, snap tail. Instead, gently stroke the underside of the tail, and when it comes up, place your hand lightly on the top as a reminder to the dog.

Lower center: This dog is now holding her tail correctly, but are you finished? Not quite. Check the dog's front again and be sure she's square. While this dog is almost correct, she has now shifted her weight slightly to the rear and is not showing much expression.

Bottom left: Linda has tossed a piece of bait in front of her dog. Note the difference in appearance that the forward shift of the dog's weight makes. Her keen expression, forward pricked ears and arched neck make her much more attractive. She looks balanced front and rear, and gives an impression of alertness and energy. (Linda will pick up the bait before she moves.)

Ch. Kaila's Paw Print and Chris Gabriel are a lesson in partnership. Chris is moving at a speed that shows his dog's power and drive but keeps his balance. The taut leash maintains contact but does not pull the dog's head up. Chris is glancing at his dog to make sure he is moving correctly. Breeder/owners, Chris and Eileen Gabriel. Perlmutter photo.

MOVING

In the ring, you always move with your Malamute on your left, and he should be kept on the mat. Hold the lead in your left hand (two hands are for obedience) and keep it taut enough for control, but not so tight that it lifts the dog's head up and restricts his front movement.

If you are at the front of the line, check to see that everyone is ready before taking off. Male Malamutes can get testy, especially if bitches in season are present, so leave ample space between dogs when you are running. Never fall into the trap of outrunning everyone or letting someone else set your pace. Move your dog at the speed at which he looks most balanced.

You must adjust your own running style to one appropriate for the show ring. If you take short, choppy, mincing strides, your dog will, too. Take long strides and move forward rather than up and down, tucking your right arm in close to your body.

Move in a straight line. The judge cannot evaluate your dog's movement coming and going if he is bobbing from side to side because you do not run straight or because he is trying to scoop up liver from the floor. To improve your own ability to run straight, take a tip from dancers: focus on some object directly ahead of you and move towards it, checking your dog occasionally to make sure he is trotting.

Always turn so that the dog is on the outside, and, as you do, glance up and make eye contact with the judge. If she is not looking at you, wait until she does, then move so that the dog is in her line of sight. A judge may shift her position to see your dog better, or she may not. Showing your dog to his best advantage is *your* responsibility.

If you mess up, or if the dog starts galloping or pacing, stop, go back to your starting position, and begin again. To correct pacing (both legs on the same side moving together), start out at a faster speed or pull up sharply with the lead to throw the dog off-stride. Jerk back sharply on the leash to check a gallop. This should be a quick, obedience-type correction, rather than a steady pull. Otherwise, your dog will pull in the opposite direction, and you will have little or no control over him.

This is your time, and you must make the most of it. A judge operates under many constraints. If she falls behind, she inconveniences a lot of people. Regardless of how much she empathizes with a novice handler, a judge does not have time to look at a dog six or seven times nor to give handling lessons. You may get a second chance because you are obviously inexperienced, but you will rarely get a third.

Judges look kindly upon handlers who save them time, whose dogs are set up and ready to be looked at, and who perform patterns correctly. While the person in front of you is moving his dog in its individual pattern, move your dog up and have him ready as soon as the judge turns around. This gives you the opportunity to fix any problem areas without calling the judge's attention to a fault.

DEALING WITH PROBLEMS

A well-structured Malamute has an upper arm about the same length as the shoulder blade. Good angulation of the shoulder and upper arm means that the legs are set directly under the withers. However, dogs with straight shoulders, short upper arms, and/or poor angulation of the shoulder and upper arm, will not be able to stand this way. If you have one or more of these problems, make the best of what you have and set the front legs perpendicular to the ground, rather than trying to set them under the withers. To do so will only make your dog look off-balance, as if he is tipping forward.

Many Malamutes are close in the rear, so when the rear legs are set in the customary fashion their hocks point slightly inward. With a dog with a close rear, set the rear legs in slightly closer than usual and just before the judge makes an examination, reset them, twisting the hocks out as you place them so the rear appears to be true.

Stretching the dog farther out in the rear may make a level topline look sloped, but stretching the dog too far will make his back sag (remember your experiment). If you need to overextend the rear to improve the look of your dog's topline, be sure that you do so very slightly.

If your Malamute is out at the elbows, either from barrel ribs or improper shoulder placement, make sure that you do not turn the elbows out when you set the front or you will exaggerate the problem. Instead, set the legs of this dog in just a little to minimize the fault.

If your dog fidgets or readjusts his position, instead of assuming he is being willful, reconsider your positioning. If you have to set him up slightly unbalanced to compensate for a structural problem, expecting him to stay like that forever is unreasonable. Use these corrections judiciously. Constant discomfort will make your dog wary and resentful.

Top winning bitch in breed history with many BIS and BISS wins, Am. Can. Ch. Williwaw's Icicle Works, owned by Alison Crouse. Breeding, grooming, and training all play a part. Photo © Animal World Studio.

SHOWING THE BITE

At some point while you are in the ring, the judge will have to check your dog's teeth. The method illustrated works well because it puts pressure on the back of your dog's head, discouraging any efforts to pull away or to back out of the collar.

Have other people check your dog's teeth, but be careful when puppies are teething. Their lips and gums are sensitive, so practice needs to be more style and less substance.

Many judges will check bites themselves. If your dog has a level bite, have the dog ready as soon as he approaches. Pull the dog's head up as much as you can before showing the teeth, since this forces the upper jaw back and makes the bite look better.

Most judges check dentition as part of the individual exam. If you are baiting your dog, do not feed him just before the exam. No one likes looking at teeth as little pieces of half-chewed liver fall out of the dog's mouth.

USING BAIT

By the time you are actually showing, your dog should be able to stand freely. You then can stand beside or in front of him and bait him so that his expression is alert and attractive. Do this when the judge is looking at his face or observing him from the side, not just before he examines teeth.

Bait can be carried in a pin-on pocket available from show vendors or in your own pocket if you have one. It can be anything the dog likes, but most people use liver fixed in some fashion. You can make it or buy it from a show vendors if they have it.

Do not aimlessly feed your dog all the while you are in the ring; make him work for it. His expression when he is anticipating a goody is much better than when he is snatching bait out of your hand. It should be a reward. Just as his interest shows signs of flagging, treat him and then let him work for it again.

SHOWING THE BITE

 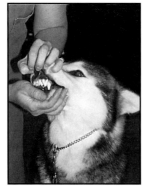 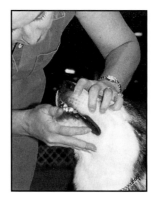 

Top left to right:
As the judge approaches, grasp the dog's collar at the throat with your right hand. Your knuckles face the throat, the palm is up.

Incorrect. If you place your palm on the dog's muzzle or pinch his nostrils shut while showing his bite, he will have trouble breathing and will fight you.

Incorrect. Be sure you do not cover the dog's eyes because he will move to try to see who is approaching. Also, keep your fingers away from the teeth.

From the side, see how the back of the collar should be just below the occiput to keep the dog from backing up. However, in this photo the nostrils are covered.

Right: The correct way. Hold the front of the collar just under the dog's mouth, allowing you to use your index finger to brace the lower jaw and your thumb to retract the lower lip. Tilt his head up and, with your left hand across the bridge of the nose, lift his upper lip. Linda Allen handling. Wallis photos.

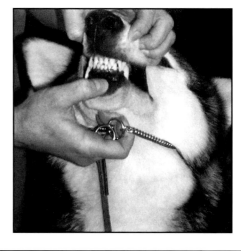

USING BAIT

Top left: The dog's alert expression is anticipation of food. This dog is well trained enough to wait and watch whenever Linda's hand is in her pocket.

Top right: Here she strikes an attractive pose for the liver Linda is holding in her right hand.

Left: For some Malamutes, the appeal of food is too strong. If food becomes a distraction rather than an aid, try something else. Here her lovely expression is directed at a sheepskin toy with a squeaker inside.

Linda Allen handles Wahkeen's Heavenly Body, bred and owned by Rick and Linda Allen. Wallis photos.

Whether you use liver, balls, or furry toys, if you throw it or drop it, you must retrieve it. Never let your dog take liver off the floor. Teaching him food manners very early will stand you in good stead for the life of the dog. Otherwise, he will become a doggy vacuum, swooping to pick up dropped bait, or he will corkscrew around your legs to see if you have food. Unless you want your fingers amputated, do not let him get into the bad habit of snatching bait; instead, make him take it gently.

You can practice baiting your dog any time, anywhere. Ch. Fate's Little Miss Priss, a multiple specialty winner and multiple group placer, owned by Lynda Birmantas has obviously had lots of practice. She was owner-handled to most of her wins.

Making Your Own Bait

Liver Bait

Wash beef, pork, chicken or turkey liver. Cut into 2-inch squares.
Method 1. Cover with water, add garlic and onion powder and bring to a boil. Simmer for 15-20 minutes. Drain and pat dry with paper towels. Do not add salt.

Method 2. If the boiled liver is too crumbly and wet, place it on a cookie tray and bake 15 minutes at 375 - 400 degrees. Turn once and bake another 15 minutes until liver is hard. To preserve, pack it in rock salt.

Freezing: Spread the liver pieces apart on a tray and put it in the freezer until all pieces are solidly frozen. This will prevent it from sticking together. Bag the frozen pieces in useable-sized portions. When thawed, it will keep three to four days in a refrigerator or ice chest.

While you can purchase various types of treats to use for baiting your dog, most exhibitors make their own. Beef liver is probably the all-time favorite. Most dogs are wild about it, it keeps fairly well, and if properly prepared, it is reasonably clean and easy to break into small bites.

Here are two of the authors' favorite recipes.

You can simply boil your liver and dry it, then chop it into bite-size pieces. Or, you can boil it and then bake it to keep it drier and easier to handle.

If you don't want to make your own, liver and other bait usually can be purchased from one of the vendors at a show.

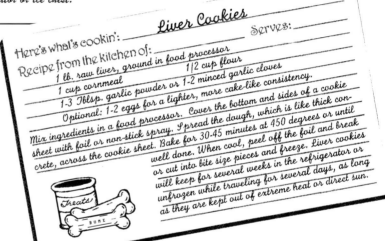

Here's what's cookin': _____
Recipe from the kitchen of: _____
Liver Cookies   Serves: _____

1 lb. raw liver, ground in food processor
1 cup cornmeal   1/2 cup flour
1-3 Tblsp. garlic powder or 1-2 minced garlic cloves
Optional: 1-2 eggs for a lighter, more cake-like consistency.

Mix ingredients in a food processor. Cover the bottom and sides of a cookie sheet with foil or non-stick spray. Spread the dough, which is like thick concrete, across the cookie sheet. Bake for 30-45 minutes at 450 degrees or until well done. When cool, peel off the foil and break or cut into bite size pieces and freeze. Liver cookies will keep for several weeks in the refrigerator or unfrozen while traveling for several days, as long as they are kept out of extreme heat or direct sun.

SPORTSMANSHIP

Today, we are inundated with an "in-your-face" attitude from the media. Television shows and even their commercials are packed with examples of ill-tempered, crude, even violent conduct towards others. Countering such a pervasive influence with good manners, kindness, and graciousness is difficult, especially when compounded by competitive pressures.

At a dog show you may hear all sorts of fabrications about fellow exhibitors, ranging from ordinary gossip to accusations of cheating, trickery, and duplicity. You may hear that the judge is incompetent, dishonest, contemptible, and a host of other adjectives.

Over time, you will find the source of the problem is usually the source of the gossip instead of its object. The same people who disparage a dog one day will breed to him the next. They will show next month under the judge they called an idiot today. Often the worst sort of slanders are tolerated and even encouraged by listeners, who never think twice about it until they become the victim.

Good sportsmanship is never out of place or out of fashion, and it extends much farther than congratulating the winner. It means not robbing someone of their pleasure in a win by casting aspersions at them or the judge. It means showing honest dogs and presenting them honestly in accordance with the rules. It means being forthright with other breeders and truthful with yourself. It means losing or winning with equal grace, and keeping some of your more biased opinions to yourself.

Although everyone has lapses, good sportsmanship does require a degree of self-discipline. Dog shows are a competition in which people invest a lot of money, energy, and emotion. At every show, a few people win and a great many do not. The only real losers are the ones who make themselves and everyone around them miserable. A good attitude will keep the sport enjoyable for you and others.

USING A PROFESSIONAL HANDLER

Showing your dog does not necessarily require your presence; you can hire a professional handler to do it for you. Most handlers take the dog before the show, keep it with them, groom it, and show it. However, you could groom the dog yourself and meet him ringside.

Your labor is free to you, but a handler's is not. In addition to a fee, some also charge a prorated share of their expenses, grooming and boarding fees, plus bonuses for wins above Best of Breed. As with any other financial undertaking, before you hire someone to handle for you, a written contract should specify all fees and obligations.

Never send your Malamute with someone without thoroughly checking out on how they care for dogs at home, on the road, and at the show. Big wins should not be your selection criterion. Get references and check on their set-ups at the show. Handlers who have air-conditioned vans where the dogs are left unsupervised or where the passengers are in another compartment while driving must have a functioning temperature sensor and remote alarm for the dogs to be safe. Never take it for granted.

You may often hear that handlers have an unfair advantage. Undoubtedly, sometimes they do. The greater part of their advantage, however, is due to hard work and experience.

UNDERSTANDING JUDGES

While judges have different levels of expertise, each has accumulated a substantial and impressive body of knowledge through years as breeders or handlers. The diversity of their experiences, fields of endeavor, and breed knowledge accounts for differences between their choices and contributes to the excellent over-all quality of judging in the United States.

The judge's mandate is to evaluate dogs against her interpretation of the written standard for the breed. Her knowledge must be coupled with integrity. She must treat life-time friends and perfect strangers with impartiality and should bring to the task a sense of humor and good manners. She must be so familiar with the breed standard, that she can act on it without a second thought. In addition to this, she has to know and be able to apply the *Rules*

Applying to Dog Shows, the *Guideline for Judges*, and procedures for disciplinary action.

When you enter under a judge, you are asking for her opinion of your dog which is expressed through her placements. You are entitled to a thorough examination of your dog, parity of treatment, and her full attention to your dog while it is being examined. Your dog should be handled well and gently, and you should be treated with dignity and courtesy.

SHOW PHOTOGRAPHS

You may request a photograph from the show photographer regardless of what your dog has won. When a judge can take pictures depends on his schedule. For special awards or large trophies, the club may have a presenter who is also in the picture, and if you want someone else in the picture besides you and the judge, feel free: It is your picture.

A regional or national specialty may have an agreement with the photographer for club pictures although such circumstances are exceptions. Normally, your request for a photograph is a contract with the photographer. If it does not turn out, the photographer will send you a note to that effect; otherwise, he will send your picture or an ordering proof along with a bill that you are obligated to pay.

Some people send the judge a photograph of particularly prestigious wins with an accompanying thank-you

Some shows are sophisticated affairs, and some trophies are quite impressive; others much more modest. Ch. Arctic Luv's Swashbuckler ROM, owned by Bernadette Quercio. Bergman photo.

note. Some judges like this; others do not, or are indifferent to it. However, when a judge specifically asks you for a picture, you should make an effort to comply.

BEYOND BEST OF BREED

At specialty shows, Best of Breed is the highest award available, although additional dogs of quality may be recognized with some special non-regular award of merit (the wording differs between breeds). At an all-breed or group show, competition continues. Each BOB winner may compete in the appropriate group competition, although participation is not required. Alaskan Malamutes are in the Working Group.

Group winners are placed first through fourth and each first place winner is obligated to participate in the Best-in-Show judging which follows the completion of the last group. Only one dog is chosen for this award; consequently, it is very prestigious and very difficult to achieve.

Ch. Kee-Too's Kougarok's Demos, bred by Kay and Linton Moustakis was the youngest Best in Show winner in breed history. He was sired by Kougarok.

ENDNOTES:
1. The Westminster Kennel Club show in fact is the second-oldest, continuously-held sporting event in the United States. The first is the Kentucky Derby.
2.   The last decade has seen the advent of the commercially-sponsored, invitational show. Invitations are issued on the basis of participants' wins over the previous year, statistics which are collected by various dog-show publications or by the organization itself. Also, the American Kennel Club has sponsored special exhibitions, such as its centennial show, and holds an obedience invitational and a show invitational.
3.   Why both sides, when all pertinent information, except for junior showmanship, is on the front? The "Agreement" is the fine print on the back that says you have had an opportunity to acquire the *Rules Applying to Registration and Dog Shows*, and are familiar with their contents. It goes with a long legalese clause indemnifying anyone associated with the show from any liability for anything that happens there. The front of the entry has another paragraph where, among other things, you say you agree to abide by the rules and regulations of the AKC and any other rules appearing in the premium list. Your signature attests to this. A copy of the *Rules* can be obtained free from the AKC, Field reps, superintendents, and club booths at shows often have copies available.
4.   American Kennel Club, *Rules Applying to Registration and Dog Shows* (January 1, 1994), 43.

Best in Show Ch. Storm Kloud's Qquest for Glory, WTD, owned and handled by Gloria Urbani, Italy. Embrione photo.

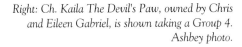

Top: Gena Box handled Am. Can. Ch. Baylor's Video King very successfully in the South during 1996 and 1997. They won several specialties and many Groups, proving that owner handlers can do very well with Malamutes. Breeders, Gary and Carol Cooper. Owners, J. L. and Gena Box. Sosa photo.

Right: Ch. Kaila The Devil's Paw, owned by Chris and Eileen Gabriel, is shown taking a Group 4. Ashbey photo.

Ch. Alcan Jack O'Diamonds was the top winning red of all time and the first red to go Best in Show. Breeder/owner, Dian McComb.

Am. Can. Ch. Chikara's Chilly Willy finished his American championship with his fifth BOB from Puppy class. Breeder/Owner, John Dewing. Booth photo.

Am. Can. Ch. Storm Kloud Valoup was the first bitch to go Best in Show in Canada. Breeder, Nancy Russell; Owners, Andre and Lise Lepine.

Ch. Snow Song's Jessica James is shown winning a Group 3, owner handled by Barbie Corwin. Booth photo.

Ch. Kaila's Meeko Starship, multiple breed and specialty winner. Breeders, Chris and Eileen Gabriel. Owner, Marie De Saules.

Baylor's Batteries Not Included places in Working Group at only ten months. Breeder/owners, Gary and Carol Cooper. Mikron photo.

THE ALASKAN MALAMUTE CLUB OF AMERICA NATIONAL SPECIALTY

A National Specialty Show is a cut above an ordinary show. The AMCA holds its annual National Specialty show and obedience trial in alternating regions of the United States. Entrants and spectators come from all over the country, and many special events are held. This show offers a unique opportunity to meet breed experts, talk to people with mutual interests, contact vendors, attend auctions, and enter raffles with products geared especially for the breed. Workshops and seminars will increase your knowledge and introduce you to new activities. Breed greats may be brought out of retirement for exhibition or special classes and futurities and sweepstakes attract the most promising youngsters.

The AMCA actively encourages owners to work their dogs and recognizes achievement in many areas. Among its special events are the Working Dog Showcase, Sweepstakes, Futurity, Veterans, Stud Dog, Brood Bitch, Team, Brace, Weight Pull, Tournament of Veterans Showcase, Parade of Veterans and Title Holders, as well as an Invitational for the top-twenty champions, Junior Showmanship, and many non-regular obedience classes, including Graduate Novice, Veteran, and Brace.

Extending over several days, the National also has many social functions, including the AMCA banquet where many of the special awards are presented. The AMCA annual membership meeting is held in conjunction with the specialty. Of special interest are the varied educational seminars offered, including ones on breeding, health problems, and sledding.

The first AMCA National Specialty was held in 1952. A list of Best of Breed winners appears in the appendices. On the following pages, some of the winners are pictured.

Multiple Best in Show and Specialty Best in Show winner, Am. Can. Ch. Sno Ridge's Tywon On, ROM. Breeder, Eileen Kinnas; Owners, Eileen Kinnas and Cindy Kinnas Natale. Raines photo.

Above: Am. Can. Ch. Poker Flat's Yukon Law CD, WTD, ROM, went BOB at the 1996 National Specialty. Breeder/Co-owner, Robin Haggard.

Above right: 1995 National Specialty BOB Ch. Ceili's Foolish Pleasure. Breeder/Owner, Pat Muchewicz.

Center Right: Am. Can. Ch. Farouk De Chabek, ROM, was 1988 AMCA Specialty BOB. Breeder/Owners, Andre and Lise Lepine.

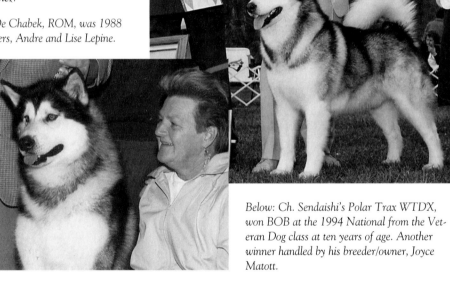

Ch. Sholyn Akala of Myakik, winner of the 1990 National Specialty, with owner Tracy Young.

Below: Ch. Sendaishi's Polar Trax WTDX, won BOB at the 1994 National from the Veteran Dog class at ten years of age. Another winner handled by his breeder/owner, Joyce Matott.

Top Left: Ch. Hug-A-Bear's Steppin Wolf won back to back National Specialties in 1986 and '87. Breeder, Cindy Elliason; Owners, Joe and Carol Hug.

Center Left: Ch. Northern Light's Togiak, winner of the 1987 National Specialty. "Togy" was the Number One Malamute for 1982. Breeder, Beverly Abbott. Owners, Joe and Carol Hug.

Bottom Left:Ch. Kaila's Wicked Witch of Inuit, a five time Specialty winner and BOS at the l977 National. She is the dam of four champions. Breeder/Owners, Chris and Eileen Gabriel.

Bottom Right: Am. Can. Ch. Kooskia's Catawba Chukchi, BOB at the l979 National Specialty. Breeders, Steve and Marianne Ross; Owners, James and Virginia Keecham.

Ch. Sno Ridge's Iron Butter Fly, a Best in Show winner and daughter of the beautiful Multiple BIS, BISS Am. Can. Ch. Sno Ridge's Blue Ice Lady O'War, ROM. Breeder/Owner, Eileen Kinnas. Booth photo.

Part II

Yesterday

The History of
the Alaskan Malamute

A working team hauling freight from the ships Alert *and* Discover *during the exploration of the Arctic. Courtesy of the Collection of Virginia Devaney.*

9

ORIGINS

The Malamute today is a product of his historical origins. His ancestors came across the Bering Strait from Siberia to Alaska during the last Ice Age with the ancestors of the Inuit[1] people who today inhabit the Arctic regions of North America and Greenland.

THE PEOPLE OF THE ARCTIC

The prehistory of these Arctic natives stretches back through many millennia and is largely a reflection of their adaptations to varying climatic conditions. Because they had no written language and virtually no contact with outside historians until the 18th century, their past is an ever-shifting puzzle defined by pieces provided by archeologist, linguists, paleontologists, and anthropologists.

The resulting picture of pre-Inuit development is one of successive waves of immigration from Asia over the Bering Strait land bridge, through Arctic North America to Greenland. During long cycles over the millennia, the weather warmed and then cooled, forcing the natives to change their lifestyle as their environment changed.

Continued existence depended on their ability to adapt. Their success resulted from technological developments such as harpoons and kayaks, which allowed them to expand their food base, as well as their use of dogs in a partnership for mutual survival. The ancestors of modern sled dogs, the northern-type dog that accompanied the pre-Inuit on their travels, represent an ancient dog strain with a long history of working for man.

The pre-Inuit's migratory lifestyle varied with the seasons. The short summer found them inland, fishing and hunting, while winter brought them back to the coast for sea mammals. Hauling their possessions back and forth as well as moving meat from the hunt back to their base took the efforts of the entire family, dogs included.

Improving portability with the development of the sled was the next natural step. Today's Inuit, direct descendants of these ancient people, maintained this subsistence hunting culture into the last half of this century. Since then, they have faced repeated incursions into their world that have changed it, perhaps forever.

THE PRE-INUIT DOGS

Until recently, interdependence between man and dog in the Arctic was complete. A walrus kill might yield a ton of meat, and the dogs were needed to transport it home. On the other hand, the food needs of the dogs increased the burden on the family. One to two pounds per feeding kept the dogs just on the border of starvation.[2]

If resources permitted, the group kept a few more dogs than were needed to pull their normal sled load. This practice allowed for illness, females with puppies, and lame or sick dogs. The number of dogs needed for a team depended on many factors: the number of healthy dogs, breed of dog, length of the trip, weight of the load, type of terrain, the depth and type of snow, and weather, to list just a few. If the load proved too much for the team, men, women, and children would take up the harness alongside their canine workers. For all the pre-Inuit (except the Aleuts who lived on rock islands with little snow), from Siberia to Greenland, dogs were an essential component of their adaptation to the harsh Arctic environment and often meant the difference between life and death.

PRE-INUIT DOG CARE

To prevent the dogs from gnawing through their harnesses, traces or tie-out lines which were made of either sinew or leather, many families filed down or pulled the dogs' teeth, especially the canines. Blunt or missing teeth also decreased the risk of injuries both in fights and to people who were bitten.

Because such dogs could not chew their food, the pre-Inuit fed them small pieces of seal meat or walrus skin which the dogs bolted whole. The pre-Inuit believed that the unchewed food lay undigested, satiating the dogs for a

An Arctic expedition prepares for its sledge journey over the ice. Harper's Weekly, July 1973. *Courtesy of the collection of Virginia Devaney.*

long period. Convinced that hungry dogs were better workers, they fed only every other day for working dogs and every third day for maintenance. If food supplies were low, the pre-Inuit advised Arctic explorers that the dogs could be driven for up to five days without food, although after that they quickly died.

Explorers who adopted the native ways to cope with Arctic conditions continued these feeding practices into the twentieth century. Much of the ferocity attributed to sled dogs, especially with regard to food, undoubtedly has more to do with their constant state of starvation than with an inherently vicious temperament.

Many tribes routinely neutered all male dogs except for the leaders. This ensured that females were bred only by the best dogs and also reduced fighting between the dogs.

In addition to pulling sleds, the dogs assisted the hunters by locating blow-holes where air-seeking seals could be harpooned. They also served as combination watchers for and hunters of the Arctic's most dangerous predators, the great bears.

DIFFERENT BREEDS

Although the pre-Inuit dogs were similar in type throughout the Arctic, considerations of work, geography, and usage as well as the type and amount of snow resulted in notable differences between them. In far northwestern Siberia, the smaller, lighter-boned dog of the Chukchi, which we now know as the Siberian Husky, was renowned for its great speed and agility. The Chukchi were subsistence hunters and fur traders who needed dogs to transport pelts from their remote, isolated settlements to far-distant trading posts. Their smaller dogs pulled less weight per dog at much greater speeds than those of the Alaskan coastal hunters, and if the load was too heavy for one team, teams might be combined.[3]

On the other side of the world, were the dogs of the Greenland Inuit. Slightly larger than their Siberian cousins, the Greenland Eskimo Dogs worked in the wide expanses of a still-glaciated land where pack ice created dangerous working conditions. Greenland dogs had to cope with heavier loads and much harsher living conditions as well as a different type and amount of snow. By all

NORTHERN DOGS

Just as the descendants of the first Indo-Europeans still have similarities in appearance despite radical divergences in language and culture, so too, certain characteristics of very different dog breeds mark them as related to these first "Northern" dogs.

From Marco Polo in the Orient to Nansen in Greenland, the descriptions of this type of dog and its work are remarkably similar. Whether they all originate from some common ancestor or whether they represent an independent adaptation to a common environment is a subject of much debate and conjecture. Regardless of their various descriptors such as "Nordic," "Northern," "Spitz-type," or "Arctic," all refer to a dog characterized by a natural, fox- or wolf-like head with erect ears; double coat with harsh, weather-proof outer coat and a dense, woolly undercoat; well-knuckled, thickly padded feet; and a tail which rises over the back to some degree.

The "Northern" breeds we know today as the Samoyed and Siberian Husky existed as working partners with the Samoyed and Chukchi peoples of Russia, respectively. Japan's dogs, ranging from the giant Akita to the diminutive Shiba Inu, are of this type, as are the Norwegians' Elkhound and Buhund, Finland's Karelian Bear Dog, Holland's Keeshond, and many others.

The persistence of these structural characteristics in today's breeds, from the tiny Pomeranian to the Alaskan Malamute, is a testimony to the vigor of these genes. Differences in coat length, color, size, proportion, and temperament are a reflection of the varied purposes for which these breeds have been used.

reports, they were tireless, willing workers but very aggressive. A favorite of polar explorers, their stamina and hardiness carried them to both Poles.

THE MALEMUTES AND THEIR DOGS

The basis of the Alaskan Malamute dog of today was the large, sturdy dog of the Malemute tribe (Mahlamuits or Mahlemuts). This Inuit tribe inhabited the area around the Kotzebue Sound of Alaska and engaged in the same hunting and fishing activities as the other coastal Inuit. The Malemutes fully realized the value of their fine animals which were reported to be of remarkable beauty and endurance. Much larger than the Siberian and slightly larger than the Greenland dogs, the Malemutes had a distinctive coat, a tendency toward more regular markings, and less variation in color. Their wolf-like appearance often led to them being called "wolf-dogs."

CROSS-BREEDING WITH WOLVES

Although wolves have been separated from dogs for longer than the dog has been associated with man, Arctic dogs certainly have a relationship with wolves much closer in time. The practice of neutering male dogs made a family's dog supply vulnerable through accidents to or the deaths of potent dogs. Eventually some sort of outside breedings would be necessary to compensate for lack of breeding stock or just to maintain vigor in a family's lines. One solution to these problems lay in the ever-present

This Malamute is following in the tradition of his ancestors, who served as bear hunters. Courtesy Mouthann of Belgium.

"Arctic," described as a Mackenzie River Malamute, at one time backpacked for Judge Henry Hildreth of Seward as he prospected for gold. Arctic ended up as the featured attraction in a petting zoo in Minnesota. When he died at age 20, he was mourned by the many thousands who had visited him. From Alaska Trail Dogs by E. N. Caldwell.

wolves. Certainly, too many accounts tell of female dogs in heat being tied out to be bred by wolves for these reports of wolf-dog crosses to be discounted.

Wolf-hybrids can be very unpredictable, however. Only the most dog-like would have been retained for breeding since the more closely the hybrid's behavior approached that of a wolf, the less likely it would be a reliable worker. These wolf-dogs would have been weeded out quickly, and, in most cases, would have been neutered and unable to breed.

To produce an effective working dog, the genetic contribution of the occasional wolf-dog hybrid would have had to have been quickly diluted. Many generations of breed-

ing for traits which made a good sled dog went into the Malemutes' dogs: body and head structure, coat, cooperation, obedience to an alpha, incredible strength, and endurance. While these are common to wolves, the Malamute is also a trainable, willing, enthusiastic worker, and affectionate and trusting by nature—definitely not wolf characteristics.

In addition, the coats of the wolf and the northern dog are slightly different, making the wolf, although an Arctic dweller, less suitable for unrelenting work in subfreezing temperatures. The Greenland Inuit told Knud Rasmussen that wolf coats were not as good for work in ice and snow as a dog's. Will Steger's problems with his wolf-hybrid Tim seem to confirm this report.

Tim had had a very successful career on Steger's team during other expeditions, but on his TransAntarctic Expedition in 1991, the unrelenting snow and prolonged cold caused problems with the ice that accumulated in Tim's leg hair. In trying to remove it, he began pulling out his hair, until he finally lost all protection from the cold. Eventually, the hair loss cost him his life.[4]

EARLY SLED DOGS

The sled dogs used on expeditions in both Polar regions during the nineteenth and twentieth century were able to perform at a phenomenal level, whether driven by Inuit, American, or European explorers. Their "sled-dog traits" were maintained by breeding under conditions very different from those of today.

The most basic criterion was survival—not the easiest task in lands of subfreezing temperatures, little vegetation, and sporadic game. To make life even more difficult, man and dog competed with fierce predators for the region's sparse resources.

Under these circumstances, breeders did not have to debate the merits of one type over another. Nature made their decisions for them, and over time, a certain type of dog prevailed because that type was ideally suited for the required work and the environment. Capable of pulling heavy loads over difficult terrain, these dogs had to be hardy and healthy and able to survive on minimal amounts of food. The resulting dogs were the most efficient size and type for this work.

Where there was competition for food, they had to be able to win it while maintaining a spirit of cooperation. The dogs had to work together as a team, with other dogs and with the people who worked side-by-side with them.

Accounts by explorers who used dogs tell of arduous

M. Robert Guggenheim's team of Alaskan Malamutes from a photo published in 1908. From the sledge forward are Jocko, Jack, Pincher, and the leader, Sneeze. Courtesy of the American Kennel Club Gazette.

journeys begun with scores of dogs and men. Air-drops were not available until after World War II, so polar explorers had to pack almost all the food for their journey. The dogs were fed the minimum amount needed to keep them going while they pulled enormous loads through the cold.

Freezing temperatures, drifting pack ice, disease, crevasses, poor judgment, bad luck, and starvation often whittled these parties down to just a few survivors—both human and dog. While the men were buried, no such fate awaited the dogs. Sometimes the difference between survival and sure death was having enough dogs. To keep going, the weak fueled the strong.

THE ALASKAN GOLD RUSH

While day-to-day life in Alaska was less rigorous than an assault on the North Pole, it was none the less difficult for man and dog. Here, too, survival often depended on using available resources, whatever they were.

In his autobiography, Leonhard Seppala recounts his early bout with "gold fever" and his attempt to stake a claim. During their trip, he and his companions encountered several "Indians"[5] who evidently were sick or dead from either white men's diseases or white men's food. One who had died in his igloo had staked his dogs outside. Seppala and his friends added these "thin and starved" dogs to their team and continued on:

> That night we ran across two other teams
> and another deserted igloo in which there was

a dead Eskimo. We wanted to occupy the igloo, so we moved the dead man to a place on the roof out of reach of stray animals, put up our stove, and made the usual preparations for the night. Soon other teams began to arrive. . . New teams kept arriving, and they all stopped. . . .

Meantime, the Eskimo had disappeared! We heard the dogs fighting outside the igloo, but thinking it was some new arrival we did not pay much attention. Some of the Malamutes, however, had broken loose, crawled to the roof of the igloo, and dragged the Eskimo down and made a meal of him. The next morning only his head and a few bones were to be found.[6]

Seppala and his friends harnessed up these same dogs and set off to strike it rich. Truly vicious animals could never have been teamed with strange dogs and driven by an unknown driver; facing starvation, the dogs merely ate what was available.

Seppala was only one of a torrent of men who poured into the Alaska and Yukon territories in the grip of the "Gold Fever" that drastically changed Alaska and its inhabitants in just a few short years. Nome, the city whose name was a contraction of the words "No Name" written on an early map, became an overnight metropolis.

Working on teams all over the area were dogs easily identifiable as Alaskan Malamutes. Men working in Alaska and the Yukon knew the character and abilities of this dog. Among them was Mr. Jackson B. Corbett, Jr. whose comments on the Malamute were a reply to a Gazette article written in 1908 by Cdr. Peary about the Greenland Eskimo Dogs he used on his North Pole expedition. Corbett said:

There are three broad divisions among the dogs of the North. . . . The malamutes have gained the widest fame of the three, their name being so closely linked to the interior that one suggests the other. They are hereditary workers, their ancestors for hundreds of years back having toiled along the frozen trails of Alaska and the British Yukon in Indian and Eskimo teams. . . . They are 'wise' in the slang meaning of the word, it being a common saying along the . . .Yukon that a malamute is 'the most cheerful worker and the most obstinate shirk; intelligent or dense, but always cunning, crafty, and wise; stealing anything not tied down.'

These wiry sled-dogs came originally from the lower Yukon country, their name, according to the Indians, being derived from the word Malamoot, the name of an Eskimo tribe living on the Bering Sea coast, the first natives it is believed to develop the sled dog in Alaska. . . .

The typical malamute's thick gray hair, his short stout neck, sharp-pointed muzzle, the erect pointed ears, and heavy forequarters suggest the gray wolf of the Far North, while the self-reliant independence of his bearing as he stands between the traces shows his descent from a long line of toiling sled dogs. With generations of workers behind him, he makes an exceptionally strong and reliable leader, in that place displaying the cunning, wisdom and trickery that characterize his breed. No smoother or smarter leader exists. No other can make life so miserable for an inexperienced or cruel 'musher.' So observant is he that once he passes over a trail its most insignificant details seem engraved on his memory, and years later, no matter how much snow has fallen or how badly the narrow road has become drifted, he will follow it with un-

hesitating certainty. He will find the way and guide the team to some lonely outpost, even when the 'musher,' . . . lies half-unconscious . . .[7]

Throughout the mining areas of Alaska and Canada, dog teams carried equipment, supplies, and the mail. In the frozen Yukon, they were the "mounts" of the famous Royal Canadian Mounted Police (RCMP). In the short summer, they did duty as pack dogs.

So many people poured into the area that the demand for dogs seemed insatiable, and the stock of native dogs was woefully inadequate. To supply the demand, dogs from "outside" (referring to the United States) were shipped to Alaska to work on teams. Some of these dogs were legitimately purchased, but many more were stolen by unscrupulous dealers with little or no concern for suitability for the work.

Judge Hildreth and Arctic start on a summer prospecting tour. From Alaska Trail Dogs *by E. N. Caldwell.*

Dog teams provided a way to
supply water for miners as far as
twenty-five miles away.
The lead Malamute on this team
shows excellent breed type.
The wheel dog (rear) is typical
of "outside" dogs brought to Alaska,
and is quite a contrast to the other
four. Photo courtesy of University
of Alaska (UAL),
Alaska and Polar Regions Dept.,
Lanier McKee Collection.

Dog teams working at a turn of the
century mining camp.Notice the
number of Malamutes
on this team.
Courtesy UAL,
Alaska & Polar Regions Dept.,
Henry L. Boos Collection.

A passenger sled, circa l920s.
Photo courtesy
of Tracy Young.

NATIVE DOGS OF ALASKA AND THE YUKON

The same differentiation of type that occurred between the Greenland Eskimo Dogs and the Siberian Husky occurred to a lesser degree among the dogs of the Arctic territories of the United States and Canada. The terrain, type and amount of snow, and uses to which dogs were put resulted in differences in coat length and texture, leg length, size, and substance. Subtle differences to an outsider, but differences nonetheless, were cemented into breeding lines because of the relative isolation of native population groups.

Accounts such as Corbett's confirm that the Inuit of the Bering Sound had a distinctive type called the Malamute. Other ethnic groups undoubtedly had their own distinct types of sled dogs; however, the miners and adventurers were largely unconcerned over distinctions between the native dogs. Consequently, few exact descriptions or comparisons exist.

Eventually, the "outsiders" who came to the area began calling all native-type dogs Malamutes regardless of their origins. The term distinguished them from the Siberians and from the outside dogs and native-outside crosses which were dispersed throughout the territories. However, to further confuse the matter, in writings about North American Arctic dogs are references to Labrador Huskies, Manitoba Huskies, Eskimos (a general term not specifically Greenland Eskimos), Malamutes or Malemutes, Mackenzie River Dogs, and a host of others. Here, "husky" is the generic term for a Northern Dog, derived from the French pejorative term for the natives, "Eskie" or Eskimo.

Because the miners scattered the native dogs all across the territories, distinctions between them are impossible to trace. The rising popularity of sled dog racing broke them down even further.

SLED DOG RACING

For the hard-bitten men of the Gold-Rush days, diversions were few and far between, and if they worked hard, they played even harder. Gambling in camps and in the towns' many saloons was a popular pastime. In the early days of the Gold Rush, skiing competitions—racing and jumping—gave those who could ski something to do, and those who couldn't something to bet on. Not everyone was an accomplished skier, and those born to it—mostly Scandinavian immigrants—had a decided advantage.

On the other hand, almost everyone in Alaska had had to put his hand to a dog sled at one time or another. That sled-dog racing would become the region's premier sport was almost inevitable.

In 1908, the Nome Kennel Club was organized, and the annual All-Alaska Sweepstakes race with a 408-mile course was inaugurated. Other kennel clubs formed and organized their own races. Winners became overnight heroes, and substantial amounts of money changed hands both as prizes and as wagers.

Alaska had succumbed to yet another fever—gambling. Every driver, regardless of his experience, tried to put together a racing sled team that could carry off the rich purses or win some money on side-bets. Dogs which had been brought up by hook or by crook from the "outside" were now bred into "inside" (Alaskan) stock in an attempt to produce faster sled dogs.

The All-Alaska Sweepstakes was quite a proving ground for the new sport of sled racing, and its stars quickly gained fame even in the United States, where their exploits were followed by a public eager for distraction from the growing troubles in Europe. John "Iron Man" Johnson, Leonhard Seppala, and Scotty Allen became familiar names to racing aficionados.

Team dogs still had to be versatile enough to go out and turn in a day's work. Few dog owners were wealthy enough to maintain a string just for racing. Even the record-holding Siberian Husky teams of the famous musher Leonhard Seppala worked on freight teams when they were not racing.

The preservation of the freighting sledge dog is undoubtedly tied to the technology of the time; had snowmobiles and tractors been in existence, the Alaskan Malamute as we know it might well have been lost in the racing craze. Even so, the years from 1909 to 1918 were among the darkest for the native Alaskan dogs. Much of this excellent stock was sacrificed in the quest to breed a better racer.

Breeding practices of the time almost ensure that some other pure- or cross-bred dogs were behind some of the dogs used to establish the breed we call the Alaskan Malamute today. Exactly what they were is open to a great deal of conjecture.

The genetic dominance of the northern-type dog makes the presence of outside breeds or wolves a moot point. The influence of a hodge-podge of dogs—from mastiff-types like the St. Bernard, herders like the German Shepherd Dog, or sporting dogs like the Irish Setter—would have quickly disappeared when the resulting crosses were bred back into the stronger Northern lines.

Summer provided no rest for working teams. This one, with several Malamutes, hauls a canoe on the Yukon River. Courtesy of UAL, Alaska and Polar Regions Dept., Lomen Family Collection.

The Malamutes which were used to establish today's breed undoubtedly had a few ancestors from the "lower 48." Their pedigree, if known, might have included an occasional wolf. However, these dogs are just as likely to have reached the "outside" directly from the Inuit's teams. Gradually, by various paths, these native dogs left Alaska for other lands. Their progeny became the breed now known as the Alaskan Malamute.

ENDNOTES

1. The Inuits are an ethnically distinct group of people who have inhabited the Arctic regions for thousands of years and continue to do so today. Until recently, Europeans and Americans have known them as Eskimos. Unhappy with this pejorative term used by the French to describe the native people, they officially adopted the name "Inuit" at the 1977 Circumpolar Conference. Inuit tribes inhabit Arctic North America, the Aleutian Islands, Greenland, Siberia, and Lapland.

2. Jean Malaurie, *The Last Kings of Thule*, (New York: E.P. Dutton, Inc, 1982), translated from the French by Adriene Foulke, 34.

3. Lorna B. Demidoff and Michael Jennings, *The Complete Siberian Husky*, (New York: Howell Book House, 1978), 40-42.

4. Steger, 141-144.

5. White men, even those who spent their lives in Inuit lands, referred to natives by a variety of interchangeable terms. Actually knowing whether the subject is an Indian or an Inuit can only be inferred, since both occupied territories in Alaska.

6. Elizabeth M. Ricker, *Seppala, Alaskan Dog Driver*, (Boston: Little Brown & Co., 1930: Boston. Reprint, Colorado: Hoflin Publishing Co., 1981), 123-124 (reprint edition).

7. Jackson B. Corbett, Jr., "Mr. M. Robert Guggenheim's Eskimo Dogs," *The American Kennel Gazette*, (Now published as *The Gazette*), (May 15, 1908), 362-363.

*Eva "Short" Seeley, matriarch of the Alaskan Malamute and the
Siberian Husky breeds. From a pastel by Dorothy Redding.*

10

THE MALAMUTE MOVES "OUTSIDE"

Alaska and the Yukon Territory exerted an irresistible pull on two U.S. groups: adventurers and missionaries. While there, like everyone else, they had sled dogs. When they eventually returned home, many brought their dogs with them. Thus the inside dogs gradually began to trickle outside to the lower forty-eight states. However, the largest exodus by far was caused by events half a world away.

WORLD WAR I

In their war against the Germans, the French government had become desperate for a way to get relief to their troops. They were cut off from supply lines by record snowfalls that had closed the mountain passes. Having heard about the Alaskan sled dogs, the French appealed to the Nome Kennel Club for help. The Alaskans responded by shipping the French army 450 dogs with their sleds and harnesses, along with two tons of dried salmon for dog food.

The French plight, along with subsequent U.S. and Canadian involvement, made the war a reality to far-away Alaska. Military enlistment eventually depleted the ranks of the racers, whose best dogs had already been sent ahead.

When the war ended, many of these men returned to their original homes. Although few needed dog sleds for survival any longer, their interest in racing remained keen, and they began to focus on ways to maintain their craft.

NEW ENGLAND SLED DOG CLUB

Outside Alaska, sled racing's strongest foothold during that time was in New England. The first recognized race was held in New Hampshire in 1921 between two three-dog teams.[1] This led to the first International Sled Dog Race in 1922, a three-day, point-to-point race held in Berlin, New Hampshire, and won by Arthur Walden.

Encouraged by the response, a group of enthusiasts formed the New England Sled Dog Club (NESDC) in 1924 with Arthur Walden as its first president.[2]

Recruiting newcomers might have been an uphill struggle for the mushers if the courage of a handful of men and dogs had not electrified the nation. Every day, men and women thrilled to newspaper and radio accounts of the greatest "race" of all time.

THE ALASKAN SERUM RUN

Attention centered once again on the little no-name city of Alaska and its inhabitants' struggle with death. In January of 1925, Dr. Curtis Welch, Nome's only doctor, saw his first two diphtheria patients and immediately recognized the danger it posed to a Native-American population with little or no immunity to imported disease.[3] Even worse, the stock of antitoxin available for vaccinations was woefully inadequate. The city sent out a desperate cry for help.

Although serum was available, getting it across a thousand miles of wilderness called for heroic measures. In one of Alaska's worst winters, mail drivers with their sturdy freighting teams and Leonhard Seppala with his team of Siberians transported the serum by relay from the railhead at Nenana to Nome. Mail transport usually took two weeks over the same route, but the serum arrived in Nome in just five days through weather so severe that the 5:30 A.M. arrival of the last driver, Gunnar Kassen, was unheralded and a complete surprise.

Unknown to the twenty men who participated in the 675-mile run, an anxious nation had followed reports from the tiny waystations and villages along the trail, spellbound by their valiant struggle.[4] When the serum reached Nome, the men and their dogs were catapulted into instant fame and controversy.

The lion's share of the work was done by Leonhard Seppala with his lead dog, the twelve-year old Siberian Husky, Togo. However, the lion's share of the publicity and the reward money went to Gunnar Kassen and his lead dog, Balto.

Kassen worked for the freighting company Seppala ran, and Balto was one of the sturdy little Malamutes that worked on its teams. Seppala was dismayed when Balto was singled out as a hero, mainly because reporters credited Balto with Togo's many race records, all of which was a bitter pill for Leonhard Seppala to swallow. He described Balto as a "scrub" dog who had never run a race in his life.[5]

Nonetheless, Balto modeled for the statue that still sits in New York City's Central Park. Erected by a grateful public to commemorate the heroes of the Serum Run to Nome, it was paid for by pennies collected from ad-

miring school children. At the base, the inscription reads "Endurance, Fidelity, Intelligence," a fitting tribute to the ordinary dogs and men who came through when the chips were down.

The Serum Run publicity revitalized sled dog racing and sustained enough interest for sledding to be featured as a demonstration sport at the 1932 Lake Placid Olympics. Many members of the NESDC entered, including a woman named Short Seeley who drove an all-Malamute team.

Sports cards popular during the era featured Seppala and other heroes. Courtesy of the Siberian Husky Club of America archives.

Above: Olympic sledge demonstration team driven by Short Seeley with Stewart Paine in the sled. Siberian Husky Club of America archives.

Below: The first relay team on the serum run at the railhead at Nenana, waiting to depart for Nome. Courtesy UAL, Alaska & Polar Regions Dept., Vide Bartlett Collection.

LEONHARD SEPPALA
Born in Skjaervoy, Norway, Sept. 14, 1877.
Height, 5 feet, 4 inches. Weight, 145 lbs.
Nationality, Norwegian
Famous Alaskan musher and the world's greatest dog-team racing driver—holder of a long string of Far North racing records over the most dangerous and treacherous trails in the Arctic regions. Won the last 3 All-Alaskan Sweepstakes, held in 1915, 1916 and 1917 (408 miles each race), and has won the Yukon Dog Derby twice. Won the Bordon Marathon, 26 miles, 385 yards, 4 times (record still standing, 1 hour, 50 minutes, 25 seconds); the Ruby Derby, 68 miles (record); the New England Point to Point race, 1927-28-29, 133 miles; the Eastern International, Quebec, in 1929, 123 miles (record); the Lake Placid race, 1928-29; the Poland Spring Maine race, 3 times, 25 miles; the Solomon burden race, 33 miles with passenger, 2 hours, 40 minutes (record standing), won twice (Nome); record between Nome and Fairbanks with passenger, 675 miles, 13 days.
Seppala was the outstanding hero of the great antitoxin race to Nome during the 1925 diphtheria epidemic, carrying the serum over the most perilous part of the trip in record-breaking time. **SPORTS CO. OF AMERICA**

IDITAROD — "THE LAST GREAT RACE"

The Alaska Serum Run followed the Iditarod mail trail. That trail is the source of the name and route for today's sled race, The Iditarod, also called the "Last Great Race." It is run each year in February from Anchorage to Nome, a distance of over 1,000 miles. Most racers today use dogs of a type called Alaskan Huskies, but the original mail-teams which carried the serum were mostly mixed-breeds, Siberians, and Malamutes.

In 1994, Nancy Russell of Storm Kloud Kennels decided it was high time that Malamutes returned to the Iditarod Trail. Her all-Malamute team, driven by Jamie Nelson, stayed in excellent condition which they maintained on a decidedly smaller calorie intake than the other breeds. The Malamutes ranged from 55 to 90 pounds; many of them were champions.

During the race, they averaged 80 miles a day over the toughest part of the trail. At the halfway point, the Malamute team had the highest percentage of dogs left running, but sadly, they had to drop out at the Ruby checkpoint, 654 miles into the race, because of foot problems.

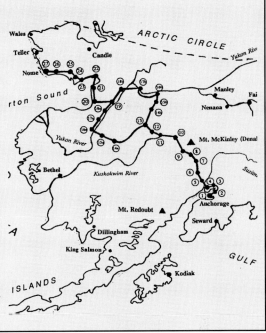

Leonhard Seppala and his lead dog, Togo, holder of many race records. Courtesy of Siberian Husky Club of America archives.

Gunnar Kasson and Balto pose after the Serum Run to Nome. Courtesy of the Siberian Husky Club of America archives.

ARTHUR TREADWELL WALDEN

by Gail Skoglund

Arthur T. Walden played a prominent role in bringing Alaskan sled dogs to the mainland. Walden was born in Indiana on May 10, 1871. He was in his twenties when he met Kate Sleeper, a relative of his stepmother, on a visit to the Tamworth area. He helped her locate a 560 acre farm for sale in Wonalancet, New Hampshire, which she told him she would buy if he would stay and manage it for her. With this agreement, Kate began running an inn to support herself, and Wonalancet became Walden's permanent home, despite frequent wanderings.

His association with Malamutes began when Arthur left Wonalancet for Alaska with only his collie, Shirley, for company. Living in the Yukon Territory, he found the dog-freighting business highly profitable and soon became a respected sledge driver. Shirley, however, suffered in the severe cold, so Walden made a quick trip home to drop her off with Kate.

By the time he got back to the Yukon, the Gold Rush had caused great changes. People were everywhere, and Dawson had grown into a city where life and property had to be watched carefully. Unhappy with this turn of events, Arthur Walden finally returned home to marry Kate in 1902.

He saw great potential for sled dogs in the woods of New Hampshire and harnessed his St. Bernard mixes to a sled to give rides to people in the area and guests at the Inn. Walden had many breeds on his teams, including some Husky-types, but he ultimately wanted a breed that had endurance, strength, tremendous power, and a friendly nature.

In 1917, he had three yellow pups from a breeding of his male Kim, a St. Bernard mix, to Ningo, a direct descendent of Admiral Peary's lead dog Polaris.[6] Walden named one of the puppies Chinook. Because of his size, power, strength and intelligence, Walden felt Chinook would be the start of his line of sled dogs. He bred females with Shepherd backgrounds to Chinook and used only tawny colored puppies like the sire to continue the line. As Chinook's progeny were trained to harness, Arthur and his dogs, with Chinook as leader, began promoting sled dogs and sled dog racing in New England.[7]

When he heard about a proposed expedition to the South Pole in 1927, the urge to explore was too much. At fifty-six, he was over the maximum age, but he and Chinook took the train to Boston to meet with Commander Richard E. Byrd. He left this meeting as lead driver and trainer of the dogs for the first Byrd Expedition (BAE I).

In 1920, Arthur Walden's Chinook team was a highlight of New Hampshire's Winter Carnival. Courtesy of Gail Skoglund.

Walden made arrangements for Milton and Eva Seeley to manage the kennel while he was away in Antarctica, since Kate had her hands full with the boarding inn. He gave Julia Lombard Chinook's puppies to raise and took Chinook and fifteen of his progeny to Antarctica.

Though Chinook had gone more as a mascot, he proved to be a hard worker. News of his exploits was broadcast by radio back to the folks at home. One night, Chinook disappeared forever, and an entire nation mourned for him. Walden was devastated at the loss of his companion. The news was particularly hard for New Englanders, for whom Chinook was a local hero.

Arthur Walden's return to Wonalancet was a grand occasion; his neighbors and friends wanted to name the road between Tamworth and Wonalancet "Walden's Highway" to show their appreciation for his achievements. Arthur asked instead to name it after Chinook. Route 113A in New Hampshire has since been known as "The Chinook Trail."

Further disappointment awaited, however. While he was away, the Depression had entered the picture, and Kate had been unable to make ends meet with the guest house. Unknown to Arthur, Kate had given a lease with option-to-buy to part of the property and had sold the kennels to the Seeleys in order to maintain the Inn and other holdings. Except for the Chinooks, all the remaining dogs went to the Seeleys, as did the name "Chinook Kennels."

Chinook at home at the kennel in Wonalancet, New Hampshire. Breeder/owner, Arthur Walden. All photos this page courtesy Gail Skoglund.

Disheartened by the twin losses of Chinook and the kennel, Arthur and Kate settled into Brook Walden, his father's summer home. Walden resumed his writing career, drawing on his memories of life in the Yukon. His books, *Dog-Puncher on the Yukon, Harness & Pack,* and *Leading a Dogs Life,* are filled with his adventures.

Walden's last battle with nature came when a fire broke out in Brook Walden. In a race against time, he saved his invalid wife by dragging her from the house to safety. As he tried to carry water to put out the fire, he suffered a fatal heart attack. On March 26, 1947, at the age of seventy-six, he died as he had lived—a hero.

Kate lingered on for a few more years, never knowing what had happened. They are buried beside Wonalancet Chapel, their names and dates carved on a large boulder used as a headstone.

Arthur Walden founded his own line of dogs, the Chinook, which, although rare, is still being bred today. He was also a key figure in the development of both Siberian Huskies and Alaskan Malamutes. About him gathered the great drivers of the past and future, and the fanciers who would shepherd both breeds to American Kennel Club recognition. Through his patronage and guidance, all the elements necessary for the furtherance of both breeds were brought together.

A recent day Chinook, Victors Umiak, bred and owned by Gail Skoglund.

A Chinook team is ready in front of the lodge at Wonalancet Farm, Wonalancet, New Hampshire.

ARTHUR WALDEN
AND THE SEELEYS

While she was helping organize her home town's winter carnival in 1923, Eva Brunelle (soon to be Seeley) happened upon a newspaper article featuring the Chinook Team in Gorham, New Hampshire's winter carnival. She decided that they were just the attraction the Worchester carnival needed and immediately arranged for two teams to appear there. One of the teams was Arthur Walden's.

When her turn came to ride across the snow-covered golf course, Eva was in Walden's sled. Suddenly, the dogs saw a cat and took off. Walden overturned the sled to stop them, hurt his hand, and was quite anxious about his passenger. His concern, it turned out, was unfounded—the diminutive Eva was absolutely thrilled. Arthur Walden did not just turn over his sled—he turned the course of the Seeleys' lives.

Before and after their marriage, Eva and Milton Seeley were frequent visitors to the Walden's Inn. They often assisted, arranging nighttime sled rides and special dinners. They even spent their honeymoon in 1924 at the Inn. Arthur gave them Nook, a Chinook son.

Several years later when he was in New York to speak at a charity event, Arthur Walden visited the Seeleys. When he learned of Milton Seeley's poor health and forced winter vacation, Walden persuaded the couple to move to Wonalancet. Preparations for the Byrd Antarctic Expedition (BAE I) were in full swing, and Walden would need someone to help with the kennels after he left for Antarctica.

Above: Milton Seeley with Gripp and friends.
Below: Short Seeley was, among other things, a model. Here she poses for a cigarette ad with one of her Siberian Huskies. Courtesy Siberian Husky Club of America archives.

MILTON AND EVA "SHORT" SEELEY

Eva Brunelle Seeley was a tiny dynamo whose stature won her the nickname "Short." Her influence on both the Alaskan Malamute and Siberian Husky breeds is incalculable and during her long life, she associated with many of the most important people involved with sled dogs, including racers, explorers, breeders, judges, and trainers.

Born in Worcester, Massachusetts, she studied at the Sargent School of Physical Education (Boston University), later working as a physical therapist with World War I veterans. She met Milton J. Seeley, a widower and professor of chemistry and physics, in a later position at Oregon State College. After their marriage in 1924, they moved to Nyack, New York, where Milton had established Seeley & Company, an extract-flavoring business.

Milton was diabetic, and by 1927, his health had deteriorated so much that his doctors advised a leave of absence. Unable to remain idle, however, the Seeleys agreed to help Walden at Wonalancet. There, Milton quickly became involved with the preparations for the first Antarctic expedition, a partner in Chinook Kennels, and the owner/operator of the Wonalancet Electric Company.[8]

In 1931, after obtaining Chinook Kennels from Kate Walden, they relocated it on 200 acres that they had purchased. Over the ensuing years, they engaged in a flurry of activity on many fronts to stay afloat financially.

Advertising Chinook Kennels as "Dogtown Village" or "Dogtown U.S.A.," the Seeleys promoted tourism by giving sled-rides, capitalizing on interest in the expedition dogs. Short became a skilled driver and trainer of sled dogs and an avid racer. Helping Walden with the first Byrd Expedition to Antarctica taught the Seeleys much about supplying dogs to explorers. Chinook Kennels subsequently supplied dogs for five other expeditions: Byrd's Antarctic Expedition II (BAE II), two U.S. military Antarctic expeditions, a U.S. Air Force weather mission, and the U.S. Army's European Search and Rescue Division during World War II. During the years they were actively breeding Malamutes, the Seeleys also bred and raced Siberian Huskies. To further their knowledge about Northern dogs, they also had Samoyeds and Eskimo dogs as well as a wolf named Wagush.

Firm supporters of children's involvement in sled dog racing, the Seeleys were instrumental in establishing the Junior Sled Dog Club. In appreciation of their service, both were made life-members of the New England Sled Dog Club (NESDC). In 1930, Short, with co-author Martha A. L. Lane, wrote the book, *Chinook and his Family, True Dog Stories*, a book full of entertaining stories about Walden's beloved Chinook and the other dogs at Chinook Kennels, including the first of her Malamutes.

Although he was a quiet, unassuming man, Milton exerted a calming influence over his exuberant bride and was well-respected by everyone he worked with. Throughout their marriage Short garnered all the publicity, but behind the scenes, Milton gave his strength and support to his wife and their projects. Dick Moulton regarded him as a mentor, and called him "the most unusual man I think that I've ever met in my life."[9] Although his contributions are largely unsung, he was truly a partner in Chinook Kennels. He made racing and breeding decisions, shepherded Chinook into recognition as a historical landmark, and helped with the campaign to make it a tourist attraction.

When Milton Seeley finally succumbed on May 28, 1944,[10] to the disease which was supposed to kill him fifteen years earlier, Short was determined to keep on with Chinook Kennels. President Eisenhower personally asked her to supply dogs for Operation Deepfreeze, and she received a military award for her service—the only woman to be so honored. After helping found the Yankee Siberian Husky Club, Short organized a group to start the Yankee Alaskan Malamute Club in 1970, serving as its first president.[11] She was also instrumental in the founding of the Siberian Husky Club of America and the Carroll County Kennel Club. When the AMCA was finally made a member of the AKC in 1953, she was its first president. That year, by vote of the AMCA, she was also the first recipient of the Dog World Award for Outstanding Service to Dogs. She is also in the Mushers Hall of Fame and was an AKC judge. Included among her many accomplishments are: being the breeder and owner of the first female Siberian Husky AKC champion, the first Malamute AKC champion, and the owner of the first registered Alaskan Malamute. Her stock helped found both the Siberian Husky and Alaskan Malamute breeds.

On October 9, 1971, in Philadelphia, Short was to be honored at a memorial dinner; however, she had fallen earlier in the week and injured her side. All attempts to get her to Pennsylvania seemed destined for failure since the ambulance service refused to take her from Wonalancet to the Boston airport. In desperation, her friend Beryl Allen called the Governor of New Hampshire, Walter Peterson, to see if he could intercede with the ambulance service on Short's behalf. He did one better. Short arrived in Boston in the governor's limousine.

An outspoken champion of the Northern dogs, Eva "Short" Seeley was a woman of incredible strength and devotion to the fancy. Her height made her hard to find in a crowd, but her lifetime of activity and accomplishment made her a giant in the world of dogs. The Mother of the Breed died December 28, 1985, in Laconia, New Hampshire, at the age of 94. Her legacy still touches us today.

This biography was compiled from several sources including material supplied by Wendy Willhauck, Carol Williams, Gail Skoglund, and the Siberian Husky Club of America Archives.

PREPARATION FOR THE
BYRD EXPEDITION

Admiral Richard E. Byrd's Antarctic Expedition had been in the planning stages for two years before its projected departure date in 1928. Although Byrd was an officer in naval aviation on active duty, the expedition was supported by private funding. (He was one of the first people to raise money by selling endorsements.) Much of his material was donated in exchange for advertising; therefore, Byrd tried to garner as much publicity as possible both before and during the operation to keep the public's interest and to generate money.

His "hook" to obtain news coverage was two-fold. In the interests of science and patriotism, a geological expedition led by Laurence Gould, second-in-command of the expedition, would map heretofore unexplored sections of the continent. This would increase U.S. knowledge of and claim to Antarctica. To capture the imagination of the public and to gain some personal glory, Byrd planned to add to the record books by being the first man to fly over the South Pole.[12]

Like the great Norwegian explorers Amundsen and Nansen, Byrd believed that the secret to success in polar exploration was meticulous planning and proper provisioning. As they did, he believed good dogs were essential for survival.

Arthur Walden was the chief dog-driver, and Chinook was the staging area for the dog preparations. Several other dog drivers destined for Antarctica were also there, including Norman Vaughan and Ed Goodale.

In 1927, Eva began to master the skills of a sled-dog driver, using Nook, the Chinook, as her lead dog. Milton, too, plunged into the preparations, tackling the problem of feeding the dogs in Antarctica. Using his chemical expertise, he developed a formula for a biscuit-type dog food that finally satisfied both the dog handlers and the dogs. Unfortunately for their future finances, he turned it over to a dog food company without obtaining a patent.

OBTAINING DOGS

Since Walden's sixteen Chinooks were hardly enough to supply the expedition, additional dogs had to be obtained. Frank Clark of the Clark Trading Co. agreed to donate 79 dogs from Labrador,[13] most of which were categorized as Greenland huskies.[14] The dogs were chosen by Dr. David E. Buckingham.

Familiar with previous South Pole exploration, Buck-

ingham and Byrd agreed that the entire fate of the expedition hinged on the health and working ability of the dogs Buckingham was to procure. Responding to telegrams, letters, and personal requests from Mr. Clark, dogs were gathered from the northernmost reaches of Labrador. From among those assembled at Harrington Bay, Mutton Bay, and Blanc Sablon, Dr. Buckingham selected those to go on to Chinook for further training.[15]

Other dogs were brought from Alaska by visitors to Chinook, among them another legend in the sled-racing world, Alan Alexander "Scotty" Allen. As they were sorting through the dogs, he called Eva Seeley over, pulling out two dogs that were larger than Siberian Huskies and told her, "This is what the large sled dog of Alaska should look like."[16] He said he wished he had been more familiar with them when he was running his All-Alaska teams.

Short was particularly attracted to a dog called Rowdy, although his name was hardly characteristic of his personality. Allen had purchased him from a Nome couple who had found him and believed him stolen. Although he was their pet, the dog had sledding experience and was a good teammate with scrappy dogs because of his sweet, gentle disposition.[17] At his first meeting with the Seeley's, Rowdy was about two years old and soon to depart for Antarctica.

In addition to Rowdy, the Byrd expedition took with it "a dozen or more large freighting dogs resembling Rowdy,"[18] which led the Seeleys to suspect that such dogs existed as a group if not a breed. They recognized that in any upcoming expeditions to which dogs would be supplied, freighting dogs that could withstand the extreme cold would be invaluable to the explorers. Moreover, Eva Seeley was fascinated by the big dog whose gentle temperament belied his wolf-like appearance. With this introduction, the idea of the Alaskan Malamute as a breed took hold.

THE FIRST MALAMUTES ARE BORN

Left to their own devices with Walden's departure to Antarctica, the Seeleys began searching for other examples of the larger sled dogs. Their involvement in sledding had put them in close contact with other people active in breeding and racing Siberian Huskies.

On a visit to Elizabeth Nansen's Poland Springs Kennel, the Seeleys came upon Yukon Jad, a dog from Dawson in Canada's Yukon Territory. Out of Grey Cloud and Pearl, the dog had been bred by Frank Gough and whelped in April, 1927. Grey Cloud was owned by another Dawson couple, Frank and Laura Berton.[19] Sold to tourists as a

Milton Seeley feeding at Wonalancet kennels. All Chinook photos this page courtesy of Carol Williams.

The museum at Chinook.

The main house at Chinook kennels.

pet, Jad ended up with Leonhard Seppala when his new owners left on a long European tour. Because he was now racing and raising only Siberians with Mrs. Nansen at her kennel, Seppala had no interest in the slower freighting-type dogs. Knowing that the Seeleys did, he gave them Yukon Jad.

Jad was the sire of the first Chinook Malamutes and was a strong dog of wolf-gray color. Like Rowdy, his erect ears were low-set, and his harsh coat, plume tail, and heavy bone, made him the type of dog the Seeleys wanted to breed.[20]

Before his departure, Arthur Walden had given the Seeleys a bitch, Bessie, whose ancestry was unknown.[21] She had been given to Walden either because of chicken-chasing or because she was stolen. Her former owner said that he was moving and could not take her. He said he had purchased her from an Alaskan.

Although she was small at 54 pounds, Bessie exemplified freighting stock. She had a characteristic Malamute coat which was harsher than a Siberian's, yet not bear-like, as an Eskimo Dog's. Bessie was gray with white legs and a slight mask. Mrs. Seeley particularly admired her "broad head, erect ears, and an EXCELLENT snowshoe foot."[22]

The Seeleys bred Yukon Jad to Bessie and whelped the first litter of Alaskan Malamutes as a proper breed in 1929. The four puppies looked remarkably alike and were named: Tugg of Yukon, Gripp of Yukon, Finn of Yukon, and Kearsarge of Yukon. Tugg was lost, and Kearsarge died on the second Antarctic expedition.

Gripp of Yukon went on to the show ring to become the first Alaskan Malamute champion, but he was a worker, not just a "pretty face." The lead dog on her Olympic sled team, Gripp lived to be 16 years old. Mrs. Seeley said she liked his "broad head, well-set ears, and tough, harsh coat. He just looked like what we thought a Malamute should be."[23]

BYRD ANTARCTIC EXPEDITION

While the Seeleys were busy with the beginnings of the breed proper in New England, Arthur Walden and the other drivers were setting up their base in Antarctica. The expedition got under way in 1928, replete with many tech-nological innovations, including "modern" ships, airplanes, and tractors. Nonetheless, the brunt of transportation work fell on the dogs and their drivers.

To reach Antarctica, the dogs were loaded on the whaler *Ross*, which crossed the tropics quickly. Problems with the ingredients of the manufactured food caused the death of five of the ninety dogs, and new food had to be made in New Zealand. [24]

On January 2, 1929, in the Antarctic summer, the dogs were released from the confines of the ship and the work of building Little America began. Haunted by the fear of having an ice section break off and drift out to sea, Byrd wanted the base located inland past an ice barrier.[25] The heavily-laden ships, however, had to tie up to the ice many miles from the chosen site, which meant that the dogs had to haul everything to the base. The trip was seven to nine miles, depending on the ice conditions, and unloading had to be completed before the summer ended and ice trapped the ships.

Every dog that could be put to harness, every hand that could drive them (including some who never thought to find themselves in charge of a team), and anyone who could backpack equipment began the arduous task of transporting the tons of material required for overwintering the expedition until summer would enable them to begin their exploration. Back and forth they traveled in the numbing cold. The "dog drivers pluckily maintained their schedules. They carried 11-1/2 tons of coal, in sacks, to the base, which is, I believe, a record of its kind," Byrd wrote.[26]

On January 16th, Byrd flew his precious Fairchild airplane to the base. By this time, Byrd writes,

> . . .dog teams were averaging two round trips per day, carrying from 700 pounds to 1,000 pounds per load. Only a person who knows dogs can appreciate what that means. Knud Rasmussen once said, 'I bless the fate which allowed me to be born in an age when the Arctic dog sledge was not yet out of date.' And after seeing them race into Little America, team after team, while the drivers fought top-heavy loads which threatened constantly to tip over into the snow, I could exclaim with him. Had it not been for the dogs, our attempts to conquer the Antarctic by air must have ended in failure. . . .

> Our sledge transport was not at all uniform. In size the teams ranged from Walden's, which was the largest, with thirteen dogs, down to four. The weight of the load hauled in each sledge varied according to the number of dogs in the team. As a rule the load averaged approximately 150 pounds per dog.[27]

DOG TOWN

Once winter set in, the dogs were kept in a snow tunnel dug out from the main quarters, called "Dog Town." "The

animals were tied to leashes that kept them apart and peaceful, and during winter were allowed to exercise individually by running up and down the corridors"[28]

During the expedition, eighteen puppies were born, and a maternity ward was set up to keep the puppies from being killed by the older dogs. These puppies had the run of the camp and several were later taken on the geological expedition.

GEOLOGICAL EXPEDITION

Planning for the geological expedition was crucial. Byrd was extremely reluctant to use his Fairchild plane for any type of supply missions, because flying in Antarctica was fraught with danger; a downed plane was a death warrant for the crew. Loss of the Fairchild also would have put an end to Byrd's planned polar flight, keeping him out of the record books once again. He had no intention of allowing this to happen.

The geologists and drivers had to compute the food requirements based on what they could cache and carry without resupply by air. They needed 1,209 pounds per man and 3,832 pounds per dog, far too much for them to carry at the outset. Although an advance support party led by Walden and his Chinooks cached food and supplies

Admiral Byrd just before taking off for the South Pole. He holds the flag and a stone from Floyd Bennett's grave, which he dropped at the Pole, BAE I. From By Dog Sled for Byrd *by John S. O'Brien.*

ROWDY OF NOME

Aside from his birth in Alaska, nothing is known of Rowdy's origins. He was a large wolf-gray weighing about 80 pounds. His brown eyes had spectacle markings, and his harsh thick coat was topped by a lovely plume tail. Rowdy had a compact body with very heavy bone, a heavy muzzle, and black nose and lip pigment. Although his ears were large and low-set, they were carried erect on his broad head. His legs were strong and straight in the front, his stifles well-bent, and his chest deep. Eva Seeley said, "He was the beginning of it all, a GREAT dog. Scotty Allen brought these dogs down from Alaska, and Mr. Walden gave Rowdy to me."[29]
Photo courtesy of Carol Williams.

along the proposed route, they were still short of enough food for all the dogs.[30] Byrd insisted that decisions about feeding the dogs would be made:

. . .[by] the inescapable economy practiced on all long-distance sledging trips—namely, the disposition of the worn-out dogs. It is more merciful to put them to death than let them die of hunger, roaming the Barrier. It may seem cold-blooded—and I suppose it really is—but a table of expectancy is worked out. . .and such a contingency must be provided for.[31]

The men who had worked side by side with the dogs for months were distraught about the decision and were afraid, also, that they could not carry out their mission in the allotted time. Gould tried to persuade Byrd that they should be resupplied by air, but Byrd refused to commit the planes except for flights to cache emergency supplies for his Polar flight.

Gould wrote that Byrd ". . .promised to leave dog food for the . . .party at his own flight depot if he could, so the sledgers would not have to kill the dogs. . . . Most of the depot goods and half the sledge loads were dog food, and the sledges were already overloaded."[32] Byrd also wrote in his diary, but nowhere else, that he planned to leave food. He never did, although he did leave other material.

At departure, the dogs carried 1,073 pounds per sled.[33] By November 18, the group had reached their halfway point. Knowing that Byrd planned a flight, Gould queried by radio, "Will you please tell me how much dog food you deposited for us? . . Several dogs will probably have to be killed within a few days and our present plans call for cutting to eighteen dogs when we arrive at the mountains. We like our dogs very much and hope we won't have to kill so many."[34]

Byrd replied, "You had better not depend on us at all. Left no dog food."[35] He refused to drop these supplies by air although it was within his capabilities.

On November 22, time and food ran out. The men selected the dogs and Norman Vaughan, as head driver, reluctantly volunteered to carry out the deed. The carcasses were cut up and the meat left at the cache for the return trip.[36]

Top left: One of the team dogs. Top right: "At the beginning of the long days, the dogs were eager to be off. Their sinuous bodies were the party's only guarantee of a safe return." Top center: "At night the dogs curled up and slept in a snow-covered ball." Bottom left: Packy was one of the dogs whelped at Little America during BAE I. Jack O'Brien took him home for a pet. Bottom right: "After a few minutes rest the dogs would be ready to go again with amazing energy." All photos from By Dog Sled for Byrd by John S. O'Brien.

BYRD'S FLIGHT

While the geological expedition made its way across Antarctica by dog sled, Byrd crossed the South Pole in the Fairchild airplane. Always wary of the possibility of a crash or forced landing, he toyed with the idea of taking a dog team with him.[37] With all his caution and preparation, the flight itself was almost anti-climactic since he encountered very few problems.

HOMECOMING

Summer was ending and the time for departure approached. The Little Americans began anxiously waiting for the geological team which reached Little America just

in time, after traveling a total of 1,600 miles. As they made plans for going home, men who had special pets were allowed to take them. Walden returned home with all his dogs except his beloved Chinook.

The first Antarctic expedition returned home in 1930 to an enthusiastic welcome. Since Byrd had paid for the entire expedition from his own pocket and through donations, he was interested in re-couping his investment in any way possible. The first of his schemes was to let the remaining dogs earn their keep by working at the Mount Cook Glacier until his next expedition, but nearby New Zealand farmers expressed reservations about having the dogs so near their sheep.[38]

Norman Vaughan volunteered to keep them at his family's farm, but the "constant flow of visitors and of let-

The Longest Dog Team Ever Harnessed

November 4, 1939, Dick Moulton, ace driver for Chinook Kennels, shouted "Yake"—and a cheer rose from the crowd of enthusiasts gathered at Wonalancet as nearly 100 trained Sledge dogs—a moment before lying quietly on the ground—jumped as one dog "into the collar." As movie cameras ground, this magnificent team drew a heavily laden army truck nearly three miles over New Hampshire's hills and dales . . . Those who were there saw history made. Here was the longest team ever hitched. Here was the culmination of the long arduous training. Two weeks later, most of these dogs were aboard the NORTH STAR sailing to Antarctica where today they are hauling heavy loads for the United States Antarctic Service . . . Such a large team may never again be assembled — but every day there's something unusual — at Chinook Kennels — In The Woods.

THRILL TO WINTER SPORT

The Tamworth Region—framed by towering Mt. Whittier of the Ossipee Range and rugged "Chocorua" of the White Mountains—has long been a mecca for winter sports enthusiasts. There are all the usual things to do that have made New England the winter playground of the United States . . . . But the ultimate in fun and pleasure is a ride behind a team of Husky Dogs. There's—

Dog Sledding From December to April

Dog sledding unites all the excitement of bob-sledding, skiing and sleighing with horses—with a thrill all its own. You can enjoy this grandest of winter sports any weekend this winter by coming to the headquarters — Chinook Kennels, where you'll find all the three recognized breeds of sledge dogs—and plenty of equipment.

LEARN TO DRIVE A DOG TEAM

So many sports-minded men and women have become dog team enthusiasts that this year Mrs. Milton Seeley has established a School for Dog Driving at Wonalancet where one can learn to handle a team of Huskies. . . . . Contrary to general opinion, this is not an expensive sport. The sleighs and equipment are reasonably priced —the team need not be too large to start. . . . Dog team driving gives one all the health and excitement of other winter sports—without the very strenuous exercise. No one is too old, or too young. Investigate this new rapidly growing sport.

CHINOOK KENNELS

WONALANCET   NEW HAMPSHIRE

SLEDGE DOGS IDEAL PETS

Fuzzy little Arctic puppies endear themselves to the heart of every lover of dogs but hardly less appealing are the grown dogs. They are not large. They are "easy" keepers. They have been bred for intelligence and strength. They are faithful to their masters but not quarrelsome with others. They are alert but still ideal companions. In short, they are

Perfectly Mannered House Dogs

There's a pride in owning a dog of any of the Arctic sledge dog breeds. They have all the virtues that have made dogs truly called "man's best friend." You'll always find a wide selection at Chinook Kennels—a dog that you'll be proud to own . . . that will become a pet within your home—one that your child or wife can drive.

This Year—Visit America's Famous
DOG TOWN

If you've seen Dog Town, you'll be coming back again soon. If you haven't, you'll have one of the most thrilling days of your whole life when you first see this village occupied by over 100 Husky Dogs—huge, powerful Alaskan Malamutes. . . strong, rugged Eskimos. . . graceful, speedy Siberian Huskies. . . All recognized breeds by American Kennel Club . . . . friendly and gentle, too. At Dog Town you'll—

— See the dogs whose litter mates are now with the United States Antarctic Expedition—hauling heavy sledges—over the frozen wastes of the White Continent where no mechanical device of man can go.
— See the Museum with its interesting exhibits of other Arctic and Antarctic Expeditions—for here was the headquarters of the sledge dog division of Admiral Byrd's First and Second Antarctic Expeditions. Here the dogs were trained.
— See the Puppy Ranch where the wooly little Huskies romp and play—possibly the cutest of all puppies.
— Meet "Rowdy"—20 years old—"first citizen" of Dog Town— a dignified veteran who dreams of his journeys to both the North and South Pole countries.
— Watch the revue, "Dog Frolic" — when the dogs exercise daily at 3:00 P. M. during the Spring, Summer and Autumn seasons.
— Thrill to "Dog Chow" — when 100 big appetites are satisfied every day at 4:30 P. M.
— See Dog Teams in Harness ready to give you a ride.

Come to Dog Town and stay as long as you like. It's a novel experience. It's something you'll talk about the rest of your life. You'll like Dog Town—and you'll like driving to it.

DIRECTIONS

Picturesque, paved New Hampshire Motor Routes (White Mountain Highway) from Mt. Washington, Cannon Mt. and Conway to Chocorua (Rt. 16) . . . from Portland (Maine), Poland Springs and Rochester to West Ossipee . . . from Lake Winnipesaukee, Wolfeboro and Meredith to Tamworth. Then —
FOLLOW THE CHINOOK KENNEL ARROWS
Along the Chinook Trail to Wonalancet — in New Hampshire's Storied Tamworth Region—5 miles from Chocorua Lake—11 miles from West Ossipee (Railroad Station: Mt. Whittier).

Above and left: Chinook Kennels' promotional brochure.

Below: Photo taken in front of the Capitol in Albany, NY. The dog standing on the left is Ch. Gripp of Yukon and the dog on the ground, front right, is Ch. Kotzebue Bering of Chinook. Photo courtesy of Carol Williams.

Yukon Jad, whelped in 1927, shown here at twelve years of age. Courtesy of Carol Williams.

Ch. Gripp of Yukon, the first AKC Champion, at twelve years of age. Courtesy of Carol Williams.

ters and of phone calls from people who wanted to come and take pictures of my well-traveled huskies," made his parents uncomfortable.[39] After four months of this, Ed Goodale offered to take the dogs to his family's farm where they were supported by tourists who paid a quarter a visit to see "Byrd's dogs." At feeding time, the fee rose to a half-dollar, and for an additional one, the visitors could feed the dogs themselves.[40]

When Goodale talked about the slaughter of the dogs in an interview, he said that he could not allow one dog that he found especially endearing to be killed. He later presented that dog to Short Seeley. She named him Rowdy of Nome.[41]

Goodale also gave Norman Vaughan six of Byrd's dogs to put together a racing team.[42] Distemper killed many of the rest within a year of their return.[43] With another expedition already in the works, Goodale returned the remainder of the dogs to Chinook to train for Byrd's next expedition. When these dogs returned home, the Seeleys incorporated some of them into their breeding plans.

AMERICAN KENNEL CLUB RECOGNITION

Their encounters with Rowdy and Yukon Jad, so similar in type and function, inspired the Seeley's dream of an American breed—the Alaskan Malamute. The acquisi-

tion of Bessie, and her litter by Jad, were the first steps in the fulfillment of that dream.

The Seeleys approached the president of the AKC, Charles Inglee, about breed recognition. The AKC was concerned that these dogs were just a variant of the Eskimo dog, and sent several people to look at Bessie and compare her to the Eskimo dogs in the area.[44] To further convince the AKC that the breed actually existed as such, the Seeleys secured an affidavit from Jad's breeder, Frank Gough, stating that the dog was an Alaskan Malamute and providing a signed, two-generation pedigree. The two breeds were deemed sufficiently different to warrant Bessie's trial breeding with Jad.

Inglee explained that the AKC would give recognition only on a tentative basis. Dogs of uniform quality would have to be shown in the Miscellaneous class until sufficient numbers were registered with the parent club to merit the AKC's opening up their stud book to the breed. To further interest in the breed and to educate the public and judges, he suggested that at least six dogs be entered in every possible show for exhibition only.[45]

In keeping with his advice, the Nordic fanciers joined together and entered seven each of Alaskan Malamutes, Siberian Huskies, and Samoyeds for exhibition at the famous Morris and Essex show. This exposure aroused a great deal of interest in these breeds.

ENDNOTES
1. Gail Skoglund, personal communication, 1993.
2. Skoglund.
3. The native population had already been decimated by a measles epidemic in 1900, followed by influenza in 1919, where whole villages died. Kenneth A. Unworn, *The Race to Nome*, edited by Walter Lord, (New York: Harper & Row, 1963), 16-19.
4. Although it received almost no publicity, a second run by dog-sled relay arrived virtually on the heels of the first delivery. Some of the same men and a few new ones braved temperatures even lower than those encountered by the first group.
5. Ricker/Seppala, 294.
6. According to Richard Tobey, Polaris was the offspring of Sipsu and Acutah, a dog and bitch pair brought back from the North Pole trip by Peary. (Tobey, "Origin," 27).
7. Michael Jennings, personal communication, 1994. The Chinooks accompanied Walden on lecture tours and gave demonstrations. He even taught one of them to trample out fire made with newspapers to demonstrate this breed's amazing abilities. As a team, they were so well trained that Walden gave demonstrations at the Inn where he would stand on the balcony and direct the dogs on the lawn by verbal commands only.
8. Nancy Cowan, "The Quiet Man," *Team and Trail*, (May, 1987), 13.
9. Cowan, "Quiet Man," 13.
10. Skoglund.
11. The Yankee Alaskan Malamute Club is still very active. It became an AMCA affiliate club and sponsored it's first Specialty on October 31, 1993.
12. Byrd had already had his fill of seconds. The second person to fly over the North Pole, his aggravation was increased even more when he was second to Lindburgh flying across the Atlantic.
13. This number plus the Chinooks coincides with the number of dogs taken on BAE 1, which lends credence to Eva Seeley's description of Rowdy as a "Labrador husky." (Eva Seeley and Martha A. L. Lane, *Chinook and His Family*, (Boston: Ginn & Co., 1930), 85. She later refers to Scotty Allen's bringing him from Alaska. Although these references seem contradictory, the problem might be more apparent than real. Although the dogs were purchased by Clark and were collected in Labrador and sent south, where they originated is anybody's guess.
14. Admiral Richard Evelyn Byrd, *Little America*, (New York: G. P. Putnam & Sons, 1930), 34.
15. "How Female Huskies Lead Byrd's Mushers," *Literary Digest*, (April 6, 1929), 71.
16. Maxwell Riddle and Eva Seeley. *The Complete Alaskan Malamute* (New York: Howell Book House, 1976), 31.
17. Pamela Mifsud, "In the Beginning," in *The Alaskan Malamute Annual*, (Wheat Ridge, CO: Hoflin Publishing, Ltd, 1988), 59-60.
18. Maxwell Riddle and Beth Harris, *The New Complete Alaskan Malamute*, (New York: Howell Book House, 1990), 183.
19. Richard Tobey, "The Origin of the Alaskan Malamute," *The Alaskan Malamute Annual*, (Wheat Ridge, CO: Hoflin Publications, Ltd., 1982), 32.
20. "Eva Seeley Interview by Kit Kirby," *Alaskan Malamute Annual*, (Wheat Ridge, CO: Hoflin Publishing Ltd., 1981), 32.
21. Richard Tobey points out that many of the dogs Peary brought back from Greenland ended up with various New Englanders. Polaris, the grandsire of Arthur Walden's Chinook, lived in Meriden, New Hampshire. In 1907, Charles Percy advertised four dogs and two bitches, an entire team from Peary, for sale in *Country Life in America* magazine. Tobey reminds us that Bessie could easily have descended from Peary's stock. (Tobey, 27). Seeley refers to Bessie as a Greenland Eskimo dog. (Seeley and Lane, *Chinook*, 94.) This may have been either her best guess as to Bessie's origins, or literary license on her part. Jad and Rowdy definitely were Alaskan/Yukon dogs. Bessie's size might indicate that she was more typical of the Greenland-type dogs, although Seeley says her coat was different. ("Eva Seeley Interview," 32).
22. "Eva Seeley Interview," 32. Seeley's delightful story of Bessie is entitled "The Dog that liked to Howl," indicating that Bessie was more than just chatty. If this sounds like someone you know, blame Bessie! (*Chinook*, 94.)
23. "Eva Seeley Interview," 34.
24. Eugene Rodgers, *Beyond the Barrier. The Story of Byrd's First Expedition to Antarctica*, (Annapolis: Naval Institute Press, 1990), 51.
25. Not entirely unfounded, as it turns out, since the original site of Little America did just that, many years later. Amundsen's camp was located in the same vicinity.
26. Byrd, *Little America*. 109.
27. Byrd, *Little America*, 107.
28. Rodgers, 117.
29. "Eva Seeley Interview," 32
30. Byrd, *Little America*, 258.
31. Byrd, *Litle America*, 257-258.
32. Byrd, *Little America*, 164.
33. Byrd, *Little America*, 261.
34. Rodgers, 202.
35. Rodgers, 202.
36. Rodgers, 203-204.
37. Rodgers, 49-50.
38. Rodgers, 246.
39. Norman D. Vaughan, *With Byrd at the Bottom of the World*, (Chicago: Stackpole Books, 1993), 152.
40. Vaughan, 152.
41. Cynthia Mekrut, "History of Famous Sled Dog Kennel Highlighted in Ceremony," *The Valley Visitor*, (Oct. 13, 1988). Goodale's account here actually says he presented Rowdy and

Holly to her. The impression left in the interview and in her own writings is that Arthur Walden gave her Rowdy. All documentation of BAE I, including Byrd's own writings and notes, indicates that except for the Chinooks, all the BAE I dogs belonged to Byrd and were never Walden's to give. It also is clear that except for personal favorites, all the remaining dogs went with Goodale.

The most likely scenario is that Allen did talk to her about Rowdy. At some point before or after Walden's trip to Antarctica, he probably told her she should get him (most likely after, since he would have seen the dog working).

As BAE II was being assembled, Norman Vaughan was purchasing supplies for Byrd, who was always pressed for money. It stands to reason that he would have asked Goodale for the return of what was essentially Byrd's property anyway. The remaining dogs were taken to Chinook for training.

Another historical oddity, though, is that Byrd himself reported that all "his dogs" died of distemper upon return. Exactly how Short Seeley actually got Rowdy is one of those mysteries left for historians to resolve.

42. Vaughan, 160.

43. Rodgers, 267. Distemper could and did wipe out many a kennel before the development of preventive vaccines. Mrs. Seeley reports loosing an average of 15 dogs per year. Losses of 30 to 75 dogs occurred during severe outbreaks.

Between the BAE I and II, the Laidlaw-Dunkin modified live-virus vaccine was tested on those Chinook dogs which had not already had distemper. It was a complete success. (Riddle & Harris, 184).

44. Jim Crowley, Vice-President, American Kennel Club, personal communication, 1994. The Eskimo breed was recognized by the American Kennel Club in 1888, but interest in the breed declined until the AKC discontinued registration and recognition of the breed in 1959. The breed is still recognized and registered in Europe and Canada, either as the Eskimo or Greenland Eskimo.

45. "Introduction," Catalog of the 1985 AMCA National Specialty, held with the Ramapo City Kennel Club.

Sno-Pak Sigdlumala with Short Seeley and John and Evelyn Barbonia.
Mala was bred by Arthur Hodgen, Sno-Pak.
Photo courtesy of Carol Williams.

11

CHINOOK DOGS:
IN SERVICE TO AMERICA

At Chinook, life settled into a rhythm built around the expeditions. The Seeleys bred and collected dogs, only to send most of them away. In the years before World War II, the Seeleys gathered the dogs that were to become the foundation of the Alaskan Malamute breed.

Because so much of the early breed history centers around the Seeleys, assuming that the converse is true seems quite natural, but the Seeleys' business was supplying and training sled dogs. To this end, they bought and bred all types of dogs for sled work, not just Alaskan Malamutes. The value of the dogs to expeditions was based on their ability, and the Seeleys had an outlet for every working dog they produced, regardless of its pedigree. Their interest in the purebred aspect of their dogs was a sideline.

As a result, breedings done for their business were often distinctly different from breedings done to further the Alaskan Malamute as a breed. That difference lay in their registration of the dogs; crossbred dogs were never registered or used for show or breeding.[1] Even within Malamute breedings, only those dogs that they considered representative of the breed were used for further breeding, and they might never be registered if their siblings were not of good type.

An example of this practice was the breeding of Holly to Ch. Gripp of Yukon. Born in Antarctica, Holly was a veteran of the geological expedition that returned to Chinook. Gripp was a son of Yukon Jad and Bessie. Their litter was born June 1, 1932, but the Seeleys did not register any of the puppies although they did keep one, Akeela of Kotzebue, for breeding.

Short described Akeela as being a "good Malamute type; grey and white with brown eyes and cap markings on a broad head with medium-set ears. She had a harsh coat and plume tail. Like her mother, Akeela was small, weighing about 55 pounds, gentle, and intelligent."[2] Her breeding to Rowdy produced Taku of Kotzebue, an important brood bitch for Chinook.

Another female important to the Seeley's early breedings was also named Taku. Heavy-boned and dark grey, Taku was large for a female. She had an excellent head with

HOLLY

Holly had many distinctions as a lead dog. On BAE I, she was Quin Blackburn's on the geological expedition and at Chinook, she ran lead for Short Seeley. Byrd, himself, credits her being lead dog on "the wildest ride I have ever had." As he describes it:

I accompanied them on a sledge drive by Siple. . . The team was made up of a number of the wild pups which had been broken, none too well, to harness, with Holly at lead. Most of the drivers were of the opinion that the pups were not capable of pulling more than four or five miles at a time, but Siple assured me they were wrong. We started down the inlet as if going to a fire.

Our troubles began. We had twice as many pups as were needed. The traces tangled, the sledge overturned and, worst of all, Holly stubbornly refused to stand still while we tried to straighten out the lines. In desperation, we fastened the dogs down with crow bars and snow shovels until we got things straightened out.

We had not gone far when the pups tangled the lines again. As I started to get off the sledge, Holly lurched forward, spilling snow shovels, crow bars, and me on the ice, and the team went off with bullet-like speed. It travelled nearly half a mile before Siple could bring it to a halt, and by that time I was marching southward with half a dozen crow bars and snow shovels under my arms. I was fond of Holly, but she was mightily in the wrong for the moment.

After this, however, the pups were on their good behavior and showed a surprising amount of speed over the last stretch; their strength was prodigious. They easily passed some of the bigger teams and carried us up the Barrier well ahead of the rest.[3]

Back home, she led Short Seeley's team in December 1933, when snow had closed the New Hampshire roads. On their sled, they carried the Tamworth district nurse to help an expectant mother. Short described Holly as being a 55 pound grey dog with brown eyes and a coat like Jad's. Holly died at the age of 9 in 1936.[4]

a mask.[5] Her pedigree shows she was inbred on Yukon Jad. She was one of many Chinook dogs sent on the second Byrd expedition, which is probably why she was called Antarctica Taku (or Taku of Antarctica, depending on the source).[6]

```
                              Gray Wolf
                    Gray Cloud
                              Susie
          Yukon Jad
                    Pearl
Antarctica Taku
                    Yukon Jad
          Waska
                    Wanda
```

ANTARCTIC EXPEDITION II

The second Antarctic expedition mounted by Admiral Byrd (BAE II) was again privately funded and, as before, had a two-fold plan for publicity and exploration. In the interests of science, Byrd stayed at a meteorology station far interior of the continent to gather data about the Antarctic weather. He endured a terrible winter alone and barely survived the ordeal. Meanwhile, the men at Little America carried out additional exploratory activities on a smaller scale than the first geological expedition.

OBTAINING DOGS

The dog drivers of the first expedition had largely moved on to other activities, and Captain Michael Innes-Taylor took over as chief dog driver. "He had served with the Royal Canadian Northwest Mounted Police and had sledged in the Yukon. He knew dogs, and was an excellent 'vet' to boot."[7]

Byrd further reports that:

We drew in all directions for dogs—the north shore of the St. Lawrence, Labrador, Manitoba, and (indirectly) from Alaska. At Wonalancet, N.H., Milton Seeley had crossed the Alaskan breed of the first expedition with Siberians and wolf, producing a stout sledging dog . . . averaging about 65 pounds. We selected some 50 of them. From the north shore of the St. Lawrence and the Labrador region we collected 76 huskies, typical Labrador dogs, motley in coat and blood history . . . stocky dogs with wide foot pads and strong legs, averaging between 70 and 75 pounds. From John Isfeld at Gimli, Manitoba, came 30 Manitoba huskies, . . . —magnificent animals, large-

boned, deep chested, heavy-shouldered and strong legged. They weighed between 80 and 100 pounds.[8]

"The *Ruppert* left Newport News with 153 dogs." They fared well through the tropics, although a few did succumb to the difficult climate or accidents.[9]

A GLIMPSE OF THE FUTURE

BAE II carried new equipment for transportation, although the snow-tractors were so unreliable that the mechanics suffered endless teasing by the dog drivers. The brunt of unloading still fell to the dogs and their drivers, but Byrd's description of the first flights during the unloading paint a vivid picture of the changes just on the horizon of polar exploration.

We decided, now to supplement the transport with aviation. During the next twenty-four hours, (his plane) made a flight an hour . . carrying a ton every flight. . . . By contrast the crawling dog teams and tractors seemed very

Seeley's dog drivers, left to right: Milton Seeley, Tom Buckly, Capt. Taylor (head of the team), Edward Moody, William Stanclife, and Stewart Paine. BAE II, 1934.

Dick Moulton and Short Seeley training puppies at Chinook.
Photo courtesy of Carol Williams.

slow and laborious. This same afternoon Captain Innes-Taylor and Al Wade drove two empty teams through the pressure (ridge) into Little America. . . . It took them an hour to make 3.3 miles. The going, they said, was hard and, in spots, dangerous.[10]

In an interview, Byrd reported that "Tractors proved successful in polar regions for the first time, covering a total of 12,000 miles. The dog men did superbly, covering a total of 7,500 miles. Dogs are still the infantry of the polar regions."[11] Nevertheless, change was coming, and hereafter, the dog would be relegated to a supporting role.

DOG TOWN REVISITED

Altogether, 121 dogs spent the long winter in the snow tunnels of "Dog Town" at Little America. In the confined quarters, the experimental wolf cross-breeds, or "wolves" as the men called them, proved to be a problem. Their fighting and slashing provoked the normally good-humored dogs into deadly fights. Of one team of nine hybrids, only five survived, and they later proved so disagreeable in harness that many were killed by their drivers.[12]

As before, BAE II had its share of puppies. No one suspected at the time, but Antarctica Taku's litter was to become important in the history of the Malamute breed. The sire was an Alaskan dog named Milt (Antarctica Taku's

Milt). The Seeleys considered him a Malamute although his parentage was unknown.[13]

In February, 1933, four females and three males produced by this breeding were born. Remarkably uniform in type and color, they were all wolf-grey and may well have been the dogs incidentally referred to in history books as the "Admiral Byrd Greys." As adults, the males weighed about 80 pounds; the females, about 65 pounds. Two, Cleo of Antarctica and Wray of Antarctica were bred at Chinook after their return from Antarctica.

DEPARTURE

In February of 1934, Little America was once more packed away, loaded onto ships, and taken home. This was to be the last major expedition of private origin. Worry about the troubles in Europe had brought the military and its interests to the forefront. The next expedition to Antarctica would be military.

THE KOTZEBUE DOGS

During BAE I, the Seeleys were just "getting their feet wet." By the time BAE II had departed, they were experienced hands and could turn more of their attention to their Malamutes. They needed more dogs, so they wrote letters to residents of Alaska and Canada, as well as explorers and travelers in the area. From correspondence and discussions

THE ANTARCTICA MEMORIAL

Admiral Richard Byrd took time to pay tribute to the foot soldiers in his polar expedition. On October 8, 1938, he dedicated a monument at Chinook Kennels to the many sled dogs that gave their lives at Little America. It reads: *Admiral Byrd Memorial to All Noble Dogs whose lives were given on dog treks during the two expeditions to Little America, Antarctica to further Science and Discovery, 1928-1930,1933-35. Dedicated October 8, 1938.*

The service was attended by New Hampshire governor, Francis Murphy, reporters, veterans of the expeditions, and, of course, Admiral Byrd, who unveiled the stone with the help of Rowdy.

Over the years, a steady steam of people wanted to see the monument, even though Chinook Kennels was no longer in existence. The owner of the property approached sledding sportswriter Nancy Cowan, who spearheaded an effort to have the monument relocated to a more accessible part of the property. On the fiftieth anniversary of the initial unveiling, the memorial stone was unveiled once again as over 100 people gathered to watch. The occasion served as a mushers' reunion and tribute to Short Seeley.

Dick Moulton gave the dedication and Ch. Kotzebue Taku of Chinook, who was out of the last litter that Short Seeley bred, pulled the cover off the granite slab which shows a sled with the bib carrying #1 over the crossbar to symbolize the missing driver. As "Taps" was bugled, a Siberian team passed by pulling a sled with the number 1 bib over the crossbars.

Rowdy looks over the original memorial plaque on a stone after the dedication by Admiral Byrd in 1938.

The new memorial unveiled at the 1987 re-dedication, with Ch. Kotzebue Taku of Chinook. Courtesy Carol Williams.

with these people, they refined their picture of the ideal Alaskan Malamute.

In a comparatively short time the Seeleys were able to develop a line which produced a uniform type of dog. Fundamental to this end was careful selection of breeding stock, using only dogs of similar appearance and strict evaluation of the progeny.

Of great significance to both the Seeley's choices and to the quality of the Alaskan Malamute was the dogs' participation on various expeditions. This provided both a proving ground for the dogs' working ability and a selection method without compromise or sentiment.

Where littermates demonstrated uniformity of type, the puppies were registered. When the puppies showed a variety of type, they were not registered, although an individual dog of merit might be retained for breeding. Applied repeatedly, these selection criteria resulted in a line of great genetic strength, easily recognized as the Seeleys'.

The now-adult puppies from Antarctica, Cleo and Wray were each bred only once; Wray, to Ch. Gripp of Yukon to produce Pandora of Kotzebue, and Cleo, to Yukon Blizzard, a son of Jad and Bessie, to produce Kotzebue Cleopatra. They are behind Ch. Toro of Bras Coupe, one of the breed's foundation sires. A study of his pedigree shows how these early dogs were entwined to produce a dog of genetic prepotency.

Ch. Toro of Bras Coupe, ROM, bred by the Hodgens of Sno-Pak.

Ch. Kotzebue Panuck of Chinook.

```
                      Yukon Jad
            Ch. Gripp of Yukon
                      Bessie
   Navarre of Kotzebue
                      Rowdy of Nome
         Taku of Kotzebue
                            Rowdy of Nome
                  Akeela of Kotzebue
                            Holly
Ch. Kim of Kotzebue
                      Yukon Jad
            Ch. Gripp of Yukon
                      Bessie
      Pandora of Kotzebue
                      Antarctica Taku's Milt
            Wray of Antarctica
                            Yukon Jad
                  Antarctica Taku
                                  Yukon Jad
                        Waska
                                  Wanda
```

Ch. Toro of Bras Coupe
```
                  Yukon Jad
      Yukon Blizzard
                  Bessie
   Kotzebue Cleopatra
                  Antarctica Taku's Milt
      Cleo of Antarctica
                  Yukon Jad
            Antarctica Taku
                        Yukon Jad
            Waska
                  Wanda
```

KENNEL NAME CONFUSION

The Seeleys finally settled on "Kotzebue" as a Malamute kennel name. Dogs that had served with Byrd had "Antarctica" as a kennel name—sometimes before, sometimes after the name. By the 1950s, Mrs. Seeley settled into a more regular pattern and named Malamutes with "Kotzebue" as a prefix and "of Chinook" as a suffix.

To further muddy the waters, however, their Siberian Huskies were named with "Wonalancet" or "Alyeska" as a prefix and, sometimes, "of Chinook" as a suffix.

FORMATION OF THE ALASKAN MALAMUTE CLUB OF AMERICA

After so much hard work, the breed soon began to attract other admirers. People interested in sledding turned to the Seeleys for dogs. As their numbers increased, the Seeleys undertook the next step in gaining AKC recognition for the breed by forming a national breed club.

On April 17, 1935, the Alaskan Malamute Club had its organizational meeting at the Seeley's home. President was Milton Seeley; vice-president, Volney Hurd; Treasurer, Miss Grace Hight; and Secretary, Eva Seeley.

Registration of dogs with at least a two-generation pedigree also began in 1935, and Rowdy of Nome became the first registered Alaskan Malamute. At first, dogs of unknown parentage were admitted for registration provided that they could win points at a dog show. This rule was changed later to allow breeding of non-registered dogs which could complete a championship. Although the dog himself could not be registered, he could be bred to one that was and the resulting offspring subsequently registered. Still later, this was changed to apply only to dogs of certain foreign breeds.

Short began showing her dogs. Gripp of Yukon showed well in Miscellaneous classes,[14] finally winning a championship after the breed was recognized in 1936. Showing took a backseat to the Seeley's business, so the next Malamute champion, Ch. Kim of Kotzebue, owned by Art and Natalie Hogdens of Sno-Pak Kennels, did not finish until 1944.

Despite Milton's poor health, the Seeleys had a very full

plate: active memberships in the two breed clubs and the sled dog club, caring for and training their dogs, welcoming tourists and reporters to Chinook, and pushing forward AKC acceptance of the Alaskan Malamute. In the midst of all of this, they also managed to send dogs off for the third Byrd expedition.

BYRD ANTARCTIC EXPEDITION III

Byrd's role in operations after BAE II was largely ceremonial, although his public image as a hero was so strong that government officials were never shy about trotting it out. With the third Byrd expedition (BAE III), the U.S. government took over Antarctic exploration. Unfortunately, this involvement came almost on the eve of World War II. By the time the expedition was actually working in 1940, the military had been forced to turn most of its attention to the ever-increasing likelihood of war.

Nonetheless, BAE III was the most ambitious undertaking to date. Two camps were planned, which meant that more dogs were needed, and the Seeley's supplied a substantial number. One base was at Little America; the other at Marguerite Bay.

While the expedition itself was fairly uneventful, winter set in early, and the leaders were very concerned about the developing ice. *Bear* and *North Star,* two whalers with years of Antarctic experience, picked up the 33 men at Little America and set off for the Marguerite Bay camp.

The ice pack brought them to a halt 200 miles out from the base. Supplies were so depleted that the 26 men at Mar-

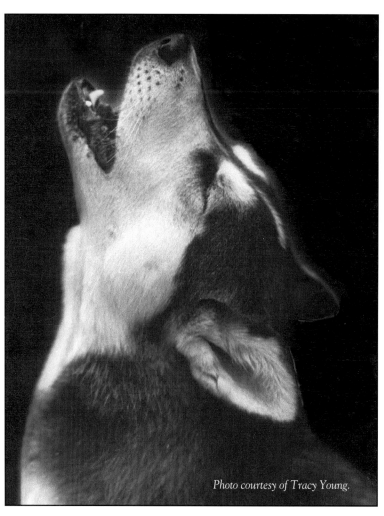

Photo courtesy of Tracy Young.

guerite Bay reported they were eating penguin eggs. The *North Star* left for Punta Arenas, a small town at the Straits of Magellan, to take on provisions, leaving the *Bear* to try to work in closer to the base.[15]

It managed to get within 112 miles of the base, but the plane at the base was not airworthy because of damage. In desperation, the pilots, Ashley Snow and Earl Pierce, fitted it with a new propeller and loaded twelve men aboard, but the overloaded plane could not gain enough altitude to take it over the mountains. Even though they dumped every spare piece of equipment, they still had to fly the more dangerous route through the foggy mountain passes. After getting as close to the ship as possible, the men had to repel 250 feet down from a plateau to the edge of the ice pack to reach it.[16]

After landing the first group, the pilots went back for the remainder, barely making it. At the base, they had to leave everything — tools, scientific equipment, and the dogs, with the exception of one litter of puppies smuggled aboard in a suitcase. Sixty-five dogs supplied by Chinook were at the Marguerite Bay base. The men shot many of the dogs because they were afraid that the dogs would suffer starvation and hardship if left alone. They then set three fifty-pound charges of dynamite in a twenty-foot triangle under the snow. The remaining three teams were staked out over the charges. "The last thing which the explorers saw of East Base . . . was the familiar upturned muzzles of Eskimo huskies, Siberians and Malemutes (sic), crouching obediently in the snow, just as their masters had ordered."[17]

WORLD WAR II

Before they had time to recover from the terrible news from Antarctica, the Seeleys were swept up in the war effort. While American involvement had not yet begun, the military was already planning for troop supply in snowy weather, and rescue of downed crews over the Arctic flight paths.

In September of 1941, the *Science News Letter* reported that the Antarctic "veterans" were being retrained for service in Newfoundland. "They didn't register for defense duty, but nearly 40 dog veterans that saw hard exploration service with the U.S. Antarctic Expedition in 1939-1940 are among the 'selectees' who will aid American defense in the North this winter."[18]

Training at Chinook, the dogs were part of a pilot program to use dogs for transportation around the Arctic Circle in the remote areas unserved by rail. Even though the Antarctic dogs had performed well under dreadful conditions, the Remount Division of the Quartermaster Corps had its own regimen specified for training.

The specially formulated pemmican, developed to meet the dogs' nutritional needs while in the south, was improved upon and officially adopted for use. Compared to life in Antarctica, these dogs were living in the lap of luxury, with special training, more suitable working conditions, and even sergeants with veterinary medical knowledge to care for them, a far cry from being stitched up by a dog driver.

DOGS FOR DEFENSE

As America moved into World War II, Dogs for Defense, Inc., recruited for many facets of military work. Their need for guard dogs was the most visible aspect of the service, but dogs worked in several other vital areas as couriers, carrying wire for communications lines, and in search and rescue missions for the Medical Corps.[19]

Among the military's most worrisome concerns was protecting the vast and inhospitable Alaskan coastline, especially the vulnerable Aleutian Islands. Although attack and sentry dogs consumed the larger portion of the military's resources and received the bulk of the publicity, dogs and men trained extensively for duties in the Arctic. These teams served in out-of-the way stations across Alaska, Greenland, along the northeastern coast of Canada, and all across the American Arctic Circle.

Like their human counterparts, most of the Dogs for Defense workers came from families scattered across the United States. However, few people at this time owned Northern Dogs, so the military sent drivers to go to Alaska and Canada to buy good animals.[20]

TRAINING CAMPS

Should the planned Normandy invasion fail, the military's alternative was to invade overland through Norway. Plans for material transportation included sleds and dogs to pull them. In addition to Chinook, the military had a training center at Hale, near Leadville, Colorado, which was the staging area for the 10th Mountain Division. With the success of D-Day, the training to accomplish "front-line supply" of the Norwegian invasion was scrapped, and the center moved to Camp Rimini, near Helena, Montana.[21]

At Rimini, dogs and drivers were trained for rescue efforts. "Planes at that time were crashing too often in the Arctic, along flyways used by the Alaska and North Atlantic wings, and some way had to be found to bring out survivors and victim's bodies, as well as secret equipment and valuable supplies. Dog transport seemed the best way," commented one reporter.[22]

Once again, the versatile northern dogs, among them Alaskan Malamutes, were working alongside their masters, toting ammunition instead of mining supplies and pulling guns instead of mail deliveries. They served from Alaska to blizzard-swept France, but were especially valuable in the icy reaches of Greenland, where they rescued countless, otherwise doomed, downed flight crews from the Greenland Icecap.[23]

Norman Vaughan's experience on BAE I made him quite valuable to the military. In July of 1942, a 25-man crew was rescued off the ice cap by dog teams. Their squadron of six P-38 fighters and two B-17 bombers had crashed after running out of fuel. Unfortunately, one of the super-secret Norden bomb sights had been left on one of the B-17s, and Vaughan was ordered to retrieve it. His success combined with his expertise earned him command of the Search and Rescue Section, Air Transport Command.

Vaughan's unit had about 300 dogs. Two nine-dog teams operated from each of the North Atlantic bases. The fast Siberians were the preferred breed for these teams, but Malamutes served on them, too, and worked as pack dogs in areas unsuitable for sled operations.

Airborne search units would use radio to locate a flyer from his SOS and, if unable to land, would dispatch a dog team to bring him in. The dogs were unflappable and learned to travel in planes and helicopters, as well as to negotiate difficult terrain on rope slings.[24]

Of the many locations where sled-dog training went on, Chinook was the best known. "[H]undreds of dogs have been trained for . . . innumerable wartime search and rescue missions. Here, too, many inexperienced GIs learned sled-dog

Tachenka learns to tolerate being dropped in a sling. Photo courtesy of Keith Hurrell.

driving."[25] An interview with Short quoted, "It's easier to train the dogs than the drivers."[26]

The military's appetite for dogs was voracious. Many who had volunteered their dogs believed that, if the dog survived, it would return home from military service just like its human counterparts. Some did want their dogs back, but many other donors died in the war or moved and could not be located. The War Department solved the problem by announcing that "dogs trained for service with the armed forces were enlisted for the duration and no appreciable number would be returned to civilian life until the war was won."[27]

However, by 1944, the number of unclaimed dogs had reached staggering proportions. The Army proposed auctioning off K-9 veterans, which brought a howl of protest from humane organizations, arguing that the dogs should be placed in appropriate homes rather than being treated like "broken-down armor and surplus food stocks."[28]

Although the war ended, the "duration" for the sled dogs was extended as the U.S. began setting up the Distant Early Warning or "DEW line" stations. Many of the dogs from Chinook spent the remainder of their lives at these installations, at U.S. Weather Stations, and at air bases continuing their service.

ENDNOTES
1.   "Eva Seeley Interview," 34.
2.   Mifsud, "Beginning," 74.
3.   Byrd, *Little America*, 286.
4.   Mifsud, "Beginning," 74.
5.   Mifsud, "Beginning," 74.
6.   Again, using old pedigrees which were kept by individuals and sometimes inaccurately passed on is always a risky business. In the AMCA Pedigree Journals, Taku of Kotzebue and Taku of Antarctic appear as sisters with Rowdy and Akeela as parents. These were two different dogs with different parentage. Other problems in these old pedigrees include nicknames, misspellings, and name changes.
7.   Admiral Richard Evelyn Byrd, *Discovery: The Story of the Second Byrd Antarctic Expedition*, (New York: G.P. Putnam & Sons, 1935), 18.
8.   Byrd, *Discovery,* 18.
9.   Byrd, *Discovery,* 18.
10. Byrd, *Discovery,* 86.
11. Richard E. Byrd, "National Geographic Honors BAE," *National Geographic*, 68:107-114 (July 1935), 107.
12. Byrd, *Discovery*, 245.
13. Mifsud, "Beginning," 74.
14. Mifsud, "Beginning," 69.
15. "26 Byrd Aides Faced Trap in Antarctic," *The New York Times*, 19:4 (April 13, 1941).
16. *Times,* (April 13, 1941).
17. "Last Antarctic Aid Went to Pack Dogs," *The New York Times*, 8:7 (December 30, 1944).
18. "Antarctic Dog Veterans Join Up for Army Service," *Science News Letter*, 40:165 (September 13, 1941).
19. "Dogs for Defense Out for Recruits," *The New York Times*, II, 4:6 (August 15, 1943).
20. Neil M. Clark, "Huskies are Something Special," *Saturday Evening Post*, 221:22, (August 21, 1948).
21. Cowan, "Quiet Man," 13.
22. Clark, 22-23.
23. "Dog's Work," *National Geographic,* 114:190-235 (August, 1958), 221.
24. "Dog Rescue Teams," *Science News Letter*, 45:230 (April 8, 1944).
25. "Dog's Work," 222.
26. "Dog's Work," 222.
27. "Army To Keep Dogs Until War Ends," *New York Times*, 3:3 (February 25, 1944).
28. "Sale of K-9 Veterans is Opposed by ASPCA," *New York Times*, 21:22 (October 30, 1944).

12

THE BREED
COMES OF AGE

After World War II, the winds of change that were everywhere touched the Alaskan Malamute. A combination of events, people, and problems changed the shape of the breed and its supporters forever.

PAUL VOELKER AND THE M'LOOTS

The recognition afforded Eva Seeley by the AKC had made her the final authority on what constituted an Alaskan Malamute. All the Alaskan Malamutes registered by the AKC before 1950 were Kotzebue dogs, descendants of the Seeley's dogs from Chinook Kennels. However, they were not by any means the only dogs referred to as Malamutes or considered so by their owners. Many of these people had purchased their dogs from Paul Voelker, who had been selling what he called "Alaskan Malemutes" for years.

During the days of the Gold Rush, Paul's father, George Voelker, supplemented his income as a Michigan woodsman by buying up dogs and sending them to Alaska. Paul spent a good share of his life raising and training dogs and other animals. Although he had worked with many breeds, by his own admission Paul was always looking for something else. He found it, ironically, in the same native dogs of Alaska that his father's earlier exports had almost supplanted.[1]

At the same time the Seeleys were acquiring and breeding dogs to establish their Kotzebue Malamutes at Chinook, Voelker was acquiring dogs for his M'Loot Kennels in Marquette, Michigan. These "Malemutes," as Voelker spelled it, came from many sources, including teams sold to Hollywood for use in movies.[2] He also traveled to Alaska and brought dogs back. One breeding pair, Dude's Wolf and Dodge's Lou, he acquired from the army at Camp Rimini, Montana, after neither made one of the sled teams.

In 1930, he obtained some dogs from Charles Nickerson who had moved to Duluth, Minnesota, from New Hampshire. Among these were some Mackenzie River Huskies. Two more females which were sired by a white Eskimo Dog

from Churchill, Manitoba, were obtained from Mike West of Hovland, Minnesota.[3]

Voelker's M'Loot dogs were somewhat different from the Malamutes being bred at Chinook Kennels. He accepted a much wider range of Arctic dogs for breeding stock than did the Seeleys, and instead of selling locally, his promotional marketing put his dogs in homes across the country from Florida to Seattle and Nova Scotia to California.

Marchetta Schmitt with Ch. Ooloo M'Loot and Ralph Schmitt with Ch. King M'Loot. Photo courtesy Delta Wilson Smith.

ALASKAN MALEMUTES
OF
M'LOOT KENNELS
(*Pronounced Maloot*)
The Home of America's Own Dog

The Alaskan Malemute, oldest breed known to man originated in western Alaska along the mouths of the Kuskwokim, Koyuk and Yukon rivers. He was and still is used for hauling supplies, carrying packs, and guarding, as well as a playfellow of the Eskimo and Indian children.

The development of that vast Territory could not have progressed without these faithful, staunch, friendly, big dogs for the intense cold of the long winters quickly eliminated weaklings, both man and beast. The value of these animals was recognized by our Government during the recent war and at this time there are several large kennels housing hundreds of Malemutes and a few of the lesser Siberian Huskies that are used primarily as lead-dogs due to their light weight and fast pace.

Rescue work could not be facilitated without the aid of the faithful teams and they are flown to the scene of the tragedy, dropped in parachutes along with sledges and first aid equipment—where they tirelessly haul the victims to safety and medical attention.

This greatest of all man's best friends could not go unnoticed here in the States, and many years ago, miners, explorers, prospectors and trappers on coming back (outside) would bring home with them some of their faithful trail partners so that both could live out their years together in memory of the grueling yet happy time spent conquering the frigid North.

We at M'Loot Kennels long ago realized their sterling qualities and could not but recognize the need for such an animal throughout our land. Slowly and carefully did we assemble the nucleus of our breeding stock for very few of the returned Sourdoughs would part with their dogs for any consideration. California and the movie industry were importing some excellent specimens and we turned to them for our first or foundation sires and a few bitches. Since that time we have travelled over countless thousands of miles, both here and in Canada in quest of better dogs, if such were to be found. These years and trips were fruitful in that for the past 5 years dogs raised and sold by us haven't been defeated at any dog show by others of the breed regardless of what part of the continent or kennel they originated in.

Famous Alaskan drivers such as the great Slim Williams, noted musher and lecturer, the man who drove a dog team all the way from Fairbanks, Alaska down through what is now the Alcan Highway and across the U.S. to Washington, D.C., have visited our kennels and pronounced publicly that our dogs are superior to those seen in the Territory. Earl F. Hammond, famous for his part in hauling serum back in 1925 to the stricken folks of Nome drives 4 of our dogs in his famous string that shows all over this country. Incidentally, Mr. Hammond is now negotiating to purchase more of our dogs to replace those growing old in his service. Dick Moulton, present owner of the famous Chinook Kennels of Wonalancet, New Hampshire, visited us and pronounced our dogs as better than any on the Eastern coast of the U.S.

Mr. Moulton had charge of about 600 Northern dogs all through World War II.

We enjoy the distinction of having sold dogs over a wider territory than any other kennel ever in existence for they have gone out to most all states plus many provinces in Canada and to parts of Alaska. Added to these glories, several youngsters were sent East and have since distinguished themselves as winning racing dogs, taking top honors in obedience trials, winning at the shows against the stiffest competition and are now retained as stud dogs at the best kennels in the New England states. Most officers of the Alaskan Malemute Club of America (in which we hold membership)[4] either own one of our dogs or use them in their business and for pleasure.

M'Loot Kennels are operated for the express purpose of raising and selling the very best dogs. We have been over 40 years in the business. If you are looking for just another good dog you have written or contacted the wrong place, for there is no satisfaction for this old Fur Trimmed Trapper in raising quantity dogs for a mass market. BUT, if you want an outstanding dog one that will stop people on the streets so that they stare at the dog and exclaim over his great beauty, you have put your sights on the right spot. We raise from 30 to 50 dogs a season only, as to do that and do it correctly, takes all our energies. Our dogs are never fed substitute feeds, we use meat and plenty of it, cooked for the puppies with lots of good rich gravies enriched with milk powder, and other nourishing ingredients. Of course, the grown dogs can get along in their new homes on the usual diet as a household generally has enough waste table scraps to generously take care of at least one pet.

Breeding stock is zealously culled so that your pup will have come from a mating that will produce the best consistently for a number of years. Experimental work goes on ceaselessly, and you are the person who benefits directly by having as a companion and playfellow one of these good natured, big gorgeously coated animals.

The Malemute has been reputed to be crossed with the wolf, this is not true except in isolated cases where a trapper crosses them to get valuable scent for use as bait. Remember the Malemute is a round eyed dog and not slant eyed as are the several varieties of Arctic Husky.

All dogs sold are absolutely guaranteed to be standard quality or better. Customers are warned against sending more than one half of the purchase price when ordering. Our local Veterinary examines all dogs before shipping, they are crated in large roomy crates with ample food and water and insured for the full purchase price. This next is very important—please have your Veterinary examine the dog BEFORE you pay charges as he will be shipped Open To Your Inspection before you pay. This method of shipping is your protection against paying for an inferior dog or one that has become sick enroute. We must protect you, the customer, for you are the one who will live with the dog for many happy years. If for some reason the dog does not measure up to what we have stated, please return him at OUR expense and your payment will be refunded or we will send you another youngster of your choice.

Weight of a mature dog is between 65 and 85 lbs. Height from 24 to 27 inches at shoulder. Good sufficient bone, excellent type with broad head and short well set, erect ears. Thick standing coat of from 2 to 3 inches and plumed tail carried over the back in an arc.

Colors range from black and white to light or silver-grey with every dog having an attractive masked face. Most dogs also have a white tipped tail and many of them have an extra white spot in center of forehead.

We are constantly asked—"will the Malemute do well in our climate?"—to which my answer is: "We have sold a great many dogs in the extreme Southern states such as South Carolina, Florida, New Mexico, and a number in the State of California and all write that the dogs seem to do better during the hot months than do the native dogs. Note:—the sun doesn't set in Alaska for about 3 months and it is very hot during that time, consequently the breed has adapted itself to the conditions and quickly shed the thick undercoat leaving a coarse long guard hair as protection against the sun."

There is no hurry in getting your dog after you order, we ship on Mondays only. This is to insure the dogs getting to your home in case of delay instead of laying over a weekend in some express office. Remember, we guarantee the dog and are constantly looking out for his welfare even after you own him so please do not hesitate in writing us and asking questions for we want you to be tickled pink with him for always.

The present season the price of a handsome well mannered youngster of 3 months or more, absolutely guaranteed, to reach you in perfect condition, is only $150.00.

We hope you have enjoyed reading this letter for it is not written as a sales talk but as a means of acquainting you with the Alaskan Malemutes of M'Loot Kennels, the finest examples of the greatest breed of man's best and most trusted friend, his dog.

Very sincerely, yours,

P.G. VOELKER, Manager M'Loot Kennels

(Reprinted from original M'Loot sales brochure.)

The M'Loot dogs, too, worked on sled teams and served with distinction in the military. Earl F. Hammond, a driver on the second Serum Run, used four M'Loot dogs on his demonstration team. One of these was Smoke, a son of Dude's Wolf and Dodge's Lou. Smoke's brother, Gentleman Jim, served in World War II and is in the Hall of Working Fame.

EARLY M'LOOT DOGS

Aside from Voelker himself, several kennels formed around key M'Loot dogs, using them as foundation stock for their breeding programs. Behind many of these dogs was Voelker's breeding of the two Camp Rimini dogs, Dude's Wolf and his great-grandmother, Dodge's Lou. Out of it came Fox; Smoke, owned by Earl Hammond; and Gentleman Jim, owned by Angel Pelletier.

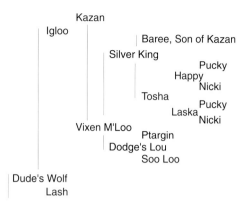

```
                Kazan
      Igloo
                    Baree, Son of Kazan
                 Silver King
                           Pucky
                      Happy
                           Nicki
                 Tosha
                           Pucky
                      Laska
                           Nicki
             Vixen M'Loo
                    Ptargin
                 Dodge's Lou
                       Soo Loo

      Dude's Wolf
         Lash
```

Fox, Gentleman Jim, and Smoke (whelped around 1944)
```
         Ptargin (Petargin)
      Dodge's Lou
         Soo Loo
```

Gentleman (sometimes Gentlemen) Jim is especially influential in modern pedigrees. Tora was out of Jim and a female named Lucky. Tosha and Jim produced a female known as Tonga, who did not have enough points for registration before the stud book closed.

Like Wolf and Lou, another breeding pair often seen at the back of old pedigrees is Silver King and Silver Girl, whose offspring include the female Noma.

```
              Kazan
          Baree, Son of Kazan
              Torno
        Silver King
                    Pucky
              Happy
                    Nicki
        Tosha
                    Pucky
              Laska
                    Nicki
```
Noma (whelped before 1946)
```
              Drift
        Tarko
              Chile
        Silver Girl
              Karluk
        Hoonah
```

Out of a different breeding of Voelker's came Mikiuk, an extremely influential early M'Loot. He was owned by Ralph and Marchetta Schmitt of Pewaukee, Wisconsin. They owned or used many of the M'Loot dogs which can still be traced back in today's pedigrees. Dogs from their Silver Sled kennel still appear in many pedigrees today.

Voelker was featured in The Escanabe (Mich.) Daily Press on Feb. 26, 1947, with Mikiuk, age 12, and Silver King, his prize lead dog. "They're gentlemen by nature,"Voelker said, and referred to his famous lead dog, Gentleman Jim. "Why, the male dogs will take care of the puppies just as the female will. And that's the mark of a gentleman."

Oomik
Tobuk
Nanook (not same as son of Mukluk)

Mikiuk (whelped late 30's or early 40's)

Peluk
Kapuk
Oolik

The breeding of Mikiuk and Noma was historic, producing two champions of importance, Ch. Mulpus Brook's Master Otter, and the first champion female in the breed, the great Ch. Ooloo M'Loot. They were bred by Voelker and the Schmitts and owned by the Schmitts. The lovely female, Chitana, bred by E. Traphagen and owned by Kenneth Smith, was produced by another line-breeding, this time, Schmoos (M'Loot) and Tora.

Nanook (Nahnook) was out of Fox. Nanook's influence was extended through his son Nanook II. Linebreeding on Dodge's Lou and Kazan continued to establish M'Loot type. Nanook's half-brother out of Fox was the early M'Loot champion, Ch. King M'Loot, who in turn produced Ch. Zorro of Silver Sled with Tosha of Silver Sled.

When the Schmitts crossed Nanook (Nahnook) to Ooloo, the breeding produced both Ch. Nanook (Nahnook) II and Ch. Gyana. Inbreeding on Nanook II produced Silver Sled Cabara and Pancho. The offspring of various combinations of these early M'Loots became foundation dogs for many later kennels. Their lines were interwoven with other strains to provide many of today's Malamutes.

Ch. Gyana of Silver Sled and Ch. Nanook II. Photos this page courtesy Delta Wilson Smith.

Notak of Silver Sled (bitch) by Ch. King M'Loot ex Ch. Gyana.

Ch. Ooloo M'Loot, owned by Silver Sled kennel.

Ch. Tuyah of Silver Sled, owned by Delta Wilson Smith.

```
                    Baree, Son of Kazan
              Silver King
                    Tosha
        Mukluk M'Loot
                    Silver King
              Vixen (M'Loot)
                    Dodge's Lou
Nanook (whelped before 1945)
                          Kazan
              Igloo
                          Vixen (M'Loot)
        Dude's Wolf
                    Lash
        Fox
                    Ptargin
              Dodges Lou
                    Soo Loo
```

Moosecat M'Loot became a foundation sire for many kennels, including Husky-Pak and Red Horse. One of his sisters was Cheechako M'Loot.

```
                          Oomik
                    Tobuk
                          Nanook (older dog, not sire of Nanook II)
              Mikiuk
                          Peluk
                    Kapuk
                          Oolik

Moosecat M'Loot, Cheechako M'Loot
(whelped 1945 or 1946)

                          Yukon King
                    Mobey
                          Star
              Unutkoot
                          Silver King
                    Miska
                          Happy
              Tosha
                    Laska
```

What happened to Paul Voelker? The back of this postcard sent to Delta Wilson Smith in 1955 tends to confirm rumors that he moved from Michigan to Arizona and changed his name to Don Pablo.

Mukluk M'Loot
Nahnook I
Fox
Ch. Nahnook II
Mikiuk
Ch. Ooloo M'Loot
Noma
Silver Sled Cabara, Pancho
(whelped 1949 or 1950)

Nahnook I
Ch. Nahnook II
Chimo of Silver Sled
Ch. King M'Loot
Ch. Zorro of Silver Sled
Nooka M'Loot
Tosha of Silver Sled
Ch. King M'Loot
Oogerook of Silver Sled
Ch. Gyana

HINMAN-IRWIN DOGS

Many of the men who returned home from Alaska to settle down brought a special team dog back with them. Although some of these were Malamutes, many passed their lives as companions and were not significant to the breed as a whole. Notable exceptions to this were the few dogs owned by Dick Hinman and Dave Irwin, now referred to as the Hinman-Irwin Dogs.

Robert Zoller began looking for Alaskan Malamutes by visiting Chinook Kennels. At the time, Dick Moulton was running the kennel.[5] After seeing the dogs, Zoller told Moulton that while he liked the look of them, he felt the Kotzebue Malamutes were too small. Moulton sent him to Dick Hinman. Of his meeting with Hinman, Zoller wrote:

Dick Hinman was a barber and when I got there, he was in the middle of giving somebody a haircut. There weren't many Malamute

Robert Zoller with Ch. Apache Chief of Husky-Pak and (clockwise) Ch. Cherokee of Husky-Pak, Ch. Husky-Pak Marclair's Sioux, and Ch. Arctic Storm of Husky-Pak. From an original by Dorothy Redding, courtesy of the artist.

people in those days, and I guess he was just as happy as I was to talk to someone about them. He sent me around back to his kennel where he had these two dogs. I looked up this hill, and there were two of the most impressive Malamutes I've ever seen in my life.

They were chained, and I knew this was what I thought a Malamute should look like. Hinman had a litter and told me that one was the sire of the litter and the other the grandfather.[6]

The father of the litter was Hinman's Alaska and the grandfather was Irwin's Gemo (also seen on pedigrees as "Erwin's" and "Gimo" or "Chimo"). Gemo's parents, Igloo and Lynx,[7] were brought from the Baker Lake area of Canada by David Irwin.

Like many dogs who ended up in New England, Gemo worked on a resort dog team owned by Craig Burt at Ranch Camp in Stowe, Vermont.[8] Dick Hinman drove the team when not plying his trade,and used Gemo for breeding. Later, Gemo was sold to Lowell Thomas, a famous writer and adventurer of the day.

Zoller felt the Hinman-Irwin dogs compared favorably with dogs of both the Seeley's and of Voelker's breedings. Also, the Hinman-Irwin dogs were similar to each other, yet slightly different in type from the M'Loots and Kotzebues. These dogs contributed an extra dash of quality to the breeding programs of several kennels. Of particular significance was the breeding of Irwin's Gemo and Hinman's Sitka, which produced Kiska. Through her two sons, Hinman's Alaska and Ch. Spawn's Alaska, came foundation dogs for several important kennels.

The Hinman-Irwin Dogs are often referred to as a "third strain," the others being Kotzebue and M'Loot. However, Robert Zoller qualifies this by saying they are "*like* a third strain." He hastens to emphasize the word "like," since too few were ever bred to justify identifying them as a strain.[9]

NEW DIRECTIONS

By 1950, the American Kennel Club became alarmed at the decrease in registered Alaskan Malamutes. Even without the devastating loss of the dogs at Marguerite Bay, Chinook's ranks had been depleted by the war. Eva Seeley's concern for the breed had kept her from selling breeding stock indiscriminately, so only a handful of registered Malamutes were in outside breeding kennels. She had very few dogs, as was true of most other kennels.

Purchasing dogs from Alaska was no longer a viable

possibility. The flurry of invention and innovation that arose after the war had a profound effect on the native Alaskan dogs. There, the very real threat of Japanese invasion had made a system of roads to reach military bases necessary. Many of these were built over the old mail-team trails linking the isolated villages of Alaska and Canada. Just as the roads replaced the sled trails, trucks, trains, and motorized sleds gradually replaced the sturdy freighting dogs who had travelled them. As a result, the native population of dogs began to decrease.

Despite the advances in motorized transportation, polar bases still kept service dogs for search and rescue and occasional sled work. Although this was laudable service, a dog in Antarctica or at a weather station was unavailable for breeding in the United States.

AKC REOPENS STUD BOOK

When the "base stock" of registered Alaskan Malamutes dropped to thirty dogs, the American Kennel Club took action and reopened the stud book for further registrations.[10] Many of the AMCA members and, of course, Eva Seeley, were aware that other people owned unregistered dogs that they called Malamutes, but none of the AMCA members considered these dogs representative of the breed. They were understandably resentful and bitter at the action of the AKC.

On the other hand, the owners of these M'Loot and Hinman-Irwin dogs were delighted. They considered their dogs true Alaskan Malamutes and had been eagerly waiting in the wings for confirmation of their belief. In their view, the new registration policy proved that their dogs were just as good, if not better, than the Kotzebue dogs since their registration had to be earned and was not granted on just one person's authority.

To gain registration, the newcomers had to pay an additional listing fee and show the unregistered dog until it had ten points. The owner then could apply for registration by sending a picture of the dog with a front, back, and side view.[11] Although none of the dogs owned solely by Paul Voelker, Dick Hinman, or Dave Irwin were ever registered, many people who bought their dogs or bred from them succeeded in winning a place in the Stud Book.

After 1950, the Alaskan Malamute began evolving into a mixture of Kotzebue and M'Loot with a dash of Hinman-Irwin thrown in for spice. The diversity of the M'Loots challenged the uniformity of the Kotzebue dogs. After an adjustment period, the additions did strengthen and improve the breed.

CHANGES IN THE AMCA

Not only did M'Loot owners begin showing, they also began joining the national club. They wanted a say in the breed, and this caught the Kotzebue camp on the horns of a dilemma.

Eva Seeley and her supporters were quite upset over the inclusion of the M'Loots. At best they considered them incorrect; at worst, another breed altogether. They certainly were not interested in sharing their breed club with interlopers.

On the other hand, they were determined to achieve AKC membership status for the AMCA, if for no other reason than to avoid surprises like the reopening of the Stud Book. One requirement was a growing, viable club, but AMCA's rosters had been growing very slowly.

Thus the new applicants were a mixed blessing, and while they were not welcomed with open arms, eventually they were accepted. Both groups had to declare a truce and get along for the good of the club and the breed.

Although the schism continued for decades, membership continued to grow. New people entered the breed, showed their dogs, and joined the national club. Some stayed with their original type of dog, but others branched out, trying new combinations. Among these innovators were the Zollers of Husky-Pak Kennels. Their combination of the various strains began the process that would ultimately change the shape of the breed.

THE ZOLLERS-HUSKY-PAK KENNELS

During the war, the young naval officer Robert Zoller was very impressed with a dog he saw in Argentia, Newfoundland. He was told it was an Alaskan Malamute. "I was fascinated by this appearance of fierceness and power, and yet the gentle disposition that the dog had."[12] Later he and his wife Laura discovered the Malamute was actually an AKC-recognized breed. They wrote for the names of some breeders which is how Robert ended up talking to Dick Moulton and visiting Dick Hinman.

Zoller was very impressed by the two dogs there, Irwin's Gemo and his son, Hinman's Alaska. Seeing them convinced him to buy his new puppy, Kayak of Brookside.

The Zollers decided they needed a second dog to keep the active Kayak company. Under consideration were a M'Loot female from Seguin, Texas, sired by Moosecat M'Loot bred to Eyak, a daughter of Mikiuk and Tosha, and a show-quality male and female, both at Hazel Wilton's kennel.

When they could not make up their minds, they

CH. SPAWN'S ALASKA

Some time after Geronimo and Storm became members of the Zoller's household, Hazel Wilton offered the Zollers their sire. The Zollers declined regretfully. They had decided they had enough males in the household.

Bob and Alice Spawn, who had used several kennel names over the years, including Spawn's, Polar (for their first dog, a white), Wilderness and Polar Den, decided to buy him. They called him Spawn's Alaska.

Like many others, the Spawns too were trying to get their dogs registered. The competition was keen, and getting points was difficult. Not only were there fewer shows then, transportation was slower, and very few Malamutes were shown. Nonetheless, Spawn's Alaska finished his championship and gained registration, taking best of breed at Westminster twice.

His influence on the breed is carried through the ubiquitous Husky Pak dogs. That he appears in pedigrees at all is doubly remarkable because he sired only the one litter.

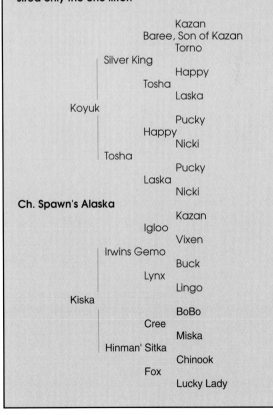

decided to buy all three. The dogs became Ch. Husky-Pak Mikya of Seguin, Ch. Apache Chief of Husky Pak (Geronimo), and Ch. Arctic Storm of Husky-Pak, respectively. All of their registrations were achieved through showing.

The Zollers bred Kayak both to Mikya and Arctic Storm, who was a daughter of Ch. Spawn's Alaska. Mikya's litter was not so satisfactory, but Arctic Storm's "B" litter had Buccaneer, Black Hawk, and Banshee, all of which became champions.

Igloo

Irwin's Gemo

Lynx

Hinman's Alaska

Douglas' Fang Silk

Hinman's Sitka

Gardner's Alaska

Kayak of Brookside

Douglas' Klondike

Keemo Chief

Douglas' Kazanne

Mayo's Nome

Mishe-Mokwa

Mayo's Reeka

Kudd-La

Ch. Black Hawk of Husky Pak, CD
Ch. Banshee, Ch. Buccaneer (whelped 1950)

Silver King

Koyuk

Tosha

Ch. Spawn's Alaska

Irwin's Gemo

Kiska

Hinman's Sitka

Ch. Arctic Storm of Husky-Pak (Whelped 7-7-48)

Mikiuk

Schmoo's M'Loot

Vixen M'Loot

Chitina

Gentleman Jim

Tora

Lucky

Kayak of Brookside, courtesy of Delta Wilson Smith.

Geronimo went best of breed the first time he stepped into the ring. He was just as accomplished a sire, producing three champions in each of his three litters, which is an impressive achievement for any dog.

Bob Zoller was well aware of the differences between the M'Loot and Kotzebue dogs, as well as the strong rivalry between the two camps that at times blossomed into antagonism. His first dogs were definitely more M'Loot in appearance. Geronimo was 27 inches at the shoulder and weighed 115 pounds, a far cry from the biggest of the Kotzebue dogs.

Zoller saw virtues in both the M'Loot and Kotzebue dogs. As well, he felt they both had major faults; they sat at opposite extremes. "The M'Loot dogs didn't look AT ALL like the Kotzebue dogs. They were SO different. The Kotzebues were a little too short and squat, I thought."[13] While they had very good rears, heads, muzzles, and ear sets, a few were too wide in the front like bulldogs, resulting in their being out-at-the-elbows.

Another asset for the Kotzebue dogs was the way the Seeley's had set their type. As Zoller said "They were a little more LIKE each other; typier and more 'fixed.'"[14]

On the other hand, the M'Loots were much larger, and often too rangy. "Stringy" in appearance, many had good fronts but bad rears with cowhocks, a lack of angulation, and what Zoller calls a "square" rear. This gave some of them a stilted gait.

The two lines varied in temperament also. The Kotzebues were less likely to be fighters and more easily stopped if they did fight.

Although Zoller felt very fortunate to have started with the Hinman/Irwin dogs, he is quick to point out that Hinman, Irwin, and Voelker were quite different from the Seeleys in their approach to breeding. Of the former three, he said he felt they were not "the kind of guys that would take a real studied approach to the dog; to their history, or background or breeding, and so on. It was kind of like they were guys that just accidentally had a dog, or two or three."[15]

He credited the presence of the Hinman/Irwin dogs in his pedigree with giving some balance to the M'Loots and making a better overall dog. Still, he admired the look of the Kotzebue dogs and was actively seeking one for use in breeding.

Someone, he thinks Roy Truchon of Roy-El Kennels, wrote him saying that he had seen the dog that Zoller needed with handlers in Nebraska. Coincidentally, the Zollers had already turned down buying the dog for the same reason that they turned down Ch. Spawn's Alaska—too many males. The dog was Toro of Bras Coupe, and

*Left: Ch. Husky Pak's Mikya of Seguin.
These two photos courtesy Delta Wilson Smith.*

Below: Ch. Arctic Storm of Husky-Pak.

Ch. Cherokee of Husky-Pak with Robert Zoller, who claimed he was "the best Alaskan Malamute I ever owned. . . . an excellent dog."

Zoller immediately wrote Earl Norris and had the dog shipped to him for breeding to Arctic Storm.

That breeding was the sort of "click" that often happens when two dogs of different in-bred lines are bred together. One puppy of the six was never shown, the rest went on to finish championships with a show record that is still enviable: Ch. Cliquot of Husky-Pak, CDX; Ch. Cheyenne of Husky-Pak; Ch. Cochise of Husky-Pak; Ch. Comanche of Husky-Pak; and Ch. Cherokee of Husky-Pak.

Unfortunately, both Arctic Storm and Comanche contracted hardpad distemper at a show and died. This tragedy left the Zollers without a breeding partner for Toro, but they did have Arctic Storm's brother. To try the same thing in reverse, the Zollers bought a female from the Norris's, Kelerak of Kobuk, out of the brother/sister breeding of Toro to Helen. Kelerak bred to Apache Chief produced Husky-Pak Eagle, Ch. Husky-Pak Echako, Ch. Husky-Pak Erok. These crosses continued to produce well, not only for the Zollers but for breeders across the country.

After so many successes, the Zollers decided to retire from breeding and showing. Their decision was based in large part on the desire to keep only as many dogs as they could comfortably accommodate as house pets.

Ch. Cochise of Husky-Pak. Courtesy Delta Wilson Smith.

REGISTERED M'LOOTS

While Robert and Laura Zoller were busy raising their dogs and children, other M'Loot owners were going their own ways. Some remained loyal to their original lines, but the success of the Zoller's crosses could not be ignored. A few repeated Zoller's M'Loot-Kotzebue cross, but many found using the Husky-Pak dogs more palatable.

Jim and Connie Lynn hold six-week-old puppies from the Husky-Pak "E" litter. Courtesy Delta Wilson Smith.

LORNA JACKSON—LORN HALL

One of the pure-M'Loot breeders, Canada's Lorna Jackson obtained her dogs directly from Paul Voelker. Ch. Oogorook M'Loot and Lorn-Hall Tonto M'Loot shared Noma as a mother. Tonto was out of Mikiuk; Oogorook, out of Gentleman Jim.

Oogorook was the first Canadian Champion, the first white champion, and the first to place in a group. He also did search and rescue after a devastating hurricane.

Oogorook's sons, Ch. Lorn-Hall's Yukon and Can. Ch. Lorn-Hall's Nordic, represented an in-breeding of two half-siblings. Yukon was the first Canadian-bred champion and was never defeated in breed.

JEAN LANE—MULPUS BROOKS

Along with the Seeleys, Jean Lane was breeding and racing both Siberian Huskies and Alaskan Malamutes under the kennel name of Mulpus Brooks. Her Siberian, Ch. Mulpus Brooks the Roadmaster, found his way into breed history, and her Malamutes, though few, are found behind many champions today. She bought Ch. Mulpus Brooks Master Otter, bred by Paul Voelker and Ralph Schmitt, and bred him to her bitch Mulpus Brooks Dusty Lane. This produced Ch. Mulpus Brooks the Bear who was owned by the Dawsons of Kobuk Kennels.

Kelerak of Kobuk.

Mrs. J. W. Dawson with Ch. Baloo, left, and Ch. Prairie Lash. Inset: Lash as a puppy.

THE DAWSONS—KOBUK

Under the name Kobuk, Bill and Lois Dawson owned and bred some of the finest and most influential M'Loot dogs. Their first Malamute was a puppy named Baloo out of Prairie Lash and Shawnee Bell. They ended up with Prairie Lash and began showing him when his original owner was transferred. Their most important purchase,

Kobuk's Dark Beauty was very influential in many pedigrees. Bred by the Dawsons and owned by Belva Rifkind of Kodara (see pg. 179).

though, came when they acquired Ch. Mulpus Brooks The Bear from Jean Lane. He finished his championship and garnered a group first at a time when few Malamutes were shown.

Through The Bear and Ch. Baloo, the Dawsons were breeders of one of the most important dams in breed history, the lovely Kobuk's Dark Beauty, who was owned by Belva Rifkind.

ELEANOR DUBUIS—SENA-LAK

In Valois, New York, Eleanor DuBuis used the kennel name Sena-Lak. She started with Ch. Kiana of Klondike, bred by Walter and Evelyn Lesh. Reflective of the first Husky-Pak dogs, Kiana combined dogs from several kennels who bred mainly M'Loot dogs with a dash of the Hinman/Irwin dogs through Kayak of Brookside.

```
                    Mikiuk
         Ch. Mulpus Brooks Master Otter
                    Noma
    Kobi of Polars Wilderness
                              Ch. Nahnook II
                    Polar
                              Kolar
         Ch. Spawn's Chee
                              Kayak of Brookside
                    Arrow of Husky Pak
                              Ch.Husky-Pak Mikya of Seguin
Ch. Kiana of Klondike (whelped 1954)
                         Ch. Nahnook II
              Eski of Silver Sled
                              Ch. King M'Loot
                    Oogerook of Silver Sled
                              Ch. Gyana
         Sno Valley Twilight
                         Ch. Nahnook II
                    Coco
                              Nooka
                    Ch. Tuyah of Silver Sled
                              Oogerook of Silver Sled
```

DELTA WILSON—TIMBER TRAIL

Delta Wilson (now Smith) was interested enough in the new breed to write Short Seeley for information about buying a female, but Short had none for sale. When she saw Marchetta Schmitt walking her Malamutes at the Chicago International Show, Delta was entranced, sure this was the breed for her. Inquiring, she found out that Nooka and Oogerook of Silver Sled had puppies. Marchetta said she would sell one to Delta to show and would even give her a free breeding to one of the Silver Sled dogs later.

Delta took the puppy, a litter sister to Tosha, and called her Tuyah. She became Ch. Tuyah of Silver Sled and the foundation of Timber Trail Alaskan Malamutes.[16]

Timber Trail Tanya, by Ch. Chinook Kotzebue Gripp out of Tuyah of Silver Sled. Breeder/Owner, Delta Wilson Smith. Tanya was on an Antarctic team during Operation Deepfreeze.

MORE CHANGES FOR THE BREED

STUD BOOK CLOSED

Just as suddenly as the American Kennel Club had opened the Stud Book, they closed it. Since the AMCA had no delegate to tell them what was happening at AKC, this came as a complete surprise. The Spawns said that many of the M'Loot owners thought they had plenty of time to get their dogs registered and had put off showing some of them. Had they known far enough in advance, many people would have made more of an effort to get these dogs finished and registered.[17]

AKC MEMBERSHIP

The AMCA members became more determined than ever to have become a member club of AKC, and their efforts came to fruition on December 15, 1953, a landmark day for the club. The secretary, Mrs. Edna Lawler, read a letter from the AKC informing the club that it had been accepted into membership. Officers at this time were: President, Mrs. Eva B. Seeley; First Vice-President, Mrs.

Delta Wilson; Secretary, Mrs. Edna Lawler; Treasurer, Mr. James Dawson. Dr. Roland Lombard was the delegate to the AKC.

Gradually, people set aside their differences and began to cooperate with each other. By 1953, the AMCA had 76 members. Most were in New England and the Eastern states, but others lived in the Midwest, California, the South and even far-away Alaska.

NEW DIRECTIONS IN BREEDING

The spirit of compromise was growing among Malamute owners—a mellow attitude reflected in their breedings. Delta Wilson Smith and Short Seeley had become close friends. Delta says that regardless of the animosity that went on from time to time between AMCA members, all of them recognized the contribution of Short Seeley and what her dogs had to offer.[18]

Although inconceivable just a few years before, Short agreed to breed Ch. Chinook Kotzebue Gripp, a son of Kim and Taku's Mascara of Chinook, to Delta's full M'Loot female, Ch. Tuyah of Silver Sled. Tuyah was a fine producer

in her own right; she ultimately had four champion progeny. From this breeding came Ch. Timber-Trail Cheechako, CD.

Several other kennels were working with their less direct Kotzebue–M'Loot crosses, using the Husky-Pak dogs as a source. Among them were Dorothy Pearson of Redhorse, Martha and Bob Gormley of Barb-Far, and Roy and Elsie Truchon of Roy-El.

NEW STANDARD

For ten years, AMCA members had been wrangling about changes to the standard. Bill Dawson finally joined the committee as a facilitator and in 1960, a new standard was adopted that better accommodated its new members. The growing influence of the M'Loot contingent was reflected in the changes regarding size which was the clearest differentiating factor between the two strains.

M'Loot owners wanted to increase the desired heights and weights. Naturally, the Kotzebue owners contested this. The compromise which is still in effect today was finally worked out and the new standard approved.

OPERATION DEEPFREEZE

Admiral George Dufek was in charge of "Operation Highjump," the military prologue to the highly publicized International Geophysical Year, which brought a multi-national scientific mission to Antarctica during the years of 1956-57. The military phase of the IGY was well-known as *Operation Deepfreeze.*

A thoroughly modern explorer, Dufek saw no need to include dogs on the expeditions. More experienced hands prevailed though, and he authorized the purchase of two teams from Chinook. Eva Seeley had so few dogs that she could not fill the need and had to call on her friends for help. The Hogdens sent some of their Sno-Pak dogs, and Delta sent a Gripp/Tuyah daughter, Timber Trail Tanya. This was the last expedition supplied by Chinook.[19]

Short Seeley with puppies. On the right is Windie, the mascot of Antarctic Deepreeze, September 1955. Courtsey Delta Smith.

THE TRUCHONS—ROY-EL

With the new standard, an outstanding young male bred by the Truchons came on the scene. He was Ch. Spawn's Hot Shot of Roy-El, and he finished his championship at the National Specialty by going Best of Breed.

Ch. Jingo's Silver Trumpet. Owner, Virginia Devaney.

```
                         Ch. Prairie Lash
            Bandit Chief of Roy El
                         Kiana of Roy-El
      Erik of Roy El
                         Ch. Apache Chief of Husky Pak
            Ch. Dakota of Husky Pak
                         Ch. Husky Pak Mikya of Seguin
Ch. Fakir of Roy El
                         Yukon King of Lunenburg
            Ch. Marclars Yukon Otter
                         Bamboo of Husky Pak
      Marclars Una
                         Ch. Toro of Bras Coupe
            Ch. Cheyenne of Husky-Pak
                         Ch. Arctic Storm of Husky-Pak
```

Ch. Spawn's Hot Shot of Roy-El (whelped 4/22/60)

```
                         Navarre of Kotzebue
            Chinook Karluk of Kotzebue
                         Taku of Kotzebue
      Musher Lane Erebus of Chinook
                         Navarre of Kotzebue
            Cleo of Kotzebue
                         Pandora of Kotzebue
Snomasque White Diamond
                         Jiffy of Kotzebue
            Igloo Paks Gripp
                         Tananna of Igloo Pak
      Musher Lane Pandora
                         Chinook Karluk of Kotzebue
            Musher Lane Ring of Chinook
                         Cleo of Kotzebue
```

He was yet another mixture of M'Loot and Kotzebue. His size and leg length were good, but unlike the pure M'Loots with which they were familiar, the Truchons said that Hot Shot never really went through a gawky stage. He was always "like a miniature Malamute." In Hot Shot, the two strains averaged. The shape of the future was reflected in the Truchon's decision to never again have pure M'Loots.

THE DEVANEYS—VOYAGEUR

H.F. and Virginia (Penney) Devaney got Ch. Husky Pak Jingo from Robert Zoller. She was out of Ch. Husky Pak Eagle and Ch. Husky Pak Marclars Sioux. This lovely female finished her championship in four shows, a remarkable accomplishment that she topped by the litter she produced with Ch. Cebas Silver Bow.

```
                         Sno Pak Kaghis Tugg
            Ch. Shuyak Caro of Cold Foot, C.D.
                         Alaskan Agnishuk of Kuvak
      Coldfoot Chikott
                         Ch. Keowuk of Kobuk
            Kiska Queen of Coldfoot
                         Alaskan Muhko-Kih of Kuvak
Ch. Cebas Silver Bow
                         Karels Buk
            Cho-Cheece
                         Chi Chi of Snow Valley
      Ceba Sue
                         Karels Buk
            Kay Buk
                         Silver Sleds Navail
```

Ch. Jingo's Silver Trumpet (whelped 1964)

```
                         Ch. Spawn's Alaska
            Ch. Apache Chief of Husky-Pak
                         Chitina
      Ch. Husky-Pak Eagle
                         Ch. Toro of Bras Coupe
            Kelerak of Kobuk
                         Helen of Bras Coupe
Ch. Husky Pak's Jingo
                         Ch. Spawn's Alaska
            Ch. Apache Chief of Husky-Pak
                         Chitina
      Ch. Husky-Pak Marclars Sioux
                         Ch. Toro of Bras Coupe
            Ch. Cheyenne of Husky-Pak
                         Ch. Arctic Storm of Husky-Pak
```

When the Devaneys bred this litter's Ch. Jingo's Silver Trumpet to Ch. Tigara's Torch of Arctica, five of the six puppies finished their championships. Pictures of Voyageur's Cougar have been used to illustrate Malamute gait.

PAK-N-PULL/KODARA/TOTE-EM

Martha Giuffre of Pak-N-Pull bought the lovely Ch. Pak-N-Pulls Dark Angel from Belva Rifkind's Kodara Kennels. She was inbred on Kobuk's Dark Beauty. Dark Beauty was both her mother and the mother of Ch. Sno-Crest's Mukluk, Angel's sire. Again, the pure M'Loot breeding was mixed with the Kotzebue through Ch. Cochise of Husky-Pak.

Dark Beauty herself is an example of a prepotent dam, whose descendants, even though several generations removed can be recognized, not so much for a specific look as an overall quality. Her offspring were the foundation for Diane Ross's Tote-Em Kennels and contributed greatly to many others.

```
                          Tobuk
                 Mikiuk
                          Kapuk
       Ch. Mulpus Brook's Master Otter
                          Silver King
                 Noma
                          Silver Girl
Ch. Mulpus Brook's The Bear
                          Koyuk
                 Chisolm's Viking
                          Kiska
       Ch. Mulpus Brook's Dusty Lane
                          Schmoos M'Loot
                 Chisholms Northern Star
                          Tora M'Loot
```

Kobuk's Dark Beauty (whelped 12/28/53) Photo on page 167

```
                          Mikiuk
                 Ch. Mulpus Brook's Master Otter
                          Noma
       Ch. Prairie Lash
                          Gentleman Jim
                 Tonga
                          Tosha
Ch. Baloo
                          Mikiuk
                 Ch. Mulpus Brook's Master Otter
                          Noma
       Shawnee Belle
                          Gentleman Jim
                 Tonga
                          Tosha
```

Kodara produced a number of champions using a mixture of the two lines. Typical of this is Minnie Graham's Am/Can Ch. Bearpaw Geena from a very tight line-breeding on Husky-Pak Dogs through Jean Clark's Erowah dogs.

```
                          Ch. Apache Chief of Husky-Pak
                 Ch. Husky Pak Erok
                          Kelerak of Kobuk
       Ch. Kodara Kodiak of Erowah
                          Ch. Mulpus Brooks the Bear
                 Kobuk's Dark Beauty
                          Ch. Baloo
Ch. Erowah Cinnaman, CD
                          Ch. Toro of Bras Coupe
                 Ch. Cochise of Husky-Pak
                          Ch. Arctic Storm of Husky-Pak
       Ch. Sno-Crest's Aurora of Erowah
                          Ch. Mulpus Brook's the Bear
                 Kobuk's Dark Beauty
                          Ch. Baloo
```

Am/Can. Ch. Bearpaw Geena (whelped 1964)

```
                          Ch. Cliquot of Husky-Pak, CDX
                 Can Ch Husky-Pak Forecast by Cliquot, CD
                          Deeka of Husky-Pak
       Ch. Amarok
                          Ch. Apache Chief of Husky-Pak
                 Barb-Far Marclar's Marook
                          Ch. Cheyenne of Husky Pak
Siska of Erowah
                          Ch. Storm King of Journey's End
                 Lad-Lin Tongass
                          Sno-Valley Chenook
       Lad-Lin Pita
                          Ch. Cherokee of Husky-Pak
                 Husky-Pak Glacier
                          Kelerak of Kobuk
```

MARILYN BAXTER—T'DOMAR

Marilyn Baxter's T'Domar Kennels combined dogs of the Spawns, Barb-Far, and Husky-Pak to produce two top winners, Ch. T'Domar's Bismarck (Ch. T'Domar's Voodoo King and T'Domar's Nootka) and his daughter by T'Domar's Taboo, Ch. T'Domar Chitina, who was BOS at the 1969 National. Other combinations fueled the breeding programs of Candee Hager's (now Becker) Karohonta Kennels.

DOROTHY PEARSON—REDHORSE

Dorothy Pearson bought Ch. Timber-Trail Cheechako, CD, from Delta Smith, and bred her to Ch. Durango of Husky-Pak to produce Ch. Dagan of Redhorse. Repeating this cross, Dorothy bred Dagan to another Husky-Pak female, Morning Star, and produced Ch. M'London of Redhorse, who later sired three champions .

DORIS KNORR—NORTHWIND/KANANGNARK

Doris Knorr had been breeding under the kennel name of North Wind with dogs that went back to the M'Loot stock of Silver Sled. However, after she bred to the Norris's pure Kotzebue, Ch. Midnight Shadow of Kuvak, she changed her kennel name to Kanangnark. Her dogs are found in many pedigrees today, especially behind the dogs of Lois Olmen of Glacier Kennels and Nancy Russell who used Timberlane as a kennel name before owning Storm Kloud and adopting that as a kennel name.

PURE KOTZEBUE KENNELS

CAROL WILLIAMS—HERITAGE/CHINOOK

Some kennels continued the pure Kotzebue lines and still do today. Of course, Chinook is one of these. Carol Williams took it over when Eva Seeley died. Her pure Kotzebue dogs have both Heritage and Kotzebue as a kennel name.

Top left: Heritage's Kotzebue Dakota, Heritage's Kotzebue Kartok, Heritag's Kotzebue Napic. Breeder, Carol and Frank Williams.

Top Right: Ch. Kotzebue Rowdy of Chinook. Bred by Eva Seeley, owned by Carol Williams.

Above: Kotzebue Muffin of Chinook, dam of some fine champions, was the last brood bitch for Chinook Kennels.

Right: Ch. Kotzebue Taku of Chinook with breeder/owners Eva Seeley and Carol Williams, winning BOB in 1979. Handled by Ed Carlson. Ashbey photo.

THE POKREKYS—COLDFOOT

Melvin and Joann Pokreky's Coldfoot Kennels, Reg., has always been known for the working ability of their dogs, which began as pure Kotzebue out of Ch. Shuyak Caro of Cold Foot, CD, bred by the Norris's. He was the sire and grandsire of two leader dogs for the blind, held a weight pull record for five years in a row, and was owner-handled to his championship and group placings. The working ability of his get was extraordinary. His dam was inbred on the Bras Coupe breeding. His sire was bred by Art and Natalie Hogden's Sno-Pak Alaskan Malamutes, the oldest pure Kotzebue kennels still breeding, outside of Chinook itself.

THE HOGDENS—SNO-PAK

Had the Hogdens never done anything else, the breeding of their Ch. Kim of Kotzebue to Kotzebue Cleopatra to produce Toro and his sisters would have kept them in the limelight. However, they continue breeding today, and many of their dogs, such as Sno Pak's Kaghis Tugg, have had quite an influence on the breed. Art and Nat have been breeding Kotzebue Alaskan Malamutes longer than anyone else living at the time this book was written.

Top: Sno-Pak Kotzebue Amorak.

Center: Ch. Sno-Pak Tanana's Mascara, bred and owned by the Hodgens.

Left: Arthur and Natalie Hodgen with several Kotzebue puppies at Sno-Pak Kennel.

THE NORRIS'S—ALASKAN/KUVAK

Before the Stud Book was reopened, Earl Norris was a well-known Alaskan with a passion for sled dogs and racing. Natalie worked for Eva Seeley at Chinook. When she decided to move to Alaska, she took a letter of introduction from Short to Earl Norris. Short had instructed her to check out Norris' dogs and see what they were like. Natalie did her one better—she married him.

The Norris dogs carried the kennel name Alaskan/ Kuvak, and later, just Kuvak. Over the years, the Norrises produced many fine Kotzebue dogs and sold some that did very well for others.

They bought Toro and his sisters, Helen, Lucy and Cookey from Chauncey Weaver, a Canadian who owned the Bras Coupe lodge in Quebec. Weaver had bought Kotzebue Cleopatra in whelp to Ch. Kim of Kotzebue. He then kept that litter and rebred Cleopatra.

These breedings gave him seventeen dogs of good

Earl and Natalie Norris.

working ability. Toro and Cookey ran on a team at the Anchorage Fur Rendezvous race, and Toro was a member of a three-dog weight pull team which won that event. Toro produced well for the Zollers and for another remarkable kennel in California, Tigara, owned by Dorothy Dillingham. He finished his life there and is buried in her yard.

DOROTHY DILLINGHAM—TIGARA

Dorothy Dillingham's Tigara Kennels is of tremendous significance throughout the history of the breed. Breedings based on the litter that produced Toro, who, along with dogs from Sno-Pak, formed the basis for one of the most consistently successful kennels of Alaskan Malamutes.

A long-time AMCA member, Dillingham produced champions of distinctive style and type, clearly true to their heritage. Among them are her foundation sires, Ch. Tigara's Torch of Arctica, Ch. Tigara's Arctic Explorer, Ch. Tigara's Dortic Shag-Luck, Ch. Tongass of Tigara, Ch. Tigara's Dortic Khan, Ch. Thor of Tigara, Ch. Tigara's Arctica Tanunak, and Ch. Rogue of Tigara, who was a National Specialty Winner, to name only a few.

Tigara's Winsome Witch was never shown but remains in many pedigrees through her son, Torch. Ch. Tigara's Arctica Eve, whose sire was Toro, was also a granddaughter of Ch. Alaskan Kuvak Nasota, another of the Toro/Helen

The Norris's Ch. Toro of Bras Coupe, the most influential Malamute sire of all time, is behind almost every modern kennel.

Dorothy Dillingham with Skilak of Kobuk at eight months of age.

offspring. She was the mother and grandmother of numerous champions.

After she retired, Mrs. Dillingham's kennel continued in the care of Sam Walden, who used the Tigara kennel name on all the pure Tigara dogs, which are still pure Kotzebue, and "Chinome" on his own dogs.

THE BREED TODAY, REFLECTED BY THE AMCA

The spirit of cooperation born in the early days of its history has set the tone for today's members of the Alaskan Malamute Club of America. Continuing a long tradition, they have banded together for the welfare of the breed whenever it has been necessary.

The versatility of the breed is reflected in the varied interests of the AMCA's members. Sledding is still important, of course, but today's Malamutes participate in dog shows, obedience trials, tracking tests, agility, backpacking, weight pull, skijouring, search-and-rescue, and therapy work. The Hall of Working Fame is sponsored by the AMCA to recognize dogs of remarkable achievement.

In response to the problems of growing popularity, the AMCA formulated a Code of Ethics for its members. It supports rescue groups and pioneered techniques to detect and solve genetic problems, looking constantly for improved testing methods. The AMCA holds a national and several regional shows. In addition, it has several programs in place to recognize, reward, and, thus, encourage working achievements as well as producing ability.

Despite its relative youth as a registered purebred, the Alaskan Malamute's service to man stretches into ancient times. The strength and purpose that made them so valuable in conquering both poles is reflected today in the joyful faces of a working team and the grim determination of a weight puller. Their history is founded in a tradition of tremendous sacrifice and hardship. Our care and love for the breed today should honor that debt.

ENDNOTES:
1. "Marquette Kennels Widely Known for Trained Malemutes," *Escanaba Daily Press*, (February 28, 1947).
2. After the heroic serum run, Seppala sold Balto and his team to Hollywood. (Ricker/Seppala, 281). Some of these dogs might well have found their way to M'Loot Kennels.
3. Tobey, "Origin" 32.
4. This statement is highly suspect. In conversations with people who were AMCA officers at the time Voelker was breed-

ing, the authors have been unable to locate anyone who remembers him as a member and all think it highly unlikely.
5. Various sources refer to Dick Moulton as the owner of Chinook Kennels. Eva Seeley was ill, and Chinook had contracted to supply dogs for Operation Deepfreeze, and Moulton, who began working for Milton Seeley when he was just a lad, was the logical person to keep the business going. Eva Seeley's illness was serious enough for her to make arrangements in case of death. Fortunately, she recovered and once again became mistress at Chinook.
6. Robert Zoller, Personal communication, 1993.
7. Richard Tobey ("Origin", 32.) records the parents of Gemo as Aguna and Guto, another source lists the sire as Irwin's Koko, while all pedigree records, including the AMCA pedigree books, list the parents as Igloo and Lynx. These may be one and the same or one source is in error. Pedigrees were loosely kept, sometimes by word of mouth, and many dogs underwent several name changes.
8. Tobey, "Origin," 32.
9. Zoller.
10. Riddle/Seeley, 42.
11. "Talks with Bob & Alice Spawn," interview by Cynthia Kerstiens, *Alaskan Malamute Annual* (Wheat Ridge, CO.: Hoflin Publishing Co., 1982), 35.
12. "Talks with Robert Zoller," interview by Lynn Snyder Hoflin, *Alaskan Malamute Annual* (Wheat Ridge, Co: Hoflin Publishing Co. 1981), 128
13. Zoller, *Annual*, 136.
14. Zoller, *Annual*, 136.
15. Zoller, *Annual*, 136.
16. Delta Wilson Smith, Personal communication, 1994.
17. Spawn, 42.
18. Smith.
19. George John Dufek, R. Admiral, *Operation Deepfreeze*, (New York: Harcourt, Brace and Company, 1957), 57. In discussing preparations for the military support aspect of the International Geophysical Year of 1957, Dufek's comments capsulize the new attitude of the military. "We had not planned to take any dogs because the huge amount of equipment. . . demanded heavy tractors and trains. But some people suggested that we should. . . I understand there was quite a hassle between the professional explorers—on the side of the dogs—and the civil engineers. The report came to me recommending that we taken four teams. The reasons given were that the dogs, sleds, and survival equipment could be dropped from an aircraft by parachute to a party in distress. . . and the dogs would be a wonderful subject for photographers and good for publicity. After all, why take the romance out of exploration?

"I cut the recommendation in half and approved the purchase of two dog teams." The contract was with Chinook Kennels, 56-57.

Freddy Demondt with a team of Akela's Song dogs. Breeder, E. Terryn, Belgium.

13

MALAMUTES
AROUND THE WORLD

As the Alaskan Malamute has grown more popular at home, he has attracted the attention of dog fanciers around the world. In some countries, the breed is rare enough to excite a lot of curiosity, while in others, it is well-established. Malamute clubs have been founded in countries with a sufficient number of dogs such as Belgium, the Netherlands, France, Italy, some Scandinavian countries, Victoria in Australia, and Canada.

Countries such as Switzerland, Germany, Spain, and Luxembourg, with too few Malamute owners to sustain an independent club, have a multi-breed Northern Breeds Club devoted to their interests. Otherwise, Malamutes are simply registered with a national kennel club or a Federation Cynoloiges Internationale-affiliated body.

The Alaskan Malamute has become quite a globetrotter, but he still functions as both a companion and a worker. In countries where sledding is common, he has gained a small but ardent following.

INTERNATIONAL SLEDDING

Sledding Malamute owners around the world have a common lament—the lack of appropriate runs for the breed. Most races favor the Siberian Husky since Malamutes of correct structure and type are not meant for competition in speed racing, a sport which has been around for quite a while in Europe.

Switzerland has had active mushers since the mid-sixties and accommodates the slower dogs at their races with longer-distance freighting classes. In France, where sledding is so common that races are held every weekend, the Alaskan Malamute Club of France (AMCF) has established the Brevet de Trail, a freight race over a longer distance designed especially for Malamutes, and the Norwegians have set up a 100 kilometer (66 mile) race for one to six dog teams.

Sled racing is so popular in Germany that sport clubs abound, and races are even held occasionally in conjunction with large track-and-field meets. Most events are

sprint races for teams in a Scandinavian, or Pulk harness, but they, too, have begun longer trail races in response to the increasing number of freighting dog owners. Two clubs there administer races, the Deutscher Schlittenportverbund (DSSV), which allows any dog to race, and the Arbeitsgemeinschaft Sled Dogs (AGSD), which restricts entries to pure-bred Northern Dogs.

Many Belgian and a few British breeders are active mushers, although in Belgium, driving requires a license, whether the vehicle is a car or a sled. Using a dog to pull is unlawful unless one has an official musher's pass.

In Scotland, the formation of the Sled Dog Association of Scotland in 1990 gave the sport a boost. They are also interested in weight pull, and their first competition was held at Aviemore in 1994.

Although sled racing is a familiar sight in Canada, few Malamute owners participated, so Dave and Pat Hardie helped start an event designed to encourage and assist newcomers to the sport of dog-sledding with Malamutes. Because of the condition of the sleds at the end, the event has become known as the Kindling Klassic. Using freight sleds over a twelve-mile course, the non-competitive, social run has become a workshop for people who want to earn WTD titles. To accommodate those who wanted more, the Kindling Klassic Challenge has been added, a seven-mile freight race on Saturday and a twelve-mile sprint race on Sunday.

In Australia, the only snow falls in high mountains, and most accessible areas are in the National Parks which do not allow domestic animals.[1] Undeterred, the plucky Down-Unders have proven that Malamutes can race in snowless lands by beginning an active program of gig and bicycle racing.

The meet season runs during the Australian winter, from late May to the end of August unless it is too hot.[2] So far, these are just for the love of the sport, and are sponsored by a combined Siberian/Malamute club in Adelaide and the Siberian Husky and Alaskan Malamute Clubs of Victoria.

Racing Around the World

Luc Verbustel from Belgium, a member of the AMCB and Inuit Trail, racing in Austria.

Mr. Lapesse, a member of the Belgian club, races in France.

Bob Mouthaan and his team of Northern Lightning Malamutes in an International race in Belgium.

Cold Valley's Mister Kandu Junior, Oenzja-Inshallah Crying Wolf, Kotzebue Trail Ozak of Cold Valley, with Gilbert Dubied, Switzerland

Left: Am. Can. Ch. Shanie De Chabek. A beautiful female from Canada bred by Andre and Lise Lepine and owned by Claude and Nicole Vaillancourt.

Right: Multi-talented Wintertrail's Cinnamon Snowbear WTDX, CGC, Certified Therapy Dog, owned by Dave Hardie, Canada.

NORTH AMERICA

CANADA

(Material for this section provided by David Hardie of Wintertrail.)

Many well-known Malamute kennels such as Barrenfield of Jerry and Sandy Musyj, Chabek of Andre Lepine, Oopik of Lorna Muir, Taolan of Ron Pohl and Lorn-Hall of Lorna Jackson are actually in Canada, a fact that often escapes notice since dogs are exchanged so freely across the U.S./Canadian border. Canadian breeders have made valuable contributions to the breed wherever it is found.

Many Canadian dogs are shown in both Canada and the U.S. Obtaining a Canadian championship requires a total of ten points from three different judges. As in the U.S., five points are the maximum available from any one show, and the award system works the same way; however, no majors are required for a championship.

The Alaskan Malamute Club of Canada holds a National Specialty and several regional boosters annually and publishes a bi-monthly newsletter. In addition to dog shows, the membership participates in obedience work, sledding, backpacking, and weight pull, breed rescue, and even therapy work.

A growing number of Malamute owners participate in agility. Fallwood's Puff the Magic Dragon, bred by Carol Ridewood and Ed Falkowski and owned by Liz and Klaus Nielson, is the first agility titleholder.

Reflecting the friendly atmosphere of the country, in early October, the Hardies and other AMCC members host an event called the Pak N Pull, which donates revenues to worthwhile dog causes. This multi-faceted event gives participants a chance to earn working certifications and includes an overnight pack trip, weight pull, puppy match, and a day-long hike. Last year, about 85 people and over 100 dogs joined the Pak N Pull weekend.

MEXICO

The Alaskan Malamute is popular in Mexico but not as a show dog. At one time, the Club Alaskan Malamute de Mexico was very active, but now it is defunct. Currently, most of the Malamutes at the Federacion Canofila Mexicana shows are U.S. dogs seeking additional championships. In Mexico, dogs can earn points towards their Mexican championships and compete in obedience trials as well as winning certificates for an FCI championship at the International shows.

The Alaskan Malamute Club in Mexico was once very active. Montoya photo.

THE PACIFIC COUNTRIES

NEW ZEALAND

(Information for this section was provided by Wilma Livingston and an article by Diana McNamara, "History of the Alaskan Malamute in New Zealand.")

Mr. H. S. Patmore of Christchurch began by importing New Zealand's first Alaskan Malamute, Gina of Clebar, from the U.K. in 1973. In 1977, he brought in Ch. Herstans Unuyuk O' Valley View from the U.S. While quarantined in the U.K., she was bred to Tigara's Farland Scot's Pride and had five puppies. A U.S. import, Ch. Kandiks Cyronak of Herstan, followed the puppies to Mr. Patmore's.

Scotland also contributed an import, Ch. Tigara Metyel of Accomac, brought to New Zealand by Mrs. Y. Harris of Auckland. She also obtained Aus/NZ Ch. HOT's Buran who went on to find fame and fortune in Australia and also imported Ch. HOT's Kiska in the early 80s. Kiska surprised Mrs. Harris with a quarantine litter born in the U.K., giving her four more Malamutes: Chinook of the Yukon, Panook of the North, Ch. Erklasook of Artic Wind, and Ch. Chimo Silver Moon, who was exported to Australia.

Mr. P. Metz of Te Puke bought Mrs. Harris's Australian import, Meryton Atasuk Nuna. Another Australian import, Whitemist Tundra Tula, went to Mrs. L. Jones of Christchurch, and Mr. J. P. Ley of Auckland imported Sea Court Icicle from the U.K.

By 1986, imports from Australian kennels had increased. Mrs. Harris brought over Daneolympus Heidi Jane, Meryton Sisamut Oona, and Ch. Daneolympus Northstar. Dogs from Huskypak (not the U.S. Husky Pak of R. Zoller), Huskypak Miss Yukon and Aus. Ch. Huskypak Tuffernhell went to Mr. M. Nicholson and Mr. B. Roberts, respectively. Another Australian import, Chuchii Apachi was brought in by Mrs. J. Musson and Mrs. D. Churcher.

Trade between the countries runs both ways, and many dogs have finished championships in both countries. In fact one of Mr. Patmore's quarantine puppies, Herstan's Whaka-Pena-Tama, was Australia's first Malamute. Two of his brothers finished championships, Ch. Herstan's Hikutawhana, owned by the breeder, and Ch. Herstan's Uguruk, owned by Diana McNamara.

AUSTRALIA

(Information for this section was provided by Wilma Livingston of Tundra Alaskan Malamutes.)

Although Australia is about the size of the continental U.S., its center is desert, clustering the majority of the pop-

Australian Ch.Meryton Makluk, owned by Ron and Wilma Livingston.

ulation in the coastal areas. The state of Victoria, located in the south-east, is home to the very active Alaskan Malamute Club of Victoria. Like its U.K. parent, Australia is rabies-free and has a costly quarantine which makes importation of new stock difficult.

Herstan's Whaka-Pena-Tama, the New Zealand import by Irene Gates, arrived in 1978. That same year, Tony and Merilyn Syme of Meryton Kennels in Victoria arranged a lease of Mrs. Harris's Aus/NZ Ch. HOT's Buran in co-ownership with Mick Mooney. Buran achieved his Australian championship in five shows, failing to win the Group once.

They also bred Australia's first litter out of their New Zealand import, Aus/NZ Ch. Chimo Silver Moon. Four of her eight puppies went on to finish championships.

One, Ch. Meryton Atasuk Chimo, was the first Malamute to win a BIS at an all-breed championship show. Her brother and sister from the second breeding became not only champions but obedience title-holders as well. Ch. Meryton Makluk Tenakee, CDX finished his obedience title before his first birthday, and sister, Ch. Meryton Makluk Panda, CDX quickly followed.

The Beverwijk Kennels of F. M. Wortman are on the Gold Coast of Queensland. In 1983, he imported three Malamutes: Miskimos Blackjack, Bar-B-R's Sugar Babe, and Rogards Shady Lady, all from the U.S.

Interest in Malamutes got a boost when Buran's head

was used on a dog-food box and his grandson, Ch. Inuk Nutara Kadluk, played a wolf in a television commercial. His son, Meryton Wsewolod (Jock), was the star of a 1987 news program on Melbourne TV which followed his exploits on an Australian Antarctic expedition.

Other imports also came to Australia. From the U.K., Mrs. W. Newton of Yarram, of Victoria imported Ch. Snow Eagle of Highnoons, Highnoons Mescalero Apache, and Highnoons Laughing Water. R. Wells, Southern River, Western Australia obtained Amerinds Bell Chyme Wolfsong (U.S.), Seacourt Fire Finch (U.K.) and Ch. Nanook of the North (N.Z.) originally owned by the T & M Syme of Belgrave South, Victoria, who also own Noataks Rajah (U.S.). Mr. & Mrs. L. Bennett of Wandiligong bought Victoria's Own Berchtenbreiter Kodiak (Can); Mr. & Mrs. E. Singer, formerly of Warrandyte, Victoria, imported Aus/NZ Ch. Eskimo Jane of the North (N.Z.). Mrs. I. Gates, Croydon, South Australia imported Tigara Sea Voyageur (U.K.),and Mrs. D. Sullivan, Sebastopol, Victoria, bought Am/Can Ch. Storm Kloud Qqwanee Song(U.S.).[3]

In the last decade, the Malamute's popularity has escalated in Australia, so that these original dogs are now foundation lines for upcoming kennels. Polstar of Mrs. D. Sullivan, Lotanpark of Mrs. E. Luke, Huskypak of Mrs. Pat Roe in New South Wales, and Whitemist of Mrs. Irene Gates in South Australia all obtained bitches from Beverwijk. The Tundra Kennels of Wilma and Ron Livingston have many champions produced from Meryton Sisamut Kara and their male, Ch. Meryton Makluk Thunder.

From a Polstar litter out of Snow Eagle, Wendy and Mick Newton of Victoria took two bitches and began their Chukchi Alaskan Malamutes. They have gone on to import many dogs from the U.S. and U.K.

The breed has become popular enough for some predictable problems to arise. The AMCV has had to form a breed rescue to deal with unwanted dogs. To help control hip dysplasia, the AMCV Hip Control Program has succeeded in getting their registering body, the Victorian Canine Council, to use an "A" suffix on the pedigrees of dogs with normal hip x-rays, which should assist conscientious breeders.

The pinnacle of the Australian shows is the Royal Melbourne, which is benched; however, shows are held every weekend within 200 miles of Melbourne. Their system for earning championships is modeled on that of the U.K., and interest in the breed has steadily grown.

One notable winner, owned by Pahrey Kennels, is Ch. Huskypak Hussybear winner of the only available Chal-

lenge Certificate (CC) for females in 1988, 1989, 1992, and 1993. In 1988, her brother Ch. Huskypak Aussie Bear joined her, winning the dog CC.

Obedience titles in Australia and the requirements for earning them correspond with those of the U.S. Growing numbers of Malamutes have achieved CD titles. In 1994, the AMCV held an obedience trial with its championship show.

JAPAN
(Information for this section was provided by Sachi Maeda of Zaverriwon Alaskan Malamutes.)

Malamutes first came to Japan with Americans who brought their dogs with them while they lived there in the sixties. The first registration with the Japan Kennel Club did not occur until 1971, when Squankan's Playboy was imported from the U.S. by Norio Iwata in Tokyo. A decade passed before the next registration.

By 1984, the Kazamas had begun importing Malamutes to their pet shop, Africa Kennel, registering them under the kennel name Dog Heart Africa. Their first breeding was between Kuuipo's Kapono and Riata's Spice on Ice. The first home-bred Malamutes in Japan were two females from this breeding.

Mrs. Kawahata began importing additional U.S. lines, a female Kanagawa MT, and Nockchin's Maximillion, who finished his Japanese championship in 1985. Another import finished his championship that year, Ch. Kimiska's Lord of the Ring.

The Kazamas then imported Am. Ch. Storm Kloud's Ooutlaw, WTD, WWPD and Am. Ch. Hug A Bear's Echo of King Togi, a pair with a profound influence on the breed in Japan. Ch. Bista of Dog Heart Africa, owned by Mr. Okubo, became the first home-bred champion.

Over the ensuing years, the Kazamas imported many American champions, including the 1984 AMCA National Specialty winner, Am. Ch. Nomarak's Kenworth, Am. Ch. Storm Kloud's Hhowling Satana, Am. Ch. Osirises Princess Nena, Am. Ch. Storm Kloud's Go West Young Man (Fujin), and Am. Ch. Sitka Tathlina. The latter two were BOB Dog and Bitch, respectively, at the JKC Headquarter's Show in 1988. Fujin had a very successful show career until his untimely death in 1990, winning the first BIS for a Malamute in Japan in 1988.

Mr. Yagai of Shingen Yagai Kennels brought over Am. Ch. Glacier's the Bearing Sea, Am. Ch. Vermer's Equalizer, Am. Ch. Vermer's Sweet Breeze of Zapada, Am. Ch. Topam's Give Me A Chance Tu; and Am. Ch. Willawaw's

Snow Dancer. Mr. T. Murase of Aikenso has also been influential in the breed, providing foundation stock for several other kennels from his importation and breedings. A slightly different strain entered Japanese Malamutes through breedings to Can/Am. Ch. Kooskia's Little Drummer Boy, last owned by Mr. Saito.

Although importations continue, mainly from the U.S., the Japanese have begun to consolidate their own breeding programs to establish their own strains. By 1990, the Saitama Kita Alaskan Malamute Club had formed under the auspices of Africa Kennels and held its first specialty show. The entry of 115 had strong support from exhibitors with ties to the Kazamas. BOB was Am. Ch. Mals About Sun Dagger of Alta, owned by Mr. Patton, while BOB at the JKC Headquarters Show was Mr. Yagai's Am. Ch. Storm Kloud's Vvanilla Snoman.

At subsequent specialties, Best of Breed was awarded in 1990 to Am. Ch. Blue Ice Ode to Storm Kloud and in 1991 to AMCA National Specialty winner, Am. Ch. Sholyn Akala of Myakik, who was imported by Mr. Inahara's Sanki Kennels. Best of Opposite Sex was awarded to Am. Ch. Keeley's Wild Trade Wind both years. She was also BOB Bitch at the JKC Headquarters show.

The Japan Kennel Club had a U.S. judge, Mr. Ed Bivin, at their Headquarters show in 1993. He chose Mr. Shindo's J/Am. Ch. Wild Wind's Viewer's Choice as BOB and J/Am. Ch. Double T's Devil in Disguise, now owned by S. Maeda, as BOS. That year Alaskan Malamute Classic Improvement, a new club, formed to revitalize interest in the breed.

The Malamute as a show-dog got a big boost when Am. Ch. Wild Wind's This Buds For You finally obtained the coveted "Supreme Dog" title from the JKC. This award is given when a dog wins five or more BIS, King, Queen, or specialty BOB awards. The second "Supreme Dog," Mrs Inaba's J/Am. Ch. Ziljo N Kasaan's Skyward Bound, obtained his title with five BIS wins.

Despite the Kazamas withdrawal from dogs, interest in the Alaskan Malamutes in Japan continues to be very strong. Unfortunately, language difficulties and distance make breed information less accessible to both the amateur breeders and pet shops which sell Malamutes. Importers are trying to diversify the lines available in Japan which should be helped by the AKC's agreement for reciprocal registration with the JKC in 1992. Before that, exported stock, for all practical purposes, was lost to U.S. breeders, since progeny bred in Japan could not be registered in the U.S.

The Japanese are also working their dogs, and the results should have some effect on their breeding choices. The first CDX was obtained by a Japanese-bred female, Ch. Cordelia Kamui I, CDX, owned by Sachi Maeda. She also runs in harness and has earned the AMCA WPD title as has domestic BIS winner, Ch. Zaverriwon Artic Reflection, owned by Mr. Takemura. Yukiko Imai's JKC Ch. TCH In Harmony's Dream of Campanella is a CDX and WPD. She is also working in agility and sledding.

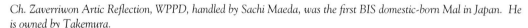

Ch. Zaverriwon Artic Reflection, WPPD, handled by Sachi Maeda, was the first BIS domestic-born Mal in Japan. He is owned by Takemura.

Japan's Ch. Zaverriwon Artic Reflection, WPD, owned by Takemura, and Ch. Cordelia Kamui, CDX, WPD, owned by the Maedas, were the first Japanese dogs to earn their working title from the AMCA.

Below:
Jap. Ch. Inharmonys Dream of Campanella CDX, is handled in the agility ring by owner Yukiko Imai.

Below left: Champaign's Cheechako with his owner Yoichi Maeda, a 1991 import to Japan.
Below right: Mom carries child while Japanese Ch. Cordelia Kamui CDX, WPD carries the package.

EUROPEAN COUNTRIES

SWITZERLAND

(Information for this section was provided by Mrs. Helly Vogt of Windy Hill Alaskan Malamutes.)

The first Malamute, Int./Swiss Ch. Wagnark of Coldfoot, arrived in Switzerland in 1965. His owner, Mrs. Helly Vogt, has been the breed warden for the Swiss Club since 1966. She established an internal studbook for the breed at the outset, and currently owns Shuyak, a Mal trained as a combination of companion, agility, and sled dog.

The Swiss club emphasizes good placement (which helps reduce the number of Malamutes turning up in shelters) and responsible breeding for the highest quality possible. They believe that each successive generation should improve on the one which preceded it.

Of the approximately 120 dogs which have been imported in the last thirty years, the first were from the United States and Canada from Sno-Pak, Kanangnark, Coldfoot, and Tigara Kennels. In the mid-seventies, these were followed by dogs from Zagoskin, Nunaga's (from Tigara lines), Tote-Um, and Tobe. Kennels in other European countries that have exported to Switzerland include Naksala, Baffin, Keewatin, and Mt. Kinley from Germany; du Grand Pierreux, Cold Valley, and WolfChorus from Belgium; Rossnisska's from Austria, and de L'Etoile from France. A combination of judicious breeding, excellent imports, and attention to working ability has made the Swiss Alaskan Malamute a quality animal.

Oki-Nuia du Grand-Pierreaux, bred by Luc and Francoise Pirick of Belgium and owned by Martin and Elke Wicki of Switzerland.

Chibougamo Furkesch, bred by Nicole Lebet and owned by Roger Fahrni, Switzerland.

Musher Kurt Benninger races Urak Du Petit Chatillon and Romy Du Petit Chatillon.

THE NETHERLANDS

*(Information for this section was provided by Mrs. Drs. H.J.C. Dub-
bledam, Secretary, AMCN, and Marijke Baas of Issumatak Alaskan
Malamutes.)*

The Netherlands' counterpart to the AKC, the Raad
van Beheer op Kynologish Gebied in Nederland, handles
all registrations and issues all pedigrees. In order to obtain
a pedigree, a puppy or dog must be tattooed by kennel club
personnel.

To maintain the quality of their excellent dogs, the
Alaskan Malamute Club of the Netherlands (AMCN)
mandates breeding restrictions. To be used for breeding,
the Alaskan Malamute must:

1) Have hip x-rays certified either excellent or good,
2) Be over 24 months for bitches or 18 months for
   dogs,
3) Not have had a litter within the previous 12
   months (bitches),
4) Have no serious genetic deformation,
5) Not be monorchid (dogs).[4]

The AMCN does not have any titles to recognize producing or working achievement, but it does encourage its
members to work with their dogs. At "activity days," members are introduced to backpacking, carting, and pulk
work. The club has held walks, weekend hikes in the Belgium Ardennes forest, and even sledding/packing weeks in
France.

The club holds its own dog show each year, although
championship points are not always available. To become a
Dutch champion, a dog must win at least four championship points under at least two different judges. In addition, the last point must be won after the dog is twenty-
seven months old.

The first Dutch Champion was Tigara's Matanuska
U-Chee, owned by Mrs. Anita Andela and bred in the
United States by Mrs. G. Schwalbe and Dorothy Dilling-
ham. Imported in 1967, U-Chee and her sister, Tigara's
Matanuska Chee-Chee, were also the first Alaskan Mala-
mutes registered in Holland.

Mrs. L. Scheffer-Pater bred the first Malamute litter,
born in March, 1972. Mrs. Betsy Ketelaar began her very
influential career in Alaskan Malamutes with a male from
this litter, Ch. Anernek. With an American import, Ch.
Jotom's Ilannak, she began her Zagoskin Maleygmyut Kennel. Her fine exports to other European countries have
started and strengthened their breedings. Currently, she is
the president of the AMCN and is still a driving force behind Mals in Holland, although she is no longer breeding.

*Come on guys, we can fit in a couple more! Photo courtesy of Chris
Eisenga, Netherlands.*

Mrs. R. Looymans-Mimpen started her Nukilik Kennel
with a dog, Ch. Zagoskin Maleygmyut's Pitlik, and a bitch,
Ch. Zagoskin Maleygmyut's Pitiksik. She then bred her
imported Ch. Inharmony's Nukilik Unayok to Ch. Inuit's
Luavik of Zagoskin, and a puppy from this was sent to
Finland.

A sister to Pitiksik, Ch. Zagoskin Maleygmyut's Sitiyok
and Nukilik's Ahre-Gay, a dog, form the basis of the Of
Narjan Mar Kennel of Mrs. F. Kerklaan. Mr. Kerklaan and
their sons run their Malamutes in two mixed teams.

Mr. P. v. Dalen of Tokositna Maleygmyut Kennel also
runs his Malamutes, Ch. Zagoskin Maleygmyut's Maitsiak
and Ch. Zagoskin Maleygmyut's Anana, in a team. So does
Mr. C. Hartveld, who imported Jotom's Paluktuk,
Amuyok's Spirit of Katum Inua, Apple Hill's Tango, and
Jotom's Issuk of Kataum Inua.

Mrs. G. Warmelink-Schaufeli's kennel Akkimayunga
began with two bitches of Zagoskin antecedents, Ayorama
v. Huis het Loo and Nukilik's Akkimayunga, as did Mrs. J.
v.d. Brink's Tareormiut Maleygymut Kennels with the
bitch, Ch. Zagoskin Maleygmyut's Yngyt, and male, Ch.
Zagoskin Maleygmyut's Atataq. Mrs. J. Algera-Verhoef of
Kiana has Ch. Zagoskin Maleygymut's Juini as well as an
import bitch, Inharmony's Teniga of Kiana.

Just beginning is the de Hamer family whose kennel
name is Mahkajo. They have a bitch, Ch. Nukilik's Nivi-
asar and a pointed male, Nukilik's Mahkajo Nakkertok.

The Hofstras started their Zharkova Kennels with the
dog, Zagoskin Maleygmyut's Koutak, and bitch, Alexej
Chirikof Tamerack. Gerke Hofstra runs his Malamutes successfully in races.

R. Servais mushes seven Malamutes and a Laika dog in the Netherlands. Photo courtesy of Chris Eisenga.

Mr. J. Maat and his daughter run a four-Malamute team. Their Of Shaktolik Kennel started with Chiminuk Thorin, G&G-1, of Zagoskin breeding, and Cold Valley's Justified Sila. Another noteworthy racer is Mrs. E. Vader, whose very successful three-dog team consists of World/Dutch Ch. Zagoskin Maleygmyut's Takuvik, a dog, World/Dutch Ch. Kataum Inua's Nunaraq and Tokositna Maleygmyut's Kuyanakuni, both bitches.

Ch. Bareebinyackzan, G&G-1, WTD, UV is owned by Mrs. Marijke Baas. Not only does he run in the pulk-class races, but he is the first Alaskan Malamute in Holland to obtain an obedience title, a Working Team Dog title and a Stamina Test title (UV). He is also trained as a Search and Rescue Dog. Her import, Ch. Inharmony Issumatak's Ikayort, G&G-1, G&G-2, UV, VZH, or "Yortok," was the first Malamute to obtain the higher-level G&G-2 obedience title and also does Search and Rescue.

Although their numbers are small, Malamutes in the Netherlands are in excellent hands. Their quality has enabled them to become foundation stock for other European countries.

GERMANY

(Information for this section was provided by Mr. Burkhard Reimer.)

Imports into Germany initially came from many different Canadian and U.S. kennels, especially from Nancy Russell of Storm Kloud. Chris Jannelli from Belgium has also sent some fine dogs.

Breeding of registered dogs is controlled through the breed clubs. Breed wardens evaluate dogs to determine if they are worthy of breeding, using requirements designed to maintain not only type in the breed but genetic health as well. In addition to considering the dog's conformation, the breed warden requires certificates vouching for the dog's hips, eyes, and physical well-being before granting ap-

proval to breed. Approval for additional breedings depends upon the results of hip x-rays on the progeny from the previous litter(s). All must be radiographed, and at least 50 percent must receive a good rating.

BELGIUM

(Information for this section was provided by Mrs. Chris Jannelli of Cold Valley Alaskan Malamutes.)

After several false starts, Chris Jannelli's very successful Cold Valley kennel began with bitches from Tigara lines through Matanuska Kennels. These were joined by American imports, a daughter of Ch. Tigara's Nordisch Kotze Tu and a bitch from Storm Kloud/Sugarbear. From the Gabriel's Kaila Kennels in the U.S., they acquired another bitch with lines back to both Tigara and Sena-Lak.

Mrs. Janelli later obtained a bitch from Blue Ice Kennels and one from Storm Kloud as well as two Kotzebue males. One, Heritage Kotzebue Youri, was out of the last litter of Ch. Kotzebue Taku of Chinook, Short Seeley's last brood bitch. The other was bred on Kotzebue and Sno Pak lines.

Chris and her friends took this stock to several dogs, including Shamrock's Shaman of Yukon; a Spanish dog, Ch. Du Paumanok Blue Ice Dragon; Ch. Baffin's Magic Dragon; Am. Ch. Sendaishi's Kandu Can Do; a Wild Wind male owned by Steffi Wassermann in Germany; and an Italian dog, The Boss, imported from Canada, owned and shown by Paola Trade.

Using these dogs with her Cold Valley/Wolf Chorus Kennel bitches enabled Chris Jannelli to produce some outstanding Malamutes. Among them are the "E" litter, with the well-known Ch. Cold Valley's Erasmus; Ch. Cold Valley Evening Song, and Fr. Ch. Cold Valley Ebraska, who was the most-titled bitch in Europe during her show career. Ch. Cold Valley's Lady Blue, who goes back to McKinley Kennels in Germany, is a multi-national champion, a best-in-show and specialty winner. Her sister, Ch. Cold Valley's

Noatak Snopak, also finished as did her brothers, Fr. Ch. Cold Valley's Last Edition and It. multi-best-of-breed winner, Ch. Magnificat Taro. Ch. Cold Valley Kodiak Explorer has championships in 13 countries as well as a CDX. Several of the Belgian bitches have been bred to dogs in the U.S., including Am. Ch. Sendaishi's Kotzebue Kotokaze, Sendaishi's Eskimo Eddy, Am. Ch. Storm Kloud's Vanilla Snoman, and Am. Ch. Nanuke's A Rushin Revolution.

The Belgians are successfully combining many American lines to produce Malamutes of quality and soundness. Luc and Francoise Pirick, Du Grand Pierreaux Kennels, have Evening Song, Ch. Cold Valley's Follow Me Furka, and Ch. Cold Valley's Frostnight Dream. They also have imports from France and the U.S., including Ch. Kandik's Kismet of Malnorska.

E. Anthonis of Borakisline (Keewatin) Kennels has imported an Italian male, For Adults Only de Lago degli Orsi. They also own Cold Valley's Ewika.

Several Belgian kennels also began with stock from Chris Janelli, including Sweet Genghis Pak of S. Diaz-Dupont and Keena's Wolf Pak of A. Gabay. Joli Mapa is the kennel name of M. and J. Lingier, whose home-bred champion Ch. Joli Mapa's Hero Boy is a multi-national champion. The Chorus Line dogs of W. & C. Bruyninckx have been making a name for themselves with Ch. Karnak of the Wolf Chorus and Cold Valley Made Another Witch.

Eugene Terryn's Akela's Song Kennels has a male import from Foxfire as well as Ch. Cold Valley's Indianak and Ch. Let Me Be Yentl of Keewatin. The Northern Lightning dogs of the Mouthaans and the Chiboui of Barnak dogs of Sloumont-Perree are starting to make their marks in the show ring also.

Above:
Ch. Karnak of the WolfChorus,
owned by Walter Bruyninckx,
Belgium.

Left: Ch. Cold Valley's Legend De
Hurtado went BOB and BIS in
Belgium under Barbara Brooks.
Legend was bred by Chris Jannelli
and is owned by P. E. Huysmans.

Top right: Young Terryn with
Let Me Be Your Yent'l of Keewatin,
owned by E. Terryn, Belgium.

Lower right: Akela's Song Ordan, bred
and owned by Eugene Terryn.

Below: Twelve-year-old Peter Mouthaan running a two-dog team
of Northern Lightning Malamutes. Belgium.

Official pedigrees for FCI shows come from the Royal Society of St. Hubert (LOSH). Currently, an independent breed club handles Malamute affairs in Belgium.

CZECH REPUBLIC
(Information for this section was provided by Michaela Purnochova' of Navarama CS Alaskan Malamutes and J. Seidl.)

Registration in the Czech Republic is through a central FCI-affiliated registry in Prague. Considering the size of the country, the breed is very popular. In 1993, the registry showed 251 breeding dogs, 442 breeding bitches and 748 registrations of puppies. Czechs show actively in other countries, such as Belgium and Italy. Imports have come from Chris Jannelli's Cold Valley Kennel in Belgium, the Di Latina Kennel in Italy, and Malamutes from Taaralaste, Kaitu, Steep Hill, Ayaluk, and Chinook have been brought in from the United States.

The Seidls imported a puppy from Mrs. Jannelli, Conny Na Horence. She has been extremely successful in the show rings of Europe, receiving seven CACIBs and becoming a champion in the Czech Republic, Poland, and Austria and winning the champion class of the European exhibition in 1993.

DENMARK

(Information for this section was provided by Birgit Hinrichsen and Niels Friis of Team Malamute.)

The first Malamute, Landsrud Alma, entered Denmark from Norway and began Moon Song Kennels which was at the forefront of Danish Malamute breeders during the 1980s. Kennel Unalaska has some very nice black Malamutes out of a Moon Song female and her daughter.

In Denmark, Malamutes are mostly family dogs, although their use as sled or cart dogs is increasing as more Danes learn about the breed. Since they have no Malamute club, Malamute owners are members of the Spidshundenklubben, a club for Northern Dogs. This was founded in 1968 and has 818 members.

NORWAY

(Information for this section was provided by Tove Tveiten of Terra Polar.)

The first Malamutes arrived in Norway in 1975-76. A four-month quarantine makes importation difficult. Most Norwegian lines arise from Oywind Moen's Topkok's Kennel. His import female, Tote-Um's Alaska Sno Bird, is behind almost all of the Malamutes in Norway today. She was followed in 1979 by Tote-Um's Ballard Queen. That same year, Mr. Moen also imported the male Orms Dorm's Moose Moose of Tote-Um from P.C. Ormiston in the U.S.

Tigara's Snow Owl of Accomac came from England to owner Magne Klep. Moose Creek Tulugak arrived from Moose Creek Kennels in Alaska for Kare Holmsen, and Moose Creek Thule came to Ole Kristensen from Stacy Lamoreux of the U.S. in 1981. Nina Overas, who had earlier imported from Wakon Kennels in the U.S., imported Alwaasen Mitzy from the U.S. in 1981.

Oyvind Moen's 1983 importation of Targhee Strawberries Shaman from Albert Holabach has had a strong influence on Norwegian Malamutes as did Inger Lise and Rune Larsen with their U.S. import, Barrenfield Lord Santana, bred by Joseph S. Huner and Robert L. Sherman. Breedings to him have introduced some new bloodlines into the Norwegian Malamutes.

In 1990, Hege and Svein Tore Boe imported a male from Denmark, Zagoskin Maleygmyut's Kre Aklak, bred in Holland by Betsy Ketelaar. In 1989, breedings from shipped semen from Int./Nl/Blg./Fr/Ger./Lux. Ch. Joli Mapa Hero Boy resulted in two bitches each having only two puppies; however one of these, Terre Polar's Delta Ka-Tuin, owned by Tove R. Tveiten received six certificates and three CACIB, two BOS and four BOB before her sec-

ond birthday. Mr. Tveiten also imported Chorus' Lines Paraded, a puppy from Belgian Chris Jannelli in 1991.

Most Norwegians have only one or two dogs. As part of the family, they join their owners in different activities such as backpacking, sledding, or just as a companion on walks. Neither weight pulling or obedience is very popular although weight pulling is held just for fun at the club's annual winter collection. For the most part, the Norwegians sled, backpack, ski, and bicycle with their dogs for recreation.

FINLAND

(Information for this section provided by Riitta and Jari Nirhamo of Samaljankan Alaskan Malamutes and Kirsi Hyttinen.)

Alaskan Malamutes arrived in Finland in the sixties and seventies. A male, Sami Silver Tip of Finland, was registered and a bitch Lupa came from the first breeding in Italy. The first kennel to breed Malamutes in Finland was Merisaimon, using two U.S. imports, the male Wonderland Toma, and the bitch, Wonderland Miksi. Serious breeding began in the eighties with imports from Norway, Sweden and England.

In November, 1992, at the biggest dog show of the year, The Helsinki International Dog Show, only eight Malamutes were shown. However, the breed is gaining ground, partly because the quarantine regulations for dogs coming from Central Europe, Canada or the United States have been lifted.

The Alaskan Malamute in Finland is well represented by an active club, Alaskanmuuttiyhdistys r,y (ALMA). ALMA publishes a quarterly newsletter and holds Camps Geld three times per year. It also sponsors weekend seminars and training camps for the Malamutes and their owners with various activities such as sledding, weight pulling, and tracking. Once a year there is a National Specialty show organized with Suomen Seurakoirayhdistys, the Finnish Companion Dog Association.

Initially, Malamutes in Finland were purely sled and house dogs; however, some new fields have opened up. At least one person has trained for tracking and search and rescue. One female has passed the Finnish novice class in Obedience and will continue into Open, and another is working in Agility.

The weight pull contest at the yearly Winter Camp has been quite popular, and skijoring and sledding are natural winter sports in this far northern country. Only a few people have more than two Malamutes, so an all-Malamute team is a rare, but welcome sight.

Top right: Samaljankan Malamutes driven by owner Jari Nirhamo, Finland.

Center right: Int. Norwegian Ch. Najanin's Country Muskie, with owner Irene Eriksen, Norway.

Right: Norwegian Ch. Totonac's Action Crying Wolf with breeder/owner Marit Trana, Norway.

Below left: Samaljankan Arctic Astral, owned by Riitta and Jari Nirhamo, Finland.

Below right: Topkok's Canadian Ike (right) with owner, Olav Tveiten of Norway and a Greenland Dog.

BIS Ch. Could It Be Magic Del Lago Degli Orsi, owned by Nadia Bersani, Italy.

ITALY

(Information for this section was provided by Gloria Urbani of Del Lago Degli Orsi Alaskan Malamutes and Giuseppe Biagiotti of Del Biagio Alaskan Malamutes.)

Mr. Camillo Grillo of Rome imported the first Malamute, Flico du Longet, from the Swiss breeder Mr. J. Paccaud of Du Longet Kennel. Flico became the first Italian Champion and sired the first Italian litter with Vega dell Alaska, owned by Rosemary Pacini.

From this beginning, the breed has thrived in Italy. Their specialty shows attract a fairly large entry, ranging from fifty to sixty dogs. Italy has both a Northern Dog Club, the Club Italiano Razz Nordische (CIRN) and a specialty club, the Club Italiano Alaskan Malamute, whose president since 1976 has been the very influential breeder, Mrs. Gloria Urbani. In addition to its shows, the CIAM recognizes top producers by awarding a Riproduttors Championship, the equivalent of the AMCA Register of Merit.

The Italian people enjoy their dogs generally both as companions and as show dogs. Although sledding takes a back seat, some Italians do use Malamutes on teams. They also have bicycle, cart, and skijor races.

BIS Ch. Kiss Me Again Del Lago Degli Orsi, owned by Gloria Urbani, Italy.

Sikoa's Dodi Monster owned by Hiram Dietah, Spain, has her wooly coat covered with snow. She was High in Trial at the 1997 AMCA National.

Top left: Aura of Splendor Del Biagio, Int. Ch. Hokie Hi Fire-Storm, Int. Ch Kiwalik's Sheoni Kimarik, & Back Fire Del Biagio.

Top center: Italian team.

Top right: Dog trekking in Italy.

Above left: BIS Ch. Storm Kloud's Ffollow My Dream WWPD, owned by Gloria Urbani.

Right: BIS Ch. The Killing Moon del Lago Degli Orsi, owned by Pietro Calcagno.

FRANCE

(Information for this section was provided by Dr. Francoise Raust, president of the AMCF and an AMCA member.)

Mrs. Michele Raust de Palma introduced the Alaskan Malamute to France in 1974 and had the first litter in 1975 out of Laska XI and Shooting Star. Two puppies were sold to Mr. Jean-Vincent Fournis as foundation stock. The second breeding produced the first French Champion, Manitou, who was also a Spanish Champion, Champion of Monaco, and International Champion.

In France, most Malamutes are placed as pets. Only a handful find their way into working or show homes; achieving a French championship is very difficult. Until 1992, only one Champion de France de Conformite au Standard was allowed per sex, per year. Increased Malamute entries now enable the breed to obtain two championships per sex, per year. An Elite A, which is the equivalent of the AMCA ROM title, is also awarded to top producing sires and dams.

Ch. Cold Valley's Last Edition, P. Dauvet, France.

Int. Am. Ch. TNT Quincy of Camps, owned by Eugeni and Helena Boix of Spain, is a top winning dog in both Spain and the U.S. Breeder, Twinkie Moore.

SPAIN

(This information was supplied by Miss Maria J. Lopez-Francos.)

The Alaskan Malamute Club de Espana was founded in October 1993. Its members are interested in establishing good working relations with neighboring European Malamute clubs. Since its formation the club has become an active member of the Northern Dog and the Akita Inu Club of Spain. Quite a number of Malamutes are shown and run on recreational and racing teams during the year. Interest in the breed is growing in Spain and show entries are large.

UNITED KINGDOM

(Information for this section was provided by Janet Edmonds.)

Dog affairs in the United Kingdom are controlled largely by The Kennel Club,[5] which is based in London. Wales, Scotland, and Ireland also have kennel clubs, but they are still subject to the rules of The Kennel Club.

Getting dogs out of the country is easy. On the other hand, importation is difficult and expensive because of a six-month quarantine period, which effectively keeps Malamute numbers down.

As a response to the volumes of bad publicity about dog bites and attacks, the government has enacted a series of very strict, breed-specific laws restricting imports of certain breeds as well as curtailing the ability to breed or even own those already in the U.K. Because of these Draconian laws, Malamute owners are very careful about the number of litters they breed and the placement of the puppies.

In the U.K., dogs become champions by earning Challenge Certificates (CCs) and the number of these available per year, per breed, and per sex varies with the number of dogs shown. The challenge-certificate format for awarding championships is not uncommon; however, it makes obtaining a championship difficult. Class competition ends with the Open Class where existing champions as well as dogs without championships compete against each other (as is done in American field trials). No Best-of-Breed Class segregates dogs that already have championships, although Group and Best-In-Show are also held. To make things even more difficult, the breed has only been able to

Tigara's Flash of Accomac, top UK Malamute 1981-83. Owner, Mrs. M. E. MacFarlane.

Highnoon's Nansamund, owned by R. Croly, England.

win a CC in the U.K. for a short time, so only few dogs have championships.

A group or even a reserve group win at a championship show is very prestigious. A recent import, Can. Ch. Oopik's Winter Excellence, is the first Alaskan Malamute to win a Working Group at a championship show and the first to win Best in Show at an open show.

The first imports came in 1959 when two Americans, William and Barbara Preston, brought their three Malamutes with them, a male, Pawnee Flash of North Wind and two females, Preston's Cheechako and her daughter. Before their return to the U.S., they bred three litters under the kennel name Kananak.

Additional imports in the mid-sixties sparked enough interest in the breed for the formation of the Alaskan Malamute Club in 1964. It has over a hundred members, and there are probably over 350 Malamutes in Great Britain today.

In the seventies, several Kotzebue dogs were imported. Subsequent imports, mainly in the eighties, have been Snowline's Polar Night, Kimiska's Arctic Sea Hawk of Highnoon, Can. Ch. Malnorska's Danikka of Highnoon, Malnorska's Gypsy Lady, Am. Ch. Fire 'n' Ice in Conclusion C.D., and Baron Von Star.

Malamutes from Britain have been exported to Australia, Austria, Norway, Sweden, Finland, Marjorca, and back to Canada. The quarantine laws, however, effectively prohibit the British from measuring their stock against that from other countries.

SCOTLAND

(Information for this section was provided by J. M. Brown of Tigara Alaskan Malamutes.)

J. M. Brown is the second oldest musher in Scotland. When he began running his dogs in 1986, he had the only Malamute team in the United Kingdom. His first dogs were acquired when he was in the U.S. Upon his return to Scotland in 1974, he brought his Malamutes back with him, a bitch, Tigara's Snow Flurry, and a male, Tigara's Sam Spade.

Although Malamutes were being shown in England when Mr. Brown's dogs came out of quarantine, in Scotland entries were so small that very few shows had separate classes for them. Undaunted, Mr. Brown showed Sam until he was let out of the yard by accident and was killed by a car.

This accident led to the importation of Tigara's Far Land Scot's Pride in 1975. He became an important sire in the U.K. In an unusual move, the Dillinghams gave Mr. Brown permission to use the Tigara name on all his Tigara-bred dogs, and now, ironically, he is the last breeder to use the Tigara name.

From the couch to the race course, Mals are at home in Scotland! Above: Tigara's Snow in Summer enjoys the "good life." Owner, Stuart Lindsey.

Right: J. M. Brown, Broadfold Farm, races his all-Tigara Malamute team at a 1991 rally in Scotland.

ISRAEL

(Information about the Israeli Malamutes was supplied by A. Schwarz.)

Israel has a northern dog club called the Israel Spitz Dog Club. The first female imported was Sasha of Chenote in 1975, following which two other males arrived between 1978 and 1981. All were AKC registered.

More recently, imports have come from Storm Kloud, including two females and a male, Storm Kloud's Ccruisin On By, imported in 1988. Jamie Nelson, who drove the kennel's Iditarod team, is sending Ch. Storm Kloud Hhere I Am for a year.

Over the years, about 19 litters with 111 puppies have been bred. Today, only about 35-40 Malamutes are in Israel but interest in the breed is increasing.

ENDNOTES

1. Wilma Livingston, Personal communication, 1993
2. Judith Blogg, "Doing What Comes Naturally," *Pedigree Pal Digest,* (Spring, 1993), 8.
3. Julie Stein, "The Alaskan Malamute in Australia." private paper.
4. Mrs. Drs. H.J.C. Dubbledam, Secretary AMCN, letter (October 31, 1993).
5. Reflecting its venerable age and its importance to the world of dogs, in the U.K., the kennel club is The Kennel Club. The Crufts Dog Show is the Kennel Club's annual show which attracts about 20,000 dogs to a four-day benched show. The Working Group has an entry of about 6,000 dogs.

Top: Mr. Jarmo Valo on the Halti Fjell, corner of Finland, Sweden, and Norway, with his three Malamutes and an Alaskan Husky mix (front).

Below: Michaela Purnochova, Czech Republic.

Ch. Wolf Pack North Star HDoo, owned by David W. J. Fourie, Republic of South Africa.

Dutch Ch. Nukilili's Ahre, owned by Mrs. Kerklaan. Photo by M. Baas. Holland

Ch. Arctic Luv's Skull Duggery played the part of "Trick" on Dr. Quinn Medicine Woman before beginning a show career. Breeder/owner, Bernadette Quercio. Photo by Missy Yuhl.

14

MALAMUTES GO HOLLYWOOD

Since wolves are unpredictable and virtually untrainable, the resemblance between them and Malamutes, coupled with the dog's friendly nature and trainability, assures the Alaskan Malamute's future in the movie and television industry. While a few directors actually use wolves or wolf-hybrids, others use a little make-up and a weight for the tell-tale tail to transform a Malamute into a well-mannered double for his wild cousin.

Malamutes will always have a place in movies that feature sled dogs. Hollywood's fascination with the Arctic and its denizens extends all the way back into the 1930s, when Leonhard Seppala sold Balto and his team to producers eager to capitalize on the public's excitement over the Serum Run. Disney's 1994 release of the animated movie *Balto* demonstrates that it continues today.

In the early days of television, before cartoons, talk-shows, and news magazines took over the airways, many children's programs were adventure dramas with live actors. Especially popular were shows in which the heros were animals. Horses were represented by Fury, Black Beauty, Flicka, and Mr. Ed. Dogs had a head start though with the German Shepherd silent-movie stars, Rin-Tin-Tin and Strongheart. Rin-Tin-Tin made the transition to television as did the collie, Lassie. Both characters are still featured today played by dogs many generations removed from the original canine actors. Dogs such as Bullet (*Roy Rogers*), Daisy (*Blondie*) and Asta (*The Thin Man*) were well-known supporting players on television series.

THE ROBELS OF RO-ALA-KEN

YUKON KING

For years during the late 1950s and early 1960s, Sgt. Preston of the Yukon shared life in the Royal Canadian Mounted Police with his "constant canine companion, the giant Malamute," Yukon King. The television series was filmed on location and ran in prime-time. Each week, Sgt. Preston, played by Richard Simmons (not the diet king), and Yukon King tested their courage and wits against the rigors of the Klondike and the "renegade lawbreakers" driven by the lust for gold.

Yukon King was portrayed by an Alaskan Malamute named Kim of the North, owned and trained by Paul Robel. While Paul was working for Rennie Renfrow, who owned Daisy in the *Blondie* series, he learned that sled dogs were needed for the movies, so he assembled a team. Kim, or Yukon King, as he came to be called, was one of the first dogs he acquired. Beulah Robel recalls Kim as a sweet, good natured, very trusting dog.[1] Unfortunately, the harmony between Simmons and Kim was as fictional as the characters they played, so Kim was replaced by another Malamute for the balance of the series.

Paul and his wife Beulah used the kennel name Ro-Ala-Ken. They showed some of their first Malamutes but were put off by the poor sportsmanship of some competitors. Paul began training and selling the dog's services to various Hollywood studios and to a dog food company for use in advertising. Feeding, cleaning, training, and overseeing the welfare of their twenty to thirty dogs was a full-time job, and Paul saw little merit in putting a dog on an unpaid leave of absence to attend dog shows. Beulah, however, was more interested in the show ring and finished several champions, some of which also worked in movies.

Often taken on location, the Ro-Ala-Ken dogs were real globe-trotters. Gray dogs like Wasco and Chena frequently earned roles as wolves. Wasco's busy career took him from Jackson Hole, Wyoming, to France where he and Chena worked on *The Christmas Tree*, with William Holden and Virna Lisa.[2] Over the years, the Robel's dogs worked on an impressive list of movies and television shows, including: *Back to God's Country*, with Rock Hudson and Marsha Henderson; *Call of the Wild*; *The Wild Country*, for Walt Disney with Vera Miles; *The Wild North*, with Stewart Granger; *Strategic Air Command*, with Jimmy Stewart; *Lost in Alaska*, with Abbott and Costello; *Mrs. Mike*, with Dick Powell and Evelyn Keyes; and *The Ice*

Chena in the movie Christmas Tree, *with William Holden and Virna Lisa.*

Beulah Roble with Sparky. All photos are from the Robel's original collection, courtesy of Tracy Young.

Paul Robel, Ro-Ala-Ken, with his movie sled dogs.

Sgt. Preston with Yukon King (right).

Palace, with Diane McBain, Robert Ryan and Carolyn Jones. *The Man from Shiloh* and *Wolf Track*, with Stewart Granger, featured Wasco and Harpy. Knick played the role of a wolf in Walt Disney's *Savage Sam* and made a pilot for CBS called *Ace of Yukon*, as well as several television commercials. He also led a studio team on *The Dean Martin Show*. Quite a bit of the Ro-Ala-Ken dogs' time was spent on the television series, *The Alaskans*, which was syndicated overseas after a long run in the U.S.

In the Munster movie, *Munsters Go Home*, Grandpa Munster was supposed to turn into a wolf, a role played by Chena. Although Chena's daughter was sold as a puppy, her true destiny was to follow in her mother's pawprints. She was returned to the Robels, and her gray color landed her a wolf role in the same Munster movie.[3]

In addition to being a star, Ch. Knik of Ro-Ala-Kan produced a multiple-group-winning son, Ch. Tenakee Chief, bred by the Robels. He is in the AMCA Working Dog Hall of Fame, had a successful show career of his own, and was a top-weight pull champion in Southern California. Paul Robel passed away in the 1970s and Beulah died in October of 1988.

Other Malamute and Malamute-cross owners have found employment for their dogs in movies. Malamutes had roles in *Niki Dog of the North*, *The Journey of Natty Gann*, and *White Fang*, as well as countless television shows and commercials.

WALT DISNEY PRODUCTIONS

Walt Disney has continued to capitalize on the public's on-going fascination with sled-dogs. In 1994, a sequel to *White Fang* appeared, along with the movie *Iron Will*. Released in January, 1994, it was filmed in northern Minnesota, Montana, and Maine during the winter of 1992-93. Based on the true story of a dog-sled race from Winnipeg, Manitoba, to St. Paul, Minnesota in 1917, the period requirements of the era and the extreme weather conditions made the movie very difficult to film.

George Gerdes is the actor who plays the movie's villain "Borg," the Swedish national champion. His seven-dog team was hired from Black Ice Kennels, owned by David and Shilon Bedford of Minnesota. They not only breed, train, and show Malamutes, but also operate a supply company for sledding equipment. Disney studios also employed teams belonging to Vicky MacLean (Trolldom), Kieth and Cindy Olson (Kingsdale), and Bill and Joyce Matott (Sendaishi) as doubles because filming took place in several different locations.

Leading the Black Ice team was Ch. Black Ice's High Speed Chase, WLDX, WTDX, WWPD. His exceptional abilities as a single leader provided the control necessary for the difficult situations and the multiple takes of the same scene needed to produce this film.

The filming locations contained several different types of terrain and some unusual settings. The breakneck run down a mountain slope was actually filmed on an expert ski slope. The scenes in which they run across crumbling ice are real; there was no way to simulate it. The dogs actually had to run to a train station complete with horses and a steam engine several feet away. Most of the film was shot from a snowmobile-mounted camera just a few feet from the dogs as they raced side by side. With typical Malamute aplomb, they kept their minds on their work and met the challenge of each new scene.

At first, the studio planned for Mr. Gerdes to drive the team as much as possible. It soon became clear that he was not comfortable handing the dogs in many of the

Actor David Bedford with the Black Ice team in the movie Iron Will. *Lead dog Am. Can Ch. Black Ice's High Speed Chase played Buster. Photo courtesy of Black Ice Kennel.*

Lead dog Am. Can Ch. Black Ice's High Speed Chase , who played Buster in Iron Will, with actor George Gerdes (Borg), and his double, David Bedford. Courtesy of S. Bedford.

Right: Inuit's Sneaky Black Pete, owned by Sheila Balch, is doing a TV advertisement for Kal Kan. Photo courtesy of S. Balch.

Far right: A scene from the movie, Kazan. Courtesy Tracy Young.

Bottom right: Short Seeley on the Steve Allen Show in 1956 with Ch. Gripp of Yukon. Photo from Seeley's collection, courtesy of Carol Williams.

Big Chena played in The Munsters. Photo courtesy Mrs. Carville & T. Young.

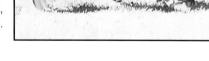

scenes, so David Bedford ended up as "Borg's" double, per-
forming all of his stunt work. The expertise Bedford
brought to driving actually allowed the director, Charles
Haid, to use the dogs under more difficult conditions than
planned and greatly added to the film's excitement. While
the film also used Siberian Huskies and Alaskan Huskies,
Mr. Haid called the Malamutes the "four-wheel drive
team" and was constantly amazed by their power and ability to work together amicably.

DR. QUINN, MEDICINE WOMAN

Another Malamute actor is Ch. Arctic Luv's
Skullduggery, or Trick, bred and owned by Bernadette
Quercio. Trick appears in the television series *Dr. Quinn,
Medicine Woman.* Like many television actors, his real-life
appearance is quite different from his screen image.

Using Malamutes to portray wolves is a mixed-blessing.
Movies and television are a potent source of advertisement, and the rise in wolf-hybrid popularity is probably
spurred on by movies that romanticize the idea of the wolf.
In shows where the dogs portray Malamutes, the character
the screen dogs display is often neither authentic nor flat-
tering to the breed.

Hollywood's influence has a way of blurring the line between image and reality, and Malamute breeders and owners need to be careful about how the breed is exploited in
media portrayals. Animal-rights advocates are always
looking for fuel for their allegations that Malamutes are
dangerous. Some areas of the country are still hot-beds of
dog-fighting activities, and Malamutes can easily become
prime targets for theft. Because these are favorite themes,
some breeders have urged that the AMCA try to persuade
the Disney studios not to show Malamutes as wolves or
fighting dogs.

Although Malamutes are not serious racing competitors, breeders involved in sledding are skeptical about the
Hollywood image of racing. Many are afraid newcomers
lured to the breed by the glamour of the movie set will try
to breed racing Malamutes, perverting their form and
function. The movies do prove that the Alaskan
Malamute is very flexible and can be trained for many purposes. Their happy-go-lucky natures and comical antics
make them natural entertainers.

ENDNOTES
1.   Beulah Robel, "Talks with Beulah Robel, Ro-Ala-Ken,"
Interview by Brenda E. Abbott in September, 1985, *The Malamute Quarterly* (Spring, 1987), 72.
2.   Robel, 70.
3.   Robel, 70.

Roger Moore in the movie
The Alaskan. *Photo courtesy
of Tracy Young.*

A beautiful head study of Am. Can. Ch. Karohonta Skymaster, ROM. "Jake" has produced more specialty winning offspring than any other Mal in the history of the breed at the time of publication. An excellent example of correct head type. Owned by Kiwalik Kennels. Photo by Krook.

Part III

Tomorrow

The Future of
the Alaskan Malamute

The breed's future lies in the hands of present and future breeders. Here, looking as if he is surveying his future, is Sno Klassic Above the Rim, bred, owned, and photographed by Tex and Patty Peel. He was three-and-one-half months old when this was taken.

15

BEFORE YOU BREED YOUR MALAMUTE

Breeding dogs can be a fulfilling, enjoyable hobby. However, before embarking on it, you should carefully consider your commitment to the breed. Breeding dogs requires a lot of hard work, dedication, and knowledge. It carries with it serious responsibilities to the buyer, the breed, and the dogs themselves.

The only justification for breeding is to improve the breed. Unfortunately, many other reasons motivate people. Some are of dubious merit; others spring from legitimate concerns or needs.

There are many sources of information on the technical aspects of dog breeding and genetics so, instead of covering the details in this book, we've chosen to direct you to the many other expert sources that are available. However, if you really think dog breeding is the path for you, your best chance for success lies in finding a mentor in your chosen breed. As his or her protege, you can benefit from experience and, in turn, you can help the breeder by becoming an extension of his or her kennel. This arrangement takes some ego restraint, since you will definitely be second-fiddle in this relationship. Eventually you will go out on your own, but you will be many steps ahead of where you would be had you started out alone, and, provided your relations are still amicable, your mentor can be a safety net when disasters occur.

THE WRONG REASONS

WE WANT A PUPPY JUST LIKE HIM

Dogs live only a handful of our years. As your pet ages, your thoughts may turn to breeding him so that you can have another dog just like the one you have. The truth is, your dog is unique, and the dogs most likely to resemble him are siblings rather than offspring. Puppies are a composite of both parents, not a copy of one.

Fortune could smile on you, of course, but the odds of getting a dog just like your dog are much better if you go "back to the well." Dogs of similar pedigree are more likely to be similar, so return to your dog's breeder or those breed-ing the same lines when you want to replace your dog with one that is most like him.

IT'S A WAY TO MAKE SOME EXTRA MONEY

Everyone can use a little extra money, and when you multiply the selling price of a puppy by the number in the litter, breeding dogs may seem like a good way to bring in some extra cash. In reality, very few breeders make a significant profit. Most consider themselves fortunate if they cover out-of-pocket expenses associated with the litter, giving no thought to the investment they have in the dam.

Mary's experience breeding her bitch is a fairly typical example of what is involved and its cost, beginning with Mary's purchase of a bitch as a show/breeding female. She paid $300 more than she would have for a pet puppy. Mary has been showing the bitch, and she is close to finishing her championship. So far, Mary has spent about $1,500 on dog shows. (Running Total: $1,800.)

In preparation for breeding, Mary paid $125 for an OFA X-ray and $65 for a CERF exam and certification. The bitch is pedigree-cleared for CHD, so Mary did not have to apply for a rating. The pre-breeding checkup and health certificate involved a $20 veterinary office call, $15 for a vaginal smear, and $20 for a brucellosis test. (Running Total: $2,045.)

Mary found two choices for stud dogs. Long distance calls, photocopies of pedigrees and certifications, and mail between Mary and their owners ran about $30. (Running Total: $2,075.) One stud is within driving distance—a top-winning champion with appropriate clearances, his stud fee is $500, payable at the time of breeding. However, Mary preferred her other choice because he had achieved an ROM bred to relatives of her bitch. Not only is he a top producer; he is also a top winning dog, with a Best of Breed at the National Specialty and several Best in Show awards. The owners quoted a stud fee of $500, half due at the time of service and the rest with the arrival of the litter. She would have had to ship her female, which would cost $420 round-trip.

Mary's foresight in having a backup dog for breeding was fortunate because, as it turned out, two days before the breeding date, the airlines embargoed all live animal shipments due to Christmas freight traffic, so Mary drove her female to the closer dog and paid the stud fee of $500. Because she stayed with a friend, her only costs were gas and food, $50; however, Mary had to take off three days from work, using up precious vacation time. (Running Total: $2,625.)

Materials for a whelping box Mary made cost $45. She also bought a heat lamp for $15, and set up the whelping area in the spare bedroom. The bitch had other ideas, however, and while Mary was at work, she climbed on the bed and shredded a custom-made bedspread that cost $250 to make a more comfortable nest. (Running Total: $2,935.)

Mary took two more vacation days when the litter was due. Like many Malamutes, her bitch easily delivered eight puppies. Her checkup after whelping cost Mary $20. Lactating females need high-quality food and a lot of it, so Mary's feed bill increased by $30 while the puppies were nursing. When they began eating solid food, increased food costs ran about $150. (Running Total: $3,135.)

The veterinarian does not charge an office visit for puppy shots, but at $15 per pup, vaccinations amounted to $120. The pups also had to be wormed. The exam was $9 and the worming, at $6 per puppy, was another $48. (Running Total: $3,312)

Mary spent $150 for an exercise pen from a pet supply store because the puppies were climbing out of the whelping box. She could have made one more cheaply, but did not have time. (Running Total: $3,462.)

She began advertising in the local newspaper when the puppies were six weeks old, $25/week, ($175) and she also took out an ad in a breed publication for $100. At first, she had a flurry of calls. The callers asked all sorts of questions and made appointments, but many did not keep them. Mary spent all her time off work either cleaning up after puppies, answering phone calls, or waiting for people to look at the puppies. (Running Total: $3,737.)

Mary sold five puppies to what seemed good homes, at $300 per puppy. One pup was returned after the veterinarian the new owners consulted for a health check told them that Malamutes were terrible pets. Mary refunded their money. (Running Total after sales: $2,537.)

By this time, the four remaining puppies needed additional vaccinations which cost $60. A monthly heartworm preventative and fecal exam for parasites ran an additional $34. (Running Total: $2,631.)

Mary planned to keep one of the two puppies that she considered show quality; the other she sold for $650 to a referral by the stud-dog owner. The last two puppies were finally placed in good homes by twelve weeks, but she reduced the price on the last one to $250. (Running Total: $1,431.)

With expenses of $3,831, or $479 per puppy, and an income of $2,400, Mary lost $1,431 on the litter (about $178 per puppy). Of course, she has a dog of her own breeding to show, a $650 asset. Valuing the puppy leaves her only about $750 in the hole—hardly a get-rich-quick-scheme.

Mary was fortunate. First, she sold all of her puppies. If the number of adult dogs (six months or older) allowed per house is restricted by the city or zoning, the situation of a breeder stuck with a group of youngsters long past the "cute" stage can quickly become desperate.

Secondly, Mary's bitch had no whelping problems. Expenses for problems can range from the price of an oxytocin shot to a Caesarean section with subsequent spaying of the mother. In the worst case, you could find yourself buying formula and bottle feeding the entire litter, which brings up another item no one ever factors into the puppy-cost equation—your own time and labor. If you multiplied just the minimum wage by the number of hours you spend taking care of a litter, the amount would be staggering.

Everyone loves puppies, but be sure to count the cost in time, money, and commitment before you decide to raise a litter. Two-week-old puppies at Wendy Willhauck's Frostfield Kennels.

Two very nice Yukon Pride puppies.

WE WANT OUR DOG TO EXPERIENCE IT

Often, owners believe their female will be missing something vital in her life if she does not have offspring. However, in the wild, nature renders most wolves sterile just as effectively as does a veterinarian. Only alpha males and females reproduce. Pack males are effectively neutered, not only because of alpha-male dominance, but because females reject their advances in favor of the most dominant male. Puppies born to another female at the same time are killed by the alpha female, but the entire pack works to feed and care for puppies.

Unlike humans, dogs do not engage in recreational sex, nor are sexual concerns the motivation for relationships. Although breeding pairs may be lifelong friends, sex is not the basis for the association. Dogs bond to one another, but friendships between same-sex pairs can be just as strong as between male and female, and often exist despite their being bred to outside dogs.

A BREEDER HAS RESPONSIBILITY

RESPONSIBILITIES TO THE BREED

You have many responsibilities as a breeder, but your highest obligation is to those lives which you bring into the world. Each generation should be an improvement over the last. Although mistakes happen, they should be through happenstance and not negligence.

To ensure that you are doing the best that you can, you need to learn about dogs in general, and Alaskan Malamutes in particular. Learn all that you can about pedigrees and the dogs in them, and familiarize yourself with basic genetic principles.

OVERPOPULATION

In many areas, the right to even own dogs is under assault by organized groups of animal rights activists, who often have the support of animal welfare workers. Ammunition for their anti-dog agenda comes from the huge number of dogs killed every day on streets and in shelters. You cannot solve the problem by not breeding your dog, but you will not contribute to it either.

Your plans for breeding should begin with a trip to an animal shelter and a conversation with someone in Malamute Rescue. Talk to them about how many Alaskan Malamutes they get and how successful they are in placing them. Walk through the shelter and look at the pleading faces of the dogs. You are looking at the doomed. Most of them will not be adopted and will have to be euthanized.

If you are still committed to breeding, give a lot of forethought to how you will find homes for your dogs. Make plans to follow up every sale and help your puppy buyers, so that none of your Malamutes end up on death row in a shelter.

RESPONSIBILITIES TO THE BUYER

When you place your puppies, you must make sure that the buyers have a suitable animal for their needs, and instruction for its care, along with the customary registration information and sales contract. The puppy should be physically and mentally healthy.

Experiential knowledge is very valuable in evaluating puppies and making deductions about how they will mature. You may not have this, but you can borrow it from a more experienced breeder. Many are happy to serve as mentors and have a wealth of knowledge to share.

The more you know, the more you can help puppy buyers with service after the sale. They should turn to you first for information and advice. Your help can be the cement that bonds them to the breed. Conversely, your failure to stand by your puppies may drive them away from Malamutes, your breeding program, or, at the least, their dog.

Anyone who breeds dogs can tell you that problems will occur despite every precaution on your part. Some dogs will be dysplastic; some will have illnesses; others just do not fit with the new family. When you have to deal with the emotional trauma of people suffering because something is wrong with their beloved pet, especially if it means euthanasia, the only shield you have for your own psyche is the knowledge that you did everything possible to prevent such an occurrence.

RESPONSIBILITIES TO THE PUPPIES

If you bring new canine lives into the world, you owe them every opportunity for happiness and health. However, once a puppy goes to a new home you no longer have control over its circumstances, so take the time to check out buyers and visit their homes to make sure they have made provisions to house and care for the dog properly. If you have any reservations, say "no". Advertise your puppies for sale to "suitable homes," which means you are not obligated to sell to just anyone who has the cash. You cannot stop poor prospects from buying a dog elsewhere, but you can stop them from buying yours.

Despite every precaution on your part, some placements will fail. You should take the dog back until you can find it a new home. In the worst case, you may have to euthanize the dog yourself or provide support by accompanying the owners to the veterinarian.

The value placed on a puppy has as much to do with your concern for the welfare of your charges as with its price. The people to whom it is sold will care more because you do.

STUD DOG OR BROOD BITCH?

Technically, by AKC definition, the *breeder* is the owner of the female at the time the breeding is accomplished. Practically, anyone connected with producing puppies may be lumped under the title of breeder—the owner of the sire, the dam, or the person who whelped the litter.

In obtaining a dog for breeding, your first decision is whether to buy a male or female. Experienced breeders will tell you to begin with a female—the best you can possibly obtain. Reasons for this are rooted in the etiquette

Will they get good homes? Beautiful five-week-old Sendaishi puppies, bred by Bill and Joyce Matott.

and customs of dog breeding. The choice of which dogs to consider and whether to proceed with the breeding lies mostly with the owner of the bitch. The stud-dog owner has the option of refusing a mating, but that opportunity comes only after he has been approached by the owner of a bitch.

An outgrowth of this practice is that females are bred up in quality, and dogs tend to be bred down. The female's owner, with his pick of dogs at public stud, will choose one better than or equal to his female in quality, since no logical reason exists to do otherwise. Therefore, the stud dog is being bred to bitches that are at best, only his equal. Since quality studs are at a premium, the better the dog, the more likely this will be the case.

Males, however, exert more influence on the breed as a whole because they can produce many more offspring than can females. In a large, slow-maturing breed like the Alaskan Malamute, this is even more the case. Under no circumstances should a female be bred before her second season, nor should she have puppies more than twice in two years. Breeding optimally should be postponed until OFA certification can be done at 24 months, a time-frame that permits her to have three or four litters at the maximum.

As the owner of the female (the "breeder"), you get

the fruits of the breeding and all the accolades for success, but the stud dog, not your brood bitch, tends to get the lion's share of the credit for the litter. A puppy out of Jack and Jill is more likely to be referred to as a "Jack son or daughter," as if Jack contributed more to the puppies. Great for Jack if the pups are good, but not so great if they are not!

Confusing the influence of the stud dog on the breed with his influence in a particular breeding is an easy mistake to make, but is a distorted perspective causing the female's contribution to a litter to be dismissed or overlooked. Actually, not only does she contribute an equal share of the genes, she is the one with the most physical and temperamental influence over her brood. Discussing the merits of a stud dog without reference to the bitches with which they were partnered is pointless.

A male is valuable because he is available to produce puppies for the owners of many bitches, whereas, a female produces only for one breeder. The dog and his owner get much of the glory; the brood bitch and her owner get the puppies.

CHOOSING A BROOD BITCH

Before she is even considered for breeding, a female should be screened for all the genetic diseases found in the Malamute. Clear ratings only qualify her; they do not make her a candidate for the whelping box. She must have a good pedigree and correct structure and, equally important, an impeccable temperament. After all, she will be teaching her offspring.

Anne Rogers Clark, a well-respected breeder, handler, and judge, says a brood bitch should have ". . . an aura of well-being and quality . . . immaculate type . . . and construction that defies serious questions and welcomes close inspection," plus "movement functional to her breed." Like other experienced breeders, Clark urges newcomers to begin with the very best bitch they can find, since the "bitch is the heart of the kennel." She must be "well-bred, sturdy, . . . and sound."[1]

A good brood bitch should be innately healthy; a dam that seems to catch every disease that comes along does not bode well for healthy puppies, or even a healthy pregnancy. While she need not be a champion, she should be of championship quality. Breeding a bitch that is anything less in quality is a disservice to the breed and to your breeding program.

She should also be from a "good family;" indeed, her pedigree is almost as important as her appearance. Her ancestors should be dogs you admire, even if some are not champions. As a general rule, breeding two good dogs with good pedigrees will produce better overall quality than breeding a good bitch to a great dog with a mediocre pedigree.

If possible, choose a bitch that is from a line of top producing bitches who were known to whelp easily. The ability to produce and sustain large litters often runs in a bloodline. A bitch with one or more ROM bitches in her pedigree will always be at a premium. Most breeders recommend that the bitch you choose for a foundation should definitely exhibit those characteristics of type which you feel are most important, and that she have a linebred or lightly inbred pedigree. This means that she at least has a good chance of passing on the genes for those important traits.

LEASING

Breeders who have a good track record and a good reputation in dogs may be willing to lease a proven brood bitch, although seldom to a newcomer. The breeder with several bitches and the means to whelp only one may welcome a lease that gives her the chance to breed a

The qualities that make good performance Mals are inherited, too. If this is your goal, look for a sire and dam with performance titles or one that has produced performance-titled dogs. Ch. Poker Flat's Love At First Bite, CD, WTD, has a beautiful, soft expression and excellent eye shape. Breeder, Robin Hagard; owner, Jane Wilson Adicks.

European champion for 1993 and 1994, World Champion 1994, American Champion, Best in Show, and Top Ten in 1995, International, Italian, Reproduttore, Bundessieger, Seiger Orteau, BIS-BOG Winner Ch. Storm Kloud's Qquest for Glory, WTD, was bred by Nancy Russell and is owned by Gloria Urbani of Italy. Expect a dog with impressive wins like this to command quite a high stud fee.

Only time will tell if a top winner can also produce those qualities in his or her offspring. Breeding to a top winning dog does not guarantee top winning show puppies. A dog or bitch that can both win and produce is a real prize to a breeder, and may come along only once in a lifetime.

bitch that might otherwise languish most of her producing life. Ill health or hectic schedules may prompt other breeders to offer a bitch for lease. Some will agree to lease to a breeder in a different area in order to more easily mate her with a stud in that area. Leasing can be a way to get a puppy from a bitch you would not otherwise be able to obtain. It is easier to choose a stud for a bitch with a proven producing record, and puppies of various ages can help you to determine traits for which she may be dominant.

Terms for leasing vary just as much as the reasons for doing so and can be a source of trouble between partners who might otherwise have remained friends. Just as with co-ownerships, make sure all the terms of the lease are spelled out and all eventualities are covered.

THE STUD DOG

If the brood bitch is the cornerstone of a kennel, where does the stud dog fit in? Someone has to own him. You, your family, and your lifestyle may well be more suited to having a male. You may have little or no interest in whether he is ever bred. If so, you should have little difficulty achieving your goals, and you will be much happier, because your aspirations are realistic and attainable.

On the other hand, if you dream of sitting back and raking in the stud fees while bypassing the effort and expense

of breeding, you are in for a rude awakening. Stud dog owners do sit back and wait, but that can be the sum total of their participation in the fancy. Many dogs are never used for breeding because the owner of the bitch decides to whom she should be bred. Choices are based on many factors such as pedigrees, conformation, availability, expense, amount of promotion, and the producing record of the sire. So, the stud-dog owner's first hurdle is getting his dog even considered as a choice. That you have the ideal breeding partner is irrelevant if the bitch owners do not know your dog exists.

You can promote your stud through advertising, which can cost from a few to many hundreds of dollars. However, examining the pages of dog publications should tell you the fact that your dog exists is not enough. This is an extremely competitive market. Since the needs of bitch owners vary, the more categories your dog satisfies, the more successful he will be. At the minimum, his eyes and hips must be certified clear, and he must have an acceptable CHD rating, so you will have to wait until he is over two years old.

Bitch owners will have more confidence in his soundness and type if he has a championship, which means the additional effort and expense of showing him.[2] However, those elusive owners have their pick of champions. To increase his appeal, you can continue campaigning him as a special to rack up an impressive show record.

From the show ring, your dog can enter performance areas such as obedience, weight pull, sledding, and backpacking. You can also get a temperament test certification and a Canine Good Citizen title to testify to his virtues in that area.

The more successful your dog is, the more likely he is to appeal to the owner of a potential mate, especially if he also has an impressive pedigree. None of this guarantees his success in the breeding arena, however. The career of a stud dog rises and falls on the quality of his get.

Once you have invested your time, money, and ego into a dog, saying "no" to the owner of a bitch is very difficult. Again, returning to Jack and Jill, when Jack's puppies are of lesser quality, people tend to blame Jack for the problems, with Jill's owner likely to be the first to do so. If the dog is heavily advertised and shown, simple jealousy may make his detractors even more enthusiastic. That the puppies are light-years better than Jill will matter not one whit.

The vast majority of successful stud dogs are owned either by experienced breeders or by a breeder's protege. Having learned their lessons, usually the hard way, these breeders know when to refuse a breeding. They also have experience in handling visiting bitches. Some Malamute females still have strong instincts regarding breeding and are interested only in alpha males. Her owner's choice of stud may not be hers, and accomplishing such a breeding can tax the abilities and resources of anyone.

Most importantly, long-time breeders have access to good bitches with which to start off a young dog. Experience allows them to discriminate between good choices and poor ones, and they know the best advertising for their dog is a good puppy.

CONTRACTS

The stud dog owner is responsible for the contract governing the breeding terms. The contract specifies the fee for the service, when it will be paid, and under what circumstances it might be refunded or a repeat breeding offered. It should contain particulars about the dog being used, the bitch (or bitches) being bred, and any fees associated with their transportation, care, and housing.

You should also discuss what to do if you cannot consummate the breeding. Does the bitch owner want you to try artificial insemination (you will need to have a veterinarian on deck for this). When you have covered all eventualities and the breeding is imminent, the owner of the stud should send a signed copy to the owner of the bitch to sign and return.

Before the bitch is shipped, the stud owner should learn all he can about her, her habits, and any quirks of her personality. He must make sure that housing for the visitor will be sufficient. Remember, you are being entrusted with the care of someone's special Malamute. Keep them informed of her well-being and the progress of the breeding. If you will be shipping the bitch, make sure that she gets on the plane and that she arrives safely.

Regardless of how excellent the sire and dam, not all puppies will be show quality, and not all show quality puppies will find a show home. Be prepared to work with pet owners, too. A home where the puppy is loved, groomed, trained and has something to do, is best. Vicky and Ben Palinkas have just won second place at a pet parade with Frostfields Douglas. Photo by Jane Palinkas.

HEALTH CARE

Dogs and bitches that will be used for breeding must be in excellent general health. Immunizations should be up to date, and the dogs should be parasite-free. Shortly before breeding, they will need a brucellosis test. Many stud owners also request a vaginal smear, which is customary, but hardly informative, since the vagina always has organisms growing in it. Healthy dogs do not need antibiotics as a preventive measure. Antibiotics kill indiscriminately and may rid the reproductive tract of helpful flora, opening the way for subsequent infection.

Your veterinarian has access to reliable ovulation tests. You may want to run several before shipping your bitch, or the stud owner may have them run after your bitch has arrived. Vaginal smears can also be a helpful tool in determining when a bitch will ovulate (and thus what days are optimum for conception) or where she is in her estrous cycle.

Breeding stock needs to be kept in prime physical condition, so a good quality, complete diet and regular exercise are vitally important. Malamutes that are kept in a kennel where all they do is eat and sleep do not make good producers.

WHAT YOU NEED TO BREED

Being a breeder requires more from you than just owning a bitch. Above all, you will need patience. A lot of your time will be spent waiting—for puppies to mature, for success in showing, or until they are old enough to sell or train. If you cannot deal with waiting, find someone who can and buy from them.

FINDING MR. RIGHT

The time to look for your bitch's ideal partner is long *before* she comes in season. Check advertisements in the AMCA *Newsletter* and the *Alaskan Malamute Quarterly*. Watch Malamutes at area shows, and try to attend the National or a regional specialty. If you find a dog you like, look at his relatives and see if you like them, too. Write the owner and ask for information about breeding, about any offspring the dog has produced, and for a pedigree. Send information about your bitch, a picture, and her pedigree with the inquiry. If the dog of your dreams is located so far away that shipping is necessary, always devise a contingency plan in case you are unable to ship at the right time.

The owner of the bitch is responsible for getting her to the stud dog just before or when she is ready to breed. Before then, you should have mutually worked out any concerns and signed a written stud-fee contract agreement.

Am. Can. Ch. Kaila's Spellbinder of Kioona is the sire of five specialty winners. Breeder, Patti Colcord. Owners, Chris and Eileen Gabriel. Ashbey photo.

STUD FEES AND RELATED MATTERS

Stud fees vary from breed to breed. For an ordinary champion, they are usually about the price of a pet puppy. This fee may increase as the dog achieves fame and fortune, especially if he proves to be a good producer.

Unless you have an exceptional bitch with fame and fortune of her own, stud-dog owners will not accept a puppy in lieu of a stud fee. If you have such a pearl, be sure that you both agree in advance on which pick the stud owner gets and who will pick it.

The fee is usually payable at the time of the breeding, although many stud owners will accept a down-payment of half, with the other half due on arrival of the litter. If no litter comes, you are still liable for the balance, since the stud fee is payment for the dog's sperm, not an advance on puppies.

Bitches are usually bred twice within a forty-eight-hour period, but do not take this for granted. If your bitch is being kept by someone else, you are perfectly within your rights in asking for a photograph of the tied dogs to assure you that your dog was indeed bred.

If no puppies result from a breeding, a return breeding is usually guaranteed. This may have stipulations: return within the year, or only on that bitch. Some breeders will guarantee one or two live puppies or allow a substitute bitch on the return service.

Very popular studs may be booked far in advance and may not be available when your bitch is ready. The owner

SHIPPING BY AIR FREIGHT

Most, but not all, airlines accept dogs for shipment as air freight. Reservations must be made in advance (the period varies with the airline, but most require 24-hours notice) because the presence of live animals restricts the amount of cargo which can be cooled with dry-ice in the same cargo hold. Too much carbon dioxide vapor from the dry-ice can suffocate the animals.

The most desirable flights are non-stop, followed by direct flights with one stop. If the dog has to change planes, aim for flights arriving at the change site during an off-period. Busy freight areas are more likely to make mistakes.

You will need a current rabies vaccination, a health certificate, and an airline-approved shipping crate large enough for the dog to stand and turn, but not so large that she bangs around inside. The crate must have containers for water and food. Freeze water in the container and put it back into the crate just before you leave for the airport. This will keep water from slopping all over your dog's crate and will cool her if the weather is hot. Attach a zip-lock bag or small container of food to the outside of the crate in case the dog encounters an emergency overnight stay. In hot weather, freeze water in flat, hard-plastic containers and put them under the crate floor. To help with any accidents, place shredded paper or wood chip bedding on the crate floor. In cold weather, this bedding will also help keep the dog warm.

Most Malamute females are comfortable in a large (#400), but if you have to use the larger size, make sure that the scheduled plane can accommodate it. Some planes have cargo doors too small for an extra large (#500) crate. In that case you will have to find another flight or give up.

Tranquilizers may depress respiration and should not be used for air travel. If you have a very nervous dog, give her a weight-appropriate dose of Benadryl antihistamine. This will make her sleepy without putting her at risk if oxygen becomes scarce.

Write your name and phone number, (as shipper or consignor) and that of the stud dog owner (consignee) in indelible marker on the top of the crate. Tape a resealable plastic pouch on the crate with your dog's name, information about her training, her medications and her habits. Write her call-name on the crate. Depending on the airport, the shipping office may require that dogs be there up to two hours before departure. Stay and make sure your dog is loaded on the plane, then call the stud dog owner and tell him she is on her way. Be sure to check back with him to ensure that she arrived safely.

Airlines are prohibited by law from accepting dogs when temperatures are very hot or very cold. Some airlines may accept dogs in borderline temperatures if a letter from a veterinarian states that the dog is acclimated to that temperature. During holidays, airlines may embargo all live animal shipments because of the high volume of mail. This means no shipments at all.

Most dogs are shipped by air without a mishap. If you have a problem, do not be shy about asking that something be done now— not later. Offices close, people change shifts, and planes depart, so the longer looking into your problem takes, the more likely something else can go wrong. If the person with whom you are dealing puts you off with assurances that everything will be okay, ask for a supervisor and start over. Eventually, you may reach a dog lover who will do a little extra.

may have other dogs, but, again, this should be worked out before you invest money in shipping or driving your bitch.

In addition to the stud fee, some stud owners want reimbursement for boarding, veterinary care, and trips to and from the airport. Also, a breeding fee may be due to a handler or a veterinarian if artificial insemination is necessary.

Another item to be worked out ahead of time is whether you are willing for the breeding to be done by artificial insemination. Discuss this possibility with the stud's owner and make sure an experienced veterinarian is available for the procedure. Although an AI is a fairly routine and simple procedure, it is not without risk to your bitch. If the semen is not handled properly, the fertility rate will be lower than with a normal breeding. Remember that a veterinarian must complete the form for AKC when artificial insemination is done. This form accompanies the litter application.

One option that has come about recently is breeding with cooled semen shipped from the stud owner's veterinarian to a local insemination center. New, easier techniques for collecting and handling semen make it possible for semen to be collected, shipped, and inseminated into your bitch within 24 hours or less. Not all veterinarians are comfortable with the procedure, so you must make the arrangements well in advance and be sure that the clinics on both end are properly trained in the procedure. Since there is no risk to the bitch, shipping charges are minimal, and there is no risk of infection or injury to either dog, this will probably be the method of choice for breedings in the future.

THE AMCA REGISTER OF MERIT PROGRAM

The Alaskan Malamute Club of America awards males that have sired at least eight champions, and females that have produced at least five, the title of Register of Merit (ROM). The initials can be used after the dog's registered name. These Malamutes have potential long-term influence on the breed. You'll find many of the earlier dogs and bitches in the background of modern Malamute bloodlines, and you can look forward to some of the most recent additions to the ROM list becoming the foundations for tomorrow's lines. If you want to know more, research the number of litters sired or whelped. Producing ability is not only tracked by numbers of champions, but also by ratio of champions to total number of offspring. Some studs have far more opportunities than others.

ENDNOTES
1.   Anne Rogers Clark sidebar in Patricia Craige, "Campaigning a Brood Bitch," *Pure-Bred Dogs, American Kennel Club Gazette*, 111:2 (February, 1994), 53.
2.   A championship has no bearing on whether a dog is a good producer. That is determined by the genetic material passed on to the progeny and is part of the dog's nature. It does, however, give outside validation to his own quality and is a selling point for his career as a stud dog.

Ch. Lorien's Man O' War of Snoridge ROM, bred by Debra Sherman and owned by Eileen Kinnas, is the second top-producing sire. Among his get is the first Malamute bitch to win a Best in Show, Am. Can . Ch. Snoridge Blueice Lady O'War, ROM.

Name		Name	
No. Chs. *		No. Chs. *	
Ch. Glacier's Storm Kloud CD	65	Ch. Toro Of Bras Coupe	15
Ch. Lorien's Man O'War Of Sno Ridge	39	Ch. Vykon Jarva's True Colours	15
Ch. Uyak Buffalo Bill	34	Ch. Williwaw's Kodiak Cub	15
Ch. Inuit's Sweet Lucifer	29	Ch. Shamrock's Kotze Tu Be Good	14
Ch. Kasaan's Fortune Hunter	29	Ch. Storm Kloud's Ximious Dream CD	14
Ch. Snopaw's Snoqualmie CD	29	Ch. T'Domar's Bismarck	14
Ch. Storm Kloud's Better Than Ever	25	Ch. Veulta Toros By Wildwind TNT	14
Ch. Williwaw's Kakooshka	25	Ch. Alcan Private Label	13
Ch. Sno Ridge's Tywon On	23	Ch. Malwood's Dirty Demon	13
Ch. J Len's Arctic Windjammer	22	Ch. Storm Kloud's One More Time	13
Ch. Wild Wind's Best Edition	22	Ch. Alyeska Su Son	12
Ch. Karohonta Skymaster	21	Ch. Baronof	12
Ch. Sarge's Bo Jangles Of O'Nan	21	Ch. Kioona's Chibouk Of Kaila	12
Ch. Aristeed's Frost Shadow	20	Ch. Poker Flat's Yukon Law	12
Ch. Kiwalik's Vykon Indiana Jones CD	20	Ch. Sendaishi's Kandu Can Do	12
Ch. Storm Kloud's Oomiak CD	20	Ch. Storm Kloud's Echo Of Bear	12
Ch. Tote Um's Cinnamon Bear	20	Ch. Storm Kloud's R Tic Sun	12
Ch. Kiwalik's Snowbear Of Kipnuk	19	Ch. Tobe's Tony Baretta	12
Ch. Tigara's Torch Of Arctica	19	Ch. Win Kre's Ace High	12
Ch. Inuit's Wooly Bully	18	Ch. Strawberry's Clyde All Mighty CD	11
Ch. Kazan's Kremlin Kylee	18	Ch. Sugarbear's Satan O Snoridge	11
Ch. Storm Kloud's Fortune O'Kasaan	18	Ch. Alcan Past Forgetting	10
Ch. Storm Kloud's Vvanilla Snoman CD	18	Ch. Bigfoot's Field Artillery	10
Ch. Taolan Flying Colours	18	Ch. Fleur De Lis El Macho	10
Ch. Wild Wind's Viewer's Choice	18	Ch. Glacier's Burbon King CD	10
Ch. Williwaw's Sunbear Of Targhee	18	Ch. Kanangnark's Wildcat	10
Ch. Atanik Awesome's I Need A Hug	17	Ch. Mushateer's Lewis Moon	10
Ch. Barrenfield's Rocket Torpedo	17	Ch. Snocre's Sun King Of Midway	10
Ch. Glacier's Santa Man	17	Ch. Zel Knoll's Speck Of Hill Frost	10
Ch. Kiwalik's Taolan Quilleute	17	Ch. Apache Chief Of Husky Pak	9
Ch. Malesa's Silver Glacier	17	Ch. Champaign California Cooler	9
Ch. Atanik's Snopaw I'm Awesome	16	Chief Michigamme	9
Ch. Kachina's Cujo	16	Ch. Husky Pak Erok	9
Ch. Storm Kloud's Keep The Win	16	Ch. Kaila's Son Of A Witch	9
Ch. Voyageur's Cougar	16	Ch. Nahnook II	9
Ch. Beowulf's Danska	15	Ch. Nanuke's Colour Me Happy	9
Ch. Inuit's Moon Unit	15	Ch. Nanuke's A Rushin Revolution	9
Ch. Nanuke's Revolutionary	15	Ch. Nanuke's Winter Magic	9
Ch. Silver Frost Bold Savage	15	Ch. Northpaw's Ghostbuster	9
Ch. Skookum's Tamon Of Onak CD	15	Ch. Sno Crest's Mukluk	9
Ch. Sugarbear's Wins Of War	15	Ch. Snow Star's Stormy Jack Son	9
Ch. T'Domar's Juneau	15	Ch. Spawn's Hot Shot Of Roy El	9
Ch. Timberlane's the Yankee	15	Ch. Storm Kloud's Emcee Of Awanuna CDX	9
Ch. Tonopaw's Awesome Ayuskeemo	15	Ch. Targhee's Kodiak	9

- continued -

*Updated through 1997.

Ch. Tiagara's Karluk Of Roy El	9
Ch. Tinut Of Fleur De Lis	9
Ch. Wild Wind's Phumphrey Bogart	9
Ch. Wild Wind's Yo Nitro Baby	9
Ch. Artic Luv's Swashbuckler	8
Aventurero De Korok	8
Ch. Cold Foot Khaibar Of Sena Lak	8
Highland's N W Black Kong	8
Ch. Kiskayo's Best	8
Ch. Kodara Kodiak Of Erowah	8
Ch. Nomarak's Kenworth	8
Ch. Nordic Kauk of Ptarmigan	8
Ch. Poker Flat's Cosmic Ray CD	8
Ch. Sendaishi's Kipkandu Kiwalik	8
Ch. Shuyak Caro Of Cold Foot CD	8
Ch. Storm Kloud's R Tic Sampson	8
Ch. Sun King's Gripp of Snow Song	8
Ch. T'Domar's Voodoo King	8
Ch. Tigara's Nordisch Kotze Tu	8
Ch. Vermar's Arclar Terrific Turk	8
Ch. Warlock's Still Smokin'	8
Ch. Wild Wind's Flashy Fanfare	8
Ch. Wild Wind's Magnum Of Veebee	8
Ch. Win Kre's Begins The Dynasty	8

Ch. Bigfoot's Field Artillery, owned by Jerry, Sandy and David Musyj.

Ch. Uyak Buffalo Bill was one of the most prepotent stud dogs of all time. Breeder, Harold Schwartzapfel; Owner, Robert Montheard. Photo by Sel Levy.

Ch. Kiwalik's Snowbear of Kipnuk. Breeder, Shelton Sewell; Owner, Kenneth Hyatt.

BIS, BISS Am. Can. Ch. Vykon Jarva's True Colour's, bred and owned by Vicky Jones. Alverson photo.

Ch. Inuit's Moon Unit, won Westminster in 1982 and again in 1988. Breeder, Shannon Sollinger; Owner, Sheila Balch.

Am. Can. Ber. Ch. Inuit's Wooly Bully was the 1975 National Specialty winner. Breeder/owner, Sheila Balch.

Ch. Sugar Bear's Win's O War. Breeder, owner, Dennis and Patti Grzyb.

Am. Can., Ch. Storm Kloud's Keep the Win, WLD, WTD, WWPDX, CGC at one time held the record for the most AKC/ CKC Best in Shows wins. Breeder/owner, Nancy Russell.

Am. Can. Ch. Williwaw's Kodiak Cub was the National Specialty winner in 1993. Owners, Al and Mary Jane Holabach.

Am. Can. Ch. Shamrock's Kotze To B Good, AMCA Specialty and Group winner. Breeder, George Arnold; Owners, Paul and Ruth Levesque.

Am. Can. Ch. Alcan Mate to Arte, owned by Jerry, Sandy and David Musyj.

Ch. Snocre's Sun King of Midway ROM, BOB at 1976 and 1978 Nationals. Breeders, John and Phyllis Schmidt. Owners, Howard and Jane Anderson.

BIS Ch. Sno-Crest Mukluk was the first Best in Show winner in the breed. Breeder, Belva Rifkind; Owner Martha Giuffre.

Ch. Apache Chief of Husky-Pak. Owner, Robert Zoller.

Am. Can. Ch. Kaila's Son of a Witch, multiple sepcialty and Group winner. Owners, Chris and Eileen Gabriel.

Am. Can. Ber. Ch. Kiskayo's Best. Owner, Ron Pohl of Canada.

Ch. Wildwinds Yo Nitro Baby ROM has been a very good producer for breeder/owner Jeannie Wild.

REGISTER OF MERIT – BITCHES

Ch. Princess Nikkita Sno Kloud	16	Ch. Hug A Bear's Kiska Tug N Chug	8
Ch. Mals About's Touch Of Frost CD	14	Kanangnark's Anna Karenina	8
Ch. J Len's Gallopin' Gimlet	13	Ch. Kasaan's Stolen Moments	8
Storm Kloud's Ddawn Of The North	12	Ch. Kiana Of Klondike	8
Kobuk's Dark Beauty	11	Ch. Koldwind's Restless Wind	8
Ch. Northeast's Scarlet Fever	11	Ch. Kutachonauu Kiva Of Kachina	8
Russell's Yveti Rose CD	11	Ch. Polarpaw's Akela Akamai	8
Ch. Storm Kloud's Fresca Of Big Paw	11	Ch. Blue Ice's The Leading Lady	7
Ch. Sugarbush Of Alaska	11	Ch. Glacier's Good Intentions	7
Ch. Skookum's Mika Of Tugidak	10	Ch. Glacier' Tisha Lyng CD	7
Ch. Sno Kloud's Shasta of Kiska	10	Ch. Greenbrier's Aims Tu Please	7
Ch. Snopaw's Champagne Addition	10	Ch. Keeley's Magic Moment	7
Ch. Snowpaw's Coco Of Arctic Pride	10	Ch. Kiwalik's Miacis Of Nerak	7
Ch. Voyageur's Winged Victory	10	Ch. Maltrail's Champagne Edition	7
Ch. Alcan Mate To Arte	9	Ch. Mushateer's All For A Dream	7
Alcan Torchfire Of Tigara	9	Ch. Sno Ridge's Conversation Piece	7
Artic Pride Gigi Of Snopaw	9	Ch. Storm Kloud's Forever Yours CD	7
Glacier's Phanny Too	9	Ch. Sugarbear The Blue Ice Queen	7
Ch. Nanuke's Seal Of Approval	9	Ch. Trillium's Cessie La Rue	7
Ch. Mals About's Star Song	9	Ch. Vykon's Jessika Jones CD	7
Ch. Storm Kloud's Hhumble Shaman	9	Ch. Wild Wind's Ghost Rider N The Sky	7
T'Domar's Taboo	9	Ch. Win Kre's Essence Of Chum Lee	7
Ch. Tote Um's Snow Star	9	Ch. Win Kre's Firestarter	7
Ch. Tuffnook's Critic's Choice	9	Ch. Aurora's Kuyana Of Windrift	6
Ch. Vermar's Arclar Shady Sadie	9	Ch. Ca Jim's Arctic Pride	6
Ch. Williwaw's Ivaloo Of Targhee	9	Chilanko's Tishka Doll	6
Aleutia	8	Cobra Of Nipigon	6
Ch. Arctic Storm Of Husky Pak	8	Ch. Contrail Carried Interest	6
Ch. Atanik's Kinda Koona	8	Glacier Hill's Snow Princess	6
Ch. Chamai's Chum Lee	8	Ch. Icefloe's North Star	6
Ch. Dorry's Sitka Of North Wind	8	Ch. J Len's Taolan Tamisan	6

Ch. Kasaan Atanik's The Seducer	6	Ch. Knotty Pine's Dark Devil	5
Ch. Malesa's Mischief Maker CDX	6	Kotzebue Muffin Chinook	5
Ch. Montak's High Sierra Tundra	6	Kumata's End Of Ennocence	5
Ch. Nomarak Sourdough Little Su	6	Ch. Lobitos Ebony Ms Chief	5
Ch. Nordic Crystal Storm	6	Ch. Lokoshi's Curio Classic	5
Ch. Polarpaw's Foxy Lady	6	Ch. Lucky Bear Of The South Wind	5
Ch. Sabre's Misty Dawn Of Snopaw	6	Malesa's More Mischief	5
Ch. Sena Lak's Thora	6	Ch. Maltrail's Double T Edition	5
Ch. Silver Frost's Kimluk	6	Ch. Midnight Sun's Winter Love	5
Siska Of Erowah	6	Misty Dawn	5
Sno Pak Kavik's Oonalik	6	Ch. Misty Pak's Toast To Nitecap	5
Ch. Sno Ridge's Mountain Lady	6	Ch. Nanuke's Driving Ms Daisey	5
Ch. Storm Kloud's Lla Paloma	6	Ch. Nor N Lit's Star T N Deering	5
Ch. Storm Kloud's Vvanilla Pudding	6	Northeast's Krystel Gale	5
Ch. Sugarbear's Tantara	6	Oakiok's Kewpie Doll	5
Ch. Taolan Snoklassic Sassafras	6	Ch. Onak's Tufferenhel	5
Ch. Taolan Taliesin Shenoa	6	Ch. O'Nan's Misty Magic Of Topam	5
Ch. Uyak Indian Inez	6	Ch. Poker Flat's Nahanni CD	5
Ch. Wenaha's Taneum Of Onak CD	6	Ch. Poker Flat's Snow Flurrie CD	5
Ch. White Hawk's Tahlequah	6	Ch. Rapid Run's Kimugeen Of Kubuk	5
Ch. Wild Wind's Quicksilver Dondee	6	Ch. Sena Lak's Beowulf Tawechi	5
Ch. Williwaw's Seahawk O Targhee	6	Ch. Sena Lak's Kiana's Black Witch	5
Ch. Alcan Forget Me Not	5	Ch. Sno Kloud's Home Free	5
Alcan The Copper Queen	5	Ch. Sno Kloud's Icily Polite	5
Ch. Atanik's Totally Awesome	5	Ch. Sno Kloud's Moka Of Storm Kloud	5
Ch. Barrenfield's Sunrise	5	Ch. Snoridge's Blueice Lady O'War	5
Ch. Byeyo's Champagne N Ice CD	5	Staghorn's Little Tootsie	5
Ch. Ca Jim's Luv Truck	5	Ch. Storm Kloud's Hharmony	5
Ch. Cetanya's Delphinus Dream CD	5	Ch. Storm Kloud's Hhell's Angel CD	5
Ch. Chena Nenana II	5	Ch. Storm Kloud's Peny Of Wild Wind	5
Ch. Cholla's Contessa Of Chupak	5	Strawberries Sable Sparks	5
Ch. Cold Foot's Chevak	5	Ch. Tikiluk's Mystic Thunderation	5
Contrail Shumagin	5	Ch. Tikiluk's Nickola Of Windrift CD	5
Ch. Copper Knight's Tundra's Dream	5	Ch. Tote Um's Kooteeyah	5
Ch. Double T Silver Mtn Echo	5	Timberlane's Heidi Jane	5
Ch. Erowah Roxanne	5	Ch. Timberlane's Tuktu Of Snocre	5
Far North's Zodiak of Aleutian	5	Timlo's Glacial Reflection	5
Ch. Goldrush's Noel Of The Yukon	5	Ch. Veebee's Daphne Of Wahkeen	5
Ch. Hill Frost Natasha A Dream	5	Ch. Veebee's Little Bit Of Asgard	5
Ch. Hill Frost's Merrifield's Jewel	5	Ch. Vermar's Here's Harriet	5
Ch. Hug A Bear's Karisma Windrift	5	Ch. Vermar's Hurricane Hanna	5
Hug A Bear's The Sweetest Taboo	5	Ch. Vermar's I'm Amazing	5
Husky Pak Morning Star	5	Ch. Vermar's Pretty Classie	5
Ch. Istari's Tinuki On Artic Wind	5	Ch. Voyageur's Elke	5
Ch. Jetadora Of Silvafrost	5	Wayeh Needa Mist	5
Ch. Jingo's Silver Trumpet	5	Ch. Wild Wind's October Frost	5
Ch. J Len's Prairie Twister	5	Ch. Wild Wind's Prelude To Gothic	5
Ch. J Len's Tigress of Kiwalik	5	Ch. Win Kre's Akamai Fury	5
Karohonta Westwind Honey	5	Ch. Wintuk's Aljawahara Of S Kloud	5
Ch. Kasaan's Blue Ice Autumn	5	Yukon's Cheyenne Autumn	5
Ch. Kasaan's Eloquent Edition	5		
Ch. Kasaan's Karizma Of Kloud Burst CD	5		
Ch. Keetoo's Alatnah	5		
Ch. Kiwalik's Nomi Of Excalibur CD	5		
Kiwalik's Zuni Of Vermar	5		

Ch. Kiwalik's Miacis of Nerak was BOS at three National Specialties. Breeder, owner, Terry Sewell.

Am. Can. Ch. Williwaw's Seahawk of Targhee ROM was BIS at Nationals in U.S. and Canada. Breeder/owners, Al and Mary Jane Holabach.

Am. Can. Ch. Toalan Taliesin Shenoa., Breeder, owner Ron Pohl.

Ch. Tikiluk Mystik Thunderation. Breeders, Grimsley and McMahon. Owner, Beverly Turner.

Am. Can . Ch. Byeyo's Champagne N' Ice, Am. Can. CD, ROM Can. CGC. Owned by Cheryl Paterson, Canada.

Ch. Tikiluk's Nickola of Windrift CD, WPD, TT. Breeder, Barbara Brooks, Owner, Beverly Turner.

Greenbrier's Kaus'N Arukus (Kizmet) is a promising upcoming bitch for breeder/owners Paul, Ruth and Kristin Levesque.

16

MAKING GENETICS WORK FOR YOU

Long before the science of genetics even existed, people realized that families had certain traits in common, traits which appeared consistently in a related group but not in the population as a whole. They thought shared blood was the mechanism by which these traits were passed from one generation to the next. Echoes of this idea still persist in our language when we talk about "blood kin," and "bloodlines," even though we now know these terms are inaccurate.

Traits which marked aristocratic or royal families were duly noted and, in an era without paternity testing, spoke to consanguinity (same blood). The Austrian Hapsburgs had a distinctive lip. Queen Elizabeth I's mother was from a family in which extra digits were common, and Queen Victoria's descendants often had hemophilia.

THE SCIENCE OF GENETICS DEVELOPS

The first organized scientific study of inherited traits was presented to a scientific assembly in 1866 by an obscure monk named Gregor Mendel. His paper summarized ten years of his observations regarding inheritance of traits in pea plants, but since he had no explanation of the mechanics of the process, his findings lapsed into obscurity until microscopes strong enough to view individual cells were finally available.

Scientists were fascinated by rod-like bodies that occasionally appeared in the cell nucleus. To make the cells easier to see, they added stains, one of which was absorbed by these fibers. Hence, they were called "chromosomes" or "colored bodies."

By the turn of the century, biologists had dusted off Mendel's papers and connected them with the curious behavior of these colored bodies, especially in the gametes or sex cells. Using Mendel's research as a springboard, geneticists defined and refined the laws which governed inheritance.

During all the decades where scientists built on Mendel's observations, biochemists and microbiologists were studying cellular material. The publication in 1953 of the investigations of James Watson and Francis Crick which identified the actual building blocks of inheritance—deoxyribonucleic acid or DNA—gave the fledgling science of molecular genetics a jump start. Since then, it has impacted studies in virology, cancer, inherited disease, and a host of other fields.

GENETICS AND DOG BREEDING

Since it has been going on for ten-thousand years, breeding dogs does not require that you know the chemical composition of DNA. You may not know how to focus a microscope or know a Punnett square from tic-tac-toe, but every time you decide to breed this female to that male, you are doing field work in genetics. Your task will be much easier if you learn something about the science and apply it to your breeding choices. The practical advantages to you as a breeder should be easy to see.

You will understand why liver dogs do not have black noses, why two long-coats produce long-coat puppies, and

Very similar five-weeks-old pure Kotzebue puppies bred by Wendy Willhauck, Frostfield Kennels.

231

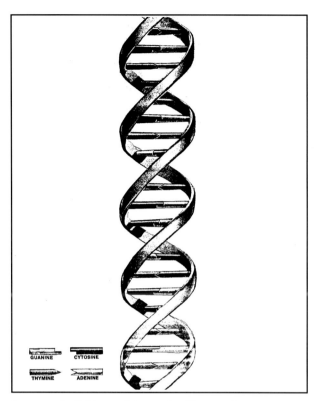

Diagram of a DNA strand showing bond between the component amino acids.

how the chance of inheriting diseases can be minimized. You can also learn to use your dog's pedigree as a breeding tool.

As an introduction or just a refresher, some functions and terms are presented here in a very basic and simplistic manner. If you want to pursue this subject in more depth, you can find excellent books on general genetics in any library. Books specifically on inheritance in dogs may be available from dog-show vendors, from the publisher, or your veterinarian.

GENETICS—FACTS AND TERMS

GENETIC MATERIAL

Chromosomes come in pairs, one from the mother and one from the father. They can be envisioned as chains of genes which are units of DNA that control a specific function and are found on both chromosome strands in the same spot called a locus (loci, plural). The gene may have different forms or alleles that produce different effects.

For instance, we know in dogs, the gene for coat length has two alleles, long and short, which are autosomal, that is, not located on one of the chromosome pairs that deter-

mine sex (X or Y chromosome). Other genes, such as one which determines the distribution of white in a dog's coat, have many alleles in one locus: no white, Irish spotting, pinto, and extreme piebald.

Regardless of whether a gene has one allele or twenty, since chromosomes occur in pairs, only two alleles of any one gene can be found in an individual. When the *same allele is found on both chromosomes, the animal is homozygous* for that gene. *If they are different, it is heterozygous.*

In that individual, the relationship of these alleles may vary. One may be dominant, which means it masks the other's presence in the individual's appearance. In that case, the masked gene is said to be recessive. A homozygous dominant animal has only the dominant form of the allele in its genetic makeup or genotype, while the homozygous recessive has only the recessive form of the allele.

Homozygous dominant and heterozygous animals are, for convenience of discussion, considered identical in phenotype (appearance) even though they are not identical in genotype, since the homozygote has only one allele present, and the heterozygote has two. In fact, geneticists say that this is never absolutely true, only that the differences may be so subtle as to be invisible to the casual observer.

You may see a slight difference, for instance, in dogs heterozygous for the long and short alleles of the coat-length gene. While the short one is considered dominant over the long, a hybrid (heterozygote) may have a slightly softer, longer, thicker coat than the pure dominant.

Some hybrids show a blend of allelic characteristics, a circumstance called incomplete dominance. White coat markings are a case in point. The most dominant allele is the self-colored or totally pigmented coat, like the Labrador Retriever; therefore, breeding Malamutes to solid colored-dogs would quickly alter the breed's appearance. That the standard prohibits solid-colored dogs (white is polygenic in origin, and a different case altogether) reflects a practical acknowledgement of this relationship even if the mechanism was not understood at the time it was written.[1] The allele present in most Malamutes is for "Irish spotting" which is recessive to self-coloring and dominant over the pinto allele.

The same practical application of genetic theory occurs when the Standard penalizes dogs with broken colors and uneven splashing, both characteristic of the Irish-spotted/pinto hybrid. Breed history shows that some early dogs or their siblings were pintos or had shawls and white splashes in their coats, confirming the presence of the pinto allele in the early gene pool. Early breeders practiced rigorous selection of symmetrically marked dogs typical of the Irish spotted allele and never bred the mismarked siblings. This practice quickly eliminated any dogs pure for pinto and most dogs with a pinto recessive.

Occasionally, a throwback occurs and normally marked dogs produce a splash-coated puppy. Dogs with pinto recessives still appear. Some phenotypic signs that a pinto gene or white enhancers are carried in the genotype of a dog are the presence of a white haw, pink splotches around the nose leather, pink pigment on the lips and on the feet, asymmetrical collars, jagged white markings that extend into the mantle, white that extends into the shoulder color on one side but not the other, and too much white on the tip of the tail. Offspring of two such dogs are more likely to show more of these irregular markings and further distribution of white into the coat color than either of their parents. To further complicate the inheritance of white markings, other genes, in locations not yet identified, seem to increase or decrease the amount of white in the marking pattern.

A trait determined by genes at different loci is called polygenic. Coat color and markings, hip dysplasia, and head growth are polygenic traits. A gene which alters the appearance of another is epistatic, which is seen when the liver allele changes normally black coat to red (liver).

FROM ONE GENERATION TO THE NEXT

Genetic material is transferred from one generation to the next when an egg and sperm cell (gametes) unite. Gametes form in a process called *meiosis*. Its execution is elegantly simple and yet marvelously intricate, opening up almost limitless possibilities.

All of the body's other cells reproduce by simple division, or *mitosis*. During both meiosis and mitosis, the cell's DNA is replicated, but in mitosis, two cells are created, each containing identical DNA.

GENETIC VARIATION

In the beginning stages of meiosis, as with mitosis, the chromosomes replicate. At this point, the cell has two sets

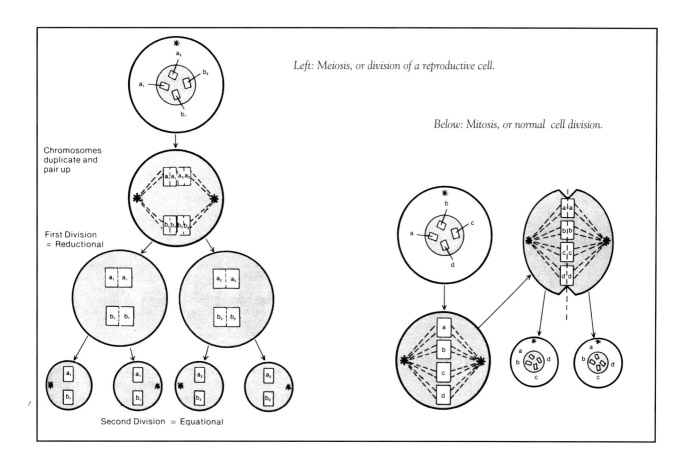

Chromosomes duplicate and pair up

First Division = Reductional

Second Division = Equational

Left: Meiosis, or division of a reproductive cell.

Below: Mitosis, or normal cell division.

of similar chromosome pairs which closely line up or twist around each other. During this process, genes on one chromosome may break off and switch places with those on the other in a process called crossing-over or recombination. During recombination genes are shuffled between the two sets of chromosomes producing a whole new mixture of genes.

For instance, from the mother may come an allele for blue eyes and one for red hair (together on one chromosome) and from the father an allele for brown eyes and black hair (together on one chromosome). While each pair's proximity on the chromosome makes it likely that they will inherit together, recombination during meiosis may result in the alleles for eye color switching places. This creates a new chromosome that is no longer identical to the original.

The sets of chromosome pairs separate and then the pairs separate, with one chromosome strand migrating to each of the four new nuclei. New cell walls are formed and four gametes result. Each gamete now has one chromosome instead of a chromosome pair. Continuing the example, after recombination and meiosis, the four gametes could have new combinations of alleles; i.e., brown eyes and red hair, blue eyes and black hair, blue eyes and red hair, and brown eyes and black hair.

When the chromosomes of the egg and those of the sperm are combined, the normal genetic complement is complete. The resulting individual has half his genes inherited from each parent in a different combination from theirs, which alone ensures that he will be different from them. Further variation results from whatever genetic reshuffling or recombination occurs during meiosis.

GENE POOL

The gene pool represents the various genetic alleles present within a population and will vary considerably in size from one trait to the next. Many different coat colors are found in dogs, for instance. Akitas are allowed in any color and have many different alleles. Rottweilers come only in bicolor black and tan, indicating that they have very few alleles for coat color in their gene pool.

Every dog breed represents a separate gene pool with a combination of alleles unique to the breed. Limitations on the gene pool occur when specific traits are specified in the standard and selected for by breeders so that other alleles are left out. For instance, Alaskan Malamutes have only an allele for erect ears because drop-eared dogs are not used in breeding.

PREDICTABILITY

Genetic variation ensures that a species can adapt to changes and therefore survive. It can play hob, however, with the breeder of purebred dogs who not only expects a Malamute from the breeding of two Malamutes, but also wants to be able to predict things about them: their appearance, temperament, and working ability, for example. In fact, most breeders are looking for even more specificity.

By decreasing the number of alleles for any trait that you think desirable, you increase the likelihood that the one you want will appear in subsequent generations. For the sake of example, suppose your female's ears were larger than you thought correct by the Malamute standard.

Your first step to remedy this would be to research the mode of inheritance where you would find that small ears are an autosomal recessive. Several scenarios are possible from here:

1.   Your female's pedigree, as far back as you can find, reveals only dogs with large ears. You assume she is a homozygous dominant (EE).[2]

2.   Dogs in her pedigree show a mixture of large and small ears. She may have inherited an allele for small ears. You assume she is heterozygous (Ee).

If she is EE, you have no chance of getting small ears in the next generation because even if you breed to a homozygous recessive (ee), all the puppies will get one gene for big ears from your female (E, because that is all she has) and one gene from the male for small ears (e, because that is all he has). Thus, they will all be heterozygous (Ee). Their ears may be smaller than hers, but not so small as you want. However, you have taken a positive step by introducing the allele for small ears into your gene pool.

The second step for case 1 and first step for case 2 is to take the heterozygote (Ee) to a dog with short ears (ee). About half their litter should have short ears. Since you are dealing with a recessive, from here on if you only breed dogs with small ears, you should keep small ears within your stock.

SAMPLE SIZE

Genetics is a statistical science, and unfortunately, nature is seldom as neat as scientific theory. In your litter, none, half, or even all of them might be pure recessives. After all, dogs produce millions of sperm and females have many eggs, and the right (or wrong, depending on the genes involved) combination just might not make it to the finish line.

Light red and white male puppies from Alcan Kennels. All turned medium red as adults. Courtesy McComb.

If you kept statistics on the offspring of a hundred litters rather than just one, the numbers would approach those of the appropriate model. If these percentages do not occur after building a large sample size, then the model is probably wrong. You may be dealing with a polygenic trait.

TEST BREEDING

Analyzing the incidence of a trait's appearance, coupled with complex test breedings is a practical method by which geneticists postulate the genes behind those traits, their alleles, and the relationships among them. Statistical analysis of the results gives them information about the most likely scenario.

The test breeding program for chondrodysplasia (dwarfism) recognizes the importance of sample size by requiring a minimum number of puppies in the litter before certification. This helps ensure that carriers do not slip through. The chance that a litter of six from a normal dog and dwarf would produce all dwarfs is extremely small, but it has been reported. The converse might also occur; a carrier and dwarf might produce six normal puppies.

Your chances of winning the lottery are probably about as likely, but the possibility does point up the need for a better screening method than either pedigree analysis or test breeding. Advances in genetics will soon replace these methods with direct analysis of the DNA molecules, and projects to do so are being funded by the AMCA and by the AKC. You can find out more about DNA testing by reading current periodicals like *The Gazette* or *Dog World*, or information your veterinarian may be able to supply.

PHENOTYPE VS. GENOTYPE

As you can see from the example, in an animal that is purely recessive, phenotype, its external appearance, and genotype, its genetic composition, are the same. Pure recessives bred to other pure recessives produce only pure recessives unless a mutation occurs. Mutations are alterations of DNA and can be due to replication errors during cell division or induced by radiation or chemicals, among other things. The altered DNA is replicated in somatic and sex cells, so it can be passed to the next generation.

An animal that shows a dominant characteristic phenotypically may be either a homozygote or heterozygote. Subtle indicators may give you hints as to which is the case, but the only way to know for sure is to breed to a homozygous recessive and see what you get. This is called test breeding, and it is the principle that governs chondrodysplasia (CHD) testing.

Nonetheless, in dogs with the same phenotype, while you may not know all the genotype, you do know they have one allele in common. Whether they are homozygous dominant or heterozygotes, you should get some progeny that show the dominant allele. This principle is the basis for what is called type-to-type breeding. Because the parents have common alleles, it lessens genetic variability in the progeny.

This still leaves you in the dark about the genotype, however. If you are trying to maintain a particular allele in your stock, homozygotes are better. They are the only way to maintain a recessive trait, like erect ears or red color. For a dominant trait, such as short coats, the homozygote will reliably reproduce itself.

Ch. Kougarok, bred and owned by Kay and Linton Moustakis, is an example of the early crosses of M'Loot and Kotzebue through the combination of Northwind and Husky Pak lines.

Breeding heterozygous animals gives a mixture. In a cross between a homozygote (dominant or recessive) and a heterozygote, half the progeny will be homozygous and half heterozygous. When two heterozygotes are crossed, half the resulting progeny will be heterozygous, one quarter homozygous for the dominant, and the other quarter, homozygous for the recessive.

If you were only looking for one thing in breeding, such as ear size or coat color, your task would be quite simple, but dogs have many genes, and you have many parameters to satisfy to breed successfully. Fortunately, there are other tools that can help you make decisions.

PEDIGREES

Alaskan Malamute breeders are lucky to have the AMCA *Pedigree Journals*. A valuable service begun years ago, these publications contain pictures and pedigrees of almost every titled Alaskan Malamute ever born. It can be purchased from the AMCA. Using the *Journals*, you should be able to trace almost any Malamute back to the beginnings of the breed. Since most of the dogs are pictured, you can also see something about their phenotype.

Using photographs and pedigrees can help you determine what type of breeding you want to do and what dogs you want to use to produce puppies that represent your idea of the perfect Alaskan Malamute.

OUTCROSSING

The simplest type of breeding is an outcross. By strict definition, it is the breeding of unrelated animals. In pure-bred dogs, however, go far enough back in a pedigree and you will see the same dogs appearing more than once. This happens quickly in Alaskan Malamute pedigrees because the breed is relatively young.

An outcross that is also a "type-to-type" breeding may give some consistency in a litter, but this is not guaranteed. Even if it does, you have no idea what genotype you are breeding. You may introduce traits that you do not want and are hard to get rid of in subsequent generations.

This is especially true if you continue to outcross. In a gene pool as restricted as that of the Malamute, sooner or later you will come across another carrier of a recessive which you have been harboring in your lines.

The allele for dwarfism is an excellent case in point. The acceptable rating for a clear pedigree is 6.25%, which means that 93.5% of the time you can be sure that your dog is not heterozygous for CHD. This means that of all the dogs that have been issued pedigree clearances, 6.25% of them may be carriers. This is not so alarming as it seems. Some of the dogs in this percentage may never be bred. If they are, the fertilized gamete may not have the CHD allele, it may have the dominant one instead. Still, if these dogs and their progeny are bred through successive generations, eventually, one will meet his genetic counterpart and dwarf puppies will result.

Continued outcrossing is the hallmark of breeders with limited or no knowledge of genetics and little purpose in breeding. Its one advantage is that genetic variability may mask deleterious genes. The serious breeder always tries to expose them so that he can eliminate them, rather than covering them up and passing them from one generation to the next.

Outcrossing can produce a good dog; however, it is less likely to reproduce itself, so it is of little use in further breeding. A breeder may outcross to correct one of the problems set in his line but, since he cannot order one part of the dog without all the other parts, such a departure may cost him several generations to return to his preferred type.

Used correctly, outcrossing is a way to dip into another gene pool to bring in a different trait; it should be used

Like many outcross breedings, this litter of six-week-old Husky-Pak puppies sired by Ch. Cochise of Husky-Pak out of Glacier of Sno-Shu is not very consistent in type. Courtesy of Delta Wilson Smith.

only when selections in your own line fail or when you want to establish a new strain. Both the Kotzebue and M'Loot lines began with outcross breedings, as did the Husky-Pak dogs, but to keep what they had achieved, all these breeders quickly began either line or inbreeding.

LINEBREEDING

To narrow the gene pool even further than a type-to-type breeding, many successful breeders use dogs with one or more relatives in common. This is called linebreeding.

Your results will be more consistent if you pay attention to the phenotype of the related dogs. Siblings from heterozygotes may be quite dissimilar genetically, since one might be homozygous for more dominant traits and the other for recessives. If they look alike and are related, they are more likely to have similar genotypes.

Linebreeding is an attempt to avoid the problems of inbreeding. When the gene pool becomes too narrow, getting rid of undesirable traits can be difficult or impossible. With linebreeding, the pool is not so small nor is it so quickly decreased in size. Although it is regarded as "safer," this depends more on the actual genotype of the animals involved rather than on their familial relationship.

INBREEDING

Inbreeding is the fastest way to concentrate a gene pool. It is breeding together dogs related within the first generation—parent to offspring or brother to sister. Of course, inbreeding dogs that are otherwise related will limit variability even more.

One of the merits of inbreeding is that it fixes type more quickly than any other breeding technique. On the down-side, however, it sets faults just as well as virtues. Without extensive knowledge of the physical qualities of the dogs in the pedigree, inbreeding can be a breeder's ruin. Inexperienced breeders or anyone who lacks the ability to be entirely objective in evaluating his dogs should never undertake inbreeding.

Inbreeding is often regarded as a controversial breeding technique, but the system is not so much at fault as are breeders who fail to use outstanding dogs. The deeper the quality of the pedigree, the more likely it is to produce that quality, since the genetic material is concentrated on the side of desirable traits which will be expressed through many future generations. Without inbreeding, significant prepotency that results in a distinct, reproducible type will never exist.

On the other hand, inbreeding unsuitable stock cements their faults into the progeny. The qualities that you want to breed must already be present in the genotype of the sire and dam; those that you do not want should not be apparent. Inbreeding cannot make the original dogs any better than they are.

Continued over generations, inbreeding can also result in a general loss of vigor. At that point, judicious use of outcrossing can bring in new genes to revitalize the line. This works particularly well if you use a heavily-linebred or inbred dog of another line.

EXAMPLES

Malamute history shows us that the Kotzebue dogs used for breeding and registered by Short Seeley were similar in appearance (phenotypically similar) and had proven working ability. At the outset, only one dog of a litter might be registered and used for breeding. Others were bred but not registered and only one or two of the puppies were used to further Malamute lines.

Once they produced dogs of consistent appearance, these dogs were linebred and inbred. This technique enabled the Seeleys to quickly produce dogs of recognizable type which bred true.

The pedigrees of two very influential Malamutes, Ch. Toro of Bras Coupe, a pure Kotzebue, and Kobuk's Dark Beauty, a pure M'Loot, are excellent examples of all three breeding techniques. Close linebreeding, exemplified by the pedigrees of Storm Kloud and Skymaster, is tantamount to inbreeding and accomplishes much the same results.

Toro

Ch. Toro of Bras Coupe's pedigree (*See page 159*) begins with the outcrossing of Jad and Bessie, Rowdy and Holly, and Jad and Wanda. Progeny from these breedings are combined, so that Taku of Kotzebue is both a daughter and granddaughter of Rowdy, while Antarctica Taku has the same relationship with Yukon Jad.[3]

The influence of Jad, Rowdy, and Bessie is further concentrated when Navarre is bred to Pandora, since they are more than half-siblings. Wray and Cleo are daughters of an outcross, which forms the basis for linebreeding, since Wray is Kim's grandmother and Cleo is the mother of Cleopatra. In Toro's five generation pedigree are seven lines to Jad and two to Antarctica Taku and Gripp.

Dark Beauty

The pedigree of Kobuk's Dark Beauty begins with the same sort of outcrosses, Silver King to Dodge's Lou, Mikiuk to Noma, Pucky to Nicki, Tosha to Gentleman Jim, and Master Otter to Tonga. As the pedigree moves forward in time, the dogs become braided together. Dodge's Lou is the dam of both Gentleman Jim and Vixen M'Loot; Chisholm's Northern Star, then, is a linebred female.

Master Otter bred to Dusty Lane represents a close linebreeding. Vixen and Noma are half-sisters out of Silver King, and Master Otter and Schmoos M'Loot are half-brothers out of Mikiuk. The breeding of Lash and Belle, however, is a brother-sister inbreeding as is the breeding which produced Beauty, since Bear is a son of Master Otter, himself the product of a linebreeding.

Kobuk's Dark Beauty

In other words, Beauty's father, grandfather, and grandmother were at least half-siblings. She has four lines to Mikiuk in six generations, three to Master Otter, and three to Noma. Note that Tosha, who appears twice in Baloo's pedigree is the product of a brother-sister breeding.

This type of concentrated breeding produces what are known as prepotent animals, which means that their progeny tend to look more like them than the other parent. The very word "prepotent" implies that the animal is somehow stronger, so falling into the trap of thinking that his genes are also dominant is easy. In fact, some of the traits that seem to always appear may be recessives. The vastly decreased gene pool and lack of variability produced by line- and inbreeding allows recessive alleles to be expressed more often than in a normal population where their presence would be masked by more numerous dominant alleles.

(NOTE: Since these pedigrees go back much further than is customary, most dogs are traced back only once. So when nothing else appears, it is either because the parents are unknown or the rest of the pedigree is already detailed. Otherwise, they get far too long to print.)

Contrast this litter of two-and-one-half- week old puppies from Hug-A-Bear Kennels with the outcross puppies on page 237. The predictability that comes from linebreeding makes breeding easier. Photo courtesy of Carol Hug.

The principle is really quite simple: the smaller the gene pool, the fewer the chances that differences will occur. Concentrating genes enables a breeder to produce consistent type which is why so many successful breeders inbreed and almost all breeders linebreed.

This cannot be done forever, though, without paying a penalty. Genetic variability is an evolutionary adaptation for survival, applicable to dogs as well as dinosaurs. When a problem arises, especially one that threatens health, the viability of a breed depends on the presence of enough outside genes to preserve the type yet steer the breed away from a calamity.

PREPOTENT DOGS

When a highly inbred (low genetic variability) animal is bred to an outcross animal with few common relations (high variability), the progeny will be more likely to look like the inbred parent unless the characteristics which contribute most to the appearance are recessives masked by the dominant genes of the outcross. They can be quickly recovered, however, by breeding back to the inbred parent or one of his relatives.

Another technique is to breed inbred dogs of different lines together. The resulting progeny can then be bred back to either line, depending on preference. This technique has produced many dogs of excellent type and producing ability in many breeds. It was the basis for the Husky-Pak line.

Kadluck

The pedigree of Kadluck of North Wind reflects such a breeding. Ch. Midnight Shadow of Kuvak, a tightly-bred Kotzebue dog, was crossed with Ch. Nome of Northwind, a tightly bred M'Loot. Their breeding, though, was a complete outcross. When its product was taken back to the M'Loot lines with the breeding of Kadluck and Ch. Glacier Lady of the Arctic, the result was the breed's top producing dog, Am. Can. Mex. Int. Ch. Glaciers' Storm Kloud, CD, ROM, ObROM.

Ch. Kim of Kotzebue
Ch. Toro of Bras Coupe
Kotzebue Cleopatra
Ch. Keowuk of Kobuk
Ch. Kim of Kotzebue
Helen of Bras Coupe
Kotzebue Cleopatra
Alaskan Kokolik (Kobolik) of Kuvak
Ch. Kim of Kotzebue
Helen of Bras Coupe
Kotzebue Cleopatra
Ch. Midnight Shadow of Kuvak
Ch. Toro of Bras Coupe
Kaghi of Kobuk
Helen of Bras Coupe
Sno Pak Kaghi's Tugg
Jiffy of Kotzebue
Igloo Paks Gripp
Tananna of Igloo Pak
Musher Lane Kila
Chinook's Karluk of Kotzebue
Musher Lanes Taku of Chinook
Cleo of Kotzebue
Alaskan Onowuk of Kuvak
Ch. Toro of Bras Coupe
Kiana of Kuvak
Taku's Mascara of Chinook
Kadluk of North Wind
Silver King
Mukluk (M'Loot)
Vixen
Nanook I
Dude's Wolf
Fox (brother to G. Jim)
Dodges Lou
Ch. Nanook II
Tobuk
Mikiuk
Kapuk
Ch. Ooloo M'Loot
Silver King
Noma
Silver Girl
North Wind of Silver Sled
Tobuk
Mikiuk
Kapuk
Ch. Ooloo M'Loot
Silver King
Noma
Silver Girl
Lobo of North Wind
Frost of Silver Sled
Kamah of Sliver Sled
Lateya of Silver Sled
Ch. Nome of North Wind
Ch. Nanook II
North Wind of Silver Sled
Ch. Ooloo M'Loot
Klondike Kate of Northwind
Nanook II
Dorries Dolly
Oogarook of Silver Sled

Am. Can. Mex. Int. Ch. Glacier's Storm Kloud, CD, ROM, Ob-ROM, top sire in breed history with 65 champion get. Breeder, Lois Olmen, Owner, Nancy Russell.

Storm Kloud

Storm Kloud's pedigree points up a pitfall of inadequate pedigree research. A four-generation pedigree, which is what most people work with, shows him to be linebred, since North Wind dogs show up twice, as do Moosecat and Flicka. The similar kennel names hint at possible relationships further back but do not confirm them.

Never assume dogs are unrelated just because a four-generation pedigree does not show common ancestors, nor should you discount the influence of dogs more than four generations back. If the same dog appears at the end of almost every line, the gene pool was restricted to begin with since that one dog could have, at most, only two alleles for any gene.

The top half (father) of Storm Kloud's pedigree shows a line inbred on the pedigree of Toro of Bras Coupe, himself the product of high inbreeding. Toro bred to his sister produced Keowuk, who was then bred back to his mother to produce Kokolik (or Kobolik, it is spelled both ways on pedigree records). Kagi of Kobuk is the grandsire of Midnight Shadow and the brother of Keowuk, since he, too, is the son of Toro bred to his sister Helen. Kiana's pedigree has several lines similar to those of Toro. Basically, all these dogs go back to Rowdy, Bessie, Jad, Wasca, Wanda, and Holly, Eva Seeley's original dogs.

Likewise, the original M'Loot dogs, Mikiuk, Mukluk, Fox, Silver King, Silver Girl, Dodge's Lou, and Dude's Wolf are behind almost all the rest of the pedigree, so it is just as tightly inbred. Storm Kloud's pedigree was a fortunate mixture, providing almost any Malamute breeder some kind of line- or inbreeding, since their pedigrees were bound to have some of the same dogs.

Kadluk of North Wind
Ch. Glaciers' Storm Kloud, CD
    Moosecat of North Wind
   Midwests Moosecat Jack
   Midwests Flicka
  Kodiak of North Star
      Ch. Nooknook II
     North Wind of Silver Sled
      Ch. Ooloo M'Loot
    Great Bear of North Wind
      Ch. Nanook II
     Dorries Dolly
      Oogarook of Silver Sled
   Shuli Brooke of North Wind
       Ch. Nanook II
      North Wind of Sliver Sled
       Ch. Ooloo M'Loot
     Lobo of Northwind
       Frost of Silver Sled
      Kamah of Silver Sled
       Lateya of Silver Sled
    Ch. Misty of North Wind
       Ch. Nanook II
      North Wind of Silver Sled
       Ch. Ooloo M'Loot
     Klondike Kate of Northwind
       Nanook II
      Dorries Dolly
       Oogarook of Silver Sled
 Ch. Glacier Lady of the Arctic
    Moosecat of North Wind
   Midwests Moosecat Jack
   Midwests Flicka
  Princess Rose of North Star
   Kim Loop
  Princess Kina of North Star
   Nome of Hales

Skymaster and Buffalo Bill

The four-generation pedigree of Am/Can Ch. Karohonta's Skymaster, a son of Ch. Uyak's Buffalo Bill, shows what seems to be a moderately inbred dog. Like Storm Kloud, these dogs are found today farther back. The significance of dogs like Storm Kloud, Skymaster, and others is easy to overlook when related dogs are dropped off a pedigree in the interest of saving space.

A study of their pedigree shows why these two dogs have proven so prepotent. Buffalo Bill's Sire, Ch. T'Domar's Kulak, was the product of the brother-sister breeding of Ch. T'Domar's Voodoo King and T'Domar's Taboo. Through their ties to the Husky-Pak dogs, these two dogs bring in both M'Loot and Kotzebue lines.

Bill's mother, Conestoga, has the same ties to the Husky-Pak dogs with the addition of several lines to Kobuk's Dark Beauty. She is the common grandmother of the sire who is out of more than half-siblings—that is,

Ch. Spawn's Alaska
Ch. Apache Chief of Husky Pak
Chitina
Ch. Daku of Husky Pak
Ch. Husky Pak Mikya of Seguin
Ch. Barb Far LooTok
Ch. Nanook II
Koonah of Silver Sled
Oogerook of Silver Sled
Ch. Spawn's Kulak
Ch. Nanook II
Polar
Ch.King M'Loot
Ch. Kola
Ch. Gyana
Ch. Spawn's Chee Chee
Kayak of Brookside
Arrow of Husky Pak
Ch. Husky Pak Mikya of Seguin
Ch. T'Domar's Voodoo King
Ch. Toro of Bras Coup
Ch. Cherokee of Husky Pak
Ch. Spawn's Alaska
Ch. Arctic Storm of Husky Pak
Chitina
Ch. Husky Pak Gazelle
Ch. Toro of Bras Coup
Kelerak of Kobuk
Helen of Bras Coup
Ch. T'Domar's Kulak
Ch. Spawn's Kulak
Ch. T'Domar's Taboo
Ch. Husky Pak Gazelle
Ch. Uyak Buffalo Bill
Ch. Apache Chief of Husky Pak
Ch. Husky Pak Erok
Kelerak of Kobuk
Ch. Kodara Kodiak of Erowah
Ch. Mulpus Brooks the Bear
Kobuk's Dark Beauty
Ch. Baloo
Ch. Kodara Kodiak Teddi
Ch. Toro of Bras Coup
Ch. Cochise of Husky Pak
Ch. Arctic Storm of Husky Pak
Ch. Sno Crest Aurora of Erowah
Kobuk's Dark Beauty
Ch. Kodara Conestoga
Ch. Cochise of Husky Pak
Ch. Sno Crest Mukluk
Kobuk's Dark Beauty
Ch. Kodara's Koona Karohonta
Pancho
Pawnee Flash of North Wind
Nome of North Wind
Ambara's Evaro (Eyara)
Ch. Cochise of Husky Pak
Preston's Cheechako
Kobuk's Dark Beauty

Am/Can Ch. Karohonta's Skymaster, ROM

Ch. Spawn's Kulak
Ch. T'Domar's Voodoo King
Ch. Husky Pak Gazelle
Ch. Karohonta Voodoo Flame
Ch. Kodara's Kodiak Teddi
Ch. Karohonta Tai-Lo-Wah
Ch. Kodara's Koona Karohonta

they have the same mother and very closely related fathers.

Two of Conestoga's grandparents, Ch. Sno Crest Aurora of Erowah and Ch. Sno Crest's Mukluk, are siblings; another sibling appears at the tail end of Conestoga's pedigree. Her great-grandmother, Preston's Cheechako is also out of Cochise and Dark Beauty.

As if this were not close enough, Skymaster's dam brings other relations to his father, Buffalo Bill. Karohonta's Voodoo Flame is a half-sister to Buffalo Bill's sire, Ch. T'Domar's Kulak. To top it all off, both Skymaster's grandmothers are full sisters: Tai-Lo-Wah and Conestoga are both out of Teddi and Koona.

This pedigree offers quite a sampling of the various Husky-Pak dogs. In addition to the often-seen Apache Chief, Arctic Storm, Cochise, and Cherokee, it has lines to Daku, Arrow, Gazelle, Erok, and Mikya.

Whether this pedigree is considered tightly linebred or loosely inbred is largely a matter of semantics. The repeated appearance of the same dogs means that genetic variability is considerably lessened. Therefore, linebreedings or inbreedings with Skymaster and/or Buffalo Bill in the pedigree should result in increasing similarity in the offspring.

Nakoah

Ch. Windrift's Leah of Aurora's paternal pedigree through Lucifer is heavily backed by Kotzebue dogs, which have a small, concentrated base. M'Loot influence comes from the introduction of Husky-Pak dogs, which were a cross between M'Loot and Kotzebue with a dash of something extra. The maternal half has a higher concentration of M'Loot dogs because the Storm Kloud and the Roy-El dogs were both partly M'Loot.

Breeding Ch. Aurora's Kuyana of Windrift (Yana) to Bowser intensified the linebreeding on the M'Loot dogs by doubling a line to Storm Kloud. At the same time, it doubled all the Kotzebue dogs found behind Kotzebue, Chinook, Sno-Pak, and Roy-El. Kuyana is a granddaughter of Wooly Bully, so her breeding to Lucifer is a classic formula for linebreeding, where the sire of the sire is the grandsire of the dam.

Two other pedigrees show how the same type of breeding works with different dogs. One is the breeding of Kuyana to her grandson, Nakoah. The other is the more current pedigree of Ch. Hug-A-Bear's All That Jazz. As you can see from the following photos, consistency of type and overall quality can be maintained through many generations by the judicious use of linebreeding.

Ch. Tigara's Arctic Explorer
Ch. Tigara's Torch of Artica
Tigara's Winsome Witch
Ch. Tigara's Prince Igor of Tumleh
Ch. Tigara's Arctic Explorer
Tigara's Thais of Artica
Ch. Tigara's Kije of Artica
Tigara's Totemtok of Blitzkrieg
Ch. Tigara's Torch of Artica
Ch. Tigara's Dangerous Dan McGraw
Tigara's Thais of Artica
Ch. Tigara's Kointa of Totemtok
Alaskana's Toby of Hercules
Ch. Totemtok's Tianna of Alaskana
Tigara's Kiana Kenai
Ch. Aurora's Noataq of Windrift
Ch. Husky-Pak Erok
Ch. Kodara Kodiak of Erowoh
Kobuk's Dark Beauty
Kiowa's Arcturas of Tikiluk, CD
Tigara's Honah Lee of Artica
Snow Bear's Royal Beauty
Tigara's Majeska of Arctica
Tikiluk's Shagaluk
Ch. Tigara's Whip of Artica
Ch. Tigara's Togiak Chieftan
Tigara's Tsena of Artica
Tikikluk's Artic Sno-Mist
Ch. Tigara's Jo-Dan of Artica
Ruby Gem of Tikiluk, CD
Silver Chablis

Ch. Windrift's Nakoah

Ch. Fakir of Roy-El
Ch. Spawn's Hot Shot of Roy-El
Snowmasque White Diamond
Ch. Inuit's Wooly Bully
Ch. Tigara's Karluk of Roy-El
Ch. Balch's Ingrid of Brenmar
Ch. Sno-Pak Nashoba
Ch. Inuit's Sweet Lucifer
Ch. Tigara's Artic Explorer
Ch. Tigara's Torch of Artica
Tigara's Winsome Witch
Ch. Voyageur's Elke
Ch. Ceba's Silver Bow
Ch. Jingo's Silver Trumpet
Ch. Husky-Pak Jingo
Ch. Windrift's Leah of Aurora
Ch. Spawn's Hot Shot of Roy-El
Ch. Inuit's Wooly Bully
Ch. Balch's Ingrid of Brenmar
Ch. Bernard
Sno-Pak Sigdlumala
Kotzebue of Chinook
Tigara's Tundra of Arctica
Ch. Aurora's Kuyana of Windrift
Kadluck of Northwind
Ch. Glacier's Storm Kloud, CD
Ch. Glacier Lady of the Arctic
Aurora's Kantishna Meadow
Kanangnark's Anna Lobo II
Winter Wind
Kanangnark's Noma
Ch. Nome of North Wind

Ch. Aurora's Noataq of Windrift, bred by Lynn Gray and owned by Barbara Brooks, when bred to . . .

Am. Can. Ch. Windrift's Leah of Aurora, bred and owned by Barbara Brooks. produced . . .

Ch. Windrift's Nakoah, bred and owned by Barbara Brooks. When bred back to his grandmother, his get were very uniform in type.

Am. Can. Ch. Aurora's Kuyana of Windrift, ROM, was the foundation bitch for Windrift. She was bred by Lake and Juengst.
"Yana" won BOS at Westminster KC in 1977.

Ch. Windrift's Chemio of Nakoah is from the breeding of Nakoah
and Kuyana which produced many champions. Breeder, Barbara
Brooks; Owners, Sherry Wallis and Barbara Brooks.

Ch. Windrift's Nakoah
RRUFF N'TUFF, CHEMIO, MON CHERI
        Ch. Fakir of Roy-El
     Ch. Spawn's Hot Shot of Roy-El
        Snowmasque White Diamond
   Ch. Inuit's Wooly Bully
        Ch. Tigara's Karluk of Roy-El
     Ch. Balch's Ingrid of Brenmar
        Ch. Sno-Pak Nashoba
 Ch. Bernard
        Sno-Pak Anvik
     Sno-Pak Sigdlumala
        Sno Pak Tacoma
   Kotzebue of Chinook
        Ch. Rogue of Tigara
     Tigara's Tundra of Arctica
        Tigara's Kazana
Ch. Aurora's Kuyana of Windrift
        Ch. Midnight Shadow of Kuvak
     Kadluck of Northwind
        Ch. Nome of North Wind
   Ch. Glacier's Storm Kloud, CD
        Kodiak of North Star
     Ch. Glacier Lady of the Arctic
        Princess Rose of North Star
 Aurora's Kantishna Meadow
        Toro of North Wind
     Kanangnark's Anna Lobo II
        Kanangnark's Silky
   Winter Wind
        Cuffy of North Wind, CD
     Kanangnark's Noma
        Ch. Nome of North Wind

Windrift's Mon Cherie, a sister of Chemio. Bred by Barbara Brooks
and owned by Leora Zook.

All That Jazz

The influence of dogs in Nakoah's pedigree is carried into the present through linebreeding on Nakoah, shown in the pedigree of Jazz. Her sire is two times Nakoah. Karisma, her maternal grandmother, is out of the breeding of Nakoah to Kuyana. While Jazz's dam brings in some unrelated lines through Legend, her maternal grandmother is also Karisma. Not only does Kuyana appear directly in this pedigree through her breeding to Nakoah; there is yet another line to her, since she is also Nakoah's grandmother.

The resemblance between Jazz, Mon Cherie and Kuyana should come as no surprise. This type of close linebreeding maintains type through many generations. Careful attention to the mechanics of genetics, familiarity with pedigrees and the dogs which appear in them, and a goal towards which to strive will enable you to develop dogs with a distinctive look that will identify them as coming from your breeding program. This kind of uniformity is the mark of a good breeder.

The striking resemblance of Ch. Hug A Bear's All That Jazz to Mon Cherie and Kuyana arises from linebreeding on both Am. Can. Ch. Aurora's Kuyana of Windrift, ROM, and her grandson, Ch. Windrift's Nakoah. Breeder/owners, Carol and Joseph Hug.

Endnotes

1. Many requirements in various standards arise from a desire to safeguard the gene pool of the breed from alteration and often display a sophistication far ahead of the science of the day.

2. By convention, scientists denote alleles with one letter, usually related to the trait. The dominant allele is shown by a capital letter and the recessive by a lower-case letter. If more than two alleles are present, the recessives are listed in descending order of dominance and denoted by the lower-case letter and a superscript. For instance, in spotting, S-no spotting is the most dominant, followed by si-or Irish spotting; sp-pinto; and se-extreme white piebald. Notations for well-researched traits are used in common by geneticists.

3. It is easy to see why so many pedigrees confuse these two females.

                Ch. Hug-A-Bear's IceBr'Ker O' Windfall, CD
        Windfall's Budd-Light
                Ch. Hug-A-Bear's De Javue of Windfall, CD
      Windrift's Discovery
                Ch. Windrift's Nakoah
        Ch. Windrift's Minx of Tikiluk
                Am/Can Ch Tikiluk's Nikola of Windrift,
                CD, WPD, ROM
   Ch. Hug-A-Bear's Last Starfighter
                Ch. Northern Light's Togiak
        Ch. Hug-A-Bear's Steppin' Wolf
                Tinka of Elkhoune
    Ch. Hug-A-Bear's Kiska O' Tug-N-Chug, ROM
                Ch. Windrift's Nakoah
        Ch. Hug-A-Bear's Karisma O' Windrift, CD, ROM
                Am/Can Ch. Aurora's Kuyana of
                Windrift ROM

Ch. Hug A Bear's All That Jazz

                Ch. Sarge's Candyman of Big Paw
        Am/Can Ch. Sarge's Bojangles O'Nan
                Yukon Kiva of Zaklan
      Ch. O'Nan's the Legend Lives On
                Am/Can Ch. Timberlane's the Yankee
        Ch. O'Nan's I'm A Phanny Too
                Glacier's Phanny Too
   Hug-A-Bear's Sweetest Taboo, ROM
                Ch. Northern Light's Togiak
        Ch. Hug-A-Bear's Steppin Wolf
                Tinika of Elkhourne
    Ch. Hug-A-Bear's Kiska O' Tug-N-Chug, ROM
                Ch. Windrift's Nakoah
        Ch. Hug-A-Bear's Karisma O'Windrift, CD, ROM
                Am./Can. Ch. Aurora's Kuyana of Windrift, ROM

17

CONTROLLING HEREDITARY PROBLEMS

Health problems, whether genetic or acquired, are eliminated or significantly decreased in wild canids because affected animals do not survive to reproduce. Once humans enter the equation, however, everything changes. Human care enables animals that cannot survive in the wild state to thrive in a domestic one. This interference is not necessarily detrimental—many modifications to the wild canine have benefitted the man-dog relationship.

An unfortunate side-effect of selective breeding, though, has been the passing of genetic disease from one generation to the next. The rigorous natural selection that was a by-product of life in harness made the Alaskan Malamute of old a hardy, healthy dog; today's Malamutes have inherited general good health, a rugged constitution, and incredible fortitude in the face of adversity. Nonetheless, several diseases of proven or suspected genetic origin have found their way into the gene pool. Although these problems are not unique to Alaskan Malamutes, or even to purebred dogs, they may sometimes seem so because breeders, individually and through dog clubs, have supplied both the impetus and funding for much of the research into these diseases. Concerned with producing the best dogs they possibly can, breeders try to identify genetic problems and eliminate them from the gene pool by screening out affected dogs or carriers.

By their very nature, purebred dogs have limitations in their genetic variability, so not all problems are found in every breed. Knowing which diseases affect Alaskan Malamutes and their symptoms is important—not only for breeders, but for pet owners as well.

Historically, Alaskan Malamute breeders have responded to difficult problems with integrity and courage. To further the welfare of the breed, many individuals have had to make painful choices at a very real financial and emotional cost. Their sacrifices have been largely unheralded, but we have all benefited from them. Their efforts have paved the way for our breed's future and, in turn, we owe it to our successors to follow in their footsteps.

To that end, we must be familiar with genetic defects and work to eliminate them. This is neither simple nor pleasant, but it is essential to preserving the well-being of the breed and assuring its future.

ORTHOPEDIC DISEASE

(Much of the information for the remainder of this chapter is provided by Randall S. Murray, DVM, of Texarkana, Texas, who points out that it is intended only as a guide to the Malamute owner and is limited to generalities. It should not be a substitute for a close working relationship with your veterinarian.).[1]

HIP DYSPLASIA

Hip dysplasia is found in almost every breed. It is particularly difficult for large dogs like the Alaskan Malamute because their weight puts more stress on their joints. Dysplasia results from an abnormal structure of the hip (coxofemoral) joint, which has a ball-in-socket formation. The ball or head of the thigh bone (femur) must rotate and support weight within the socket or pelvis (acetabulum).

The mechanics are simple. Alteration of the shape of the ball or socket begins a chain of events that leads to degenerative joint disease and eventual bony change, called osteoarthritis.

Currently, diagnosis is done by radiograph (X-ray) of the pelvic area. While preliminary radiographs can be done earlier, OFA certification is not done on dogs less than twenty-four months old. Research into earlier detection and more precise evaluation is being done by the University of Pennsylvania School of Veterinary Medicine. They have developed a program from measuring joint laxity which is implemented under the name PennHip by veterinarians trained by International Canine Genetics Corporation (ICG).

It takes sound limbs and joints to race. Alecho Sabugo of Spain, a European champion, runs an all Malamute team. Photo by Chris Eisenga.

Several differences exist between the OFA and PennHip programs. PennHipp exams can be done at any age. Instead of examining the actual formation of the hip, measurements of joint laxity are compared with a database compiled for each breed, and dogs ranked above a certain percentile are predicted to have normal hips that will be free of change as the dog ages. All PennHip results are reported; OFA participation is voluntary

In dogs with profound abnormalities, symptoms frequently will be present early in life. These include stiffness at as early as five to six months of age, with severe lameness in one or both hips appearing soon afterward. An animal with mild abnormalities may never show lameness; instead, he may have difficulty getting up from a prone position, may show stiffness in the hindquarters, or a reluctance to stand without frequently shifting his feet. Eventually, the front may appear more obviously muscled while the rear appears skimpy. Affected dogs may gallop with both rear feet together in a "bunny hop" in which both rear legs move as if tied together.

Unfortunately, hip dysplasia does not follow any set of rules or regulations regarding presentation, age of onset, visual conformation, or degree of pain upon movement. Understanding that a lame dog has an orthopedic problem is easy. On the other hand, believing that a dog with no symptoms has severe joint problems is more difficult. Almost every veterinarian has radiographed a dog for something else and found such severe deformity of the hip joint that the dog should be unable to walk. Yet, walk they do! The sometimes poor correlation between observable symptoms and radiographic evidence is one reason why many people have trouble understanding the problems associated with hip dysplasia and the need for radiographs on all breeding stock.

Canine hip dysplasia is believed to be an inherited disease caused by the interaction of many genes, which also

may be influenced by environmental factors such as nutrition, amount of exercise, and excess weight. However, no exclusively environmental cause has been found. The only proven way to reduce the frequency of hip dysplasia from one generation to the next is selective breeding for normal hips.

Although dramatic advancements in treatment have developed over the last decade, dysplasia cannot be cured. If diagnosed early before bone begins to change, a popular treatment is surgical correction to the shape of the joint. Injection of polysulfated glycosaminoglycan (PSGAG) temporarily results in improvement and may lessen the osteoarthritic changes that occur in dysplastic dogs over time. Old standby techniques include removal of the femoral head (head and neck osteotomy), as well as total hip replacement with prosthesis. Both of these are drastic and expensive measures.

Prevention of hip dysplasia can only be achieved by using unaffected and genetically clear dogs for breeding. Even then, affected progeny may still appear. With each successive generation of normal parents, however, the likelihood of producing dysplastic puppies decreases.

As a guideline, OFA recommends breeding only normal dogs, which should have normal parents and grandparents. Dogs used for breeding, in addition, should come from litters where at least seventy-five percent of the siblings were normal. If information is available, choose dogs that are already proven to produce good hips consistently, and when you keep a bitch for breeding, always select one with better hip conformation than her parents.

ELBOW DYSPLASIA

Elbow dysplasia is a term used to describe a poorly understood condition of the elbow joint which results in chronic pain and/or chronic degenerative arthritis. An umbrella term for an elbow-joint incongruity of some type, elbow dysplasia may include ununited anconeal process and osteochondrosis (OD) of the humerus, and possibly fragmented coronoid process of the ulna as well.

Affected Malamutes commonly show some degree of pain and lameness in one or both of the front legs. Some may only have an altered gait in which they may carry the elbows and possibly the paws further away from the chest than normal. Crepitation and degenerative joint disease may be present in the more advanced cases. Treatment should be determined by the attending veterinarian and may include surgical removal of anconeal fragments and/or coronoid fragments from the joints, along with anti-inflammatory therapy.

Whether elbow dysplasia is an inherited disorder is a subject of debate. Many experienced breeders believe it shows a familial tendency, but a metabolic developmental problem currently is suspected as the most likely culprit. However, since an incongruity is an obvious part of the scenario, genetic factors could exist.

Radiographic screening can be done at the same time as the hip X-ray and sent to the OFA's elbow registry. Although the Alaskan Malamute is not listed as an "affected breed" (at least fifty animals must have been identified by the OFA for a breed to be considered affected), vigilance seems in order.

Two important reasons to screen for elbow problems are: the possibility that the low incidence is merely a reflection of the lack of screening, and the second is the likelihood that an undiagnosed condition will result in a veterinary consultation only when it has progressed to degenerative arthritis. Then, the impetus to report to the OFA is lost.

CHONDRODYSPLASIA

Chondrodysplasia, or dwarfism, is an inherited condition of the Alaskan Malamute which may be similar to dyschondroplasia in humans. Although other breeds exhibit simple dwarfism, the condition in the Malamute is much more complex, involving related anemia which can exist partially in seemingly-unaffected carriers.

The largest body of research comes from the Ontario Veterinary College at the University of Guelph in Guelph, Ontario. Their well-published findings have helped the AMCA initiate programs to try eliminating the gene from the breeding population. Potential breeders should make every effort to communicate with the AMCA about pedigree analysis by the Chondrodysplasia Certification Committee.

Breeders should be able to recognize a dwarf puppy. Dwarfs have angular limb deformities early in life which vary in severity and can be diagnosed radiographically between three and twelve weeks of age. The front legs are usually shortened and the radius and ulna of the forelegs are often markedly bowed. In comparison to unaffected littermates, most pups are uninterested in exercise. By maturity affected animals may weigh as much as normal counterparts, although they are shorter in stature because of their truncated legs. Pups suspected of chondrodysplasia should be diagnosed by a veterinarian, and information and a pedigree should be sent to the Certification Committee of the AMCA.

Many people would not recognize this dog as a chondrodysplastic, but she is. Breeders still encounter the genes for this problem in the Malamute.

CHONDRODYSPLASIA—A HISTORY
by Linda M. Dowdy

The effort to control chondrodysplasia in the Alaskan Malamute is somewhat routine today, but it wasn't always so. Its history has been written through the pain and perseverance of many, many people. A story of denial evolving into acceptance and determination—it should never be forgotten.

About thirty years ago, breeders in the Pacific Northwest began to see an occasional "odd" puppy in their litters. They were generally smaller than normal littermates. Their legs were not straight, and they sometimes had a "reverse" topline with the rump higher than the withers. Although their bodies were of normal size, the crooked legs made them shorter than a normal Malamute, thus they gradually became known as "dwarfs."

Over the course of time, perplexed breeders sought the help of the Washington State University at Pullman. At first these dwarfs were thought to be the victims of vitamin-D-resistant rickets, but this was not the case. Attempts were then made to alleviate the deformation and bowing of the legs through surgical intervention, but this, too, proved futile.

As the problem became more widespread, breeders predictably tried to disassociate themselves from it, but the dwarfs continued to appear. Breeders disavowed all knowledge of them. Amid a witch-hunt atmosphere, charges and counter-charges flew about the country at an amazing speed. In the midst of this hysteria, Minnie Graham, a Canadian breeder, first suggested that the problem might be genetic.

The daunting challenge of proving or disproving this genetic hypothesis was undertaken by the University of Western Ontario at London, where it captured the attention of two researchers, Dr. Sheilah Fletch and Dr. Meg Smart. Proving a genetic link was a long and arduous process. They had to try every possible combination of breeding pairs, and the number of breedings had to be sufficient to remove the results from the realm of statistical anomaly. After what seemed an interminable passage of time to anxious breeders, the results were published: the genetic transmission of the disease most closely resembled an autosomal simple recessive. To put it simply, the gene was not sex-linked, and it had to be carried by both parents.

Once the genetic hypothesis was established, the AMCA faced an even more difficult task. They had to find a way to use this genetic information to control the problem with nothing but the power of persuasion. How could it convince several hundred disparate breeders (going in several hundred disparate directions) of its importance? Five people were given the task of creating a battle plan. They were Dr. Ken Bourns, Dr. Henry Dodd, Alice Jean Lucus, Linda Dowdy, and Dot Pearson.

This group's plan was a four-pronged attack: 1) a screening process to determine the likelihood of any normal Malamute carrying the recessive gene, 2) a test-breeding process to establish the status of "suspect" dogs, 3) a certification system for "safe" dogs, and 4) education of both owners and the veterinary community about the problem.

The screening process consisted of a mathematical probability analysis of a dog's pedigree. Based upon a continually expanding database of information on affected dogs, the dog's chance of being a recessive carrier of the gene was calculated. A value of 6.25% was chosen to be the largest acceptable probability. A value above 6.25% made the dog ineligible for certification by the AMCA.

The test-breeding process was the deliberate mating of suspect dogs to either known carriers or actual affected dogs. The resulting litter, if large enough to be statistically significant, would establish the genetic status of the suspect dog. If the suspect animal was indeed a carrier, one or more dwarfs should be present in the test litter.

The certification system was administered by the AMCA to identify participating breeders. Initially, certification was divided into three categories: provisional certification granted on the basis of pedigree analysis; test-bred certification granted on the basis of successful test-breeding; and genetically-uninvolved certification granted to dogs of a pure Kotzebue background. Today, there is a single certification.

The AMCA's implementation of the plan in the early 1970's instantly fueled a cauldron of heated emotions throughout North America. Some breeders embraced it wholeheartedly, while others viewed it as an anathema and swore they would never cooperate.

Slowly and inexorably the plan gained credence, but the price was high. Entire kennels were test-bred, and some of the finest representatives of the breed were found to be carriers of dwarfism. Some kennels were unscathed, while others were literally decimated. The number of breeders voluntarily cooperating with the project continued to swell.

The AMCA developed brochures for Malamute owners and gave presentations at the annual meeting, in the *AKC Gazette*, and in the *AMCA Newsletter*. Both the American Veterinary Medical Association and the American Animal Hospital Association presented research on dwarfs at their national conventions so that veterinarians could acquaint themselves with the problem and with the Malamute Club's efforts to control it. Through the vet-

erinarians it was possible to reach many owners who were not AMCA members.

Dr. Fletch and Dr. Smart coined a new term for the problem—chondrodysplasia, meaning "faulty cartilage"—because the term "dwarf" was confusing for both owners and veterinarians. Veterinarians associated it with the dwarfism found in Hereford cattle while owners thought that it meant a miniature Malamute.

Today the project has become far more successful than its authors ever dreamed possible. It has reached breeders and owners around the entire globe and gained the admiration of the veterinary community. It has become a landmark for other breed clubs. Much of its success, however, results from the early support and cooperation of some of the most influential people in the breed. Many of these breeders went through the arduous and sometimes heartbreaking task of test-breeding their entire kennel. They provided a magnificent example of courage and vigorous action in those early days, and their contribution to the success of the project and the welfare of the breed cannot be measured.

Dozens of people have donated, and continue to donate, significant amounts of time to administer the project. These unsung volunteers are the soul of the program, and it is through their efforts that this unwieldy project continues to benefit the breed. The story is one in which breeders and owners can take unabashed pride. Like the phoenix, the fight against chondrodysplasia rose out of the ashes of despair and confusion and became one of the great success stories of purebred dogs.

Note the high rear, short, bowed legs, and Basset Hound look of this moderately chondrodysplastic female. Courtesy Sally Stephens.

OPHTHALMIC DISEASE

The Canine Eye Registry Foundation (CERF) was established in 1975 to collect research and disseminate information about canine eye diseases. Like the OFA, they issue clearance certificates based on ophthalmic examination reports submitted to them. Eye exams must be done by a certified veterinary ophthalmologist and, unlike OFA, can be done on puppies but need to be repeated annually.

HEMERALOPIA

Hemeralopia or "day blindness" is a hereditary disease of the retina involving a partial or complete lack of cone development and eventual degeneration of those which do develop. This leads finally to a retina with only rod photoreceptors, resulting in a classic set of symptoms.

Between two and four months of age, affected dogs usually begin bumping into objects. On very sunny days they demonstrate sight deficits which obviously improve in low light. The condition will gradually worsen.

Because the symptoms are similar to central progressive retinal atrophy (CPRA), dogs suspected of vision abnormalities should be seen by a veterinary ophthalmologist. With hemeralopia, no lesions are identifiable through normal ophthalmic examination; whereas, in CPRA (which is not reported as frequently in Alaskan Malamutes), characteristic lesions are visible.

Hemeralopia has an autosomal recessive inheritance mode and can be eliminated by sound breeding practices. The attention drawn to this ailment by the AMCA and responsible breeders has significantly reduced its occurance in the breed. To prevent its proliferation in the gene pool, the need for constant surveillance of breeding stock is obvious.

PROGRESSIVE RETINAL ATROPHY

Progressive Retinal Atrophy (PRA) is caused by cellular degeneration in the retina. It is transmitted genetically by what researchers believe to be an autosomal recessive gene. The first symptoms are slight night blindness that worsens as the disease progresses. The dog may hesitate to go out at night or to enter a dark room. He might go up stairs but refuse to go down them; he may not want to jump inside a dark car. Eventually he will become blind.

Ophthalmic examination will detect PRA, but only after symptoms begin. Until then, the eye will be normal.

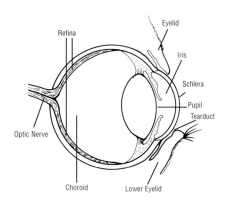

The structure of the canine eye. Light enters the eye through the pupil. Images are focused on the retina and transmitted via the optic nerve to the brain.

The age of the dog at onset is quite variable, so periodic eye examinations for Malamutes are essential. This is why CERF certification, unlike the OFA's, must be renewed periodically.

Affected dogs should never be bred. Part of the problem with current methods of detection is that older dogs may have already been bred before any signs appeared. In such a case, the owners of the progeny should be notified. Ongoing genetic research is under way to develop a DNA test to identify carriers as well as affected dogs not yet exhibiting symptoms.

OTHER INHERITED EYE DEFECTS

Many other inherited disorders impair canine vision including central progressive retinal atrophy, retinal dysplasia, microphthalmia, and congenital cataracts. None of these are particular to nor reported in high incidence in the Alaskan Malamute to date.

However, breeders must always remember that the gene frequency within the breeding population can be dramatically affected when two carriers are bred and the resulting progeny are incorporated to a breeding plan. The following experience is a dramatic example of how dormant genes can suddenly come to the forefront and why exams of breeding stock are valuable. Any suspected vision or other hereditary problem in a young animal should be pursued to a definitive diagnosis by a qualified veterinarian.

CATARACTS IN THE ALASKAN MALAMUTE
by Linda M. Dowdy

I had heard that Malamutes did not have eye problems so many times; I just assumed it to be true. Consequently, I never bothered to have my dogs' eyes checked.

About two years ago my naive faith was shattered when a bitch from my kennel was diagnosed with cataracts. Horrified by the revelation, I started contacting owners of dogs I had sold, making arrangements to have an ophthalmologist check their eyes. As I spent that entire summer shepherding dogs through her clinic, each trip became an ordeal of suspense. I dreaded the results but knew I had to ascertain the status of those dogs.

During that agonizing summer, a total of thirty-four Malamutes from my kennel had their eyes checked. Of those, six were diagnosed as having cataracts and one was termed "suspicious." The "suspicious" reading was on a nine-year-old bitch, whose eyes were also showing the normal changes associated with aging. The natural aging of her eyes prevented a positive diagnosis.

According to the ophthalmology texts, posterior subcapsular cataract occurs in Malamutes and is similar to that seen in Siberian Huskies. They usually appear by the dog's first birthday as a triangle in the subcapsular area which slowly expands to cover much of the subcapsular cortex. After a variable time of expansion, the cataract stabilizes, so complete blindness is unusual. Those few with extensive cataracts are usually in the younger group (one year to eighteen month), or in older dogs (eight years or older), that have had intraocular inflammation. Affected dogs do not necessarily have visual deficiencies, but when they do, veterinarians can remove the lens.

Although a genetic mode of inheritance has not been established, breeders report a familial tendency. Veterinarians advise against breeding affected animals and suggest screening all siblings and closely related animals.

After recovering from the initial shock of finding cataracts in my dogs, I began trying to make some sense of the results. Although thirty-four dogs do not constitute an adequate statistical population, I made the following observations:

• Both parents of every affected dog had clear eyes,

• Every affected dog but one had a common grandmother. The exception had a grandfather which was a sibling to this common grandmother,

• The common grandmother was the older dog that was screened as "suspicious."

Even though the mode of inheritance is not yet understood, a few measures seem logical and desirable for my future breeding plans. All affected dogs have been removed from consideration as future breeding stock. The sons and daughters of the common grandmother have been removed from my breeding program. Even though they themselves have clear eyes, experience has shown their offspring can be affected.

Future breeding plans will minimize or remove the suspected transmitter from my pedigrees. Whether these actions are sufficient remains to be seen. Only time will tell. At least I can face the future with the knowledge that I am attempting to deal with the problem.

It is wildly improbable that I am the only breeder whose dogs are affected by cataracts. It is much more likely that the problem is present throughout the breed. Because cataracts are hard to detect without professional examination and visual impairment is minimal, assuming, as I did, that Malamutes don't have eye problems is very easy.

More than twenty years ago, Malamute breeders came face to face with the problem we know today as chondrodysplasia or dwarfism. Because it wasn't swept under the rug, we now have a successful program to control it. Cataracts are another problem that breeders must acknowledge. Ignoring it, or using the excuse that nothing can be done because the mode of inheritance is unknown, will do nothing more than carry the problem downstream and make it harder to control in the future.

We, the breeders, have replaced the laws of natural selection. As such, we now bear the responsibility of keeping the breed as free as possible of genetic problems. Accepting that responsibility means adding cataract screening to all the other tests which we currently do. The eyes of your dogs may appear to be clear, but if you don't have them checked, you will never know for certain.

IMMUNE-MEDIATED DISEASE

HYPOTHYROIDISM

Both adult and juvenile onset hypothyroidism results from a lack of circulating thyroid hormone. Juvenile onset is so rare that only six cases are reported in the literature. Adult onset is primarily the result of lymphocytic thyroiditis (an immune-mediated disease) or idiopathic atrophy of the thyroid, which means that the cause has yet to be determined. Both forms probably affect the Alaskan Malamute equally.

Many breeders feel the incidence of thyroid problems is fairly high. However, until recently, no central collating organization has collected statistics or compiled reports, so this belief is only speculative. The open thyroid registry begun in 1996 by the OFA should provide valuable and valid information about the problem at last.

Recognizing the clinical signs is important. Most of them relate to the involvement of thyroid hormone in basic metabolism. The most common signs are lethargy and dullness, hair loss, and obesity. Some animals also have no heat cycles or abnormal ones, darkening of the skin, and/or cold intolerance, and a few have a lowered heart rate. The gradual degeneration of the thyroid means that signs of disease may not be recognizable as such until the dog is between four- and ten-years of age.

Diagnosis of hypothyroidism by blood tests (T3, T4, and Free T4 and TSH) should be carried out on any suspected animal. Treatment is with a synthetic hormone given orally.

Immune-mediated hypothyroidism results from abnormalities of the dog's immune system. Other causes of thyroid atrophy are not known but may possibly be of familial origin. In all breeds, certain lines of dogs have been incriminated as being "carriers," but no concrete proof supports this contention. Until absolute evidence of the underlying mechanism is found, it should be assumed to have some genetic origin. Affected individuals should not used in a breeding program.

AUTOIMMUNE SKIN DISEASE

Autoimmune skin diseases fall into two major categories: 1) the pemphigus (Greek for blister) or pemphigoid diseases, and 2) the erosive-ulcerative diseases such as systemic lupus or discoid lupus erythematosus. To diagnose this, your veterinarian will send skin biopsies to a laboratory for examination.

Pemphigus—The different types of pemphigus are classified according to the location and severity of the lesions. They are unsightly and can be painful for the dog. Most common is pemphigus foliaceous. In both foliaceous and pemphigus erythematosus, a scaly rash occurs around the eyes, ears, and nose. It is not unusual for the foot pads to become thickened and scaly.

Pemphigus vulgaris also has red, oozing lesions that crust and scale, but in addition to being found on the head and neck, lesions occur on the mucosal areas of the body, including the lips, nostrils, eyelids, prepuce, vulva, and anus. Even the nailbeds can be involved.

In pemphigus vegetans, the skin on the body is affected with wartlike growths. These become covered with pimples and ooze fluid.

Pemphigus can be treated by suppressing the immune-system response that caused the problem in the first place. Antibiotics also may be used to treat the lesions. Abatement of symptoms, however, means only that the disease is in remission, not cured, and relapses may well occur.

Lupus Erythematosus—Dogs have two lupus erythematosus diseases, systemic, which is like that found in humans, and discoid. In systemic lupus erythematosus or SLE, many organs are affected, including the joints, kidneys, blood, and skin. Eventually, affected dogs succumb to the disease.

On the other hand, the discoid variety (DLE) is more benign and seems to affect mainly the tissue of the nose, although other areas can be involved. The dog looks as if it has a very bad sunburn, and the nose may have loss of pigment and a "cobblestone" appearance. Exposure to sun and stress may worsen the condition. DLE may be controlled with Vitamin E supplementation or with tetracycline and niacinamide.[2]

What causes autoimmune problems to arise remains the topic of much medical research. They may be triggered by external factors—stress, environment, exposure to chemicals, vaccinations, viruses, or a host of other agents. Regardless, many scientists feel that the ability to trigger the disease is carried genetically, and until further research proves otherwise, affected dogs should never be bred.

DEMODECTIC MANGE

Demodectic mange is caused by a tiny mite which is found on the skin of many animals and is a harmless parasite most of the time. In dogs with weakened immune systems, whether from genetic propensity or stress, the mites may cause a reaction that can vary in intensity. Slight patches of hair loss in the head area or feet are often the earliest signs. Untreated, it may stay confined to the extremities, or it may generalize over the body.

The stress of pregnancy may induce symptoms. When it appears on the mother, some or all of the puppies may also be affected, although their symptoms do not usually appear until after they are subjected to stress. If weaning does not bring it out, going to a new home will.

Demodectic mange is diagnosed by microscopic examination of skin scrapings. It is usually treated with a special dip available from your veterinarian. Supplementation with Vitamin C sometimes helps in conjunction with other treatment. Reports of successful treatment with daily, high doses of Ivermectin have given hope to dogs with severe cases resistant to treatment. Some dogs still must be euthanized.

While the mite is not inherited, the sensitivity to them seems to be, a proclivity which is probably related to an underlying immune problem. Certainly, a female that demonstrates demodectic mange once may exhibit it again, and affected puppies may repeat the cycle if they are bred.

SKIN DISEASES

SUPERFICIAL PYODERMA

Superficial pyodermas are lesions commonly called "hot spots" because of their appearance, although the clinical description is "cutaneous abscess." These lesions tend to appear rapidly. The most common infective agent is staphylococcus bacteria, which is exacerbated by other predisposing factors such as fleas, matted hair, allergies, and even hormonal imbalances. Hot spots are most often seen during shedding season. They may develop in Malamutes fed high-protein, high-fat diets during very hot weather. Whether directly inherited or secondary to an inherited condition, the tendency toward hot spots can run in families.

The dog's incessant licking removes all hair from the lesion itself and keeps it moist, while hair around the margins is frequently matted. Treatment consists of cleansing the affected area with antibacterial shampoo, often accompanied by antibiotic therapy. However, chronic recurrence indicates the need for a definitive diagnosis through blood tests and skin biopsy.

ZINC RESPONSIVE DERMATOSIS

Once common in the Malamute, zinc responsive dermatosis (ZRD) has been greatly reduced in recent years according to most dermatologists. Typical signs are crusty lesions that appear on the nose, around the eyes and lips. Several littermates are usually affected, beginning at just a few months of age.

These lesions are caused by either a zinc deficiency or an inability to absorb zinc. In either case, treatment consists of supplementation with zinc sulfate. Reformulation of some commercial food formulas has corrected the former problem. The ability to absorb zinc is thought to be genetic in origin, although this has never been proven in Malamutes. Until more information is available, affected dogs should probably not be bred.

ALASKAN MALAMUTE COAT FUNK

Alaskan Malamute breeders have been talking for some time about a recurring type of coat problem. Their shared information indicated that it appeared with enough frequency to warrant further investigation. For want of a better name, the syndrome has been called "coat funk." Whether this is a new disease or related to an old one is unknown.

The symptoms seem to appear primarily in males, beginning in mid to old age, although an affected female has been reported. As youngsters, the dogs have typical, healthy coats, but as they age, the guard hairs around the neck begin to break off. At first this may appear to be damage from a collar, but eventually the rest of the guard coat breaks off or falls out, leaving behind only the woolly-undercoat, giving the dog a sheep-like appearance. (The undercoat is not shed like normal coat.) The head, face, and spinal area may continue to be unaffected, but the guard coat will be sparse in those areas. The tail may be affected at any time, early or later, depending on the dog. Since the coat does not shed normally, the old hair takes on the reddish tinge of dead or sun-damaged hair. This may be connected with the disease, or may be unrelated.

Once shaved or plucked, the dog may grow in a normal coat, but symptoms eventually reappear. Interestingly, the same process occurs with castrated dogs.

Some symptoms resemble those associated with hypothyroidism, but testing reveals affected dogs with both normal and abnormal thyroid levels. Investigators are trying to see if diseases with similar symptoms found in other breeds are the same as this one.[3]

This once-normal-coated dog now has a bad case of "coat funk." There is nothing to do but remove the dead coat and wait to see if it will grow back normally. However, the disease nearly always recurs.

OTHER HEALTH PROBLEMS

POLYNEUROPATHY

Polyneuropathy is a disease of possible genetic origin that has been observed in Alaskan Malamutes. Symptoms consist of progressive weakness in the hind legs, sometimes resulting in paralysis. In some dogs these symptoms begin as early as seven months of age, but are more commonly seen between twelve to eighteen months.[4]

The disease is devastating, since it causes temporary if not permanent paralysis of the dog's hindquarters. Hopefully, further research will reveal more about its symptoms and causes. Most sources assume it to be a recessive autosomal condition. Dogs with symptoms should be suspended from breeding until conclusive studies prove otherwise.

IDIOPATHIC EPILEPSY

Assuming a genetic cause for every case of epilepsy can be "dangerous for breeders. . . Only when other possible causes have been checked as far as possible and have been eliminated should the breeder begin to consider idiopathic epilepsy."[5] However, when the search for underlying causes of recurrent seizures offers no answers, a breeder faced with this diagnosis must consider the likelihood of genetic origin.

The Alaskan Malamute is among the breeds with a higher than normal incidence of inherited epilepsy. Research on inherited epilepsy has been done in many breeds, and the findings are not always consistent from breed to breed or study to study. However, clearly the mode of inheritance is quite complex, possibly "involving at least six gene pairs [taking] three matches out of those six pairs to produce epilepsy. . . . In plain language, . . . you can breed two normal dogs and get all epileptics, or you can bred two epileptics and get all normal dogs."[6]

Seizures are generalized and in about a quarter of the cases begin between twelve- and twenty-four months of age which means that dogs may have been bred before any symptoms appear. Some studies suggest a correlation between early onset and an increasingly high degree of inbreeding on a carrier or carriers.[7]

Inherited epilepsy appears more frequently in males than females. This may be due to a sex-linked suppressor on the X chromosome or to differences in hormones. Reported ratios range from five to one to three to one, depending on the breed.[8]

"[M]ost seizures will occur in the home or kennel, and only rarely when the dog is under stress at a show or other function. In this respect idiopathic epilepsy may differ from seizures induced by flashing lights and other stress factors. It does, however, mean that dogs may have fits in the privacy of their kennel without the owner being aware of the problem, and it means the epileptic can be shown (knowingly or otherwise) and win in the show ring."[9]

The only real way to reduce the risk is to "isolate and identify problem animals and then avoid or reduce risks by not inbreeding to these dogs or by not doubling up on them."[10] Unfortunately, epilepsy is more often a secret than an acknowledged problem, and identification of carriers may be done only by inference, observing affected progeny, and seeing what common ancestors recur.

GASTRIC DILATATION–VOLVULUS

Also known as "bloat" and/or "torsion," gastric dilatation-volvulus (GDV) is an acute, life-threatening emergency which almost always requires surgery. It occurs in many deep-chested breeds, including the Alaskan Malamute.

Despite extensive research, an absolute cause has not been discovered nor has a genetic mode of inheritance been identified, although it is frequently seen in related dogs. For some reason, the dog swallows excessive air or produces excessive gas, causing the stomach to bloat (dilatation) and sometimes twist on its long axis (volvulus).

Recognition of its onset is extremely important and immediate veterinary care is imperative. Initially, there will be an abnormal enlargement of the dog's abdomen at the rear of the rib cage characteristic of the "bloat" stage of the disease. The bloating is normally followed by non-productive vomiting and rapid deterioration of the animal's condition.

Opinions about effective treatment vary. Generally, everyone agrees that GDV patients must receive rapid intravenous fluid as well as treatment for shock. Decompression of the bloated stomach must be accomplished rapidly, and may be all that is necessary. However, when bloat is accompanied by a twisting of the stomach, surgical treatment is required. Seventy to seventy-five percent of dogs treated with medical therapy alone will have another episode of GDV.

Since gulping air is recognized as one cause, the logical conclusion is that gobbling food may contribute to bloat. A large percentage of animals prone to GDV are kenneled in an environment which encourages "competition" for food. This or any condition which causes rapid food consumption, should be avoided. Males kenneled with or next to females in season tend to "inhale" their food and over-indulge drinking water so they can turn their attentions to the female more quickly. Careful management, limiting the amount of food and water, giving water before, not after feeding, and avoiding rapid changes in diet will help prevent the occurrence of bloating. When operating on a dog with GDV, veterinarians can stitch the stomach in place to prevent rotation should the problem occur again.

ENDNOTES
1.   Sources used are: Kirk & Bonagura, Current Veterinary Therapy XI *Small Animal Practice* (1992); Robert L. Peiffer, Jr., *Small Animal Ophthalmalogy: A Problem Oriented Approach* (1989); Muller, Kirk, Scott, *Small Animal Dermatology* (1989); Ettinger, et.al., *Textbook of Veterinary Internal Medicine*, third edition (1989); Birchard & Sherding, *Manual of Small Animal Practice* (1994).
2.   Jocelynn Jacobs-Knoll, DVM, "Health Column—Autoimmune Skin Diseases," AMCA *Newsletter*, 43:3 (March, 1995), 25-27.
3.   Jocelyn Jacobs-Knoll, DVM., "The Coat Funk," *Malamute Quarterly*, 12:3 (Spring, 1994), 8-9. Dr. Knoll is currently researching coat funk and welcomes information on affected dogs. If you have one, contact the AMCA secretary for further information.
4.   Polyneuropathy has been reported in Norway (12 cases, 10 dead); in the U.S. (10 cases, 9 dead), and in Australia.
5.   Malcolm B. Willis, *Genetics of the Dog*, 181.
6.   Roger M. Clemmons, D.V.M., quoted in Owen, 9.
7.   Willis, 184.
8.   Willis, 187.
9.   Willis, 182.
10. Willis, 187.

The future of the breed lies in the quality of today's upcoming sires and dams. Adair N Hug's Strategic Move has an exceptionally good profile an excellent tail, correct ears, lovely neck, correct coat and dark pigment. Breeder/owners, Joe and Robin Hug. Cott photo.

18

THE ALASKAN MALAMUTE PUPPY

At birth, Malamute puppies weigh only about a pound and look more like guinea pigs than dogs. Their eyelids are sealed and do not open until they are about two weeks old; their ears are closed and pinned up close to their heads. As the ears open, the ear flaps drop. They should begin rising again from the age of four weeks on. The needle-like first or "milk" teeth begin appearing between three and four weeks.

Puppies have a short, soft, dense, fuzzy coat with scattered guard hairs sticking out from the body. Replacement by an adolescent coat begins at about twelve weeks. Heralded by a band of slicker, darker hair ringing the base of the tail, the new hair growth continues forward from the tail, along the back, down the sides, and across the front. Eventually the only remaining puppy fuzz is on the ears and behind the cheeks. During this process, the remaining puppy coat becomes brittle and dull and may even change color slightly. The new coat is slick and lies flat.

While some breeds display drastic changes in color from puppy to adult, the Alaskan Malamute's puppy color somewhat resembles that of the adult dog, although even experienced breeders may have trouble predicting *exactly* what color an adult will be, especially if they are unfamiliar with the lines.

The distribution of white remains fairly consistent, although narrow blazes on the head and dark markings under the eyes may gradually disappear, as will tan on the backs of the ears. Some puppies have muddy-looking, dark hairs around the front and sides of the leg that extend almost to the elbow, and dark hairs on the sides of the face. Scattered throughout the sooty color are a few longer, silvery-white hairs. This muddy color usually disappears by the time the puppy is six months old, although the resulting white will probably be a light cream rather than a bright white.

A dark stripe down the back of a puppy tells you that the adult will be seal color. Gray puppies, the most common Malamute color, may darken or lighten with maturity. White puppies will stay white, as will reds, although the intensity of the red color may change.

The term "pigment" most commonly refers to skin color, especially that of the nose, lips, eye-rims, and pads. Here, newborn puppies should have black pigment, although some have pink, especially on the nose. This fills in with dots of black until it is completely colored, but the pads may be pink or have pink splotches into adulthood. Some sled dog breeders prefer black pads because they believe the darker pads are tougher and more readily withstand punishing trail conditions.

As the puppy grows, his muzzle and stubby little legs begin to lengthen. Development is from the head back, so puppies begin pulling themselves around by the front legs almost as soon as they are born. Soon they are rising on

A ten-day-old white puppy. Eyes and ears are just opening. Photo © Mormont de Henau.

A mother and her young litter. Note the nice-size, homemade whelping box. Photo by F. Seidl, Czech Republic.

Right: Individual attention will help overcome the independent nature of loners. These pups are often found away from the others.

Far right: The large dorsal stripe on this puppy's back indicates that it will be a dark seal color at maturity.

A new litter of reds and grays. There are more puppies than nipples, so they need close observation to make sure each puppy has it's turn nursing. If there is a disparity in size, you can remove the larger pups periodically while the small ones nurse. Photo courtesy Hug A Bear Kennel.

OH, THOSE EARS!

Developmental timetables are subject to a great deal of variation, and the age at which ears become erect varies between lines. Many factors contribute to their rising. Among them are: the size and thickness of the ear, ear placement, shape and set. Ear cartilage can be damaged or torn during rough play or it may not stiffen quickly because of the growing dog's metabolic demands.

Many puppies have erect ears by the age of eight weeks, some as early as four. However, pups with very heavy or very thin ear leather may still have soft ears at three months. Ear placement, especially a very low-set, can exacerbate the difficulties. If you are worried, you should consult your breeder who can give you a better idea of what to expect for your dog.

When teething begins between four and six months, many dogs relax an already-erect ear to relieve the pressure on swollen gums exerted by the muscle which runs from the jaw to the base of the ear. If the ear was up and the puppy dropped it, you needn't worry; it will return to its erect position once he has his teeth. However, if the ears are still not up and teething begins, worry is appropriate. Problem ears continuing into this developmental phase may worsen. A consultation with the breeder is definitely in order.

This seal and white puppy's ears are just starting to stand erect. Courtesy Chris Eisenga.

Eight-week-old Frostfield puppy. This pup was born solid black.

Four-week-old males at Arctic Legend Kennel have drop ears characteristic of this age. Photo courtesy of Chris Eisenga.

Stormy Monday's Hurricane, a four-month-old puppy bred by Parry Douvet. The ears are fully erect and the puppy has good proportions and substance for this age.

Although still a patient mom, the dam is probably getting anxious to wean these puppies. Puppies learn from their dam—a good reason for leaving them with her rather than placing them at six weeks. Photo courtesy of Del Biagio.

A long, low pan, or a circular pan with a hole in the center, allows all puppies equal access to the food. Photo courtesy of Del Biagio.

the front legs and eventually taking tentative steps with very wobbly rears. Some puppies are stumbling about at two weeks, while others are still scooting. By four weeks all the puppies should be up and walking well.

From six to sixteen weeks, puppies literally explode with growth, and a shadow of the adult can be seen in the form of the youngster. Some changes are so rapid that the pup looks different from day to day. Such a high metabolic rate requires a great deal of rest and a good diet. Bursts of energetic play may well be followed by an almost comatose sleep.

PUPPY BEHAVIOR

The rapid physical growth rate would be totally eclipsed by the changes which occur in the brain, could these be seen as easily. Assuming a normal gestation period, the brain of a puppy is not fully functional until the dog is about seven weeks old. Because his inherited temperament is almost untouched by his experiences up to this point, this age is the ideal time to do a Puppy Aptitude Test or some other form of evaluation.

Puppyhood is the most critical period of a dog's life. The breeder has an enormous responsibility for and influence on his charges, which is why the breeder from whom

you acquire your puppy can be just as important as which puppy you choose. During this time span the puppy begins his relationships with other dogs, people, children, and the world around him.

The litter forms his first pack, where Mom is the leader. The rough-and-tumble play between siblings teaches the puppy how to interact with other dogs, while his mother teaches him proper dog manners, what to fear, and whom to trust. While a puppy can be removed from his litter and mother at seven weeks without physical detriment, he will miss many valuable lessons that a good home with his mother and siblings can provide.

Puppies will accommodate changes well from seven to twelve weeks of age and can easily go to a new home, but breeders often keep puppies longer to better evaluate their show potential. Some breeders believe that the enriching experiences which they can provide will offset the heightened separation anxiety the older puppy experiences upon leaving his canine companions.

Kennels raising working sled dogs may keep puppies for training and sell them as young adults once their working ability is confirmed. If you are interested in serious sledding, you should check with this type of breeder but be prepared to accept an older dog.

CRITICAL PHASES OF DEVELOPMENT

(Contributed by Carol Williams, Kotzebue-Heritage Malamutes.)

Whether breeder or buyer, the owner's responsibility to the Malamute, to himself, and to his family is to know the innate potential the seven-week-old puppy offers their common future. A puppy's greatest potential is multifactored, having genetically clean parents, being raised in a balanced environment of food, shelter, exercise, training, and love. This is a sound basis for any dog, whether he is to be a pet, show, working, obedience, or therapy dog.

Breeders need to ensure that their puppies make the difficult adjustment of leaving the litter with the least chance of developing behavior problems later. As the breeder cares for the new brood, her actions influence their behavior. The seeds of adult behavior tend to be implanted during highly critical, formative periods in both children and puppies, except that with puppies, time is measured in weeks and months, rather than years. Insight into these periods of development give the breeder and new owner a broader understanding of puppy behavior and development.

NEONATAL: BIRTH TO 2 WEEKS

Even though the mother tends the puppies almost all the time, handling should be done twice daily by lifting the puppies to weigh them. Cradle each one on his back in your arms for about a minute while rubbing his belly gently with your fingers.

TRANSITION: 2 TO 3 WEEKS

Eyes and ears are open. Puppies try to walk, wag their tails, and join in group howls. Continue with gentle handling. Young children can also gently handle the puppies once a day to give the pups a pleasant experience with preschool children, who smell and move differently from adults or adolescents.

CANINE SOCIALIZATION: 3 TO 7 WEEKS

The pups bark, bite, chase, play games, and mount one another. Some breeders separate the mother from her puppies at four weeks. This is not recommended—do not buy a puppy from this type of breeder. At this stage, the pup needs its mother for the discipline and training she imparts. If the pups are deprived of this, behavior problems will occur. Continue to handle the pups as often as possible.

Weaning starts at about four weeks. The mother settles into more set feeding times and spends more time away from the litter. Facilitate this by giving her access to an area away from the pups. From four to six weeks, puppies begin eating human-made food. Around this time, mother stops her cleanup efforts because of the food change and the puppies' age. Set regular feeding times to help regularize bowel movements, and if possible, make the out-of-doors available to the pups after feeding, before bed, and upon awakening. When a pup eliminates in the proper place, make sure someone is present to praise him. No scolding, hitting, rough handling, or rubbing the puppy's nose in the excrement will help at this stage, or any other for that matter. If the puppies cannot go outside, line a far corner of their pen away from their sleeping area with newspapers.

Among the social practices which may cause permanent trauma and should be avoided are: rough handling by anyone at any time; preferential treatment toward any puppy, creating "outsider" puppies, and overexposure to people.

ATTRACTION: 5 TO 7 WEEKS

The puppy notices other things and begins to form attractions to people. Threatening sounds, gestures, scolding, punishment, physical force, or the loud whap of a newspaper roll violates the concept of social attraction. Introducing new people at this time will help the puppies make successful adjustments to their new homes.

HUMAN SOCIALIZATION: 7 TO 12 WEEKS

At this age, a puppy has the brain waves of an adult dog and the intellectual capacity to process his experiences. Ask an experienced administrator to give the Puppy Aptitude Test, then use the information it provides to match your puppies and buyers. Few buyers will be sophisticated enough to equate puppy behavior with adult temperament, so you will need to explain a lot to them.

While emotional attachment has its place in puppy selection, the significance of puppy behavior must be an aid to placement. Attention to both will promote a long life of human/canine companionship.

FEAR IMPACT: 8 TO 11 WEEKS

Adventurous puppies will be wandering far from the security of the den and mother by ten weeks. An animal this young is incapable of much in the way of self-defense, so to counter the drive to explore, nature has given the youngster a pre-programmed fearfulness. Bad experiences at this age will be indelibly fixed in the dog's memory and although his fears can be allayed, they will never entirely disappear.

SENIORITY CLASSIFICATION: 12 TO 16 WEEKS

At this stage the puppy puts humans to the test. He will either become your leader or you will become his. A puppy should never win this contest. Tug-of-war is not a good game to play; winning such a contest only encourages dominance.

FLIGHT INSTINCT: 4 TO 8 MONTHS

This period varies with the individual, but it usually occurs during the teething period when teeth and jaws are developing. No matter what his behavior before this time, when he enters this stage the puppy will push at his boundaries. Do not trust him off-leash; even if he came before, he is likely to assert his freedom now. If you allow him to get away with this, you will struggle with this issue indefinitely.

FEAR OF THE UNKNOWN: 6 TO 14 MONTHS

The formerly curious puppy again reacts to new situations, sights, and sounds with fear. This can be a stressful time since the puppies are still teething as well. Reprimanding or scolding the pup will only heighten his fear, while petting him and reassuring him will reward his response. Instead, allow him time to see that his fear is unjustified and treat him with tolerance.

YOUNG ADULTHOOD AND MATURITY: 1 TO 4 YEARS

Continue training. Attend classes on a building block method and use instructors who understand that independence is part of what makes a Malamute a Malamute.

A litter of Poker Flat puppies practice being sled dogs in their invisible harness. Photo by Jim Kuehl.

19

EVALUATING ALASKAN MALAMUTE PUPPIES

Observing generations of dogs teaches those especially devoted breeders who continue to breed year after year to translate a puppy's appearance and personality into that of an adult dog. When you are just starting out you will not have the benefit of this experience and must rely on other resources such as your dog's breeder, friends, and information in books and magazines.

Look at puppy pictures of adults you know to see how the puppy developed into the adult. If other breeders working with your lines keep records, refer to them, and begin keeping records of your own. They will yield reliable yardsticks for the future.

EVALUATING CONFORMATION

Your puppy selection priorities will be weighted by what you want to do with your dog, although soundness should take precedence over everything else. An attractive dog is an asset in the conformation ring, but cosmetic considerations are secondary to structure and temperament in a working breed. In the same vein, a submissive dog will probably lack the sparkle needed in the show ring but may make a great team dog. An independent dog may become a great lead dog but is a poor choice for obedience. Keeping your intentions in mind and choosing a puppy that fits them will make both of you happier in the long run.

SOUNDNESS

To be sound, a dog must first be healthy. Positive genetic screens on the parents will decrease the probability that puppies will be affected. Some physical characteristics remain constant throughout the different growth stages, while others change with the dog's changing body. Between seven and nine weeks is probably the best time in which to evaluate a puppy. After that, rapid changes occur until the dog is a young adult.

Regardless of age, the Malamute puppy's legs should be straight columns of support, both when moving and standing. The forelegs, when viewed from the front, should form a straight line from the elbow to the foot; viewed from the rear, the hind legs should also form a straight line from hip joint to hock to foot. Elbows, toes, hocks, and stifles should point neither in nor out.

From the side, the slope of the pelvis should almost parallel the slope of the shoulder. The angle which forms the stifle or knee in the rear is analogous to the angle which forms the point of shoulder. An additional angle forms in the rear where the upper and lower legs meet at the hock joint.

When I grow up, what will I be? Artwork by Dorothy Redding.

An adult will probably have less angulation in the rear than he shows as a puppy. In some lines, the shoulder layback and the angle formed at the point of shoulder, (where the upper arm and shoulder meet) remains constant, while in other lines the angle decreases. However, a puppy with steep shoulders and a straight rear will be just as straight, if not straighter, as an adult.

Light eyes will always be light, although they may darken somewhat with age, and eye shape is fairly constant despite the head's many changes. While a dip in the spine of a puppy will be present in the adult, a slight arch or "roach" may remain or may straighten out with maturity.

Unfortunately, uneven growth patterns may make the topline impossible to assess and also influence the dynamics of the dog's gait. When the slope is back-to-front rather than front-to-back, the puppy will move differently. Other characteristics which are difficult to assess in the young dog are height and size, length of ears, feet, and head shape.

THE PICK PUPPY

Choosing a conformation show puppy can be quite difficult, as is describing what you should look for, since different lines develop differently. In one line a youngster with front legs too close together may be fine when his chest drops and broadens in adulthood. In another, the chest may broaden early, so a youngster with a narrow chest and close front legs may stay the same in adulthood. Some lines seem to come together at certain ages, and knowing this can help you determine the best time to choose. Heed the advice of breeders experienced with your bloodline.

Assuming that the puppy is in a "together" growth phase, the most important single factor in selection is balance. All parts of the dog should fit together well and be in proportion. The well-balanced puppy stands squarely from all angles and moves with a free and easy gait.

Soundness is paramount no matter what you want to do with your dog. Good feet and a proper coat are important to a show dog, and essential to a sledder. A show puppy should walk and carry his tail with confidence; even better, he should have a cocky attitude. A scissors bite is a must, and dark eyes and symmetrical markings, definite pluses for the show puppy.

Be wary of a pup with several minor faults such as light eyes and a splash coat, even if he looks like a perfect Malamute in miniature. If these minor problems are compounded by others that emerge later, you will be disappointed in the show ring.

Future champion Fate's Little Miss Priss at five weeks of age. Owned by Lynda Birmantas.

Some people have an excellent eye for puppies. If you know accomplished breeders, exhibitors, or mushers, ask them to look at your litter and give their opinion, but steel yourself. The apple of your eye may not even be on their list. Listen to them as objectively as possible and try to understand their viewpoint. Whatever you think at the time, wait a few days, then examine the puppies individually again and see if your opinion has changed.

"Amos" at six weeks. Bred by Linda Allen.

"Amos" at three months old.

"Amos," Ch. Wakeen's A Touch O'Texas, full grown. Owned by Lynne Anderson.

The true movement shown by twelve-week-old "Moochie," will help him win Best in Shows in three different countries as an adult.

At four months Moochie is still very balanced. He will grow into his ears and pasterns, and his topline will change. Breeder, Sam Walden.

Better known as Ch. Chinome's Arctic Invader, Moochie is already a winner at six months old.

Adulthood is worth waiting for. Moochie has fulfilled the promise he showed as a youngster and become the most titled Malamute in history.

Right: A typical Kiwalik puppy at eight-and-one-half weeks old.

Far right: Snowbear at five months of age.

Below: Ch. Kiwalik's Snowbear of Kipnuk, ROM, all grown up at four years of age. Breeder, Terry Sewell; Owner, Kenneth Hyatt.

Ch. Hug A Bears Icebr'ker O' Windfall, CD as a puppy. Carol A. Hug, owner.

ANYONE CAN MAKE A MISTAKE

Take comfort in the knowledge that even skilled, experienced breeders can make mistakes. Leonhard Seppala sold his great lead dog Togo as a puppy to Victor Anderson because he "was spoiled and hard to handle."[1] Anderson considered him difficult and mischievous and returned him to Seppala.

Seppala then gave Togo to a friend who was moving to the States and wanted a pet, but the poor woman had nothing but trouble with him. Finally, Togo jumped out her window and ran back to Seppala's kennel. He was caught and returned, only to repeat his performance, breaking loose from a stake-out chain.

Togo ran along beside the team when he was loose and generally made a pest out of himself. As they embarked on one trip, Seppala left instructions that Togo was to be secured in the corral and not to be let out for a day or two.

When the household was asleep, Togo tried to jump the seven-foot wire fence and gashed his leg. His cries awakened the kennel boss, who got him down, but Togo ran away. When Seppala set off the next morning, he thought his team was on the scent of a reindeer, they moved so quickly. It turned out to be Togo, who then spent the entire day harassing the dogs and making mischief. Finally, Seppala wrote,

> I had decided that there was nothing to do but get out an extra harness and give Togo a chance in the team. . . .I put him in close to the wheel in order to watch him carefully. He was working harder than any dog in the team. . . . He was taken out and promoted up toward the lead. By the time we pulled in at

the mouth of the Koyuk he was actually in the lead beside old Rusty. . . . I had found a natural-born leader.[2]

Perhaps more suitable wording would be that a natural-born leader found him. How Leonhard Seppala's life might have been different without his great dog is an open question; certainly the Siberian Husky breed and the race world would have been poorer for the loss of a once-in-a-lifetime sled-dog. Today, a dog like Togo would end up in a shelter, dead on the highway, or at a rescue.

TOOLS FOR TEMPERAMENT EVALUATION

Fortunately, some helpful tools are available to keep this sort of mismatch from happening. The Fishbacks' test is obviously a one-time thing, but a puppy attitude test can be administered several times. It will give you a good idea of what a puppy's basic nature is like and how he is being affected by his training and environment.

PUPPY APTITUDE TESTING

Your observations of puppies with their littermates and other dogs can tell you a lot about how they react with other dogs. The Puppy Aptitude Test (PAT), developed by Volhard, can be used to augment the information that you have about a puppy by revealing how he reacts to people (see Appendices, p. 296). The series of exercises helps an experienced tester to assess a puppy's innate temperament. With it, you can gain valuable insights that will help a new owner maximize the puppy's strengths and bolster his weaknesses.

If no one in your area does temperament testing, a friend can help, although the results will not be as dependable as with an experienced tester. In either case, you should review the procedures yourself and make sure they are carefully followed. After you have had the puppies tested, go over the results of the testing with potential buyers and explain what the evaluation implies about the best ways to work with each puppy. The test procedure is outlined in the Appendix. Further information is available from many sources.

The Dominant Malamute—At the top of the scale are very dominant dogs. Breeders must pay special attention to their placement. Not only should the owners be very assertive, but they should also be thoroughly familiar with

the ways in which dominance is communicated between dogs and able to adapt these methods to their relationship with their pet.

Vicky Jones's article on training in Chapter 3 describes a technique for establishing human dominance early by using the puppy's feeding time. In the wild, the alpha dog gets his pick of the kill, an important indicator of social status. A Malamute that thinks he runs the house will display dominant behavior most obviously and strongly regarding food. When you gain the upper hand at feedingtime you send the dog an important message about his place in the household.

MEL FISHBACK'S PUPPY SELECTION METHOD

Mel and Lee Fishback are well-known mushers who have written extensively about the sledding world. They had a simple test to select puppies with good working attitude. Mel says, "Once a litter of pups is old enough to learn one thing (usually around seven weeks), they're all individually leash tested." This test does not work well on older pups or ones raised apart.

The only equipment needed is a small leather collar (no chokers or chains) and a light leash. Pick up the puppy and take it well away from the pen. "Instead of familiarization with the collar or leash, put the collar right on the pup and snap the leash to it. Then, simply walk away (not backwards, not crouching, not doing any fancy coaxing). Tug the leash lightly and start walking. By doing this, you will quickly see which group each pup falls into." says Mel.

Puppies in Group 1 get the idea almost immediately. Although they may dash here and there, they quickly realize they need to go with you. Occasionally, they might need coaxing, but for the most part, other pups being walked or shouting in the pen draw only curious glances.

From this group came almost every lead dog the Fishback's ever trained, dogs that were leaders for other people, and almost all the best team dogs they had. She says, "These are the real learners and level heads." Even extra shy pups, she said, "took off like rockets during the leash work. They showed plenty of 'go' and ability to cooperate even though they didn't trust the handlers."

The Group 2 pups are often reluctant to walk at first and plaster themselves to the ground. They fight the leash, scream, and throw themselves around. However, continuing to pull on the leash will bring the pup to you. You should pet him, go a few more steps, and repeat. In about ten minutes, he should be doing nicely. These dogs

can make team dogs. As Mel says, "fighters and active resistors can make good dogs as long as they are good active resistors."

Group 3 pups are passive resisters who try to crawl off whenever the leash is slack. If they don't go towards the pen, they try to get under an object, and may whimper or shriek. When the leash is tight, they reluctantly follow, often whimpering, gagging, etc. Eventually, they will follow, but, as Mel describes them, "they want to cuddle up in a sort of sad, hang-dog way when you stop, or they may just sit or stand at a short distance yearning toward the pen or staring into space." Here, "active fighters" will make it on teams, although it takes patience.

The Fishbacks caution against using Group 4 puppies, calling them "anathema" because they are quitters. When the puppy is pulled, he lays down, perhaps even closing his eyes and letting his nose drag in the dirt. If you stop, he'll get up but go down again when the leash tightens. Even after several training sessions when he's following well, he'll still go down when confronted with a new or strange situation.

Of group 4s, Mel says: "You see pups of this disposition constantly in fun matches and even in the puppy classes at dog shows. Usually they are there 'for experience' because the owner has had a previously unhappy experience with the pup on leash. Sometimes it's a shock to the owner who has subscribed to the 'gradual method' of leash training to discover that the pup has been essentially untrained all his life. . . . you cannot 'gradually' introduce a six-month old to a neck line in a team! It's all there from the first moment you hook up the pup, and he'd better by accustomed to obeying tugs on his neck—or else."

Whenever asserting your position becomes necessary, although he may object, turn the puppy on his back and do not release him until he is accepting and calm. Mal puppies should be carried around occasionally. Pick a pup up from behind and hold him off the ground. When he is older and better trained, you can enforce your position by putting him on a Down Stay. These are all non-forceful methods of making your point—you are alpha, boss, master—and enforcing your position and his place in the pack. This should be repeated by every person in the household, not just the primary caretaker.

Very few children have the psychological strength to dominate a Northern dog with an alpha personality. Even a very tough child lacks the physical strength to enforce his will; therefore, dominant dogs should rarely be placed in a home with small children.

Taken as a breed, most Malamutes fall just to the dominant side of average, with fewer individuals at either extreme. Among the many dog breeds, the degree to which dominance is expressed may be quite different. Dealing with a strongly alpha Malamute is light years away from dealing with his Chihuahua counterpart, because selective breeding has encouraged some responses and extinguished others entirely.

Like humans, dogs use both verbal and physical discipline. If a growl does not suffice for a dog, the next step is a nip or a bite. A disciplinary bite from a Malamute (or any other large breed) poses a much more potent danger than a bite from a small dog. In the wild, such an action is entirely natural and is never motivated by cruelty or viciousness. However, it is absolutely unacceptable in a pet, and any tendency to express dominance in this manner must be inhibited by training.

The Malamute bias towards alpha behavior is undoubtedly the natural outcome of their origin. During the centuries in which the Inuit refined their dogs, selection for this type of dog provided them with their leaders. Sled-dogs are not driven like horses. A dog team has no reins. Control rests in the bond between the musher and his leader, and that bond can be as strong as any between people. In a world with few second chances, a musher's survival lies in the abilities of his leader, and the literature and lore of the Arctic abound with stories about this relationship.

The Independent Dog—Another heritage of life in the Arctic is the core of independence found to some extent in all Northern dogs. Malamutes are certainly no exception. They are quite capable of making up their own mind, a necessity for leadership and survival.

The very independent puppy is better placed where he will live inside with the family. Leaving him in a backyard will only reinforce his natural tendency to get by on his own. Even the most independent dog needs companionship.

Raised in close contact with people, these dogs can be very satisfying pets. Since he can be left to his own devices during the day without being miserable, the independent dog thrives in a home where the owners work all day, as long as he receives enough attention at night and on weekends.

The Submissive Dog—The alpha dog has its submissive counterpart in the omega animal. Submission is shown by a variety of expressions, including pawing, licking, tucked tail, lowered gaze, and lowered ears. Confronted with a more dominant animal, the submissive dog lays its ears back, tucks its tail and may raise a hind leg. It may roll onto its back, exposing the neck and belly, wag just the tip of its tail, or urinate.[3]

The submissive dog is a good choice for families with small children. New owners of extremely submissive dogs should be given some guidelines for training. The omega dog seldom requires any kind of harsh correction; a quick, growly "No" usually suffices. In fact, a heavy hand may exacerbate the dog's lack of confidence and cause more problems.

Drawing by Linda Duke.

The submissive Malamute's most annoying traits are pawing and submissive urination. Since these are elicited by circumstances in which the dog feels threatened, any correction only makes the dog more unsure and more likely to repeat its actions.

Obedience training is one of the best ways to build the dog's confidence, since it offers him structure in an uncertain world. Submissive dogs need direction and reassurance. They are eager to please and are very responsive to attention.

The In-Between Dog—Of course, most Malamutes are neither extremely assertive nor extremely submissive, but fall somewhere in-between. The people who belong to these dogs have to be prepared to respond appropriately to the dog's personality. One day, they may have to reinforce their position by putting the dog in a sit or down-stay; the next day they may be cleaning up puddles. Everything depends on circumstance and the temperament of the dog.

ENDNOTES
1.   Ricker/Seppala, 283.
2.   Ricker/Seppala, 286-287.
3.   Carol Lea Benjamin, *Mother Knows Best*, (New York: Howell Book House, Inc., 1987), 53-54.

Ch. Hill Frost Dream Extreme, CGC, was the top AMCA puppy in 1996 shown winning Best of Breed over specials from the Puppy class. Breeder/owners, John and Laura Swire. Photo © Booth Photography.

20

FROM TEENAGER TO ADULT

The horrible truth is that the canine adolescent is not much different from the human one. From the standpoints of both appearance and behavior, this is probably the most challenging growth stage. The young dog is undergoing many exciting changes which are reflected in his maturing body and developing mind.

THE CANINE ADOLESCENT

By adolescence, the puppy coat has been replaced, although traces may still remain around the ears. Like the dog himself, the coat is at an in-between stage. Much coarser than the puppy coat, it usually lies flat and has little undercoat, especially if the weather is warmer.

Exceptions do exist. Some lines have a thick, puffy, stand-out coat at this age which helps mask the teenager's awkward edges. If this is a show-puppy, the owner is lucky indeed, since most of his competition will still be waiting for their swans to emerge!

The Alaskan Malamute should have what is called a "scissors" bite, which means that the insides of the upper front teeth (incisors) meet and engage the outer surface of the bottom front teeth. In addition, the molars on the sides should mesh with the upper teeth, fitting into the nitch between the bottom teeth with equal space on either side.

When the bottom jaw is slightly longer or shifted slightly forward, the teeth, especially the front incisors, may sit one atop the other. This is called an "even" bite, and generally is regarded as less desirable because the teeth tend to wear down more quickly. When the upper ones are so far forward that the surfaces of the incisors do not engage, the bite is overshot. This is analogous to an overbite in humans. On the other hand, when the position of the teeth is reversed, and the lower teeth protrude past the upper teeth, the bite is undershot. According to the standard, the Malamute should never be undershot or overshot.

A correct bite is especially important if the dog is to be shown. A Malamute puppy with an even (level) bite at eight weeks runs the risk of being slightly undershot. Any puppy with a markedly over- or undershot bite should not be selected for a show or breeding quality puppy, especially the latter, for while a judge may overlook a less than perfect bite, no dog with a bad bite should be used in a breeding program. While these conditions can change with maturity, the one to take a chance on these puppies should be the breeder. An unacceptable bite may make an otherwise quality animal available for sale as a pet.

While most dogs lose and grow teeth with no problems, occasional help may be necessary. Sometimes, the adult canine teeth erupt before the baby teeth are shed. If a generous supply of chewies doesn't take care of this, the baby teeth need to be pulled by a veterinarian before they force the adult canines out of alignment.

As the lower jaw grows, forward growth is halted when the lower incisors meet and engage the upper ones. If the upper incisors are too small, this occlusion may not occur, and the resulting bite may appear to be level or even very slightly undershot. This type of occlusion is not uncommon in the Alaskan Malamute. When evaluating the bite, look carefully at the way the upper and lower molars mesh, since this portrays the bite most accurately.

ADOLESCENT GROWTH

Alaskan Malamutes grow rapidly between six and eighteen months. Although most growth occurs during the first year, during the second year the Mal begins filling out. Unfortunately, not all parts grow at the same rate which makes for some very disproportionate animals. For a long time, his feet will look like the dog version of clown shoes, and his ears may make him look like Dumbo. Both these appendages grow to their adult length very quickly; whereas the bones of the legs and skull take much longer to lengthen and broaden.

Sometimes the puppy's legs will be far too long for his body. Other times, his rear will be so high that his tail seems to be on the wrong end! His body will fill out faster than his leg bone, and he'll look like a barrel on sticks. All this just means your dog has still more to grow. Have faith. One day, your gawky teenager will become a mature dog whose parts all fit together.

If you are unfamiliar with large breeds, you may be unprepared for the amount of time they spend sleeping as puppies and adolescents. The high metabolic demands of their rapid growth rate make their sleep much sounder than that of older dogs, who tend to doze or nap.

Because the longitudinal growth of a bone occurs at the ends (epiphyses) rather than in the middle of the bone, when growth is occurring, the epiphyseal plates tend to be enlarged. The degree of the enlargement is often an indication of the eventual size of the dog. While bone growth is occurring, bumpy areas can be felt, especially on the cheeks and skull, and seen, most noticeably at the front pastern. These knobby wrists may cause concern to a person more familiar with medium or small breeds.

Many an owner of very large dogs has made a panicky trip to the veterinarian after seeing a picture of a dog with rickets in a breed book. Even worse, a few veterinarians unfamiliar with large breeds have failed to recognize these growth bumps as normal. Medical treatment is not needed, and any suggestion that the dog needs a cast or wrapping should send you speeding to another veterinarian.

What is not normal or desirable is any *bending* of the pastern or *bowing* of the legs, either in or out. These conditions would certainly warrant a trip to your veterinarian and/or a consultation with your breeder.

ADOLESCENT BEHAVIOR

Like his human counterpart, the teenage dog is busy experimenting with different roles and behaviors. One day he may be cock-of-the-walk, full of swagger and bluster; the next, he may be a shrinking violet. You need to meet these changes with stability, tolerance, and love.

Between four and six months is a good age to start your Mal puppy in obedience classes. Although you may decide to continue in obedience competition, your first classes should be aimed at helping you establish control over your dog, as well as teaching the dog the basics of good manners. He should learn to come when called, heel, sit and down, and stay in those positions. Going to class with other dogs will teach him to respect others and pay attention to you. He will learn to behave with strangers and gain experience about the world outside your house and yard.

If you are interested in other dog sports such as dog shows, weight pull or agility, some introductory training at this age is also appropriate. The control and deportment that you and your puppy have gained from obedience training will help prepare you for all kinds of activities you do together.

Ch. Windrift's Minx of Tikiluk, bred by Beverly Turner and owned by Barbara Brooks, shown as a promising six-month-old and (below) as an adult.

Am. Can. Ch. Barrenfield's Rocket Torpedo ROM, age five months. He has good bone, balance and angulation, along with a typical puppy topline.

As a mature adult, Rocket has all the quality he promised as a puppy, plus the proper topline. Breeder/owners, the Musyj family.

Some puppies do not go through radical changes as they mature. Leah, at six months, is a less filled out version of the adult.

Am. Can. Ch. Windrift's Leah of Aurora as an adult. Breeders, Barbara Brooks and Judith Lake. Owner, Barbara Brooks.

Ch. Kioona's Chibouk of Kaila, ROM, ("Paws") bred by Patti Colcord and owned by Chris and Eileen Gabriel, shown in the large photo as a fully mature five-year-old. Counterclockwise: Chibouk at six months, one year, and two years of age.

BEST OF
BREED
THE WESTMINSTER
KENNEL CLUB
FEBRUARY 11-12, 1980
ASHBEY

THE ADULT ALASKAN MALAMUTE

The adult Alaskan Malamute is definitely worth waiting for. Here is an animal of impressive stature, whose strength is tempered with gentility. Although much more dignified than in his youth, the mature Malamute rarely loses his sense of humor.

ADULT GROWTH

Your Malamute may continue to develop until he is four or five years of age. However, maturation in the adult dog is far less dramatic than in adolescence and usually involves increases in bone diameter rather than length, and gains in overall body depth and width.

The head will become distinctly adult, filling in above and below the eye, and fleshing out on the top of the skull. The muzzle and skull broaden and deepen, and the cheeks fill out slightly. The planes of the jaw and skull become smooth and strong, and all the parts begin to fit together in good proportion.

ADULT COAT

The coat of the adult Malamute is one of his crowning glories, and it comes in after the adolescent coat is shed. The outer guard coat is thick and coarse and stands out from the body to some degree. While the hair is long, it is not excessively so, and is longest on the shoulders, neck, down the back and over the rump, and in the breeches and tail. The hair on the face, legs, and sides of the body is shorter. Short, thick tufts of hair also grow between the toes.

The outer coat is protection for the thick, woolly undercoat which provides valuable insulation. In cold weather areas the undercoat should be about one to two inches in length. Its presence enables the dog to withstand subarctic temperatures.

In warmer areas, most dogs will have less undercoat, even when they are in full coat. They will shed what they do not need and keep the remainder to serve as insulation and protection from the heat.

From the plume-like tail to the thick neck fur, the luxurious, weather-proof Malamute coat is a pleasure to touch and see. Keep this in mind while you sweep up the copious amounts of hair during the Mal's two shedding cycles. Spring comes and the coat goes, and when winter arrives, the summer coat is replaced. The former is by far the more dramatic. The undercoat comes out so fast and is so profuse that your yard may look like someone unstuffed a mattress in it! Fortunately, this massive shed comes only once a year, since the summer coat has much less hair involved.

Because hair growth is at least partially light-cycle dependent, dogs which are kept inside most of the time tend to grow less undercoat and to shed slightly all year round. As some males get older, their coat becomes heavier and they shed less frequently. Unspayed females, on the other hand, shed seasonally around their estrous cycle. With less time to grow, their coats are seldom as plush as their male counterparts.

Adult dogs sometimes develop calluses on the pressure points of the elbows and lower legs from lying down. Padded pallets, crate bottoms, and dog beds will help minimize these. Vitamin E oil will soften the skin and may allow hair to regrow if the calluses are not too advanced.

THE OLDER DOG

As he ages, the dog may begin graying around the muzzle. His teeth will begin to show wear, and he will lose some of the padding on the head. Older dogs also lose muscle mass in the rear and may look disproportionate in later years.

Generally, Malamutes age well. Many work in harness into their teens. Veterans at dog shows are dogs over seven years of age, but many Malamutes are showing and winning long past this. Sheila Balch's Am/Can/Ber Ch. Inuit's Wooly Bully and Bill and Joyce Matott's Ch. Sendaishi's Polar Trax were both over ten when they won the National Specialty from the veterans class.

Older dogs may not shed or may do so less frequently. Their thicker coat may be very difficult to brush. Because

Am. Can. Ch Barrenfield's Kings Excalibur winning the Veteran dog class as the National Specialty. Breeder, Barrenfield Kennel. Owners, Gary and Carol Cooper.

Ch. Hug A Bear's Where Eagles Dare finishing his championship. Breeder/owner, Carol Hug.

natural hair oils are trapped close to the skin, the hair becomes dry and brittle on the ends. A water-soluble coat oil misted on lightly will help with brushing and protect the hair. Joint soreness or stiffness can make standing in a tub for long time periods difficult for an older dog. Therefore, brushing becomes doubly important.

Very old dogs may have changes in their coat quantity and texture. It may become sparse overall, or just in certain areas, usually at the base of the tail and along the back and haunches. If so, they will need more protection from cold than when they were younger.

INSTINCTS AND DRIVES

Your understanding of how instincts and drives influence and motivate your dog will help you to channel them constructively and communicate with him more effectively.

Northern dogs generally are regarded as more "natural" or "primitive," which is another way of saying they retain more of the instinctive behaviors present in wild canines. Presented with the right set of stimuli, an innate response in the dog's brain tends to govern its behavior. These responses can be altered, rechanneled, or enhanced, however, depending on the training and experience the dog receives during his lifetime. They can also be eliminated from future generations by selective breeding.

Instinctive behaviors are not bad per se; they enable the dog to survive in the wild. Trouble can arise when strong drives are thwarted or when inappropriate cues are provided.

AGGRESSIVE TRIGGERS

Triggers for aggressive behavior can be found in any area where dogs have instinctive behavior patterns, especially in those involving dominance, fear or pain, prey, or

parenting. Dogs have no tools with which to communicate except the body-language and vocalizations which they use among themselves. Our greater abilities place the burden of understanding on us.

PACK ORDER

His original environment and intended work determine much of the Malamute's personality and behavior. He is foremost a pack animal, very conscious of his place and happy to work. Malamutes are the perfect team players. Very respectful of authority, they are cooperative within an established group. The operative words here are "authority" and "established," and they can make the difference between a delightful pet and a monster.

Dominance behavior begins just after birth. The most dominant puppies lie atop the others. Dominant puppies are first to the food, to greet people, and to get a toy. The litter forms the initial pack and the hierarchy is quickly worked out. The most dominant dog is referred to as the "alpha," and the most submissive, the "omega."

Dogs have individual personalities just as people do, and like people, their behavior is relative to the conditions in which the dog finds itself. Thus, on an absolute scale, the bully of the litter may actually be fairly submissive by comparison with puppies from another group. Also, how a dog reacts with other dogs may not adequately reflect the way he will interact with humans. This has special import when children enter the picture.

The dominant puppies lie on top of their littermates, almost from the day they are born.

Children must be taught, and dogs must learn to accept, that the child is the dominant partner.

MALAMUTES AND CHILDREN

Many Malamutes work for youngsters on teams or tag along as willing playmates. In mixing Malamutes and children, especially very young ones, thought must be given to the Mal's independent nature, his dominance level in the pack, and his hunting instincts. Care must be taken by the parents to ensure that the child is the dominant partner in the relationship and that the child respects the dog.

Infants have no status in the family and should never be left alone with any dog. Dominance discipline administered by an adult dog to a human infant can be fatal. An infant crying seems particularly disturbing to some Malamutes and may activate a prey response.

Some breeds seem capable of tolerating any behavior from children and loving them in spite of it. A Malamute is likely to endure only so much ear-pulling, climbing, or squeezing before expressing his annoyance. Few will accept outright abuse, especially from children who do not "belong" to them. Therefore, you should never stake out a Malamute where children might tease or torment him.

Just as the dog must be taught to respect people, any child living with a dog must learn to treat the dog with care and love. Parents with children who are rough or unthinking with animals, and breeders who observe such behavior from the children of potential puppy-buyers, should have huge reservations about Malamutes being the right breed. Such families should not have any pet until their children learn to respect them. In this less-than-perfect world, one can only hope they decide on a more suitable breed or that they end up with an extremely submissive Malamute.

PAIN OR FEAR

Any animal can be provoked into an aggressive response—an entirely natural and normal survival characteristic. Provocation can come in response to pain or fear. The old saw about "being as angry as a wounded bear" has considerable basis in fact. When the threshold for aggression is lower than normal, the dog may be more easily provoked into an aggressive response. Such lowered sensitivity can be inherited, induced, or a combination of the two.

Fear-Induced Aggression—Dogs are born understanding their own language and are ignorant of the fact that humans do not understand it as well. They react to humans much as they would to another dog, and errors of interpretation lead to misunderstandings on both parts. When the tools they have available for coping with their world no longer function effectively, the same thing happens to dogs that happens to humans—they become neurotic and fearful.

For example, when a submissive dog lives in constant fear, he becomes generally fearful, so that his response to anxiety-producing situations may be far out of proportion to the actual stimulus. If the response is to bite, it almost always seems unjustified by the circumstances, yet such behavior arises from a massive misreading of the dog by the human and vice versa.

In nature, the rituals of dominance behavior are well-established, understood, and respected. Submission has its basis in fear, and when two dogs face each other, the more fearful submits, whereupon the more dominant, having made his point, moves on to other activities.

When an extremely submissive dog is subjected to a fear-inducing correction, such as hitting, yelling, or shaking, his instincts tell him that the way to escape the fear is to exhibit submissive behavior. If this does not result in a cessation of the punishment, the dog becomes confused. When the punishment is evoked by the very behavior with which the dog is using to avoid it, the resulting loop can destroy the animal's trust. Fortunately, Malamutes are very resilient, and this trust can be restored by better communication and consistent treatment.

Chronic Pain—Cheerfulness, liveliness, and friendliness are difficult when one is confronted with chronic pain. Humans can always complain, take medication, and go to bed. Sometimes the only clue a dog gives that he is suffering is a seemingly inexplicable irritability which can occasionally blossom into aggression.

Again, the Malamute is the product of his heritage, and life in the Arctic has produced a stoic dog. Puppies usually demonstrate a high tolerance to pain on the Puppy Aptitude Test, so, as a general rule, by the time a Malamute displays pain, the dog's physical condition is rather severe.[1] The culprit is often arthritis, sometimes induced by hip dysplasia. Aggressive behavior has also been linked to untreated thyroid imbalance.

PREY DRIVE

Every dog has some degree of prey drive. Dogs first served man on the hunt; the Malamute helped the Inuit locate seals and fight off bears. In the busy summer season while the Inuit fished and trapped, the dog's food was often his own responsibility. The resulting breed has finely-honed skills as a hunter and a very strong prey drive.

Malamutes do not make good "farm" dogs. The same instinct that encourages them to kill farm vermin—rats, mice, gophers, moles—can also drive them to dispatch a prodigious number of chickens, ducks, geese, and rabbits to animal heaven. If they have a willing companion or can coerce an otherwise proper dog into it, they may even tackle livestock such as goats, calves, or horses.

Robert Frost might have been speaking directly to Malamute owners when he said, "Good fences make good neighbors!" Allowed to roam free, Malamutes can become more than just pests. They can easily unite neighborhood dogs into a pack that can pose a danger to area pets. Malamutes can live on a farm as long as they are safely confined away from farm critters and vice versa. A puppy raised with other animals, other dogs, cats, or caged birds, can be trusted inside. Outdoors, all bets are off, and the rules may change. Such cohabitation may require a bit of training.

Take a puppy everywhere that he can go and introduce him to a variety of experiences: different people, places, objects, car rides, outside malls, public parks, the veterinarian, and schools. Well-socialized puppies learn to get along with people and other animals, and quickly learn the boundaries of acceptable behavior. Any sign of or attempt to chase other animals should be strongly discouraged.

An older dog may accept the introduction of a new animal, but this should be gradual. You should crate the newcomer and allow him out when both animals are on leash or, in the case of a cat, with the dog on leash. This way you can stop hostilities before they become serious, and then separate the animals for a later try.

TERRITORIAL IMPERATIVE

Animals are territorial, and dogs are no exception. They "fence" the area which belongs to them, by marking the boundaries with urine. Even a well-housebroken dog may succumb to the urge to mark, especially during periods of heightened sexual activity. These markings are as obvious to a dog as a fence is to people. Dog (and occasionally, but not reliably, human) intruders into this area are as alarming and threatening to the dog as a burglar is to the homeowner. Depending on their sex and attitude, the intruder may be welcomed or dealt with violently, even killed.

Other animals, such as squirrels, cats, turtles, chipmunks, rats, mice, gophers, skunks, moles, opossums, snakes, chickens, ducks, geese, or any other animals that wander through your property, are not intruders or cause for alarm. They are prey. Your Malamute will use them to hone his infrequently-used hunting skills. He even may try to share his trophy with his best buddy—you.

This territoriality, however, rarely extends to keeping out people. Exceptions to every rule can be found, but the typical Malamute makes a poor guard dog. A sled dog that only worked for one driver would have had little value to a tribe, so Malamutes are not "one-man dogs." Some will bark when cars come into the driveway or when people are on the porch. A few stories have been related of Mals guarding the home when their owners were away.

Jenny raised her Malamute, Blackie, as a house dog from puppyhood. When he was nine, Jenny was awakened by knocking at her bedroom door that she assumed was one of her teenagers. Without a thought, she unlatched the door only to find Blackie standing right next to a stranger who had climbed in through her living room window. She slammed the door and called the police while the intruder crawled back out the window.

Telling this story, Jenny said, "I know everyone says Malamutes aren't really protective, but in my heart, I was sure that if push came to shove, I could count on

Blackie."[2]

While many people are afraid of any large dog, particularly one with such a wolf-like appearance, relying on a Malamute for personal protection is risky. Protective behavior is seen most often when a Malamute confined in a small area, such as a crate, car, or his own kennel, feels trapped and threatened. He may also be protective of a mate or a youngster, but such aggression has its roots in a parental drive.

DOG AGGRESSION

From their wolf ancestors, Malamutes have a strong sense of pack order and the urge to protect the pack from outsiders. In the world of today's dog, the Malamute's family and its other animals form the pack. Other dogs assume the role of intruders, giving rise to aggression, especially between two dogs of the same sex (intrasexual aggression).

Accounts about Northern dogs from anthropologists, explorers, mushers, and pet owners always discuss their scrappy nature, although in earlier times it was exacerbated by hunger and could be quite ferocious. Modern dogs display a toned-down version that is usually directed towards dogs of the same sex, depending on the circumstances. However, it can be extended to humans of the same sex or to strange dogs of either sex (non-pack members). Males usually will not fight with females; females on the other hand are not quite so gracious and may fight with males as readily as females. Fights between warring females are the fiercest of all.

When sexual drives are factored into the equation, the results can be truly fearsome. Seemingly inseparable males may end a friendship over a female, especially one in season. Likewise, being in season may cause a female and/or other females to become generally more aggressive to other dogs, although they may be quite affectionate to people. [3]

PARENTAL PROTECTIVENESS

Parental drives, especially those of the mother, are very strong and necessary for species survival. Mothers may react quite strongly to any perceived threat to their young, particularly when the pups are very young. No child should ever be allowed around a mother and her young, regardless of breed, without close adult supervision.

Adults, too, need to be considerate of the new mother. Allowing a parade of people through to see the puppies can make her very anxious. A few females will not tolerate

---

SALLY'S GUARD DOGS

Unlike Jenny, Sally never expected either of her Malamutes to protect her, although in their own way, they did. As she told it, after having a tooth pulled, she took a strong pain-killer. When she got groggy, she went upstairs to her bedroom, taking her dogs with her.

When Sally repeatedly failed to answer the phone, her mother became concerned and called Sally's building security. The guard checked and found Sally's car in its space. He became increasingly suspicious when ringing the doorbell and banging on doors brought no response. Accompanied by his guard dog, he opened Sally's door with a passkey and went inside. The guard suspected the worst when his calls got no response from either Sally or her dogs. Drawing his gun, he and the dog proceeded to the door of Sally's bedroom which was just at the head of the stairs.

Sally awoke to her worst nightmare. Her door was being pushed open to reveal a stranger with gun in hand. She screamed and her two trusty protectors launched themselves off the bed and onto the German Shepherd. Caught in the fray, the security guard, his gun, and all three dogs went tumbling down the stairs. Fortunately, no one was hurt.

"The moral to this story is" says Sally, "if a strange dog breaks into your house, your Malamutes will definitely protect you!"[4]

---

anyone touching their newborns. This parental drive is so strong it must be respected and tolerated. It cannot be corrected.

Males living in a pack atmosphere may become very protective of young dogs. Females with strong maternal instincts may extend solicitous behavior to all puppies, not just their own.

PROBLEM DRIVES

DIGGING

Wild canines, like wolves and foxes, are denning animals. They may dig or find small caves to whelp their young, to hide, or seek shelter from the elements. The urge to dig is still present in Malamutes, especially if they need a hiding place for a special treasure or a protected resting spot. No matter what you think of your landscaping, an unsupervised Malamute will have his own ideas about what to do with deliciously soft, rich-smelling soil. Tasty plants will probably not fare well either. If you have a fortune invested in your yard, a separate fenced area or run for the dog will make both you and your dog much happier.

ACTIVITY LEVEL

The Inuit had little use for couch potatoes, so Malamutes are active dogs by nature. They are not hyper but need short bursts of activity throughout the day. Idle paws are truly the devil's workshop.

A morning and evening walk will benefit both you and your Malamute immeasurably. In between, if he is left in the yard during the day, the dog needs something to play with. He can sharpen his hunting skills and amuse himself with a few toys, which need not be expensive. A clean plastic bottle with an attached rope can provide a lot of entertainment. Rawhide chewies can help keep teeth clean, but do not be surprised if your Malamute buries them.

A few walks with a couple of short training sessions interspersed will probably keep the house-dog's interest. Older dogs can be conditioned beside a bike, or hitched to a cart, or sled. Regardless, some exercise will keep your dog happier and make both of you better companions for each other.

VOCALIZING

The bored Malamute may become a noisemaking nuisance, since he is capable of a wide variety of sounds, running the gamut from yips and barks to long, mournful howls. Many Mals are quite chatty, with a whole series of verbalizations directed at people. These "woofs" or "woo-woo" sounds are usually an invitation to play.

CLEANLINESS

Wild canines housebreak themselves. Once they are able to leave the nest, they keep it clean. Malamutes retain a desire for good housekeeping. You may even see one licking and washing himself like a cat! They are easy to housebreak unless early training has overridden their natural tendencies, as is often the case with puppies raised in pet shops. Kept in cages, they learn to eliminate in their "den," which makes housebreaking them more difficult if not impossible.

INDEPENDENCE

In the past, survival often depended on the Malamute's ability to make a decision and stand by it, despite his master's wishes. A Malamute is not going to sit at your feet with shining eyes, begging you for instructions. If you want that kind of obedience, another breed is in order.

Malamutes can certainly be trained but the key lies in their learning to respect you as a pack leader, rather than a desire to perform repetitive tasks. Successful owners learn to work with his independent nature. Trying to squelch it makes for a spiritless dog and a frustrated master.

ENDNOTES
1. Malamute puppies, tested by one of the authors, routinely scored in the upper ranges on pain sensitivity. Some never showed any response regardless of how hard the tester pinched; whereas, my Papillons never scored above a four on a ten-point scale, and most rated a one or two.
2. All names have been changed, but this story is a personal communication to the authors.
3. Children should not be allowed around a pair engaged in breeding behavior. If you want them to watch, let them do so from inside. No child should ever be left alone with such dogs.
4. Again, the names have been changed, but this story is a personal communication to the authors.

21

WOLVES, DOGS, AND WOLF-DOG HYBRIDS

A ttitudes in the United States about wolves have undergone quite a turnaround in the last decade or so. The mostly-European immigrants who populated this country carried with them the wolf-lore of their homeland and passed this on to their children. The villainous wolf of fairy tales—the big, bad wolf of *Peter and the Wolf* and *Little Red Riding Hood*—became the steadfast enemy of the western farmers and ranchers.

Today, in a culture ever conscious of environmental issues, wolf faces grace the fronts of T-shirts and howl at the moon on countless pieces of southwestern art, furniture, and accessories. Television specials on wolves abound, newspapers run stories about reinstating wolves in national parks, environmental and wildlife organizations have made them the poster animal for endangered species. Wolves are "in."

WOLVES AS PETS

However, the wolf's nature makes him unsuitable as a pet. Lori Schmidt, a wolf curator, says, "The wolf is a top-level predator which has survived due to its sensory abilities and predatory instincts."[1] The socialization of a captive wolf may lull non-professionals into a false sense of security. In fact, wolves are extremely dangerous to anything that triggers hunting behavior, including livestock, small animals, and children.

Able to work with a wolf pack because the wolves accepted her as a member, Schmidt relates a story from her own experiences as a wolf curator in Ely, Minnesota:

I had a female wolf under my care who showed indifference towards children well into adulthood. She was an educational display animal exposed to hundreds of children during the summer months until, one day, a toddler waddled in front of her, fell down, and began waving his arms and crying. The wolf stalked down the hill of the exhibit and

pounced towards the child. Fortunately, she was stopped by a ten-foot chain link fence. This offered a great educational moment, but far too often pet wolves or hybrids are kept on the end of a chain within reach of a child. This is the situation which makes headlines. By the way, the female wolf who was indifferent to so many children cannot be exposed to a single child without motivating a predatory instinct.[2]

She goes on to say that, "In most states, pure wolf ownership is not allowed, but personnel to enforce these laws are few and far between."[3] Federal law prohibits taking an endangered species from the wild, but the Federal Endangered Species Act does not apply to wolves bred in captivity. While most organizations raising wolves are respectable and responsible, some dealers are less than scrupulous.

THE NEXT BEST THING

If ownership of wolves is difficult, owning the next best thing is very easy. Wolf-hybrids are bred and sold all across North America. For some people, the wolf-hybrid fulfills the need for the thrill of manageable fear like a roller-coaster ride or a fright movie. Reluctant to own a pure wolf, they think that the mixture of wolf and dog will give them the living equivalent of a teddy bear—a belief that is often a prescription for disaster.

For others, the wolf-hybrid answers "an obsession to be close to an animal who represents true wildness,"[4] in what they think is a manageable version. Ownership and control of a wild, untamed animal gives some people a sense of empowerment, a visible symbol of their importance and strength.

According to Scott Barry, who has worked with wild canines, dogs, and hybrids for over twenty years, these individuals "rarely exhibit responsible pet-ownership, and attempt to attract as many onlookers and potential 'ad-

The totally straight tail and huge feet are the only real indicators that Aero is a Malamute-wolf cross. Her owner bought what she was told was a pure Malamute. It was only when she heard Lori Schmidt speak on wolf behavior that the owner realized what she had purchased. "Whatever her breeding might have been, her brain was wolf."

mirers' as possible—which in reality, translates to attention for themselves. . . . These hybrid owners, very often out of ignorance, or a general laissez-faire attitude . . . do not properly confine or leash them; rather, the urban/suburban hybrid is treated like any pet dog; and quite often, with potentially disastrous results, the rurally owned wolf-dog hybrid is allowed to roam free in areas where the animal can or will eventually threaten livestock, as well as children."[5]

WOLF-MALAMUTE CROSSES

These wolf-hybrids as a group have much more to do with Alaskan Malamutes than proponents of the breed would like. Possibly, wolf-poodle crosses do exist, but the vast majority of wolf-hybrids are wolves crossed with either German Shepherd Dogs, Siberian Huskies, or Alaskan Malamutes, undoubtedly because of their more wolf-like appearance.[6]

In one attack that received national attention, a hybrid jumped the fence into the neighbor's yard and attacked a girl playing there. Her six-year old brother tried to help her. When he ran between the hybrid and the girl, the hybrid redirected its attack and ripped off his right ear. The hybrid was referred to as a "moof;" he was a wolf/Malamute cross.[7]

Because they are one of the breeds commonly crossed with wolves, wolf-hybrids are a concern to all Malamute breeders, and yet another reason for careful screening of prospective buyers. Potential buyers need to know why wolf-hybrids are not a wise choice to breed or to keep for a pet. Recognizing and understanding the differences be-

A pure wolf.

This Malamute-wolf cross looks just like a wooly Malamute.

tween wolves, dogs, and wolf-dog crosses is an important educational tool for all Malamute fanciers.

PROBLEMS WITH WOLF-DOG HYBRIDS

Dogs and wolves both have the same number of chromosomes and can interbreed freely. In fact, they have received a new taxonomic classification as one species. However, ten-thousand years of selective breeding in dogs have eliminated behaviors that make the wild wolf dangerous in a household setting.

In the wild, the wolves' elaborate social structure makes them uniquely suited for survival. They are the Cadillacs of the predator world. Only pale shadows of the wolf's instincts survive in the dog. Even the most natural dogs, of which Malamutes are an example, display a stunted instinct development which never matures past the juvenile stage of the wolf. This inherited inability to mature is the essential difference between a wild and domestic animal.

A wild animal socialized by people from birth may be tame, but it will never be domesticated. Behavioral modification produces the one, but genetic modification produces the other. Crossing the wolf and dog, then, combines genes for a wild animal with those of a domestic one, creating a very unpredictable animal.

UNPREDICTABLE BEHAVIOR

Scott Barry says where the wolf-hybrid is concerned, the sum is greater than the parts—that the behavior they exhibit is neither like the dog's or wolf's, nor is it in between the two. He says, "the combination of the two, often produces individuals who can be characterized in the following behavioral terms:

1. General and/or extreme hyperactivity,

2. Potential aggression, caused by severe shyness, coupled with varying degrees of quick, defensive responses to outside stimuli,

3. Unpredictability in any given stressful or potentially stressful situation (i.e., loud noises, crowds, confined areas, extremes of climate, such as hot summer weather)."[8]

IMMUNIZATIONS

Captive wolves and wolf-hybrids present a little-known health problem. Federal veterinarians do not recommend rabies vaccinations in wolves or wolf hybrids, nor do they know whether they are effective.[9] In fact, while dosages, safety, and efficacy of drugs and vaccines are determined for most medicines given to domestic animals, no scientific evidence exists regarding their efficacy on wild canids.

In 1993, rabies reached such epidemic proportions in the state of Texas that a quarantine went into effect. The health department reported at least one wolf-hybrid that contracted the disease even though it had a current rabies vaccination. If vaccines are indeed ineffective in some or all of these animals, they pose a significant danger to the public and other animals, not just for rabies but for other canine diseases as well.[10]

BEHAVIORAL DIFFERENCES

The biggest concern with hybrids, though, lies in the discrepancy that can exist between the hybrid's appearance and his temperament. While behavior and appearance may correlate, so that wolf-looking hybrids act like wolves and dog-looking ones like dogs, assuming that appearance will predict behavior can be extremely risky.

Determining the actual wolf content of a hybrid is difficult. As Schmidt explains,

> Hybrids will be advertised as a percentage or fraction of wolf content. Breeders arrive at these numbers by adding the wolf percentages of parent animals together and dividing by two. The number is supposed to represent the content of wolf in the litter. . . .Unless one breeds a pure wolf with a pure dog creating a true 50% hybrid, certainty on percentage of wolf genes in a hybrid may be questionable.[11]

What genes actually affect behavior are unknown, although genetic research is being done to try to identify the proportion of genetic material hybrids retain from their wolf ancestors. The mechanics of genetics make using percentages an extremely unreliable method for predicting whether an animal will be more like its dog or its wolf ancestors.

A large component of the relationship between dog and man is the residue of the wolf's pack instinct. Most dogs accept their owners as leaders without much of a challenge. The same is true of the juvenile wolf, who "readily accepts the parents . . . as alphas. (As) the wolf matures to adulthood, the natural process is to test or identify weakness in the order and move up in rank or to disperse."[12]

In competitive situations, dominance takes the form of privileges, with the dominant animals showing the initiative and claiming whatever is desired. To get along in the pack, subordinate wolves try to do what the alpha sees as right. When they are involved with wolves, trouble occurs because humans, especially those without a strong background in canine behavior, do not always know what seems right to the wolf.

Disciplinary action for transgressions against the alpha wolf are administered by grabbing the offender by the scruff of the neck and pinning him to the ground. Although this behavior is sometimes seen in dogs, it is a much milder response and may discourage another challenge forever. Wolves, however, never quit testing and challenging. "If the alpha is weaker, a stronger subordinate can test and move up to keep the pack strong and viable. These behaviors should not be seen as good or bad. They are behaviors of a wild animal trying to stay alive in the wild."[13] This behavior will not change because wolves are captive instead of free or because the target is a human instead of another wolf.

WOLF OR DOG? HOW TO TELL?

Life in the wild has resulted in physical adaptations in wolves that are different from those of dogs. Pure wolves breed between January and March, depending upon the latitude, so that litters are produced in the early spring. Estrus occurs only at this time; whereas, the dog can breed throughout the year.

Growth patterns are also quite different. To keep up with the pack during winter, wolf cubs must attain adult size by eight months. This is a prodigious growth rate when the adult wolf weighs between seventy and one-hundred-fifty pounds.

This three-and-one-half-month old wolf hybrid could easily be mistaken for a German Shepherd puppy.

Despite this rapid growth, sexual maturation is slow in the wolf. Dogs reach puberty and achieve sexual maturation before a year of age; wolves may not reach this stage until two or even three years of age. In the hybrid, this detail is quite significant, since the mature animal may undergo drastic changes in behavior long after the family has accepted him as if he were a dog.

Differences in physical appearance between a Malamute and a wolf may not be so pronounced as those between a German Shepherd and a wolf, but they are there. Most dogs have some curve to the tail, while the wolves' tails are straight, and they have disproportionately large feet. Their chests are narrower, resulting in front legs that are closer together.

Wolves have more muscle mass; a seventy-five-pound wolf is much stronger than a seventy-five-pound dog. A wolf's skull is broader overall, more so at the base of the eye sockets. They have a pronounced sagittal crest to accommodate increased jaw pressure, and much larger teeth with "elongated canines, and pronounced peaks of the carnassial."[14] Wolf eyes are more almond-shaped than most dogs. Almost all wolves have yellow eyes as adults.

Wolves and Malamutes both have facial masking which may aid in communication. However, in the wolf, the pattern is created by the hair itself, while in the dog, it results from the hair color, as though painted.[15]

When Malamutes are crossed with wolves or wolf-hybrids, the resulting animal may be virtually indistinguishable from the purebred Malamute on first sight. Close examination, however, may reveal some subtle differences. Differences in behavior also offer clues as to whether the animal is truly a hybrid and how much wolf influence is present.

Wolf hybrids that come in season in the fall or were born in the fall or winter are probably more dog than wolf, as are puppies that mature more slowly. The hybrid probably will have larger feet than a dog, but not so large as the wolf's. Likewise, the teeth and head may be larger. The hybrid's ears may be larger than that of either parent, even when northern wolves and northern dogs are crossed, a maladapted result of hybridization.[16]

Most wolves are fearful of man, although Schmidt feels this may result from natural selection during the long history of bounties on wolves and the extensive measures used to hunt them. Typically, wolf cubs, even if handled from birth, become fearful of humans and retreat from them at the age of three to eight weeks. Hybrids which display this behavior are probably more

A wolf/Malamute/Siberian mix, Max was picked up by a Mala-mute Rescue, covered with mange (note sores on forelegs). He was so aggressive that he had to be euthanized.

wolf-like. "A hybrid with predominant dog genes usually has no difficulty accepting humans as a young pup."[17]

HYBRID OWNERSHIP

Many people who obtain wolf-hybrids are strongly attached to their pets both because his wolf-instincts cause the animal to establish strong social bonds and because ownership furnishes support for the person's own emotional needs. The relationship may be highly satisfactory until the hybrid reaches two or three years of age, when, with full maturation, he becomes pushier, challenging the owner and anyone else. He may also begin killing livestock or dogs, and may end his tenure as a household pet by injuring or killing a child.[18]

This sudden personality shift is yet another clue that the animal is more wolf than dog. The temperament the owners had found so amenable was in fact that of the immature wolf. Puberty brings not only sexual maturation but triggers the emergence of adult wolf behavior. As Schmidt says, "Juvenile animals may be easy to manage

and even train; but when adult behavioral characteristics are evident, you may only be able to train a wolf to do what it wants to do."[19]

If the initial acquisition of a wolf-hybrid is based in ignorance, continuing to keep the animal or attempts to place it after it has displayed aggression are mired in the psychological state known as denial. Schmidt reports that she receives many calls from people with two- or three-year-old hybrids, and that wolf organizations receive hundreds of calls a year from owners attempting to find new homes for the "pets;" unfortunately, very few homes are available.[20] So few people have the resources to build or maintain facilities that can reliably house a wolf-hybrid that they pose a potential threat wherever they live. In fact, "many owners keep their animals on the ends of chains without any physical barriers. This is the most dangerous situation when children are able to approach a chained animal"[21]

Many shelters will accept wolf-hybrids only for euthanasia, a decision prompted by experiences like that of the Humane Society shelter that in "1988 placed a hybrid with a family. Two hours later, the hybrid, which had been advertised as the pet of the week, killed a four-year-old boy. The animal shelter was sued and finally settled the suit for $452,000."[22]

Owners who are too attached to their animals to consider this alternative have dealt with the problem by releasing their hybrids into the wild, where they pose a significant danger to the genetic purity of the wild wolf population. This is neither a personally, socially, ethically, or environmentally responsible solution.

LEGAL RESTRICTIONS

Aware of the threat released hybrids posed to the established wolf population of the New England/Eastern Canadian area, wildlife biologist Jean Mattos petitioned the legislature to pass a bill which prohibited the possession, sale, trading, breeding, importing, exporting or release of a wild canine or feline hybrid in the Commonwealth of Massachusetts. It was signed into law on January 10, 1994, receiving strong support from many victims of wolf-hybrid attacks.[23]

Liability claims paid homeowner's insurance for damage caused by dogs have caused some companies to only cover homes with certain breeds of dogs when precautions have been taken by the owners. Other companies have refused to cover them at all. They are certainly looking at the issue of wolf-hybrids. If dogs like the "moof" become common, the difficulty in differentiating between a real Malamute and a Malamute/wolf hybrid may make Malamute ownership too much of a financial liability.

When the issue of the wolf-hybrid presents itself, all dog lovers need to take a stand like that of Mrs. Mattos. Existing animals should be humanely but safely maintained. Traffic in both wolves and wild canid/dog crosses should be unlawful.[24] As Dr. L. David Mech stated in a 1991 *Minneapolis Star and Tribune* article, "I see no reasons for people to raise a wolf or a hybrid. If someone wants an interesting animal that's similar to the wolf, it's called a dog."[25]

ENDNOTES

1.   Lori J. Schmidt, "Major Project in Issues relating to Management of Wolves or Wolf/Dog Hybrids in Captivity." Manuscript for University of Minnesota Program for Individualized Learning (April, 1992), 11.

2.   Schmidt, 12.

3.   Schmidt, 30.

4.   Schmidt, 26.

5.   Scott Ian Barry, "Wolf-Dog Hybrids. Legal Briefing." Manuscript, 3-4.

6.   Barry, 5.

7.   Barry, 2.

8.   Barry, 1-2.

9.   Schmidt, 31.

10.   Schmidt, 31.

11.   Schmidt, 4

12.   Schmidt, 13.

13.   Schmidt, 14.

14.   Barry, 6. Carnassial molars are the large teeth on the side of the jaw with sharp points. Common to carnivorous animals, carnassial teeth are adapted especially for cutting and tearing rather than crushing.

15.   Schmidt, 5-6.

16.   Barry, 6.

17.   Schmidt, 9-10.

18.   An argument can be made that domestic dogs, including Alaskan Malamutes, have been implicated in all these activities. However, aggression in the domestic dog is often motivated by dominance behavior and stops once the dog has administered what it considers an appropriate correction. Administered by a wolf, this dominance correction is much more severe and may not stop until the offender has made appropriate response which the victim is unlikely to understand.

Another factor to be considered in evaluating reports of attacks by Malamutes, especially on children, is whether the dog is actually purebred or is a hybrid. After an attack, the owners may not want to admit the potentially incriminating presence of wolf genes or may not actually know. DNA testing would be valuable in such situations.

19.   Schmidt, 33.

20.   Schmidt, 33.

21.   Schmidt, 33.

22.   Schmidt, 33.

23.   Brian Lowney. "Steadfast and Determined," *The Wolf Hybrid Times* (February, 1994), 22.

24.   Although it is more difficult, dogs and coyotes have also been crossed.

25.   Schmidt, 37.

ALASKAN MALAMUTE RESCUE

For years, responsible breeders have taken dogs back from people who were unable to keep them. Doing so kept those dogs from ending up abandoned on the streets or at a shelter where they would become a statistic. The statistics are certainly grim. Each year in the U.S. alone, public and private shelters euthanize between thirteen and twenty-seven million animals. Humane workers, staggering under this unwelcome burden, have become increasingly resentful of anyone who breeds dogs. As a result, anti-breeding legislation in local areas has found firm support from shelter staffs, providing a wake-up call to purebred dog fanciers.

Responsible breeders account for only a small part of the problem, but they recognize that shelter workers need help. Across North American, national and local breed clubs, kennel clubs, and caring dog lovers have banded together to save the lives of purebred dogs. These dedicated volunteers not only care for the dogs' immediate needs but also raise funds to provide for continued rescue operations, interface with the public to let them know dogs are available for adoption, and screen potential adopters for suitability. It is emotionally wrenching and physically hard work.

Rescue groups interact with people in their own breed to provide long- and short-term care and medical treatment and to find suitable homes for the dogs where the dog and the people are a good match so the dog doesn't get shuffled again later. Rescue workers try to rehabilitate dogs that have been abused or neglected or which have behavior problems. Most dogs can eventually be placed in a caring environment.

As lovers and protectors of the Malamute, we must take it upon ourselves to care about all Malamutes, not just the ones we breed and love. We must educate the public that not everyone should own a Malamute. This breed digs, sheds hair, hunts small animals, howls, and

This chapter was contributed by Susan Ingersol Cloer.

chews. They don't guard your property, hang on your every word or instantly obey your commands, nor will they bring your slippers in the evening.

Breeders must be even more careful when placing puppies. The time has come for all of us to use the limited registration AKC now has available as well as to sell puppies with spay/neuter contracts. We can also withhold papers altogether until the new owner presents proof that the puppy has been altered.

WHY DOGS END UP IN RESCUE

Dogs end up needing rescue for all sorts of reasons. People move around a lot in our society, and many will not move with their dog. When faced with a major change in their lifestyle, they may not call the breeder to say they can't keep their dog, even if it is in their sales contract. Some just forget that it's an option; others are afraid to admit they have a problem or that they've made a mistake.

Families who relocate may not be able to keep a dog in their new housing situation or regard taking the dog as just too much bother. Teddy Bear's owners thought they had a solution when they gave him to neighbors, but they forgot to mention how much an Alaskan Malamute sheds. The new owners turned him in to a shelter.

Mattie was turned in to rescue at eleven weeks of age when her owners were transferred because of their work. Pet shops don't take these dogs back.

Divorce also sends many dogs to shelters. Yukon Girl was housebroken, obedience trained, and loved children. Her owners turned her in not because she had a problem, but because they did.

Tok was not so lucky. Although he was the husband's dog, he ended up with the wife who didn't really like him. When Tok growled at her, he ended up at a shelter, frightened, confused, and not very fond of women in general. The female rescue volunteer could not even get close to him, which made him impossible to place. He was euthanized.

A portfolio of rescued Malamutes. Right: Cody was picked up by animal control and Houston Mal Rescue was called. His right leg was gangrenous and he had to be euthanized.
Far right: Taylor was found beside a road, very ill with parvovirus. He is now in a happy home.

Below: Victoria when she was rescued by Susan Cloer, and below that, Victoria in her new home. Susan kept her. Some dogs steal your heart.

The lovely Smokey, adopted by Karen and Gil Borgardt.

Many dogs end up homeless because the new owners did not learn what a Malamute is like before they got one. Malamutes are very adept hunters. Laika's owners chained her and another Malamute in a barn with fifty ducks, geese and turkeys and left for a week-long cruise. The dogs slipped out of their collars and killed all the fowl. Shocked that their beloved pets could behave so savagely, the owners did not want them any longer.

Malamutes can also be exceptional escape artists, quickly testing the owner's patience. Czar was just such a dog. When animal control officers picked him up for the fifth time, his owners told the Delaware SPCA just to

Kena is now happy with new owners Ron and Terry Lerner.

keep him.

Finally, some people obtain dogs on a whim. When they discover that owning a dog involves more than putting food down once a day, they decide the dog would be better off in a home where he gets more attention. Some will drop the dog off at a shelter. Others just turn him loose hoping a kind soul will take him in; picnic and rest areas are a popular spot for abandoning dogs. Maintenance crews clean many of these unfortunate dogs off the roads every morning.

WHY ALASKAN MALAMUTE RESCUE?

If you truly love Malamutes, you don't want any Malamute abused, abandoned or killed, regardless of whether you know its pedigree. As responsible breeders, we have always taken care of the puppies we have produced and have followed the rule, "Create a life and you are responsible for that life." Unfortunately, not everyone believes this. We cannot save all the unwanted Alaskan Malamutes, but we must make the effort to try to save all that we can.

Rescue dogs are often wonderful ambassadors for our breed. Many people with a life-long commitment to the breed obtained their first Malamute from a shelter or from someone who could no longer keep it. Some of these peo-

ple will become lifelong fans of the breed and will seek out responsible breeders from whom to buy a puppy later on.

Over the past several years, these unwanted dogs have proven to me that the Malamute is not only adaptable but very resilient. We should be proud of that. Mattie, Max, Smokey, Teddy Bear, Czar, Yukon Girl, Jake, Baron Oonak and a host of other Malamutes have all survived neglect, uninformed owners, and abandonment. They have put the past behind them, making their new owners enthusiastic supporters of our breed in the process.

Time and again, I have watched grossly abused dogs come into rescue who were able to understand that just because one person has beaten or starved them, does not mean all people will do the same. Two examples of this are Sierra and Victoria.

Sierra was confiscated from a puppy mill in Minnesota several years ago. The starvation, filth, and abuse she endured in the first two years of her life do not show today; she has gained a second chance to love!

Victoria had a very different beginning. The neighbors told us she been had placed through a "free-to-good-home" newspaper ad when she was seven. Her new family kept her for five more years, giving her only minimal care and leaving her alone in the yard. When she was twelve, they moved and abandoned her. For the next two years,

Max was adopted by Tom Cena.

Victoria wandered the streets, living off the neighbors' leftovers and out of garbage cans. She suffered terribly with arthritis of the spine and was severely hypothyroid, so she lost most of her fur. In the summer, the flies ate into her bare skin; in the winter, she had no way to keep warm. When mange and a staph infection caused sores to appear on her body, the neighbors called us at Malamute Rescue.

When we arrived to get her, she was curled up on a twelve inch square of muddy carpeting, asleep. When we touched her shoulder to wake her, she raised her head and wagged her tail. In her eyes, we could literally see the regal dog she had once been.

We knew the rescue could never afford to pay her massive bills or hope to place her at nearly fourteen years of age; so my husband Dan and I undertook her rehabilitation. When I looked at Victoria, I was ashamed that I was a human and that others of my species had allowed this to happen to this poor creature. Victoria was the epitome of that one dog every rescue worker encounters at some time—the one that looks up and begs for just one small chance to live, even in the face of little hope. We expected her to live only about six months, but for over two years, she was our cherished house-pet.

HELPING WITH RESCUE

Few rescue groups have the luxury of full-time workers. Instead, they function by having many people contribute a little time, material, or money. You might think your contribution is too small to matter, but if everyone does something, we can turn the tide and help solve the problem of pet overpopulation. You might have space and time to foster a dog. Veterinary care is a substantial expense;

perhaps you could persuade your veterinarian to donate a free spay or neuter or heartworm treatment for rescue. Donations of food are always welcome.

Another drain on rescue workers' time is checking on dogs in area shelters. Many shelter workers are volunteers unfamiliar with purebred dogs and need help with breed identification. Perhaps you could volunteer some time for this or spare a few hours to shuttle Malamutes from area shelters to a rescue worker's home.

A critical part of rescue work is fund raising because more money is always needed. Auctions, raffles, and garage sales are all potential income sources. A dog wash can bring in needed funds. Several clubs have held weight-pulls where sponsors donate money to rescue based on the participating dogs' performances. Some breeders donate a small amount from each puppy sale to rescue.

Finally, you can help publicize the availability of rescue dogs. Many people inquiring about a puppy are more suited to an older dog. Rescue workers often have calls for puppies, although they rarely come into rescue. They are happy to pass these calls on to someone whom they know is a responsible local breeder.

Despite your best efforts, the possibility is always there that one of your puppies will end up in a shelter. Now, thanks to the efforts of people who love Alaskan Malamutes, a rescue chapter may be there to take him in and give him a second chance.

For more information, contact the Alaskan Malamute Club of America or a local club for information.

THE LAST WORD

"Thus it has been down through the ages. Animals have been domesticated and have helped us in all of the important undertakings in the settlement of this great country. We are now learning to show our appreciation of the debt we owe by giving them more humane treatment. This in itself is one of the best indications of our progress in civilization. Ours is a machine age and, however much we may regret it, the need for animals is rapidly disappearing. Some we will keep to minister to our pleasure as companions of our leisure hours. But the days of their usefulness are numbered. Like the knight in armor let not their memory be forgotten."

– Arthur T. Walden

In 1906, Roald Amundsen's team of sled dogs carried him across the icy reaches of Antarctica to the South Pole. In 1994, in accordance with an international treaty designed to protect the delicate environment of Antarctic, the last sled dogs left Antarctica for their Inuit home in northern Quebec, ending a century-long partnership on the white road.

Painting of BIS, BISS Ch. Windrift's Nakoah by Carolynn Bullock.

SELECTED BIBLIOGRAPHY

Many areas discussed in this book are covered more exhaustively in other publications. Full references and occasional comments are provided for additional material, as well as for all books cited in the text.

DOG BOOKS
The Alaskan Malamute Annual. Wheat Ridge, CO: Hoflin Publishing, Ltd., yearly from 1981.
Brearly, Joan M. *This Is the Alaskan Malamute.* New York: T.F.H. Publications, 1975.
Demidoff, Lorna B. and Michael Jennings. *The Complete Siberian Husky.* New York: Howell Book House, 1978.
Riddle, Maxwell and Beth Harris. *The New Complete Alaskan Malamute,* New York: Howell Book House, 1990.
Riddle, Maxwell and Eva Seeley. *The Complete Alaskan Malamute.* New York: Howell Book House, 1976.
Seeley, Eva B. and Martha A.L. Lane. *Chinook and His Family.* Boston:Ginn & Co., 1930. Seeley's book about sled dogs, written for children.

GENETICS AND DOG BREEDING
Battaglia, Dr. Carmelo L. *Dog Genetics. How to Breed Better Dogs.* Neptune, N.J.: T.F.H. Publications, Inc., 1978.
Hutt, Frederick B. *Genetics for Dog Breeders.* San Francisco: W. H. Freeman and Company, 1979.
Little, Dr. Clarence C. *The Inheritance of Coat Color in Dogs.* New York: Howell Book House, 1971.
Onstott, Kyle. *The New Art of Breeding Better Dogs.* New York: Howell Book House, 1971.
Willis, Dr. Malcolm. *Genetics of the Dog.* New York: Howell Book House, 1989.
Winge, Dr. Ojvind. *Inheritance in Dogs With Special Reference to Hunting Breeds.* Ithaca, N.Y.: Comstock Publishing Company, Inc.,1950.

HEALTH AND WELFARE
Kirk, Dr. Robert W. *First Aid for Pets.* New York: E.P. Dutton, 1978.
Lanting, Fred. *Canine Hip Dysplasia and Other Orthopedic Problems.* Loveland, Co: Alpine Publications, Inc., 1981.
McGinnis, Terri. *The Well Dog Book.* New York: Random House, 1991.

PERFORMANCE EVENTS
Coppinger, Lorna. *The World of Sled Dogs From Siberia to Sport Racing.* New York: Howell Book House, 1977.
Collins, Miki and Julie. *Dog Driver: Guide for the Serious Musher.* Loveland, Co.: Alpine Publications, Inc., 1991.
Flanders, Noel. *Joy of Running Sled Dogs.* Loveland, Co.: Alpine Publications, Inc., 1989.
Labelle, Charlene. *Backpacking With Your Dog.* Loveland, Co.: Alpine Publications, Inc., 1993.
Milon, Ellie. *201 Ways to Enjoy Your Dog. A Complete Guide to Organized U.S. and Canadian Activities for Dog Lovers.* Loveland, Co.: Alpine Publications, Inc., 1990.

POLAR EXPLORATION AND LIFE IN THE ARCTIC
Amundsen, Roald. *The South Pole. An Account of the Norwegian Antarctic Expedition in the 'Fram,' 1910-1912.* Translated from Norwegian by A.G. Chater. London: John Murray, 1912. Volumes I & II. Volume I in particular is full of observations about the dogs, their behavior and use. Amundsen is a witty, observant writer, so despite their age, the books are easy and entertaining to read.
Byrd, Richard E. *Alone.* Covelo, Ca.: Island Press, 1938, renewed 1966. Originally published New York: G. P. Putnam's Sons, 1938. Byrd's account of his time spent alone at a weather observation hut on BAE II.
___. *Discovery. The Story of the Second Byrd Antarctic Expedition.* New York: G. P. Putnam's Sons, 1935.
___. *Little America. Aerial Exploration in the Antarctic. The Flight to the South Pole.* New York: G. P. Putnam's Sons, 1930. Byrd's own account of the first expedition.
Dufek, George John. *Operation Deepfreeze.* New York: Harcourt, Brace and Company, 1957.
Flaherty, Leo. *Roald Amundsen and the Quest for the South Pole.* New York: Chelsea House Publishers. World Explorers, General Editor William H. Goetzmann.
Gladych, Michael. *Admiral Byrd of Antarctica.* New York: Julian Messner, Inc. 1960.
Gould, Laurence McKinley. *Cold. The Record of An Antarctic Sledge Journey.* New York: Brewer, Warren & Putnam, 1931. Gould was second in command of BAE I and was in charge of the geological expedition.
Hoyt, Edwin P. *The Last Explorer. The Adventures of Admiral Byrd.* New York: The John Day Company, 1968.
Kirwan, Laurence Patrick. *A History of Polar Exploration.* New York: W.W. Norton & Company, Inc., 1959. Previously published as *The White Road.* England: Hollis & Carter, 1959. Excellent early history.
Malaurie, Jean. *The Last Kings of Thule.* New York: E.P. Dutton, Inc., 1982, translated from the French by Adriene Foulke. The author lived with the Polar Inuit in Greenland.
Nansen, Fridtjof. *Farthest North. Being the Record of a Voyage of Exploration of the Ship 'Fram' 1893-96 and of a Fifteen Months' Sleigh Journey by Dr. Nansen and Lieut. Johansen.* New York: Harper & Brothers Publishers, 1897. Volumes I & II. Nansen provides many profound observations about his dogs and their journey.
O'Brien, Jack. *Alone Across the Top of the World. The Authorized Story of the Arctic Journey of David Irwin As Told to Jack O'Brian.* Chicago: E.M. Hale and Company, 1935. The dogs Irwin brought back from this trip are foundation dogs for Malamutes.
O'Brien, John S. *By Dog Sled for Byrd. 1600 Miles Across Antarctic Ice* Chicago: Thomas S. Rockwell Company. 1931. A surveyor for the first Byrd Expedition, O'Brien participated in the mapping expedition.

Ponting, Herbert and Frank Hurley. Text by Jennie Boddington. *1910-1916 Antarctic Photographs. Scott, Mawson and Shackleton Expeditions*. New York: St. Martin's Press, 1979. Ponting was a photographer whose pictures tell a more vivid story than words alone can convey from a time when Polar exploration was fraught with danger.

Ricker, Elizabeth M. *Seppala, Alaskan Dog Driver*. Boston: Little Brown & Company, 1930 *reprinted* Wheat-Ridge, Colorado: Hoflin Publications, Ltd., 1981.

Rodgers, Eugene. *Beyond the Barrier. The Story of Byrd's First Expedition to Antarctica*. Annapolis: Naval Institute Press, 1990. An excellent, thoroughly researched history told by a non-participant. Rodgers takes advantage of many recently released papers and paints an unbiased, unvarnished portrait of the people involved.

Rose, Lisle A. *Assault on Eternity. Richard E. Byrd and the Exploration of Antarctica 1946-47*. Annapolis: Naval Institute Press, 1980. A history of Operation Highjump.

Siple, Paul. *90 South. The Story of the American South Pole Conquest*. New York: G. P. Putnam's Sons, 1959. Paul Siple was a Boy Scout chosen to accompany the first Byrd Expedition where he became an expert at musher. He returned with Byrd on BAE II, Operation Highjump, and was in charge of the Operation Deep Freeze.

Steger, Will and Jon Bowermaster. *Crossing Antarctica*. New York: Alfred A. Knopf, 1991. A wonderful account of the Trans-Antarctic Expedition, an international group who made a trip across the continent by dog sled. Includes many excellent observations about the dogs and their performance under the extreme conditions of the Antarctic.

Ungermann, Kenneth A. *The Race to Nome*. Editor, Walter Lord. New York: Harper & Row, 1963. A story of the Serum Run.

Vaughan, Norman D. with Cecil B. Murphey. *With Byrd at the Bottom of the World. The South Pole Expedition of 1928-1930*. Harrisburg, Pa.: Stackpole Books, 1990. An entertaining, modern account of Vaughan's work as a dog driver for Byrd. Another view of the mapping expedition.

Walden, Arthur Treadwell. *A Dog-Puncher on the Yukon*. New York: Houghton Mifflin Company, 1928.

____. *Harness & Pack*. New York: American Book Co., 1935.

____. *Leading a Dogs Life*. Cambridge: Houghton Mifflin, Col, 1931.

Walden, Jane Brevoort and Stuart D.L. Paine. *The Long Whip, The Story of a Great Husky*. New York: G.P. Putnam's Sons, 1936.

SHOWING

American Kennel Club Complete Dog Book. New York: Howell Book House, 1994. Contained in this book are the standards for all AKC-recognized breeds as well as information about dogs, showing, and performance events sponsored by the AKC.

American Kennel Club. *Rules Applying to Dog Shows*. New York: American Kennel Club, 1994.

Brown, Marsha Hall and Bethany Hall Mason. *The New Complete Junior Showmanship Handbook*. New York: Howell Book House, Inc., 2d ed., 1979.

Harmar, Hilary. *Showing and Judging Dogs*. New York: Arco Publishing Company, Inc. 1977.

Nicholas, Anna Katherine. *The Nicholas Guide to Dog Judging*. New York: Howell Book House, 1979.

Spira, Harold R. *Canine Terminology*, New York: Howell Book House, 1982.

TRAINING AND BEHAVIOR

Benjamin, Carol Lea. *Mother Knows Best*. New York: Howell Book House, 1987. Any book by this author will be chocked full of advice and a joy to read.

Campbell, William E. *Behavior Problems in Dogs*. Santa Barbara, Ca.: American Veterinary Publications, Inc., 1975.

Dunbar, Dr. Ian. *The Sirius Puppy Training Manual: How To Teach a New Dog Old Tricks*. Oakland: James & Kenneth Publishers, 1991. Dr. Dunbar also wrote an excellent series of articles on various aspects of behavior for the *Gazette* and has a series of booklets on training problems available from the same publisher; e.g., Preventing Aggression, Fearfulness, Chewing, Digging, etc.

Fox, Dr. Michael W. *Understanding Your Dog. Everything You Want to Know about Your Dog But Haven't Been Able to Ask Him*. New York: Coward, McCann & Geoghegan, Inc., 1972.

Milani, Dr. Myrna M. *The Invisible Leash. A Better Way to Communicate with Your Dog*. New York: New American Library, 1985.

Monks of New Skete. *How to Be Your Dog's Best Friend. A Training Manual for Dog Owners*. Boston: Little, Brown and Company, 1978.

Pfaffenberger, Clarence. *The New Knowledge of Dog Behavior*. New York: Howell Book House, 1986.

Rutherford, Clarice and Dr. David H. Neil. *How To Raise a Puppy You Can Live With*. Loveland, Co.: Alpine Publications, Inc., 1992. Puppy development and training from birth to one year. Contains information on temperament testing puppies

Sautter, Fredrick J. and John A. Glover. *Behavior, Development, and Training of the Dog. A Primer of Canine Psychology*. New York: Arco Publishing Company, Inc., 1978.

Scott, Dr. John Paul. *Animal Behavior*. Chicago: The University of Chicago Press, 2d ed., 1958.

Volhard, Joachim and Fisher, Gail. *Train Your Dog: The Step-By-Step Manual*. New York: Howell Book House, 1983.

Whitney, Dr. Leon. *The Natural Method of Dog Training*. New York: M. Evans and Company, 1963.

WOLVES

Harrington, F. H. and P. C. Paquet (Eds.) *Wolves of the World*. Park Ridge, N.J.: Noyes Publications, 1982.

Mech, L. David. *The Artic Wolf. Living With the Pack*. Stillwater, Mn.: Voyageur Press, 1988.

_____. *The Wolf: Ecology and Behavior of an Endangered Species*. New York: Doubleday, 1970.

Appendix

ALASKAN MALAMUTE CLUB OF AMERICA SPECIALTY BEST OF BREED WINNERS

Year	Dog	Owner
1952	CH. Toro of Bras Coup	Earl and Natalie Norris
1953	CH. Arctic Storm of Husky	Robert Zoller
1954	CH. Mulpus Brooks the Bear	James and Lois Dawson
1955	CH. Cherokee of Husky Pak	Robert Zoller
1956	CH. Cherokee of Husky Pak	Robert Zoller
1957	CH. Cherokee of Husky Pak	Robert Zoller
1958	CH. Mister Yukon of Tobuk	Mr./Mrs. Robert Hall
1959	CH. Aabara of Redhorse	H. B. Pearson, Jr.
1960	CH. Rogue of Tigara	Glen E. Hull
1961	CH. Spawns Hot Shot of Roy-El	Mr. /Mrs. Robert Spawn
1962	Panuck	Dr. B. Weininger
1963	CH. Eldor's Little Bo	Mr. and Mrs. D. E. Tarr
1964	CH. Spawn's T"Domar's Panda	Alice Spawn
1965	CH. Sno Crest's Mukluk	Dr./ Mrs. Leo Rifkind
1966	CH. Tigara's Eskimo Eddy of Kayuh	Ralph Roger
1967	CH. Kodara Kodiak of Erowah	Mrs. Martha Guifffre
1968	CH. T'Domar's Genghis Kim Shadow, CD	Donald Mull
1969	CH. Glacier's Burbon King, CD	Lois Olmen
1970	CH. Glacier's Storm Kloud, CD	Robert/Nancy Russell
1971	CH. Burbon's Aristocrat of Brenmar	Frank/Claire Bongarzone
1972	CH. J.Len's Captain Koriak	Leonard/Joyce Fahlsing
1973	CH. Lobito's Cougar Cub, CD	Dr./Mrs. Dawn Woods
1974	CH. Inuit's Sweet Lucifer	Sheila Balch
1975	CH. Inuit's Wooly Bully	Sheila Balch
1976	CH. Snocre's Sun King of Midway	Howard/Jane Anderson
1977	CH. J.Len's Tribute to Mundy	Joyce Fahlsing
1978	CH. Snocre's Sun King of Midway	Howard/Jane Anderson
1979	CH. Kooskia's Catawba Chukchi	Jim/Cindy Kirkham
1980	CH. Inuit's Sweet Lucifer	Sheila Balch
1981	CH. Chamai's Chum-Lee	Betty Sconce
1982	CH. Northern Light's Togiak	Joe and Carol Hug
1983	CH. Northeast Lucan	S. L. Foster/ S. A. Wright
1984	CH. Nomarak's Kenworth	Marilyn Curtis
1985	CH. Sendaishi's Dan of Kennebec	Bill/Joyce Matott
1986	CH. Hug a Bears Steppin Wolf	Joe/Carol Hug
1987	CH. Hug a Bears Steppin Wolf	Joe/Carol Hug
1988	CH Farouk De Chabek	Andre /Lise Lapine
1989	CH. Alcan Private Label	Dian McComb
1990	CH. Sholyn Akala of Myakik	G. Bayer/Sholyn Knls.
1991	CH. Storm Kloud's Exotic Shayle	Sharon/Larry Kalous
1992	CH. Alcan's Simply Snazzy	Dian McComb
1993	CH. Williwaw's Kodiak Cub	Al/Mary J.Holabach; Frank/Lynn Sattler
1994	CH. Sendaishi's Polar Trax	Bill/Joyce Matott
1995	CH. Ceili's Foolish Pleasure	Pat Muchewicz
1996	CH. Poker Flat's Yukon Law CD, CGC	K. Stortzum/ B. McKiernan, DVM/ Robin Haggard
1997	CH. Nanuke's Take No Prisoners	Dr. William Newman/ Kathy Leuer/ Sandra D'Andrea

PUPPY APTITUDE TEST

(Circle one item in each group)

	Puppy #					
COME (Attraction to people)	1	2	3	4	5	6
Comes rapidly, nipping at hand	A	A	A	A	A	A
Comes happily, may lick hand, jump in lap	B	B	B	B	B	B
Comes slowly but willingly	C	C	C	C	C	C
Comes very hesitantly, or shyly sits and watches	D	D	D	D	D	D
Doesn't come, may look at you and go his own way	E	E	E	E	E	E

STROKING (Attitude toward social activities)						
Very excited, bites, growls	A	A	A	A	A	A
Jumps and paws, happily	B	B	B	B	B	B
Squirms and licks hand	C	C	C	C	C	C
Rolls over or slinks away	D	D	D	D	D	D
Walks away and stays away	E	E	E	E	E	E

FOLLOWING (Desire to stay in a social environment)						
Pounces on feet, bites pantleg, underfoot	A	A	A	A	A	A
Follows happily, underfoot	B	B	B	B	B	B
Follows slowly but willingly	C	C	C	C	C	C
Doesn't follow, slinks away or sits shyly	D	D	D	D	D	D
Doesn't follow, more interested in going elsewhere	E	E	E	E	E	E

RESTRAINT (Acceptance of human dominance)						
Struggles fiercely, bites, growls	A	A	A	A	A	A
Struggles then settles, or wiggles the whole time	B	B	B	B	B	B
Settles, then struggles	C	C	C	C	C	C
No struggle	D	D	D	D	D	D
Wiggles occasionally	E	E	E	E	E	E

RETRIEVING (Concentration and desire to please)

PINCH (Pain tolerance and forgiveness)

ANALYSIS OF THE PUPPY TEST

Extremely shy		Strong desire to please in this range				Extremely aggressive	
3 or more exaggerated "D" responses	3 or more "D" responses	3 or more "C" responses with 1 "D"	3 or more "C" responses with 1 "B"	3 "B" responses with 1 "C"	4 "B" responses	3 "B" responses with "A's"	4 exaggerated "A" responses
Shies away for no reason. Retest 2 times to verify. This pup is virtually untrainable. 2 or 3 "D" responses with 1 or 2 "A's" is a potential fear biter.	Highly submissive. Will not socialize easily. Needs much gentle but firm training and confidence building over long period of time. Not good for young children.	Needs much praise and confidence building. Not good for an impatient person. Good with elderly and handicapped.	Good with children. Good for the inexperienced trainer, will let you make a lot of mistakes.	Outgoing & fairly dominant. Fits in most homes. Very people oriented. Very eager to please but needs a firm hand or will make a pest of himself	Learns quickly and needs firm, consistent training but not harsh physical training.	Contests for pack leadership. Makes a good watchdog. Can be trained into a faithful family dog with consistent repetition in training and minimum of physical punishment.	Will not socialize. Not good with children. Untrustworthy around strangers. Needs special training with very experienced dominant trainer.

① Social Attraction

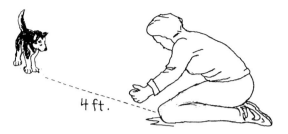

4 ft.

The tester sits on her
heels & calls the puppy to her

⑤ Elevation Dominance

The tester laces her fingers
under the puppy's rib cage
and lifts the puppy so that
all four feet are off the
ground. The puppy is held
in this position for
30 seconds

② Following

Come on,
Puppy,
puppy

The tester walks away,
verbally encouraging the
puppy to follow.

⑥ Retrieving

After the puppy starts
towards the paper,
the tester moves back
and encourages
the puppy

2-4 ft.   2 ft.

After getting the puppy's interest,
the tester tosses the crumpled
paper 2-4 feet away.

③ Restraint

Neutral
expression

only enough force
to hold puppy
in place.

The puppy is gently rolled onto his
back and one hand gently
restrains him for 30 seconds.

⑦ Touch Sensitivity

The tester cradles the leg
n one hand and squeezes
the webbing between the toes
th the other. Squeezing with
icreasing pressure, the tester
ounts to ten.

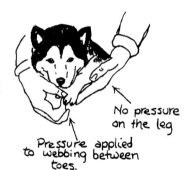

No pressure
on the leg

Pressure applied
to webbing between
toes.

④ Social Dominance

head low
enough
for puppy
to lick

Stroke puppy
with one hand

45°

With the puppy sitting at a
45° angle in front of the
tester, he is stroked gently
from head to tail.

⑧ Sound Sensitivity

Puppy faces away
from tester

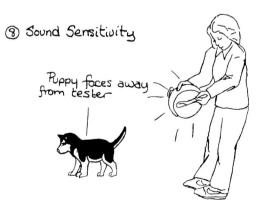

CODE OF ETHICS
(As Approved by 1992 Annual Election Membership Vote)

In accordance with the ideals set forth in the Preamble, the Alaskan Malamute Club of America, Inc., herewith sets forth the following as its Code of Ethics, and states that violation of any provision hereof by a member could constitute grounds for suspension of membership or expulsion from the Club:

1. No member shall knowingly be involved in the sale of dog(s) through pet shops or any other type of wholesale outlets, including but not limited to mail order houses, dog agents, or federally licensed dog dealers in the U.S. or any foreign country, or act as finder for agent/broker, or sell to institutions involved in research.

2. No member shall knowingly become involved in the sale of any dog(s) to any individual or outlet whose main reason for purchase is for resale.

3. No member shall sell any dog or bitch (of any age) without furnishing proper transfer papers, unless at the time of sale, both parties sign a written agreement of sale in which a stipulation is made concerning when said papers will be furnished.

4. It is recommended that any puppy sold with the designation pet/companion be sold on a spay/neuter contract with the Limited Registration now supplied by AKC. It is recommended that adults sold as companions be sold on a spay-neuter contract. The breeder may retain the registration papers until proof of sterilization.

5. No member shall be involved in the breeding or selling of wolf-hybrid dogs, and no member shall knowingly sell a Malamute or provide stud service to any person known to breed wolf-hybrids.

6. No member shall offer for use at stud or use at stud any dog who has not been certified clear of hip dysplasia by the Orthopedic Foundation for Animals, a qualified veterinarian, or a certified radiologist without a written stud contract stating that the stud has not been certified as indicated above.

7. No member shall sell any puppy whose sire and dam have not been certified clear of hip dysplasia by the Orthopedic Foundation for Animals, a qualified veterinarian, or a certified radiologist unless there is a written contract of sale for said puppy which has been signed by both buyers and sellers and which sets forth that the sire and/or dam have not been certified as being clear of hip dysplasia as provided above.

8. If the CHD probability number of any puppy or dog being sold or any dog used in open breeding is higher than 6.25%, or if no CHD number has been applied for, there shall be a written contract so stating, unless the animal is neutered or sterilized permanently.

9. Breeders should accept responsibility for those animals that are the results of their breedings, abandoned, or found in shelters.

10. Advertising should be factual. It should not be worded so as to attract undesirable buyers nor to encourage raising and selling dogs for profit. Care should be taken to evaluate buyers with regard to the suitability of the home being offered.

11. AMCA members will exhibit good sportsmanship at all times.

Sources of Information

CLUBS AND ORGANIZATIONS

AMERICAN KENNEL CLUB
Executive Office, 51 Madison Ave, New York, NY 10010

All other departments, including registration:
5580 Centerview Dr., Suite 200, Raleigh, NC 27606
Webpage: http://www.akc.org

CANADIAN KENNEL CLUB (CKC)
Commerce Park, 100-89 Skyway Ave.
Etobicoke, Ontario M9W 6R4 Canada

FEDERATION CYNOLOGIQUE INTERNATIONALE
13 Place Albert I
B-6530 THUIN, Belgium

THE KENNEL CLUB
1-4 Clarges St
London, England W1Y 8AB, UK

THERAPY DOGS INTERNATIONAL
6 Hilltop Rd., Mendham, NJ 07945

UNITED KENNEL CLUB
100 East Kilgore Rd., Kalamazoo, MI 49001-5598

ALASKAN MALAMUTE CLUB OF AMERICA
Corresponding Membership Secretary
Stephen Piper, 3528 Pin Hook Road, Antioch, TN 37013-1510

ALASKAN MALAMUTE RESEARCH
Foundation Ways & Means,
P.O. Box 675, Rosemead, CA 91770

WEB PAGE:
http://members.aol.com/amcahome/amcahome.htm

ALASKAN MALAMUTE CLUB OF CANADA
Corresponding Secretary
RR 4 Site 1 Compartment 73
Havelock, ONT K0L-1Z0   CANADA

LOCAL ALASKAN MALAMUTE CLUBS

The following is a list of local area Malamute Clubs. Those affiliated with
the Alaskan Malamute Club of America are followed by the letters AF; others are not. Some are licensed by the American Kennel Club to hold independent specialties (denoted by L), while others sponsor shows under the aegis of the AMCA. To contact a club, obtain the secretary's name and address from the AMCA or from the Club Relations Department at the AKC.

AMA of Long Island, AF
AMA of South Puget Sound (Washington)
AMC of Greater Detroit, AF, L
AMC of Greater Houston, L
AMC of Eastern Pennsylvania, AF
AMA of Wisconsin, Inc., AF
Bluegrass AMC (Kentucky), AF
Cascade AMC Enthusiasts Organization (Oregon)
Chicagoland AMC, Inc, L
Columbine Country AMC (Colorado), AF
Empire AMA (New Jersey), AF
Golden State AMC (California), AF
Greater San Fernando Valley AMC, (California), AF
Minnesota Malamutes, AF
Muddy Mukluk Hiking Club of Virginia
Northern California AMA, AF
Potomac Valley AMA (Maryland), AF
Southern California AMC, L
Snow King AM Fanciers (Washington), AF, L
Wasatch AMC (Utah), AF
Yankee AMC, (Massachusetts), AF

ALASKAN MALAMUTE RESCUE

Contact the AMCA for current addresses.

SLED DOG EQUIPMENT SUPPLIERS

This list was compiled by the AMCA Working Promotional Committee as a service to interested people. The AMCA does not necessarily endorse these products. Most of these suppliers offer a variety of dog sledding equipment.

Those marked with a ** also supply hard-to-find utility/horse-type carts suitable for one dog.

Adanac, 4108 Hwy 93 N, Kalispell, MT 59901

Alyeska Sled Dog Products, 1628 8-1/2 St. SE #A, Rochester, MN 55904

Black Ice, 3820 Yancy Ave., New Germany, MN 55367

Halls Sleds, 5875 McCrum Rd, Jackson, MI 49201

Ikon Outfitters, 7597 Latham Rd., Lodi, WI 53555**

Jim Malcolm Dog Sleds, 3350 Greensferry, Post Falls, ID 83854

Kaleb's Kart Co., Rt 3, Box 89, Chapel Ln., Neilsville, WI 54456

Konari, Box 752, Middlebury, VT 05753

Mel's Custom Harnesses, 9875 Hwy 2 W, Marion, MT 50025

Nooksack Kennel, RFD #1, Box 3261, Mechanic Falls, ME 04256

Nordkyn, P.O. Box 1023, Graham, WA 98338-1023

Raceway Products Corp., 2708 Walnut St., Muncie, IN 47303**

The Real Alaska Mushing Co., 471 Fleshman St., Fairbanks, AK 99712

Rae's Harness Shop, 1524 Dowling Rd. #6, Anchorage, AK 99507

Resha, SR1, Box 112, Lewis Run, PA 16738

Risdon Rigs, Cylde Risdon, Box 127, Lainsburg, MI 48848

Rustic Outdoor Supply, RR2, Shanty Bay, ONT, CAN. L0L-2L0

Sacco Dog Carts, Box 71599, Fairbanks, AK 99707-**

Sawtooth Mtn Sled Works, Rt 3,Box 693, Grand Marais, MN 55604

Tundra, 16438 96th Ave., Nunica, MI 49448

Windigo Outfitters, Rt 1, Box 536, Solon Springs, WI 54873

DOG MAGAZINES

Gazette, AKC, 1001 Madison Ave, New York, NY 10010 (Official publication ofthe American Kennel Club, monthly, all-breed)

Dog World, Primedia Publications, 29 N. Wacker Dr., Chicago, IL 60606-3298 (Monthly, all breed)

Dogs USA, P.O. Box 6040, Mission Viejo, CA 92690 (Annual, special issue on purchase, selection, and care of puppies)

Dog Fancy, P.O. Box 53264, Boulder, CO 80323-3264 (Monthly, all breed)

Malamute Quarterly, Hoflin Publishing Ltd, 4401 Zephyr St, Wheat Ridge, CO 80033 (Quarterly, Malamute specific)

Malamute Annual, address same as above.

Mushing, P.O. Box 149, Dept. XM, Ester, AK 99725 (Monthly, dog-sledding)

AUTHOR

Sherry Wallis (Sherob's Akitas) rwallis@infocom.net
http://www.infocom.net/~rwallis/index2.html

OTHER TITLES OF INTEREST
AVAILALBLE FROM ALPINE PUBLICATIONS

All Breed Dictionary of Unusual Names. Jarret, Gloria. Unique suggestions for naming your puppy.

A Fan's Guide to the Iditarod. Hood, Mary H. 1996

Backpacking with Your Dog. LaBelle, Charlene G. 1993. Author is a Malamute breeder.

Canine Reproduction, A Breeder's Guide. Holst, Phyllis, DVM.

Dog Driver, A Guide for the Serious Musher. Collins, Miki and Julie. 1991.

Guide to Skin and Haircoat Problems in Dogs. Ackerman, Lowell, DVM. 1995.

The Health of Your Dog. Bower, John, and David Youngs. 1989.

How to Raise a Puppy You Can Live With. Rutherford, Clarice, and David H. Neil. 1993.

Joy of Running Sled Dogs. Flanders, Noel. 1989. The basics of sled dog training.

Love on a Leash—Giving Joy through Pet Therapy. Palika, Liz. 1996

The Mentally Sound Dog. Clark, Gail, and William Boyer 1995. Understanding and shaping behavior.

Owner's Guide to Better Behavior in Dogs. Campbell, William. 1995. Correcting problems, discipline, etc.

Preparation and Presentation of Show Dogs. Brucker, Jeff and Betty. Handling and developing a winning attitude.

Scent: Training to Track, Search and Rescue. Pearsall, Milo, and Hugo Verbruggen.

INDEX

Hogden's, Art and Natalie, 159, 177, 181

Holly, 153n, 155

Hot spots, 16, 89, 253. See also Skin Problems

Housebreaking, 30, 35, 261, 278, 280

Housing for dog, 25-28; fencing, 25-27; invisible fencing, 27; shelter, 27

Husky-Pak Malamutes, 171-174, 176, 177, 178, 179, 236p, 237, 239, 240, 241

Identification, 28, 247

Iditerod Trail, 141

Iditerod Race, 141, Malamutes on, 61p, 141

Immunizations, 17-18, 283

Inbreeding. See Types of breeding

Indefinite Listing Privilege (ILP), 11

Innes-Taylor, Capt. Michael, 156, 157

Inuit, dogs of, 129-132; feeding, 129, teeth, removal of, 73, 129; teams, 129, treatment of, 129-130; uses of, 129. See also Inuit people; Malemute people

Inuit people, 129-132, 137n; dogs of, 129-132; Greenland, 132; history of predecessors, 129; lifestyle, 129-131; use of dogs, 129-131

ISDRA (International Sled Dog Racing Association), 57, 64

IWPA (International Weight Pull Association), 57

Irwin, Dave, 169-170

Irwin's Gemo, 170

Israel, Malamutes in, 203

Italy, Malamutes in, 185, 199

Jackson, Lorna, 175, 187

Jannelli, Chris, 194-195, 196, 197

Japan, Malamutes in, 189-191

Jogging with dog, 25

Johnson, John "Iron Man." 136

Judges, 102, 106, 107 109-110,112 114-115, 116, 118, 119-120

Junior Showmanship, 103, 104p

Kadluck of North Wind, 239

Ch. Karohonta's Skymaster, 240-241

Kassen, Gunnar, 139-140, 141p

Kelerak of Kobuk, 174, 175p

Kennels. See Housing

Ch. Kim of Kotzebue, 159

Ch. King M'Loot, 163p, 167

Knorr, Doris, 179-180

Kobuk's Dark Beauty, 175p, 176, 238

Kotzebue Malamutes, 157-159,163, 170, 172, 178, 180, 180-183, 236p, 237-238. See also Chinook Malamutes

Kotzebue Sound, 131

Lane, Jean, 175

Leasing, 217-218

Linebreeding. See types of breeding

Little America, 148, 150, 150n,

Mackenzie River Dogs, 136, 163

Malemute people, 123, 131. See also Inuit

Markings, 70, 77, 81, 82 83n, 232-233; genetics of, 232-233. See also coat color

Matches, sanctioned, 101

Medical problems and treatment, 20-25, 245-255; autoimmune skin disease, 252-253; bites, insect, spider, snake, and dog, 20; bloat, 256; cars, hit by, 20; cataracts, 250-251; chondrodysplasia, 247-249; coat funk, 253, 254p; demodectic mange, 252-253; diarrhea, 20-21, 106; elbow dysplasia, 246-247; epilepsy, 23-24, 254-255; frostbite, 21; gastric dilatation-volvulus (GDV), 255; heat stroke 21; hemeralopia, 250; hip dysplasia, 245-246; hypothyroidism, 252; inherited diseases, 245-255; lupus erythematosus, 252; mange, 252-253; pad damage, 25, 50, 51, 257; pemphigus, 252; polyneuropathy, 254; poison, 21-23; progressive retinal atrophy (PRA), 250; reproductive system, 23; superficial pyderma, 252; toad poisoning, 25; torsion, 255; zinc responsive dermatosis, 253. See also Hotspots; Pads; Parasites

Medications. 20; and seizures, 24. See also Medical Supplies

Medical supplies, 19-20; for pack trip, 51;

Mexico, Malamutes in, 187

Mikiuk, 166p, 167

M'Loot Malemutes, 163-166, 170, 171, 172, 174-176, 177, 178, 179, 236p, 237, 238, 240, 240; sources of dogs, 163, 183n

Moosecat M'Loot, 168

Moulton, Dick, 145, 151, 158, 164, 169, 171

Movies, Malamutes in, 204, 207-208

Moving dog, 114-115

Nails, trimming, 85, 88

Nanook, 167

Ch. Nanook II, 162

National Speciality, AMCA, 40, 50, 102, 123; winners of, 295; Working Dog Showcase, 50, 123

The Netherlands, Malamutes in 185, 193-194

Neutering. See Sterilization

New England Sled Dog Club (NESDC), 139, 140, 145

New Zealand, Malamutes in, 188

Noma, 166

Nome, Alaska, 133, 139, 140

Nome Kennel Club, 136; 139

Norris, Earl and Natalie, 174, 182,

Northern Dogs, 72, 75, 129, 130-131, 136, 185, 201, 269, 276; clubs for, 185, 197, 198; differentiation between, 130, 136

Norway, Malamutes in, 197

Novice Class: at Agility, 44; at Obedience Trial, 38

Obedience trials, 37-41, 190; A & B classes, 38-41; awards, 37-38; Companion Dog (CD), 37, 38; Companion Dog Excellent (CDX), 37, 38-39; levels, 37; Malamute history in, 40; Obedience Trial Champion (OTCH), 37, 41; Utility Dog (UD), 39, 41; Utility Dog Excellent (UDX), 37, 41;

Obtaining a Malamute, 4-7, 10-11, 264, 267-270, 271; best age, 5-6; choosing, 264, 267-270; considerations in selection, 4-6, documents with purchase, 10-11; pet shops, 7, 280; show puppy or dog 10;

Orthopedic Foundation for Animals (OFA), 245, 246, 247

Ch. Ooloo M'Loot, 163p, 167

Oonanik Memorial Award, 40

Open Class: at Agility, 44; at Obedience Trial, 39

Operation Deepfreeze, 176p, 177, 183n

Outcrossing. See Types of Breeding

Ownership, disputes over, 13; types of 12-13

INDEX OF PEDIGREES

LIST OF EARLY KENNELS AND OWNERS